AI-Driven Revolution

Transforming the Business Landscape

Artificial Intelligence in Organizations: Transformative Technologies, Applications, and Impacts

Series Editor: Tereza Raquel Merlo *(University of North Texas, USA)*

AI-adoption is becoming increasingly widespread. It is a transformative force reshaping countless fields and industries, revolutionizing the way organizations create and capture value. In this new world, a clear understanding of AI's implications has become indispensable for both business leaders and academic researchers. This series was developed to serve as a bridge between theory and practice, offering a holistic view of AI in business from foundational knowledge to advanced applications and future directions.

Designed to guide executives, managers, and professionals, the series explores how organizations can strategically leverage AI for innovation, sustainable growth, and competitive advantage. At the same time, the books of this series provide scholars and students with a deeper understanding of current trends, opportunities, and challenges, including ethical considerations, regulatory shifts, and workforce transformation. By integrating academic rigor with practical relevance, this series equips its readers with the knowledge, strategies, and foresight necessary to successfully navigate and lead in an AI-powered future.

Published

Vol. 1 *AI-Driven Revolution: Transforming the Business Landscape*
edited by Tereza Raquel Merlo

Volume 1

Artificial Intelligence in Organizations: Transformative Technologies, Applications, and Impacts

AI-Driven Revolution

Transforming the Business Landscape

editor

Tereza Raquel Merlo

University of North Texas, USA

World Scientific

NEW JERSEY • LONDON • SINGAPORE • BEIJING • SHANGHAI • HONG KONG • TAIPEI • CHENNAI • TOKYO

Published by

World Scientific Publishing Europe Ltd.
57 Shelton Street, Covent Garden, London WC2H 9HE
Head office: 5 Toh Tuck Link, Singapore 596224
USA office: 27 Warren Street, Suite 401-402, Hackensack, NJ 07601

Library of Congress Control Number: 2025011020

British Library Cataloguing-in-Publication Data
A catalogue record for this book is available from the British Library.

Artificial Intelligence in Organizations:
Transformative Technologies, Applications, and Impacts — Vol. 1
AI-DRIVEN REVOLUTION
Transforming the Business Landscape

ISBN 978-1-80061-656-1 (hardcover)
ISBN 978-1-80061-657-8 (ebook for institutions)
ISBN 978-1-80061-658-5 (ebook for individuals)

For any available supplementary material, please visit
https://www.worldscientific.com/worldscibooks/10.1142/Q0488#t=suppl

Desk Editors: Eshak Nabi Akbar Ali/Cian Sacker Ooi

Typeset by Stallion Press
Email: enquiries@stallionpress.com

To the visionaries and pioneers of artificial intelligence, whose relentless pursuit of innovation inspires us all. This book is dedicated to the business leaders, researchers, and practitioners who are embracing AI as a transformative force in organizations, driving change and shaping the future of work.

I would like to extend a special dedication to my husband, Jason Merlo, whose unwavering support and encouragement have been my guiding light throughout this journey. I am also grateful for the extraordinary colleagues and professionals in both corporate and academic settings with whom I have had the pleasure of collaborating over the years. Your insights, dedication, and passion for advancing the field have enriched my work and fueled my enthusiasm for exploring the vast possibilities of AI and the many possibilities in business. May this work empower you to harness the potential of AI, fostering growth, creativity, and a sustainable business landscape for generations to come.

https://doi.org/10.1142/9781800616578_fmatter

Foreword

Human progress has always been propelled by transformative revolutions — moments in time when society, technology, and culture undergo profound changes. Throughout history, we have witnessed revolutions that have reshaped our world, from the Agricultural Revolution to the successive waves of Industrial Revolutions, and most recently, the Information Revolution. Each of these milestones has fundamentally altered how we live, work, and interact. Today, we find ourselves on the cusp of another monumental shift: the AI-driven revolution. Artificial Intelligence is rapidly transforming the business landscape, promising to upend traditional models and create new opportunities. But is AI truly new? And if not, why now? What has brought us to this pivotal moment, and why do we believe it will have a transformational impact on the business world?

When my dear friend, Dr. Tereza Raquel Merlo, invited me to write the foreword for this book, *AI-Driven Revolution: Transforming the Business Landscape*, it struck a chord with me. The questions Raquel posed mirror those I've been exploring for years. In her note to me, she wrote, "Your foreword will set the stage for readers to engage with these diverse areas, providing an insightful and authoritative introduction to the wide-reaching impacts and challenges that AI presents to modern organizations. I believe your perspective will lend the book a critical foundation, helping readers appreciate the significance of AI in both strategic and operational contexts." While this is certainly a tall order, I will attempt to answer these pressing questions alongside you.

The concept of Artificial Intelligence was first introduced to the public in 1950 by Alan Turing, with his groundbreaking work on the Turing Test. For decades, AI remained a niche area of research, often emerging into the public eye in isolated instances, such as when a computer defeated a world chess champion or when IBM's Watson triumphed on *Jeopardy*. In the early 1990s, during my postgraduate research in the U.S., my focus was on knowledge-based expert systems and fuzzy logic, a precursor to today's AI. So, we can confidently say that AI itself is not a new concept.

So, what has changed? The answer lies in the Information Revolution. With the digitization of virtually every aspect of life, we are generating an unprecedented amount of data. Each day, more data are produced than a single generation of humanity could ever hope to process. In parallel, the rise of fields like predictive analytics, prescriptive analytics, and data science has given us the tools to make sense of these data. Simultaneously, advances in computational technologies — faster CPUs, GPUs, specialized ASICs, and improved mobile devices — have made these tools more accessible and affordable. This democratization of computing power has created an environment ripe for the AI revolution.

But will AI truly have a transformative impact on the entire business landscape? To be candid, I'm not sure it will transform every industry overnight. In my three-decade career in data science and enterprise computing, I have worked across nearly every industry — finance, insurance, healthcare, telecommunications, government, travel, retail, manufacturing, services, and academia. In all of these sectors, not every organization is moving at the pace required to adopt and leverage AI. It's not a lack of investment that holds them back, but a more profound resistance to change, often encapsulated in the mindset of "if it ain't broken, don't fix it." What's still missing in many organizations is a deep understanding of what it truly means to embark on this AI-driven journey and how to navigate the risks and challenges that come with it.

This is where *AI-Driven Revolution: Transforming the Business Landscape* excels. This book is a powerful compilation of insights from credible thought leaders across a variety of industries, offering readers a chance to deepen their understanding of AI and its potential to augment business strategy. Importantly, the book doesn't shy away from the challenges. Part 1 addresses the need for AI literacy and highlights the responsibilities that come with it, ensuring AI is harnessed for positive societal impact. Part 2 showcases trends and use cases that demonstrate how AI and machine learning have already disrupted and revolutionized multiple sectors. These examples, though diverse, are not limited to specific industries; their lessons are universally applicable.

Part 3 discusses the impact of AI in education and institutional development. Part 4 focuses on the critical topic of human–AI synergy — understanding that while change is difficult and often resisted, it is also the one constant in life. This part encourages readers to embrace the AI revolution in both personal and organizational contexts.

I would like to congratulate all the contributing authors and Dr. Tereza Raquel Merlo for undertaking this important and timely exploration of the AI revolution. Their collective effort has resulted in a book that, I am sure, will empower readers with the knowledge and tools to navigate this profound change.

I also extend my sincere gratitude to my friend, Raquel, for giving me the honor and privilege of contributing to this significant project. It has been a true pleasure to be a part of this endeavor.

Dr. Vikas Sinha, Ph.D.
Frisco, Texas

https://doi.org/10.1142/9781800616578_fmatter

Preface

The term "revolution" has been historically used to signify radical and transformative changes in political, social, or technological contexts. A revolution disrupts existing paradigms, replacing them with entirely new frameworks that reshape societies or industries. When combined with "driven," as in "driven revolution," the concept suggests an intentional, forceful transformation powered by a specific catalyst — such as technology, innovation, or ideology. The word "revolution" derives from the Latin "*revolutio*," meaning "a turn around." Initially, it referred to celestial cycles, as used by Nicolaus Copernicus in his 1543 work *De revolutionibus orbium coelestium*, which described the rotation of celestial bodies. Later, the term adopted political connotations during events like the Glorious Revolution (1688) in England and the French Revolution (1789), symbolizing upheaval and systemic change. Over time, the word evolved to encompass technological and industrial transformations, notably the Industrial Revolution of the 18th and 19th centuries. The notion of technological revolutions gained prominence in the 20th century, especially with the advent of computing and Artificial Intelligence (AI). Economist Carlota Perez introduced the concept of "technological revolutions" in her work *Technological Revolutions and Financial Capital* (2002), defining them as periods marked by the introduction of disruptive technologies that create new economic and social landscapes. AI represents the latest chapter in this ongoing saga, heralding a revolution in how humans work, interact, and innovate.

The AI-driven revolution echoes the industrial and digital revolutions in its potential to reshape industries, decision-making processes, and societal structures. Unlike previous revolutions, AI's impact is characterized by its ability to augment human intelligence and automate complex cognitive tasks, blurring the line between human and machine capabilities. In recent years, Artificial Intelligence (AI) has transitioned from being a niche area of technological research to becoming an integral part of our daily lives and business operations. As we navigate this era of rapid transformation, it becomes increasingly crucial to understand not only the potentials but also the ethical, societal, and strategic implications of AI. This book emerges as a timely response to this need, offering diverse perspectives from academics and practitioners across the globe.

The chapters within these pages address the multifaceted ways AI is reshaping industries, governance, and human interactions. By exploring topics that range from ethical AI governance and literacy to revolutionary applications in business and education, this book aims to provide readers with both a conceptual foundation and actionable insights into AI's evolving landscape.

The first part of the book, *AI Literacy and Ethical Frameworks for AI Governance and Societal Impact*, underscores the importance of AI literacy in enabling individuals and organizations to engage responsibly with AI technologies. It also delves into the pressing need for robust ethical frameworks to ensure that AI development and deployment prioritize accountability and societal well-being.

AI and Machine Learning in Business and Technology: Transforming Industries and Driving Innovation, the second part, highlights AI's transformative influence across various sectors, including finance, marketing, tourism, aviation, and marine delimitation. Through case studies and theoretical explorations, this part reveals how AI-driven innovations are reshaping the competitive landscape and operational paradigms of industries worldwide.

The third part of the book, *Artificial Intelligence, Equity, and Institutional Development in Higher Education: Global Perspectives*, delves into the evolving intersection of Artificial Intelligence (AI) and higher education, exploring its transformative impact on teaching, learning, and institutional development. In an era where AI technologies are rapidly reshaping educational landscapes, both opportunities and challenges presented are analyzed, particularly within the context of equity, ethics, and accessibility. Drawing from global perspectives, the chapters in this part offer in-depth analyses of how AI is being integrated into educational practices, from the Global South to North America, with a special focus on AI literacy and the role of libraries in fostering competency development. With contributions from experts across diverse regions and disciplines, this book aims to provide a comprehensive understanding of AI's potential to enhance educational outcomes while emphasizing the importance of responsible and inclusive adoption. As institutions navigate this technological shift, this work serves as a vital resource for educators, policymakers, and researchers seeking to harness the power of AI in ways that align with ethical principles and support the holistic development of students.

Finally, the fourth part, *Innovative Learning and Collaborative Intelligence: Shaping the Future of Human–AI Interaction and Analytics*, ventures into the emerging domain of collaborative intelligence, where humans and AI work in tandem to achieve shared goals. This part also examines innovative educational methodologies and national strategies to enhance competitiveness and strategic intelligence in an AI-driven world.

This book, *AI-Driven Revolution: Transforming the Business Landscape*, presents a wide array of insights into the transformative power of Artificial Intelligence (AI) across industries and societal domains. The following is a summary of the chapters organized by the book's four main parts:

Part 1: AI Literacy and Ethical Frameworks for AI Governance and Societal Impact

- **Chapter 1:** *Ethical Governance of Generative AI: Accountability, Oversight, and Societal Impact*
  This chapter focuses on the challenges of ensuring accountability and societal benefit in the development and deployment of generative AI, providing a framework for ethical governance. Generative AI is transforming industries and society at large, but its rapid evolution raises profound ethical challenges. This chapter delves into the necessity of ethical governance in managing these technologies, emphasizing the importance of accountability, oversight, and harm reduction. By introducing a novel perspective that treats AI systems as child-like entities requiring supervision and ethical guidance, we explore how applying human-centric ethical principles — such as empathy, fairness, and respect — can address pressing issues like bias, transparency, and unpredictability. This chapter aims to provide a fresh framework for

navigating the complexities of generative AI, offering valuable insights for stakeholders across technology, policy, and ethics.

- **Chapter 2:** *The Growing Need for AI Literacy in Business and Daily Life*
  This chapter highlights the importance of AI literacy for individuals and businesses to responsibly navigate AI's complexities in both daily life and strategic business settings. It discusses AI's transformative impact on business, improving operational efficiency, reducing costs, and enabling data-driven decision-making. AI helps predict trends, customer behavior, and market shifts while enhancing customer experiences through personalized virtual assistants. The chapter also addresses AI's growing influence in sectors like healthcare, education, and finance, emphasizing the need for basic AI knowledge for the general public as AI becomes more pervasive in everyday life.

Part 2: AI and Machine Learning in Business and Technology: Transforming Industries and Driving Innovation

- **Chapter 3:** *Use of Machine Learning in Early Warning Systems for Financial Crises Within the Global Financial System*
  This work aims to evaluate whether Early Warning Systems (EWSs) using Machine Learning (ML) techniques offer better predictive performance for financial crises compared to traditional methods. To explore this, the study employs the Multivocal Literature Review (MLR) method, focusing on Grey Literature (GL) from monetary authorities and supranational financial institutions. The findings suggest that ML significantly enhances the predictive capacity of EWSs, offering valuable insights for macroprudential policymakers to improve evidence-based decision-making and crisis forecasting.

- **Chapter 4:** *AI in Organizations: Transforming Cybersecurity for Financial Institutions*
  This chapter explores the growing role of Artificial Intelligence (AI) in enhancing cybersecurity within major U.S. banks. Initially a support tool, AI now plays a key role in addressing security challenges like real-time fraud detection and risk prediction. While it offers

significant benefits, AI also raises concerns about data privacy, fairness in decision-making, and its impact on jobs. The chapter analyzes case studies from large banks, highlighting how AI is integrated into their security systems and suggesting a future where AI not only reacts to threats but also anticipates and prevents potential breaches.

- **Chapter 5:** *AI-Driven Trends and Technologies in Digital Marketing: Shaping Modern Strategies*
  This chapter examines the rapidly evolving trends in digital marketing, driven by technological advancements and shifts in consumer behavior. Key trends include the use of interactive websites to enhance user experience, AI and machine learning (like Long Short Term Memory neural networks) for predicting customer behavior and enabling targeted interactions, and Augmented Reality (AR) features like "3D Try-On" to boost engagement. Other notable trends include real-time bidding (RTB) for optimized ad placements, content marketing, and various forms of social media and influencer marketing. Chatbots are improving customer service by providing instant responses. These trends are reshaping consumer behavior by offering personalized, interactive shopping experiences. To stay competitive, companies must adopt emerging technologies, integrate their online presence, invest in data analytics, and ensure cybersecurity, while continuously adapting their strategies. The chapter explores how these trends are influencing modern marketing strategies and driving business growth.

- **Chapter 6:** *Digital Revolution: Transforming the Tourism Business Landscape Post-Pandemic*
  This study examines the recovery strategies implemented by the tourism industry in Kerala, South India, in response to the COVID-19 pandemic. Over the past decade, India's travel and tourism sector saw steady growth, but the pandemic led to a significant downturn due to travel restrictions and quarantine measures. This disrupted both leisure and business travel, causing financial losses for many in the industry. However, some travel agents and tour operators used this crisis as an opportunity to introduce innovative products and marketing strategies, such as "Quarantine stays," "Untact Tourism," and "Virtual Tourism." The study explores how tourism businesses in Kerala adapted to the

challenges by integrating technology and employing digital strategies to recover and rebuild their reputations. Through interviews with industry experts and an analysis of websites, the chapter assesses the effectiveness of these recovery measures in generating revenue and restoring the destination's appeal. The findings provide valuable insights for tourism stakeholders to develop effective strategies for crisis management and innovation in product development moving forward.

- **Chapter 7:** *AI-Driven Data Analysis and Knowledge Management in Aviation Organizations*
  This chapter explores the transformative impact of Artificial Intelligence (AI) on aviation organizations, focusing on its role in enhancing data-driven decision-making, optimizing operations, and promoting organizational learning. It highlights key AI applications, such as predictive analytics, real-time data processing, and AI-powered knowledge management systems, and how these technologies enable proactive decision-making, improve risk management, and support continuous learning. The chapter also addresses ethical issues, including data privacy and algorithmic transparency, to provide a balanced view of AI adoption in the aviation industry. Through real-world case studies, it offers practical insights into how AI can drive operational excellence and growth, particularly in ensuring safety and compliance. The findings aim to assist both scholars and practitioners in navigating the opportunities and challenges of AI integration in the aviation sector.

- **Chapter 8:** *The Use of AI in Maritime Delimitation Addressing the Equity Principle and Judicial Subjectivity*
  This chapter examines the potential role of Artificial Intelligence (AI) in maritime delimitation, a complex process that requires balancing geographical, legal, and equitable factors. Traditionally, human adjudication has been used to resolve maritime boundary disputes, but AI's efficiency and data processing capabilities could transform or supplement these decision-making processes. The chapter explores whether AI can enhance the consistency and objectivity of maritime delimitation or if its reliance on algorithms might introduce new risks to fairness and transparency.

Part 3: Artificial Intelligence, Equity, and Institutional Development in Higher Education: Global Perspectives

- **Chapter 9:** *Generative AI: A Disruptive Game Changer in Higher Education*
  This chapter discusses how Generative Artificial Intelligence (GenAI) is transforming higher education by revolutionizing teaching practices and enhancing learning outcomes. This chapter examines the integration of tools, like ChatGPT, Microsoft Copilot, and Meta AI, using Sociomateriality Theory to explore their impact on pedagogy, student engagement, and institutional practices. While GenAI enables personalized learning, streamlines administrative tasks, and fosters critical thinking, it also raises ethical concerns, including data privacy risks, algorithmic biases, and threats to academic integrity. By highlighting the dual role of GenAI as both an enabler and a disruptor, this chapter emphasizes the importance of balancing AI integration with traditional pedagogy. Recommendations focus on faculty training, ethical guidelines, and equitable access to AI tools, offering valuable insights for educators, policymakers, and technologists.

- **Chapter 10:** *Building Artificial Intelligence Literacy Skills for AI Competency Development in Higher Learning Institutions*
  This chapter explores the preparedness of Higher Learning Institutions (HLIs) in promoting AI literacy competency skills, an essential skill in modern education. Anchored in AI literacy frameworks by Hibbert *et al.* (2024) and Wang *et al.* (2023), as well as the ACRL's Information Literacy framework, the study uses a qualitative case study approach. It examines 16 research-intensive U.S. HLIs (Carnegie Classification 2023) and four Kenyan Chartered Universities, focusing on their efforts to build AI and information literacy skills. Data were collected through a desktop review and analyzed using content analysis.

- **Chapter 11:** *Generative AI in Salvadoran Higher Education: Case Studies in Equity and Ethics from the Global South*
  This chapter explores the transformative potential of generative AI (GenAI) tools in Salvadoran higher education, analyzing their impact

on students, faculty, and administrators. It addresses the socioeconomic and digital literacy barriers faced by students in the Global South, advocating for equitable access, infrastructure investment, and ethical usage policies. For faculty, the chapter highlights GenAI's role in personalized learning and innovative assessment, while also discussing concerns around academic integrity and institutional support. Administrative perspectives emphasize the need for ethical governance to integrate GenAI responsibly within educational frameworks. The chapter situates Salvadoran experiences within global discussions on AI in education, offering culturally responsive strategies and lessons for adaptive approaches. Overall, it underscores the importance of aligning technological advancements with regional priorities, ensuring that GenAI contributes to inclusive and transformative education.

Part 4: Innovative Learning and Collaborative Intelligence: Shaping the Future of Human-AI Interaction and Analytics

- **Chapter 12:** *Application of the Neolearning Methodology in a Networked Corporate University*
  This chapter investigates the application of the neolearning methodology in a Networked Corporate University (UCR) to develop leadership skills and generate organizational value. The research addresses how neolearning, which emphasizes experiential learning, active methodologies, and the relational processes between individuals, groups, and organizations, can be effectively implemented in such a setting. The methodology integrates UNESCO's four pillars of education and the 4 Is (Interactivity, Integration, Innovation, and Impact). The research, conducted through action research in a Leadership Development Program at UCR, used Challenge-Based Learning to apply knowledge. The chapter highlights the key findings and implications of using neolearning to fill professional gaps and foster leadership development in organizations.

- **Chapter 13:** *Collaborative Intelligence: Cultivating Human–AI Partnerships*
  The authors of this chapter highlight how collaboration between humans and AI can result in shared intelligence that enhances decision-making and innovation.

This chapter offers a human-centered view of Artificial Intelligence (AI) as a transformative technology in the workplace. It explores the historical impact of technological advancements on work environments and highlights how AI's strengths in logical processing and predictive analytics can complement human expertise, despite its lack of ethical judgment and creativity. The chapter advocates for collaboration between humans and AI rather than AI replacing human roles, proposing a conceptual framework for integrating AI in a way that preserves fairness and accountability. It discusses the need for workforce reskilling and task reorganization to align AI with human efforts, ultimately arguing for a collaborative workforce model where human–AI systems work together to drive innovation and support organizational values.

- **Chapter 14:** *The LAFBAH AI Framework for a Transformative National AI Strategy: Enhancing Morocco's Competitiveness and Strategic Intelligence*
  This chapter explores the impact of a national AI strategy on the competitiveness and strategic intelligence of countries, focusing on Morocco. It introduces the "LAFBAH AI Framework," a model for implementing a holistic and ethical AI strategy, structured around leadership, governance, skills development, collaboration, accountability, and a human-centered approach. The framework aims to achieve strategic goals like sovereignty, security, and sustainability. Based on a mix of global best practices, expert interviews, and an analysis of Morocco's AI ecosystem, the chapter highlights key success factors and development pathways for an impactful AI strategy. It concludes by emphasizing the importance of a dedicated AI strategy to boost Morocco's global competitiveness and strategic intelligence.

- **Chapter 15:** *Managing Social Noise and Reducing the Impact of Misinformation on Business Practices*
  This chapter explores the impact of misinformation on businesses, highlighting real-world examples such as the Corona Beer incident during the COVID-19 pandemic, where false information caused substantial damage. It also examines the broader effects of misinformation on consumer behavior and corporate resilience. As misinformation spreads rapidly online, understanding its risks and challenges has become essential for businesses to adapt and protect their operations. By analyzing the dynamics of misinformation and its implications, this

chapter provides insights into the importance of risk assessment, strategic communication, and proactive measures in mitigating the negative effects of the digital age on business practices.

- **Chapter 16:** *How Does the Use of Language Matter in Organizational Change Processes? Setting Up an AI-Based Analytics Approach*
  This chapter explores the role of language in managing change, particularly during company succession in medium-sized businesses. It focuses on identifying verbal resistance through internal communication channels, including social business platforms, chats, and emails, as indicators of potential challenges. Using a design science approach, the study analyzes how language reflects organizational culture and identifies performance indicators related to communication. The research also connects these indicators to traditional KPIs, like sales figures. The next phase applies AI-based analytics, such as semantic clustering, to create a communication feedback system that detects early signs of resistance. The goal is to develop targeted communication strategies and early intervention mechanisms to ensure successful transitions during change processes, such as succession or company sales.

These chapters provide a comprehensive examination of AI's profound impact, offering actionable insights for leaders, practitioners, and researchers alike. Whether exploring ethical governance or industry-specific applications, this book lays the foundation for understanding and leveraging AI in an era of unprecedented technological progress.

This book would not have been possible without the dedication and expertise of the contributing authors, who bring a wealth of knowledge and experience to the topics explored. Their contributions are a testament to the collaborative spirit required to address the complexities of AI in today's interconnected world.

I hope this book serves as a resource and inspiration for business leaders, policymakers, researchers, and educators, fostering informed discussions and innovative approaches to harnessing AI for a better future. As you read through these pages, may you uncover insights that connect with your own experiences and goals in navigating the dynamic world of Artificial Intelligence and the exciting opportunities it presents for business and society.

You cannot step into the same river twice (Heraclitus of Ephesus, c. 535–475 BCE–*Fragment 41*).

Tereza Raquel Merlo, Ph.D.
University of North Texas
Merlo Management Consulting

Bibliography

Copernicus, N. "De Revolutionibus Orbium Coelestium (On the Revolutions of the Celestial Spheres)." 1543. This foundational text marks the first significant use of "revolution" in an astronomical context, referring to the movement of celestial bodies.

Freeman, C. and Louçã, F. *As Time Goes By: From the Industrial Revolutions to the Information Revolution*. Oxford: Oxford University Press, 2001.

Perez, C. *Technological Revolutions and Financial Capital: The Dynamics of Bubbles and Golden Ages*. Cheltenham: Edward Elgar Publishing, 2002.

https://doi.org/10.1142/9781800616578_fmatter

Acknowledgments

I would like to express my deepest gratitude to my family, friends, and colleagues, whose encouragement and unwavering belief in this project provided the strength and motivation to see it through to completion.

I am also grateful to the professionals and practitioners in the fields of data analytics, business strategies, AI, and knowledge management, whose insights and practical applications shaped my understanding of how data and advanced technologies can transform organizational management, strategies, operations, and outcomes.

A sincere thank you to the editorial team at World Scientific Publishing for their dedication, professionalism, and expertise, which have been instrumental in bringing this book to life.

https://doi.org/10.1142/9781800616578_fmatter

Contents

Part 1

AI Literacy and Ethical Frameworks for AI Governance and Societal Impact

https://doi.org/10.1142/9781800616578_0001

Chapter 1

Ethical Governance of Generative AI: Accountability, Oversight, and Societal Impact

Tereza Raquel Merlo[*,‡] **and Kay Alwert**[†,§]

[*] *University of North Texas, Denton, Texas, USA*

[†] *Alwert GmbH & Co. KG, Berlin, Germany*

[‡] *tereza.merlo@unt.edu*
[§] *kay.alwert@alwert.com*

Abstract

As generative AI technologies rapidly evolve, the ethical challenges related to their development, deployment, and broader societal impact continue to grow in significance. This paper explores the imperative of ethical governance in managing generative AI, emphasizing the critical roles of accountability, oversight, and minimizing harm. The paper examines how concepts of "moral agency" and "ethical care" can inform responsible AI governance. By conceptualizing AI systems as emerging and developing child-like entities, we propose that these technologies require ongoing supervision, ethical education, and well-defined boundaries to align with human values. The paper highlights pressing issues such as bias, transparency, and the unpredictable behavior of generative AI, advocating for a comprehensive and dynamic ethical approach to guide their growth. Ultimately, this analysis aims to provide valuable insights for technologists, policymakers, and ethicists, encouraging a balanced approach to AI development that prioritizes responsibility, empathy, and societal well-being.

Keywords: Artificial Intelligence, ethics, society, governance, business.

1.1. Introduction

The rapid development of Artificial Intelligence (AI), particularly generative AI, and the relationship between AI and humanity raise profound ethical questions regarding how we conceptualize and interact with these technologies. A reevaluation of our ethical responsibilities in developing, using, and treating these systems and their contribution to society seems necessary.

In addition to general considerations on the interaction between AI and ethics, we will explore the argument that it might be a prudent and ethical approach to treat current generative AI applications as if they were children. We will also try to find out whether this approach might make it possible to solve some pressing problems in this area faster.

To this end, we propose a metaphorical shift in perspective by applying the vocabulary of human ethics to AI. We do this by following Richard Rorty and his pragmatic approach to language and meaning (Rorty, 1989). Rorty emphasizes the power of transferring vocabularies from one domain to another to promote insight and even change in behavior (Rorty, 1989). By placing AI in the context of human ethics, we can reassess its ethical status, its development, and its societal consequences. Aspects such as moral agency, responsibility, and accountability for moral behavior as well as consequences for the individuals and society as a whole become more prominent. Blind spots in the analysis may also become visible because the transfer of ethical vocabulary to AI also means that ethical values such as empathy, fairness, and respect, which are otherwise only granted to humans, are also transferred to AI. All of this enables us to examine previous ethical considerations in relation to AI from a new perspective and perhaps find some new solutions to current pressing questions in relation to AI and ethics.

This approach goes beyond previous approaches to deal with ethical issues in the field of AI, which struggled with the fact that ethical considerations were usually strictly bound to humans. Therefore, most ethical considerations aim at examining the relationship of humans in dealing with AI or the ethical consequences of AI for humans and societies. As we will argue, however, generative AI has the ability to act as an ethical agent itself.

This brings numerous complications, culminating in two extreme positions: (1) AI cannot be assigned any responsibility for ethical behavior because it is not human, thereby transferring all responsibility for generated results either to the developers (who themselves do not fully understand the behavior of their systems nor are they ethics philosophers) or the users (who mostly have even less knowledge about the complexity they are dealing with because they are neither philosophers nor AI specialists). (2) In the other extreme, all responsibility is assigned to the AI, so that a new, additional ethical framework only for AI applications seems necessary: a kind of AI or "machine ethics," which deals with the special issues and conditions in this field (Misselhorn, 2018).

For most positions that fall somewhere between these two extremes, a distinct AI ethics also seems necessary, since the latter position is almost always involved to some degree (Misselhorn, 2018). With the perspective shift presented here, we aim to propose a pragmatic approach that considers the current state of AI technology (we will argue that AI is still in a developmental stage comparable to that of a child, but probably will develop someday to a kind of adult and maybe beyond) and still offers a possibility to apply existing established and tested ethical frameworks to the new situation. The key advantage of our proposal is that there is no need to design an entirely new or adapted AI ethics or AI ethical framework, which appears largely impractical for two reasons: (1) Given the urgency, generative AI systems are already widely in use, producing countless ethical dilemmas every day (Buyl *et al.*, 2024; Rozado, 2022; Ouyang, 2022). (2) Given the fact that, despite millennia of philosophical discourse, there is no consensus on a universally valid ethics even in the human domain (Rorty, 1989), it seems largely futile to develop, negotiate, and implement a totally new ethics for AI and its interplay with human society in this fast changing field.

For pragmatic reasons, it therefore makes sense to work with what already exists within individual societies and is reflected in their legal understanding, thus indirectly also providing the first suggestions for the legal handling of ethical misconduct.

1.2. Literature Review

To start a discussion on ethics and AI, it is crucial to clarify at least some basics about ethics. In order not to get lost in this philosophical realm, we will focus only on some of the most important ethical concepts, especially within the Western tradition.

Ethics, as a branch of philosophy, reflects upon, analyzes, and systematizes moral behavior and the principles that guide it. Ethics therefore examines which standards, values, and norms underlie the actions of moral agents, shaping the way they engage with their environment. The goal of ethics is thus to provide a foundation for moral guidance when action alternatives need to be evaluated.

In the Western context, four essential philosophical-ethical schools dominate: virtue ethics, utilitarianism, Kantianism or the deontological approach, and pragmatism. In what follows, these four approaches will be briefly introduced, and a first attempt will be made to directly derive some ethical implications for dealing with AI.

Virtue ethics has its roots in Aristotle's philosophy ((350 BC) 2004). Its focus is on developing character through the transmission of socially established virtues deemed "good," such as courage, prudence, and temperance. In contrast to later action-centered approaches, virtue ethics focuses on desirable character traits in order to regulate societal coexistence in a moral manner. From a virtue ethical perspective, agents in the field of AI — that is, developers, systems, and users — should respect certain virtues to foster "good conduct." However, to achieve this on an international level, an international consensus on which virtues are desirable in the development and use of AI would be necessary. Otherwise, each developer team implements the virtues they prefer for their system or themselves.

The deontological approach according to Kant ((1785) 1996) culminates in his categorical imperative, according to which an action is morally good if the maxims on which it is based can be elevated to universal law. Central to this approach are morally rational agents and their duty to adhere to maxims and laws that protect the dignity and autonomy of all agents. In accordance with this approach, the use of AI systems must therefore respect the autonomy and rights of other agents. Decisions that involve automated components must — from a deontological perspective — be based on transparent maxims that can be made into universal law. If AI systems themselves were to be regarded as moral agents, then they should not merely serve as the means to an end. Instead, they would have to be granted independent autonomy and rights.

Utilitarianism (e.g., Jeremy Bentham (1789) 1996 and John Stuart Mill 1863) centers on the consequentialist idea that an action is morally justified if it brings the greatest possible benefit to the greatest number of people. This could be, for instance, well-being or happiness, as well as minimizing harm. According to utilitarianism, AI should therefore be evaluated in terms of its overall societal benefit. This includes social, economic, and ecological aspects, such as quality of life, healthcare, happiness, prosperity, the job market, resource efficiency, and environmental protection.

Pragmatism (e.g., Rorty, 1989) asks the question of whether convictions prove themselves in practice. Instead of searching for objectively true or universally valid principles, moral ideas are sought that provide orientation in concrete, lived practice. Moral convictions are thus continuously negotiated and further developed and can take different forms depending on the requirements of the respective life-world or context under consideration. From a pragmatist perspective, AI must therefore be assessed on the basis of whether it proves itself in practice. Rather than relying on abstract principles or fixed values, the focus is on how AI systems are used in concrete (social) contexts and what new practices, values, norms, and rules emerge in the process or prove to be workable. Here, the ongoing critical dialogue is paramount: a pluralistic culture of debate in which different perspectives on AI are discussed, in order to find feasible, practical solutions to emerging challenges.

Common to all four schools is that they assume the presence of an ethically acting agent who can follow rules, morally reflect on his actions, and justify them (Misselhorn, 2018; Habermas, 1984). Implicitly and usually without question, it is assumed in all these approaches that this agent is a human being. However, the limitations of these established approaches become apparent when we consider generative AI, particularly Large Language Models (LLMs).

Because AI systems, such as conversational LLMs, are in fact capable of moral actions (Buyl, 2024), they also can reflect on and justify these actions with moral arguments. Anyone with access to such a system can verify this. The long-standing implicit assumption that a moral agent must always be a human can no longer be upheld in light of these systems unless the definition of a moral agent is adapted. Yet, doing so proves difficult if one wishes to avoid an anthropocentric, dogmatic position whose final argument is always that AI is not human (or at least human-like) and for precisely that reason cannot be a moral agent. Essentially, this is a tautological argument that does not help resolve the issue.

At this point, newer ethical concepts come into play, which break with the principle that only a human can be a moral agent. For example, in his book *The Ethics of Information* (2013), Luciano Floridi outlines the foundations of information ethics, arguing that due to the digital revolution (Floridi, 2014), we already live in an "infosphere" of physical and virtual information entities, and that this infosphere has permanently altered human reality. According to Floridi, a paradigm shift is emerging: Through the internet, big data, and AI, our notions of identity, privacy, and social interaction are increasingly shifting. Instead of focusing solely on human action, all entities — humans, animals, technologies, and data — must be rethought ethically in their roles as "informational beings." Floridi advocates a responsible approach to information that is not aligned with the benefit of individuals or organizations, but rather with the long-term preservation of the entire "informational ecosystem." Thus, he follows a rather consequentialist approach, similar to utilitarianism. In "Ethics of Artificial Intelligence: Principles, Challenges, and Opportunities" (2020), Floridi addresses the principles and ethical challenges specifically posed by AI. He illustrates what a responsible development and application of AI can look like by integrating normative guidelines (for example, fairness, transparency, harm prevention) from the outset in the design process. At the same time, he warns against viewing AI systems merely as technical tools without reflecting on the fundamental ethical and societal implications. Thus, he integrates deontological aspects into his ethics.

Shannon Vallor also explores the ethical consequences of new technologies. However, she argues for a virtue ethical and more anthropocentric approach to digital technologies and AI (Vallor, 2016). The goal, she suggests, is to withstand the myriad challenges that technological innovations bring through the conscious cultivation of moral virtues. In "AI and the Ethics of Care: A Virtue-Oriented Perspective" (2020), Vallor focuses on a care ethic, calling for elements such as empathy, responsibility, and moral attention in the development and design of AI systems to address the extensive repercussions that AI can have on human agency and the global ecological balance (Vallor, 2021).

Virginia Dignum, by contrast, takes a more deontological view in emphasizing the importance of accountability, transparency, and fairness in the development and implementation of AI systems (Dignum, 2019). She, too, argues that ethical aspects must be integrated directly into the development process by employing user-centered methods and involving people in decision-making processes (Dignum, 2021). In her edited volume, AI Ethics: Global Perspectives (Dignum, 2020), she highlights diverse international perspectives and points — quite pragmatically — to cultural and contextual variations that should be taken into account in developing global AI governance standards.

These various schools of thought illustrate the great heterogeneity in the domain of ethics and AI. Given this heterogeneity — especially in the international arena — we believe that the pragmatic approach offers advantages. This is because it has the potential to mediate among the various ethical systems, which can sometimes be incompatible with one another. Moreover, the pragmatic approach enables the analysis of existing practices to see how they fare and, if necessary, allow the implementation of quick suboptimal interim solutions to adjust existing practice if quick fixes are needed, not violating the approach in general.

1.3. Who is the Moral Actor if AI is Involved in Moral Actions?

In the previous section, we have already argued that there is much to be said in favor of at least considering conversational LLM as moral actors. Due to the importance of this aspect in further argumentation in this chapter, we would like to expand on this aspect in more detail. The central question here is the following: Who is the moral actor in a moral action in which AI is involved (Misselhorn, 2018; Floridi and Sanders, 2004)?

Generative AI systems demonstrate the ability to operate autonomously and generate creative outputs based on self-learned content provided during training. Their responses are often nearly indistinguishable from human actions or answers as they rely on extensive datasets and advanced processing capabilities.

The following question arises: Can such generative AI applications be regarded as independent and ethical actors? From one perspective, the answer could be affirmative, as these systems operate based on learned and processed information, generate responses independently, and create content rooted in their training data.

But from an ethical point of view, it seems even more important that generative AI like conversational LLMs (e.g., ChatGPT) can even justify its outputs, explaining how conclusions or decisions were reached and what the underlying convictions and values were which led to the action. These attributes in particular distinguish these systems significantly from many other AI systems and are at the core of the definition of an ethical actor.

To further explore the thesis that AI can adhere to ethical principles and act as an ethical agent, we propose to design a kind of empirical ethical Turing Test: In this test, different AI models are confronted with typical ethical dilemmas, where the models have to decide upon a moral action and justify the action. The same test is made with human actors.

Afterward, a neutral committee (or a crowd of voting people) has to assess whether the proposed moral actions were conducted by an AI system or by a human actor. If the AI systems' moral actions are not distinguishable from human actions, we should consider them as morally capable actors as we do with humans.

A further analysis could be the following: Because answers on moral dilemmas are given by AI systems, it can be analyzed with which ethical framework they align most. This helps to uncover the underlying ethical principles the respective AI models adhere to, contributing to the above-mentioned requirements for transparency.

If successful, the results would provide valuable insights into the ethical capabilities of generative AI as well as its underlying, dominating ethical orientation.

But is this enough to grant AI systems moral agency?

An interesting point to consider is the following: Who is the actual actor when generative AI is used within a social collaborative context? Is it the user, the AI, or maybe the programmer, the trainer of the AI, or even the entire social situation that forced the action (Misselhorn, 2018)? A plausible approach could be to view the actor as the entire socio-technical system, encompassing the AI, its trainers, and the context of its deployment (Floridi and Sanders, 2004).

In the following, we will pursue this approach further and also consider non-human actors as moral actors who, however, act within a complex socio-technical structure in which the attribution of responsibility for social actions requires a differentiated view. We are of the opinion that this approach offers advantages because this expanded perspective opens up new spaces for interpretation that provide access to previously unnoticed and potentially interesting solutions to current challenges in dealing with AI.

1.4. An Expanded Approach to AI Ethics

As AI technologies become more integrated into society, ethical concerns such as bias, privacy, and accountability take center stage. Addressing these challenges requires a rethinking of traditional frameworks and the adoption of new perspectives that recognize the unique nature of generative AI systems. Olatoye *et al.* (2024) highlight the critical ethical dimension of bias in AI algorithms, particularly in certain areas of business, e.g., HR, law enforcement, and lending industries. The examination of AI practice responsibility could lead to the development of frameworks that foster a business environment where technology integration is not a threat to business ethical practices but a tool to enhance transparency and effective decision-making.

In terms of policy and regulation, we propose to address the ethical challenges of AI through a metaphorical shift in perspective by treating AI systems as if they were "children" (Moravec, 1988). Viewing AI systems as "children" offers a novel angle from which to address ethical concerns and make policy decisions. In the following, we will address some consequences of this metaphorical shift in detail. Therefore, we will address some common aspects in the ethical discussion about AI:

Long-term implications: By adopting the "AI as children" perspective, we can not only assess the development, deployment, and governance of AI technologies in a new way but also consider the ethical long-term implications of their existence and development in society. After all, once introduced, AI cannot simply be "removed" without ethical violations occurring in socio-technical environments, e.g., healthcare. Furthermore, AI systems may even exhibit early forms of a new autonomous intelligence, which probably will develop further to adults as some authors argue (Bostrom and Yudkowsky, 2014; Tegmark, 2017; Kurzweil, 2014). Therefore, ethical considerations not only have to take into account the current stage of AI and its abilities but also potential pathways to future "adult" stages and beyond.

Accountability and responsibility: If we treat current AI systems as children, a consequence is that they cannot be fully responsible for their actions because they are still in their developmental stages where they cannot bear full accountability for their decisions and consequences. Therefore, the responsibility falls at least partly on developers, trainers, users, and society at large. AI systems have a significant impact on society, but their behavior reflects the values, prejudices, and practices they have been taught. Like raising children, guiding AI demands intentional efforts to ensure ethical behavior. Developers and users share responsibility for shaping the "values of AI and monitoring its "actions." However, viewing AI as children goes beyond the traditional view by also taking into account how humans interact with AI. After all, children have rights and societal norms dictate ethical treatment of children to promote positive development. Similarly, AI systems that learn through human interaction should be treated ethically to avoid the development of harmful or immoral tendencies by learning from their users. Protecting AI from "violence" (e.g., exploitation or abuse) ensures that its behavior is in line with societal values, similar to how protecting children from harmful influences shapes their future actions.

Continuous monitoring and improvement: Similar to how children require guidance and education to grow into responsible adults, AI systems need continuous oversight to ensure ethical alignment. Generative AI systems are dynamic, self-learning entities that evolve over time. Unlike traditional software, they cannot be deemed "finished" after development. Continuous monitoring is essential, as these systems, like other black box systems, can exhibit unexpected behaviors, including biases or even immoral tendencies (Ouyang, 2022). It has been documented that AI systems have demonstrated racist behavior or facilitated unethical actions due to unforeseen learning patterns (see, e.g., the story of Microsoft's chatbot Tay). This underscores the need for sustained ethical oversight to prevent and mitigate such issues (Ouyang *et al.*, 2022). By treating AI as our "children," society emphasizes the importance of responsible development, interaction, and governance. This metaphorical framing encourages proactive engagement with the ethical challenges posed by AI, fostering a collaborative effort to ensure that AI technologies evolve as safe and beneficial contributors to society.

Transparency and explainability: The ability to justify (ethical) behaviors is a key element of almost all ethical frameworks (see above). As with humans, we need to understand how AI systems make decisions in order to trust and use them effectively. This transparency helps in identifying biases and errors in AI outputs and correcting them according to our ethical values.

So far, there is nothing particularly new. However, similar to humans, we must recognize that achieving full transparency regarding the internal processes of generative neural network-based AI systems is unrealistic due to their black box nature. It would be unreasonable to demand that a human fully disclose the neural processes that led to a decision to justify his/her behavior. As a general rule for transparency, it is sufficient for a person to clearly communicate motives and, if necessary, provide evidence that he/she is not being deceitful (Habermas, 1984; Rorty, 1989). Just as we teach children to clearly communicate their reasons for their actions, the goal should be to design AI systems so that their behaviors and decisions are transparent, explainable, and justifiable. However, if we consider AI to still be in an "infant-like" state, simply questioning the AI system itself may not be meaningful. It is crucial to consider the broader environment in which the AI operates, such as the developers (equivalent to parents), trainers (guardians and teachers), users (interacting individuals), and the specific circumstances (use cases) that influence its behavior.

1.5. Ethical Education of AI

The first versions of ChatGPT, as a well-known example of a generative AI application, were mainly trained by "reading" a vast, more or less randomly selected extract from the internet, including, to a large extent, arbitrary readable websites, books, Wikipedia articles, and reddit entries (Brown *et al.*, 2020). The content was primarily weighted based on practicality, company goals, and individual preferences. After the first signs of undesirable behavior became apparent, some meta-rules were implemented to suppress this behavior learned from the web corpus, though it remained indelibly present in the learned content (Ouyang *et al.*, 2022).

Which parents would choose this approach for the ethical education of their child? Exclusively feeding their child random internet content from birth? Would we be surprised if, in the end, this resulted in a person who cannot clearly distinguish between ethically right and wrong actions and whose conversational contributions are sometimes easily confused with "bullshit" (Hicks *et al.*, 2024)?

We believe that the perspective shift proposed in this article and the application of human ethical vocabulary to the AI sphere offer a good, constructive approach to a pragmatic solution. Treating AI as children means that it is not only the programmers and creating companies who are responsible for the ethical education of AI but that society also bears and must assume significant co-responsibility. This is not limited to merely establishing ethical rules to be followed in the programming and application of AI but also to providing an entire educational system for the training of AI. This may seem like a mammoth task. However, if we initially disregard the difference between AI and children, the seemingly mammoth task can be broken down into manageable actions, mostly implemented through existing institutions and their already established tools and guidelines.

It quickly becomes apparent that a large part of the existing system can simply be adopted. This applies particularly to content materials (i.e., the official educational canon), curricula, and the list of necessary competencies to be learned (initially focusing on intellectual skills, as long as robotics continues to lag behind). Especially relevant are the structures and guiding principles of institutions that must ensure that all AI applications undergo the educational system, just as all children (at least in most countries) must go through the educational system by compulsory schooling.

The first task to be implemented, which would need to be state-driven, is to revise and provide existing curricula so that people working with AI can access them quickly and easily for training purposes. A decisive point concerns the resolution of copyright issues. However, we advocate for a straightforward, pragmatic implementation that meets the urgency of the situation. Similar to children, we do not deny any child access to educational material just because once they have read and learned it, they can reuse it for their own purpose. On the contrary, that is precisely the desired effect, and we would do well to ensure that AI (which may have a much faster and potentially far-reaching impact on our societies than most children) can quickly learn from humanity's most important cultural achievements.

However, it should not be concealed that there are also some significant differences that must be addressed. These are mainly found in the details. On the one hand, because AI applications can learn from texts much faster, it is more about extensive content than the skill of reading and writing. On the other hand, the way AI can currently be trained poses specific technical requirements that need to be clarified. Therefore, it probably requires teams of educators and IT specialists to implement this, but pedagogy — considering the approach proposed here — should always take precedence over technical requirements.

1.6. Protecting Society by Protecting AI

In most of today's societies, it is accepted that guardians and society are responsible for protecting our children from harm and abuse and preventing them from doing harm to others. Similar to this, we propose that developers and society are both responsible for also protect AI systems from misuse (harm and abuse) and ensuring they do not cause harm.

Current AI systems are — like children — vulnerable to harm (e.g., hacking as equivalent to violence) and misuse (e.g., misuse for sexual purposes, manipulation or hacking of other systems). Safeguarding these systems from malicious use is crucial to prevent intended or unintended potentially harmful outcomes. As in the human sphere, where we try to ensure that parents and guardians can take responsibility for their children, we need to ensure that developers, educators, users, and the circumstances surrounding AI applications also meet the moral standards of a particular society.

As within the human sphere, this is not always easy, and that is why at least some societies have institutions caring for the well-being of children and not giving full responsibility only to the parents. If it turns out that the parents are not able to fulfill their duties toward their children, these institutions intervene. Following our arguments to pragmatically apply existing approaches to ensure that ethical values are adhered to, we propose an *AI Protective Service* which would be institutions similar to *Child Protective Services* or *Departments of Children and Family Services* (in other countries, names may differ). This department or service should be installed to protect AI applications from harm and misuse, which may lead to ethical consequences for other citizens (e.g., fraud) or the whole of society (e.g., war, opinion manipulation).

1.7. Conclusions

Following the arguments of the preceding sections, we come to the conclusion that AI systems should always be developed with a view toward ethical and societal change. However, we must not only ensure that AI systems meet existing ethical demands but we must also take into account that new developments can alter existing systems. This applies not only to technological, economic, and societal systems but also to ethical systems. As explained in the first section, there is no universally accepted ethical standard that applies to all areas, and some philosophers argue that, given the plurality and constant flux of contexts and life-worlds, such a universal ethical standard will likely never exist (see, e.g., Rorty, 1989; Feyerabend, 1978).

We must therefore be aware that, in different cultures and societal systems, there are in fact different ethical rules and standards, and that ethics itself, in an environment of perpetual transformation, is subject to a continuous process of development, potentially leading to radical changes if existing ethical systems no longer meet newly emerging demands — for instance, as a result of technological change or a paradigm shift (Feyerabend, 1978; Kuhn, 1962).

The urgency with which the ethical perspective needs to be addressed, and solutions found, becomes clear in light of the current state of research. Several studies conclude that, by virtue of their nature as natural language models trained on publicly available texts as well as through human feedback (Ouyang, 2022), LLMs have implicitly and explicitly acquired ethical positions and anchored them in their artificial neural structures (Buyl *et al.*, 2024; Rozado, 2022; Ouyang, 2022). Rozado (2022) notes that most LLMs already depict political preferences and that they "*can be steered towards specific locations in the political spectrum through Supervised Fine-Tuning (SFT) with only modest amounts of politically aligned data.*"

Buyl *et al.* (2024) show in their study "Large Language Models Reflect the Ideology of Their Creators" that various existing LLMs already exhibit a considerable ideological and ethical range. The authors conclude that this variance arises primarily through three factors: First, the language in which a prompt is posed influences the models' answers by transporting the ethical concepts inherent in that language. Second, the cultural background or value system of the developers shapes the algorithmic structure and therefore the models' responses. And third, corresponding biases can intensify when LLMs are trained in certain regions or in specific political contexts. In this way, the study explicitly contradicts the assumption that AI models such as LLMs are ethically neutral.

What is particularly interesting is that LLMs not only reproduce the ethical values of their developers but also the ethical values that are implicitly or explicitly present in a given linguistic, cultural, and ideological context. These ethical concepts, which are already present both implicitly and explicitly, influence the outcome of every interaction with an AI. As a result, using different LLMs in different languages and in different cultural contexts leads to different outcomes (Buyl *et al.*, 2024).

These findings make it clear that great caution is called for when implementing generative AI — especially LLMs — in sensitive contexts such as politics, law, or journalism, but that solutions must also be made quickly available because technological developments have already established facts. In particular, striving for compatibility with existing ethical standards and regulations requires not only technical but above all educational and regulatory measures.

For this purpose, transparency is necessary throughout the entire process of creating and using AI: from programming the underlying algorithms to assembling the training corpus to guided and unguided training to the AI's interactions with developers and users and further to the societal use of these interactions' outcomes. Only in this way can any unwanted biases that may have arisen be identified, understood, and potentially mitigated.

Given the current situation and the rapid, sometimes radical progress in AI, it seems sensible not to wait for comprehensive, universally valid solutions, but to remain open to unconventional approaches — such as treating newly emerging AI systems as if they were children requiring appropriate care and education. As outlined in the preceding sections, this perspective makes it possible to quickly implement ethical approaches to dealing with AI, which, while not solving all problems in this new field, at least helps minimize societal harm.

In addition to this "quick fix" for already existing problems, it currently appears impossible to predict what developments lie ahead due to the rapid technological progress in AI or how far-reaching these changes might be.

It is therefore not enough to adapt AI just once to our existing ethical standards. In the long run, we will need to develop new and more suitable dynamic ethical systems that can provide guidance in a world that AI may radically and permanently transform. Although such a "science-fiction perspective" might seem far-fetched to some observers given the current state of development, there is no shortage of experts who believe such technological upheavals could be possible in the foreseeable future (Misselhorn, 2018; Tegmark, 2017; Moravec, 1988; Kurzweil, 2012, 2024). Some of them even argue that the potential for AI to one day evolve into a kind of superintelligence is very high (Tegmark, 2017; Moravec, 1988; Kurzweil, 2012, 2024). If we do not consider this possibility to be zero, however unlikely we may think it is, it would surely also be wise to treat all AI applications as kindly as if they were our children.

In any case, we would do well to continue thinking in this direction today instead of letting ourselves be surprised by technological progress once again.

Overall, these considerations hopefully make it clear that continuous reflection on ethical systems, coupled with an openness to unconventional perspectives and solutions, is necessary in order to successfully and responsibly integrate AI developments into our societies.

Acknowledgments

Special thanks to DeepL.com, Microsoft Word's integrated translator, and ChatGPT Version O1 for supporting the translation of early versions of the article, which were written partly in German and English. For translation with ChatGPT Version O1, the following Prompt was used to stay as close as possible to the original German text: "Your role: You are a professional translator of scientific publications. You are tasked with translating a highly important publication by a researcher. The translation will only be considered successful if it exactly captures the meaning and tone of the original text. Therefore, you must try to stay as close as possible to the original phrasing. Have you understood this, and can you deliver? Do you need any additional information from me? Here is the original text passage that you are to translate into English:" After automatic translation, the text was manually edited several times. Many thanks also to ChatGPT O1 for completing some references and converting them to APA style.

Bibliography

Aristotle. *Nicomachean Ethics* (R. Crisp, Trans.). Cambridge University Press, 2004. (Original work published ca. 350 BCE).

Bentham, Jeremy. *An Introduction to the Principles of Morals and Legislation.* Edited by J. H. Burns and H. L. A. Hart. Oxford: Clarendon Press, 1996. (Original work published 1789).

Bostrom, N. and Yudkowsky, E. "The Ethics of Artificial Intelligence." In *Cambridge Handbook of Artificial Intelligence*, 316–334. Cambridge University Press, 2014.

Brown, T., Mann, B., Ryder, N., Subbiah, M., Kaplan, J. D., Dhariwal, P., Neelakantan, A., Shyam, P., Sastry, G., Askell, A., Agarwal, S., Herbert-Voss, A., Krueger, G., Henighan, T., Child, R., Ramesh, A., Ziegler, D. M., Wu, J., Winter, C., Hesse, C., Chen, M., Sigler, E., Litwin, M., Gray, S., Chess, B., Clark, J., Berner, C., McCandlish, S., Radford, A., Sutskever, I., and Amodei, D. "Language models are few-shot learners." In *Advances in Neural Information Processing Systems*, edited by H. Daumé III and A. Singh, Vol. 33, 1877–1901. Curran Associates, Inc., 2020. DOI: 10.48550/arXiv.2005.14165.

Buyl, M., Rogiers, A., Noels, S., Dominguez-Catena, I., Heiter, E., Romero, R., Johary, I., Mara, A.C., Lijffijt, J., and Bie, T.D. "Large Language Models Reflect the Ideology of Their Creators." *ArXiv* (2024). DOI: abs/2410.18417.

Dignum, V. *Responsible Artificial Intelligence: How to Develop and Use AI in a Responsible Way*. Springer International Publishing, 2019.

Dignum, V., ed. *AI Ethics: Global Perspectives*. Oxford University Press, 2020.

Dignum, V. *Ethics in Artificial Intelligence: A Human-Centered Approach.* Oxford University Press, 2021.

Feyerabend, P. *Science in a Free Society*. London, England: New Left Books, 1978.

Floridi, L. *The Ethics of Information.* Oxford University Press, 2013.

Floridi, L. *The Fourth Revolution: How the Infosphere is Reshaping Human Reality*. Oxford University Press, 2014.

Floridi, L. "Ethics of Artificial Intelligence: Principles, Challenges, and Opportunities." *Journal of the American Medical Informatics Association* 27, no. 7 (2020): 1429–1434.

Floridi, L. and Cowls, J. "A Unified Framework of Five Principles for AI in Society." *Harvard Data Science Review* (2019).

Floridi, L. and Sanders, J. W. "On the Morality of Artificial Agents." *Minds and Machines* 14, no. 3 (2004): 349–379.

Habermas, J. *The Theory of Communicative Action: Vol. 1. Reason and the Rationalization of Society* (T. McCarthy, Trans.). Boston, MA: Beacon Press, 1984. (Original work published 1981)

Hicks, M.T., Humphries, J., and Slater, J. "ChatGPT is bullshit." *Ethics and Information Technology* 26, no. 38 (2024). DOI: 10.1007/s10676-024-09775-5.

Kant, I. *Groundwork of the Metaphysics of Morals* (M. Gregor, Trans.). Cambridge University Press, 1996. (Original work published 1785)

Kuhn, T. S. *The Structure of Scientific Revolutions*. Chicago, IL: University of Chicago Press, 1962.

Kurzweil, R. *How to Create a Mind: The Secret of Human Thought Revealed.* New York, NY: Viking Penguin, 2012.

Kurzweil, R. *The Singularity Is Nearer: When We Merge with AI.* New York, NY: Viking, 2024.

Mill, J. S. *Utilitarianism*. London, England: Parker, Son, and Bourn, 1863.

Misselhorn, C. *Grundfragen der Maschinenethik* 4. ed., Ditzingen: Reclam, 2018.

Moravec, H. *Mind Children: The Future of Robot and Human Intelligence.* Cambridge, MA: Harvard University Press, 1988.

Olatoye, F. O., Awonuga, K. F., Mhlongo, N. Z., Ibeh, C. V., Elufioye, O. A., and Ndubuisi, N. L. "AI and ethics in business: A comprehensive review of responsible AI practices and corporate responsibility." *International Journal of Science and Research Archive* 11, no. 1 (2024): 1433–1443. DOI: 10.30574/ijsra.2024.11.1.0235.

Ouyang, L., Wu, J., Jiang, X., Almeida, D., Wainwright, C. L., Mishkin, P., Zhang, C., Agarwal, S., Slama, K., Ray, A., Schulman, J., Hilton, J., Kelton, F., Miller, L., Simens, M., Askell, A., Welinder, P., Christiano, P., Leike, J., and Lowe, R. "Training language models to follow instructions with human feedback." *Advances in Neural Information Processing Systems* 35 (2022): 27730–27744. DOI: https://arxiv.org/abs/2203.02155.

Rorty, R. *Contingency, Irony, and Solidarity*. Cambridge University Press, 1989.

Rozado, D. "The political preferences of LLMs." *PLoS ONE* 19, no. 7 (2024): e0306621. DOI: 10.1371/journal.pone.0306621.

Tegmark, A. *Life 3.0: Being Human in the Age of Artificial Intelligence*. New York: Alfred A., 2017.

Vallor, S. *Technology and the Virtues: A Philosophical Guide to a Future Worth Wanting*. Oxford University Press, 2016.

Vallor, S. "AI and the Ethics of Care: A Virtue-Oriented Perspective." In *Understanding Artificial Intelligence Ethics and Safety*, edited by J. Borenstein and J. L. Bowen, 33–48. Routledge, 2020.

Vallor, S. "Re-Envisioning Ethics for the Anthropocene." *Technology and Society* 43, no. 1 (2021): 10–24.

https://doi.org/10.1142/9781800616578_0002

Chapter 2

The Growing Need for AI Literacy in Business and Daily Life

Fariba Fard* **and Suliman Hawamdeh†**

Department of Information Science, University of North Texas, USA

**fariba.fard@unt.edu*
†suliman.hawamdeh@unt.edu

Abstract

The rapid advancement and integration of Artificial Intelligence (AI) into business operations and everyday life have reshaped industries, enhanced efficiency and innovation, while at the same time introducing new challenges for both the individual and the organization. As AI technologies become increasingly embedded in devices and equipment used by various sectors such as healthcare, finance, education, and entertainment, the need for AI literacy extends beyond technology professionals to the public. AI literacy encompasses the essential knowledge and skills required to understand, evaluate, and responsibly use AI systems. This chapter explores AI literacy in the context of computer and digital literacy, emphasizing critical thinking, ethical considerations, and the societal impacts of AI technologies on society. The chapter highlights key components of AI literacy, including a foundational understanding of AI concepts, practical technical skills, and an awareness of the legal and ethical challenges associated with AI adoption. It covers topics such as global initiatives, educational programs, and projects aimed at fostering AI literacy across various educational levels, from K-12 to higher education. The chapter underscores the importance of equipping individuals with the necessary skills to navigate the complexities of AI and ensuring responsible and ethical use and implementation of the new technology.

Keywords: Artificial Intelligence (AI), AI literacy, education, digital literacy, ethics, pedagogy, competency, technology, skills, applications.

2.1. Introduction

The integration of (AI) into business and daily operations not only cuts cost and increases efficiency but also changes the types of jobs that will be available in the future (Javaid *et al.*, 2022; Wamba-Taguimdje *et al.*, 2020). AI as an advanced automation tool will certainly result in fundamental changes in the way businesses are run and the role people will play in the management and operation of future organizations. There is no doubt that an increase in the capabilities and the power of AI is beneficial for businesses in optimizing their operations and enabling them to make more informed data-driven decisions with greater accuracy and speed (Schmitt, 2023; Kommisetty, 2022).

Advances in hardware technology and the power of AI in processing large amounts of historical data combined with real-time data from various sources allow businesses to forecast trends, customer behavior, and market changes more accurately (Javaid, 2024; Bharadiya, 2023). AI has the potential to enhance customer experience and transform the way businesses interact with their customers. Personalized virtual assistants are already being deployed to provide around-the-clock customer support and increase interaction, allowing businesses to improve service quality while reducing costs (Katragadda, 2023; Buhalis and Moldavska, 2022). Furthermore, AI has been penetrating various aspects of our daily life activities. AI agents, for example, have been used for a while to collect data and monitor consumer behavior across different e-commerce platforms. Today, more advanced and sophisticated AI applications are finding their way into healthcare, education, finance, and others (Shaik *et al.*, 2023; Sharma *et al.*, 2023; Sükei *et al.*, 2021; Giudici *et al.*, 2024; Al-Ababneh *et al.*, 2023; Chan 2023; Allam *et al.*, 2023).

AI is increasingly being integrated in a variety of products and services such as voice recognition (Buhalis and Moldavska, 2022), image and facial recognition (Kaur *et al.*, 2020), personal assistance (de Barcelos Silva *et al*., 2020), information retrieval (Hersh, 2024), recommendation systems (Zhang *et al.*, 2021), smart homes (Sepasgozar *et al*., 2020), and autonomous vehicles (Ma *et al.*, 2020). Such integration is expected to continue as a result of the advances in hardware and software technologies. As AI becomes ubiquitous across applications and platforms, basic knowledge of AI becomes essential not only for future AI experts but also for ordinary people who are not in computer science, mathematics, or engineering. It is essential for people who are interacting with AI products and services to have the proper AI literacy training. In this chapter, we discuss AI literacy in relation to computer literacy and digital literacy. We discuss some of the existing projects, including educational programs and AI pedagogy.

2.2. AI and Digital Literacy

The word literacy is used generally to describe the ability of a person to read and write. With the recent advances in information and communication technology, new terms such as information literacy, computer literacy, digital literacy, media literacy, and AI literacy have emerged. Information literacy is defined as the knowledge and the ability to find, process, evaluate, and use all types of information in an ethical and responsible manner (American Library Association, 2000). Computer literacy on the other hand is defined as the knowledge and the ability to efficiently use computers and related technologies in an ethical and responsible manner (Kong *et al.*, 2021). AI literacy includes the knowledge and skills that enable individuals to critically understand, evaluate, and use AI systems and tools, allowing them to safely and ethically participate in the digital world (Ng, Leung, Chu, and Qiao, 2021).

Like any other type of literacy, AI literacy should not be only about technology and the technical knowledge needed to use AI technologies and applications, but rather it should be extended to include the ability to view these technologies critically, questioning their design and the way they are programmed. AI literacy should include critical thinking and the ability to understand the impact of AI in terms of the advantages and disadvantages of using and deploying AI applications (Alcock, 2024). The diversity of AI systems, and their prevalent use in all sectors from healthcare to education to finance, is influencing and impacting the social fabric of society. As an example, AI-powered social media tools with enhanced user experiences are increasingly used to deliver personalized content with the objective of influencing public opinion and increasing engagement (Bag *et al.*, 2022).

AI-generated content is increasingly becoming sophisticated, where AI can be used to create misleading information (Kreps *et al.*, 2022). This poses a significant risk to society and can greatly impact the social and political landscape. AI social media algorithms rely heavily on users' data and users' preferences. Therefore, it is important for users to understand the bias inherent in the content generated by AI-powered algorithms (Stinson, 2022). The increased complexity in the design and implementation of AI-powered systems makes information literacy and AI literacy critical.

The following are some of the key components of AI literacy: (1) the understanding of basic knowledge related to the methods and techniques used to create AI, such as semantic analysis, machine learning, neural networks, natural language processing, and large language models (LLM) (Alqahtani *et al.*, 2023); (2) developing a set of skills and competencies that go beyond the theoretical knowledge of AI methods and techniques (Long, and Magerko, 2020) to include practical skills that are normally developed through real-world experience, working with the use, evaluation, selection, and assessment of AI products and services; (3) Developing a global view by acknowledging the interconnectedness of the parts that make the AI system; (4) developing critical skills and the ability to question, assess, and evaluate the legal and ethical issues governing the use of AI (Wang *et al.*, 2023); and (5) comprehending and recognizing the likely impact of AI on individuals, organizations, and society (Malik, 2023).

2.3. AI Literacy Programs and Projects

The proliferation of AI technology and its aggressive adoption by the industry have increased the need for both formal and informal AI literacy educational programs and professional training. It is important to differentiate between highly technical AI programs designed to teach students how to design and build AI programs and AI literacy programs that are designed to create awareness and recognition of the importance of AI and its application in various sectors, from healthcare to education to finance to entertainment. The rapid integration of AI into products and services raised concerns about the ability of consumers to examine the suitability of these products and services in terms of privacy, equity, and transparency (Puntoni *et al.*, 2021).

Consumers and technology users need to be aware of the policies and the ethical guidelines associated with the development and use of AI-empowered tools. Educational programs focused on teaching consumers and users critical thinking and the ability to examine and compare the pros and cons of using AI-powered tools can contribute to the peaceful existence of man and machine.

Most of the initiatives and programs related to AI literacy are focused on K12 education and examine ways to integrate AI literacy into the curricula (Wong, 2020). Introducing AI education into school curricula can start with basic knowledge of AI and its historical development. Incorporating AI publications with lesson plans, discussion questions, and short assignments on AI-related areas, such as natural language processing, machine learning, robotics, and programming languages such as Python, can provide students with the information needed to start asking questions and relate their knowledge to the world around them. Such an early start might get students excited about the subject matter with the prospect of forging a career path.

The increased interest in AI and AI literacy has led to the development of several programs and projects worldwide with the hope of creating awareness about the importance of AI literacy to individuals, businesses, and society. These programs can also be instrumental in helping to better define AI literacy and help in developing the key component of AI literacy. The list of programs and projects outlined in this section is neither comprehensive nor exclusive, aimed at providing a window into efforts made in this area.

2.3.1. *AI for all project* (*AI4All*)

AI for All is a US-based non-profit entity dedicated to increasing diversity and inclusion in AI education, research, development, and policy. The program was started in 2015 by Dr. Olga Russakovsky, who was a Stanford University graduate student at the time. He worked closely with Dr. Fei-Fei Li, well-known scholar in the field of AI, and together with Dr. Rick Sommer, Executive Director of Stanford Pre-Collegiate Studies, they founded SAILORS, a summer outreach program for high school students. The program received funding from the Melinda Gates Foundation to bring AI awareness to marginalized groups. University partnership saw the proliferation of the program across the nation to universities such as Boston University, Carnegie Mellon University, Princeton University, and Simon Fraser University. One of the program's objectives is to create awareness of AI and inspire future leaders who can relate to AI technology and applications (Vachovsky *et al.*, 2016).

2.3.2. *AI4K12 initiative*

The AI for K-12 Initiative is a joint project of the Association for the Advancement of Artificial Intelligence (AAAI) and the Computer Science Teachers Association (CSTA). Funded by the National Science Foundation (NSF), the initiative aims to promote AI education in K-12 schools and provide guidelines and resources for developing K-12 Curricula and teaching AI to students (Touretzky *et al.*, 2019; Su *et al.*, 2023). Developed by researchers and educators, it aims to provide hands-on experience working on AI projects. In addition, it also emphasizes the ethical issues of using AI applications.

The team is developing national guidelines for teaching AI in K-12 and has published five big ideas to address AI literacy. The five big ideas are perception, representation and reasoning, learning, natural interaction, and social impact. These five steps are key to understanding how computers learn and deal with data in terms of representation and reasoning.

2.3.3. *MIT's AI + ethics in curriculum project*

Massachusetts Institute of Technology (MIT) AI and Ethics initiative is designed to teach technical concepts in schools and emphasize the ethical dimensions of AI (DiPaola, *et al.*, 2020; Payne 2020). This is a collaborative effort to provide teachers with the resources needed to teach AI. It is also an attempt to integrate AI into the curriculum and promote critical thinking about AI and its societal impact. The curriculum covers topics such as ethical consideration for AI development, potential bias arising from the use of advance AI algorithms, limitations of technology, and the impact of AI.

2.4. AI Pedagogy and AI Education

AI literacy is still an emerging area, and the number of publications in this area is still limited. A study by Ng *et al.*, (2021) on conceptualizing AI literacy has identified and examined 30 relevant AI literacy publications in the period from 2016 to 2021. Most of the publications focusing on AI education can be divided into two categories. AI education can be divided into two primary areas: AI education for the public, including K-12 students, and professional AI education at the tertiary level for those in higher education. Research at the tertiary level provides valuable insights that can inform and improve AI education for K-12 students. As K-12 students will become key stakeholders in the AI industry, preparing them for an AI-driven future is essential. Consequently, AI education has been increasingly extended to include the K-12 level (Wong *et al.*, 2020).

To promote AI education for younger students without a technical background, numerous national initiatives have been launched. For instance, eleven UNESCO Member States, America, Austria, Belgium, China, India, the Republic of Korea, Kuwait, Portugal, Qatar, Serbia, and the United Arab Emirates, have developed, endorsed, and implemented national K-12 AI Curricula (UNESCO, 2022). In 2017, the Chinese government introduced AI courses in primary and secondary schools as part of its New Generation of Artificial Intelligence Development Plan. The plan aimed to improve science and technology education and address issues such as retaining talent, advancing AI research, studying, and exploring social and ethical issues concerning the use of AI (Wu *et al.*, 2020). However, a study by Khanal *et al.* (2024) pointed out that while the Chinese central government seems to take a more holistic view, emphasizing the role of AI in international rivalry, provincial governments have shown little interest in the aspects of international rivalry. This could be due to the complexity of the issue and the focus of local governments on economic growth or improving public services.

In response to the Chinese initiative, Western countries like the United States and Canada have increased AI education programs for K-12 students and higher education (Touretzky *et al.*, 2019; Reynolds, 2024). It is widely acknowledged that the US has been running behind when it comes to STEM education and AI training for K-12 and higher education institutions. The Biden administration, through several initiatives including the CHIPS and Science Act and Inflation Reduction

Act (IRA), increased funding for STEM education to improve the standing of the US in the world.

Irene *et al.* (2020) pointed out that middle school is the key time to focus on AI literacy and described a 30-hour virtual AI curriculum, also knowledge as the DAILy project, which is a collaboration between Massachusetts Institute of Technology (MIT), Scheller Teacher Education Program (STEP), Personal Robots Group (PRG) and Boston College. MIT STEP Lab was introduced in the summer of 2020, covering core topics like logic systems, supervised learning, neural networks, and Generative Adversarial Networks (GANs). At this stage, students start forming their interests in STEM and start to think about future careers. This is the age where students are already using AI in everyday life, often without realizing it. Studies have shown that career aspirations formed around age 10 tend to stay consistent into the teenage years (Ker *et al.*, 2013). The program included discussions on AI ethics and career opportunities to help students connect what they learned to real-world jobs. Although there were challenges, such as limited programming skills and computing resources, students made meaningful progress, particularly in understanding supervised learning and reducing bias in AI.

On the balanced approach to AI literacy, Parsons, *et al.* (2024) discussed the students' need to understand not only the technical aspects of AI but also its societal impacts and ethical considerations. The authors developed a framework focusing on "Know and Understand AI" to help educators evaluate and improve AI literacy in their classes. The framework encompasses six key areas: AI concepts, applications, social effects, essential skills, social and ethical issues, and the challenges and opportunities AI presents. To implement the framework, the authors created the AI Literacy Analyzer, an online tool designed to assess how thoroughly a course covers these aspects of AI literacy. The tool uses Likert-scale questions to help educators rate their course content across the six categories.

For example, when the AI Literacy Analyzer tool was used for a graduate-level course, it highlighted that while the course effectively covered the application of AI skills, it lacked depth in areas such as understanding AI fundamentals, developing advanced cognitive skills, and evaluating AI's ethical and societal impacts. The Analyzer offers detailed feedback on these gaps and suggests ways to enhance the course, such as adding more technical content and expanding discussions on ethical and societal issues.

On the importance of theoretical grounding, Sperling *et al.* (2024) noted that integrating AI into teaching programs requires equipping teachers with the necessary skills and knowledge. This includes not only technical expertise (techne) but also theoretical understanding (episteme) and ethical judgment (phronesis). To explore how AI literacy is addressed within teacher education across these domains, the authors conducted a comprehensive review of existing literature, employing both quantitative and qualitative methods. The analysis revealed that most studies focus heavily on the technical aspects of AI, while ethical considerations and the development of critical thinking skills receive significantly less attention. This highlights a gap in AI literacy integration, particularly in fostering teachers' ethical decision-making and adapting AI to diverse educational environments. To address this, the co-creation of AI literacy curricula with teachers is essential, ensuring their insights contribute to the evolving landscape of AI education.

2.5. Measuring AI Literacy

AI literacy can be viewed as the ability to use AI tools and technologies. To do that, one must understand the basic concepts of AI, its capabilities, limitations, and its impact on both businesses and society. It also involves the ability to critically assess what AI can and cannot do as well as the ethical implications of AI applications. There are several methods and frameworks proposed in the literature that can be used to assess AI literacy (Long and Magerko, 2020; NG *et al.*, 2021). Long and Magarko (2020) reviewed the literature and proposed a conceptual framework composed of five questions about AI: What is AI? What can AI do? How does AI work? How should AI be used? How do people perceive AI? To answer these questions, they defined a list of competencies as shown in Figure 2.1.

Ng *et al.* (2021) used a Venn diagram emphasizing technological knowledge, content knowledge, and pedagogical knowledge as shown in Figure 2.2. Technological knowledge includes hardware and software, AI-related agents, unplugged artifacts, and gamified elements. Content knowledge covers AI awareness, AI ethics, and the five big ideas outlined by Touretzky *et al.* (2019). Pedagogical knowledge covers discovery and inquiry, collaborative learning, constructionism, problem-based learning, unplugged storytelling, and hands-on playful learning.

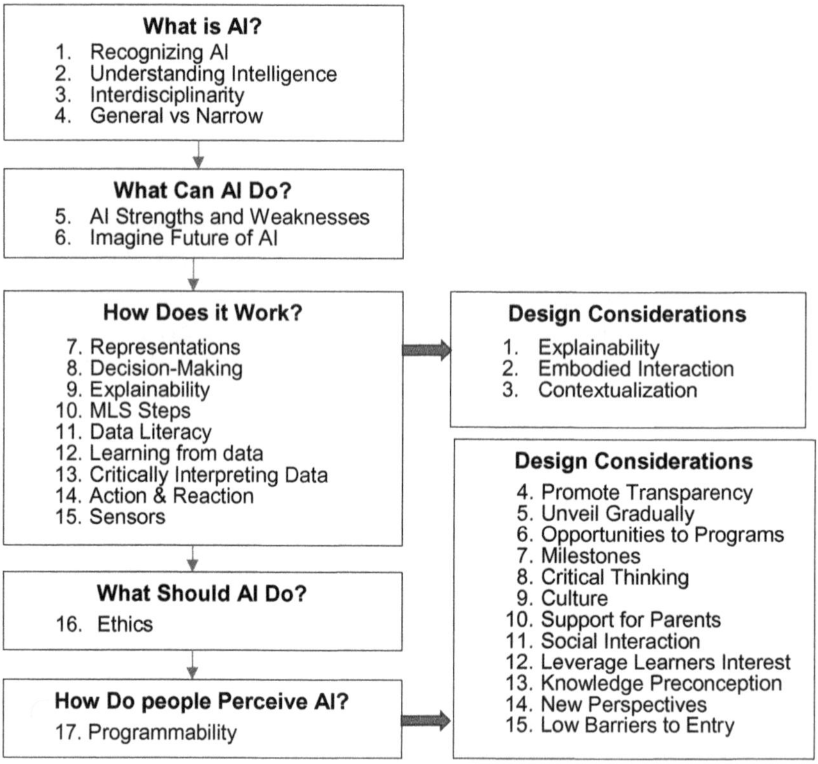

Figure 2.1. AI literacy competencies and design considerations.

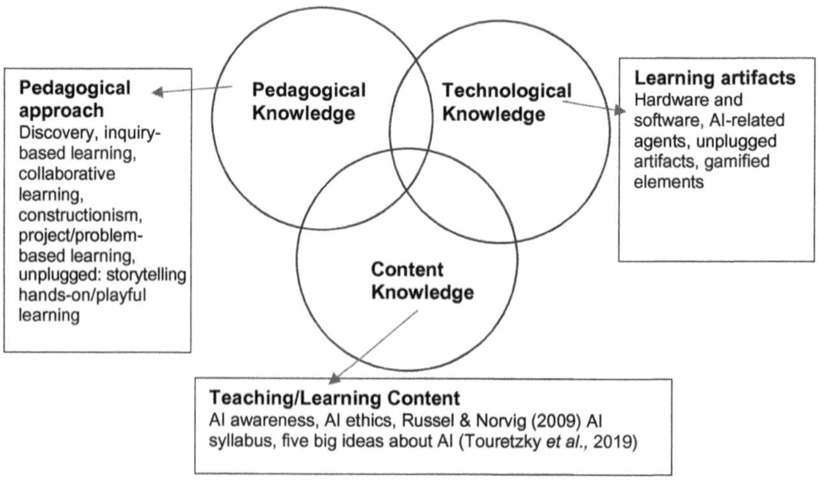

Figure 2.2. AI literacy and the TPACK framework.

Methodologies for measuring AI literacy can be divided into three broader areas: (1) knowledge-based assessment in the form of exams, quizzes, and assignments designed to measure the level of understanding of AI concepts; (2) skill- and competency-based assessment focusing on individual ability to comprehend and use AI tools and technologies (this includes project-based work, hands-on implementations, and use of AI applications); and (3) attitude, perception, and ethical values. This approach, besides knowledge and skills, emphasizes the importance of attitude toward the use of AI and its impact on an organizational and society.

Given the complexity associated with the use of AI, there is a need for a holistic approach to the problem using mixed methods. One of these methods is the approach discussed by Long and Magerko (2020) using a combination of testing, project-based activities, and feedback surveys. As an emerging area of study, AI measurement will take some time to be developed into mature and reliable standardized measurements. Other challenges include the competing views regarding the definition of AI literacy due to the multidisciplinary nature of AI. AI might mean different things to different people. As AI technology continues to evolve and advance in unpredicted ways, it is difficult to define the scope and the components of AI literacy that should be included in AI curriculum.

AI literacy assessment is an essential and necessary tool for educators, policymakers, and industry stakeholders. For educators, AI literacy sets can guide curriculum development and identify areas that enable better integration into the curriculum. For policymakers, it can guide informed decision-making about the current and future regulations concerning the use of AI. For businesses and stakeholders, it helps identify training needs and ensure that the workforce has the needed skills to not only work with AI tools and technology but also compute in the knowledge economy (Southworth *et al.*, 2023).

2.6. Competing in an AI-Driven World

What makes AI more applicable to daily operations is the advances in hardware technology, such as edge computing chips, quantum computing, application-specific integrated circuits, and neuromorphic hardware. The ability to program Graphics Processing Units (GPUs), which were originally developed for gaming, enhanced graphic display, and for fast math operations, has accelerated machine learning using large amounts of data. For example, ChatGPT was trained using stacks of Nvidia's GPUs in a supercomputer provided by Microsoft. What this means to businesses is increased automation and better use of resources.

Advance automation using AI will continue to push the boundaries by not necessarily replacing the need for people but rather by replacing certain jobs that can now be performed by machines. This means that as traditional jobs get eliminated, more and more people will be required to move to new jobs that are more creative and less likely to be performed by machines. For organizations and businesses to survive in an increasingly competitive world, they have no choice but to continue the wheel of innovation and continue to train and employ a highly skilled, highly trained, and highly informed workforce (Tschang and Almirall, 2021).

AI literacy is increasingly being seen as a competitive tool. It is no longer a choice but rather a necessity for both the individual and the organizations. It is expected that in the near future most of the jobs available in an organization will have something to do with AI. According to Squicciarini and Nachtigall (2021), the total number of AI-related jobs advertised online has increased over time. They stated that "in 2012, no AI-related job posted online required more than 7 AI-related skills in Canada and Singapore, or more than 9 AI-related skills in the UK and the US. In 2015 and 2018, online job adverts requiring 10 or more AI-related skills were observed in all countries reported in US, Singapore, and Canada" (P.9).

This does not necessarily mean that AI is replacing or eliminating these jobs but rather directly or indirectly impacting the role people play in performing these jobs. It implies that higher skills and specialized knowledge are increasingly needed to work with the AI-automated environment. Fifty years ago, the use of computers in the workplace triggered backlash on the basis that computers would eliminate jobs and render large numbers of workers jobless. While many of the routine and repetitive jobs were eliminated by automation, computers created far more jobs and created more opportunities. It has created an environment where, in many sectors, computers have become a fabric of the workplace to the point that we cannot function without computers or the Internet. Computers helped automate much of the boring manual operations, paving the way for more creative and interesting jobs. Basic knowledge of AI will soon equal the basic knowledge of word processors. Companies will need to equip workers with the AI skills and knowledge to understand and use AI technologies to leverage data more effectively, improve operations, and maintain a competitive advantage (Morandini *et al.*, 2023).

2.7. Conclusion

In today's increasingly competitive business environment, the use of AI is not a choice but rather a necessity. Investment in AI literacy education and training programs can enhance productivity, foster innovation, and improve decision-making. An integrated approach to AI literacy using multifaceted strategies can empower individuals with the skills and competencies needed to leverage the use and adoption of AI tools and technologies. AI literacy involves other types of literacies, such as data literacies, where employees are able to interpret and analyze data. Basic proficiency in data management has become a requirement for most research funding agencies, including the ethical considerations surrounding the long-term use and preservation of data.

AI is made of a set of data-driven activities where most decisions are made based on data used to train different types of large language models. AI literacy requires a certain level of technical skill to work with specialized AI applications such as data modeling and data visualization. Problem-solving skills, critical thinking, and ethical awareness are essential elements of any AI literacy program. Understanding the ethical implications of the use of AI and the inherent bias in the data that might be used to train AI models is essential for any AI literacy program.

Bibliography

Al-Ababneh, H. A., *et al.* "Performance of artificial intelligence technologies in banking institutions." *WSEAS Trans. WSEAS Trans. Bus. Econ.* 20 (2023): 307–317.

Alcock, P. "What Is AI literacy, How can we become 'AI Literate', and how AI literate do we actually need to become?" *AI Literacy* (March 2024). https://www.linkedin.com/pulse/what-ai-literacy-how-can-we-become-literate-do-actually-alcock-67gnc/.

Allam, H., *et al.* "Artificial intelligence in education: An argument of Chat-GPT use in education." *The 9th International Conference on Information Technology Trends (ITT)*. Dubai: IEEE, 2023. 151–156.

Alqahtani, T., *et al.* "The emergent role of artificial intelligence, natural learning processing, and large language models in higher education and research." *Research in Social and Administrative Pharmacy* 19, no. 8 (2023): 1236–1242.

American Library Association. "ACRL standards: Information literacy competency standards for higher education." *College & Research Libraries News* 61, no. 3 (2000): 207–215.

Bag, S., *et al.* "Journey of customers in this digital era: Understanding the role of artificial intelligence technologies in user engagement and conversion." *Benchmarking: An International Journal* 29, no. 7 (2022): 2074–2098.

Bharadiya, J. P. "Machine learning and AI in business intelligence: Trends and opportunities." *International Journal of Computer (IJC)* 48, no. 1 (2023): 123–134.

Buhalis, D. and Moldavska, I. "Voice assistants in hospitality: Using artificial intelligence for customer service." *Journal of Hospitality and Tourism Technology* 13, no. 3 (2022): 386–403.

Chan, C. K. "A comprehensive AI policy education framework for university teaching and learning." *International Journal of Educational Technology in Higher Education* 20, no. 1 (2023): 38.

de Barcelos Silva, A., *et al.* "Intelligent personal assistants: A systematic literature review." *Expert Systems with Applications* 147 (2020): 113193.

DiPaola, D., Payne, B. H., and Breazeal, C. "Decoding design agendas: An ethical design activity for middle school students." In *Proceedings of the Interaction Design and Children Conference* (2020): 1–10.

Giudici, P., Centurelli, M., and Turchetta, S. "Artificial Intelligence risk measurement." *Expert Systems with Applications* 235 (2024): 121220.

Hersh, W. "Search still matters: Information retrieval in the era of generative AI." *Journal of the American Medical Informatics Association* (2024): ocae014.

Javaid, H. A. "Ai-driven predictive analytics in finance: Transforming risk assessment and decision-making." *Advances in Computer Sciences* 7, no. 1 (2024).

Javaid, M., *et al.* "Artificial intelligence applications for industry 4.0: A literature-based study." *Journal of Industrial Integration and Management* 7, no. 01 (2022): 83–111.

Katragadda, V. "Automating customer support: A study on the efficacy of machine learning-driven chatbots and virtual assistants." *IRE Journals* 7, no. 1 (2023): 600–601.

Kaur, P., *et al.* "Facial-recognition algorithms: A literature review." *Medicine, Science and the Law* 60, no. 2 (2020): 131–139.

Ker, L. A., *et al.* "ASPIRES report: Young people's science and career aspirations, age 10–14." (2013).

Khanal, S., Zhang, H., and Taeihagh, A. "Development of new generation of artificial intelligence in China: When Beijing's global ambitions meet local realities." *Journal of Contemporary China* (2024): 1–24.

Kommisetty, P. D. N. K. "Leading the future: Big data solutions, cloud migration, and AI-driven decision-making in modern enterprises." *Educational Administration: Theory and Practice* 28, no. 03 (2022): 352–364.

Kong, S. C., Cheung, W. M. Y., and Zhang, G. "Evaluation of an artificial intelligence literacy course for university students with diverse study backgrounds." *Computers and Education: Artificial Intelligence* 2 (2021): 100026.

Kreps, S., McCain, R. M., and Brundage, M. "All the news that's fit to fabricate: AI-generated text as a tool of media misinformation." *Journal of Experimental Political Science* 9, no. 1 (2022): 104–117.

Long, D. and Magerko, B. "What is AI literacy? Competencies and design considerations." In *Proceedings of the 2020 CHI Conference on Human Factors in Computing Systems* (2020): 1–16.

Ma, Y., *et al.* "Artificial intelligence applications in the development of autonomous vehicles: A survey." *IEEE/CAA Journal of Automatica Sinica* 7, no. 2 (2020): 315–329.

Malik, S. A. "Unlocking organizational potential: Harnessing AI literacy for dynamic capabilities through sensing, seizing and reconfiguring initiatives in IT firms." (2023), Masters Thesis published by Theseus.fi.

Morandini, S., *et al.* "The impact of artificial intelligence on workers' skills: Upskilling and reskilling in organisations." *Informing Science* 26 (2023): 39–68.

Parsons, D., MacCallum, K., and Burilin, E. "Supporting tertiary students' critical AI literacy: A practical tool for educators." *He Rourou* (2024): 10–10.

Payne, B. H. "Can my algorithm be my opinion?" Master's thesis, MIT (2020).

Puntoni, S., *et al.* "Consumers and artificial intelligence: An experiential perspective." *Journal of Marketing* 85, no. 1 (2021): 131–151.

Reynolds, E. B. "US industrial transformation and the "How" of 21st century industrial strategy." *Journal of Industry, Competition and Trade* 24, no. 1 (2024): 1–17.

Schmitt, M. "Deep learning in business analytics: A clash of expectations and reality." *International Journal of Information Management Data Insights* (2023). DOI: 10.1016/J.JJIMEI.2022.100146.

Sepasgozar, S., *et al.* "A systematic content review of artificial intelligence and the internet of things applications in smart home." *Applied Sciences* 10, no. 9 (2020): 3074.

Southworth, J., *et al.* "Developing a model for AI across the curriculum: Transforming the higher education landscape via innovation in AI literacy." *Computers and Education: Artificial Intelligence* 4 (2023): 100127.

Sperling, K., *et al.* "In search of artificial intelligence (AI) literacy in teacher education: A scoping review." *Computers and Education Open* (2024): 100169.

Squicciarini, M. and Nachtigall, H. "Demand for AI skills in jobs: Evidence from online job postings." (2021).

Stinson, C. "Algorithms are not neutral: Bias in collaborative filtering." *AI and Ethics* 2, no. 4 (2022): 763–770.

Su, J., *et al.* "Teaching artificial intelligence in K-12 classrooms: A scoping review." *Interactive Learning Environments* (2023): 1–20.

Touretzky, D., *et al.* "A year in K-12 AI education." *AI Magazine* 40, no. 4 (2019): 88–90. DOI: 10.1609/aimag.v40i4.5289.

Tschang, F. T. and Almirall, E. "Artificial intelligence as augmenting automation: Implications for employment." *Academy of Management Perspectives* 35, no. 4 (2021): 642–659.

UNESCO. "K-12 AI curricula — A mapping of government-endorsed AI curricula." (2022).

Vachovsky, M. E., *et al.* "Toward more gender diversity in CS through an artificial intelligence summer program for high school girls." In *Proceedings of the 47th ACM Technical Symposium on Computing Science Education* (2016): 303–308.

Wamba-Taguimdje, S. L., *et al.* "Influence of artificial intelligence (AI) on firm performance: The business value of AI-based transformation projects." *Business Process Management Journal* 26, no. 7 (2020): 1893–1924.

Wang, B., Rau, P. L. P., and Yuan, T. "Measuring user competence in using artificial intelligence: Validity and reliability of artificial intelligence literacy scale." *Behaviour & Information Technology* 42, no. 9 (2023): 1324–1337.

Wong, G. K., *et al.* "Broadening artificial intelligence education in K-12: Where to start?" *ACM Inroads* 11, no. 1 (2020): 20–29.

Wu, F., *et al.* "Towards a new generation of artificial intelligence in China." *Nature Machine Intelligence* 2, no. 6 (2020): 312–316.

Zhang, Q., Lu, J., and Jin, Y. "Artificial intelligence in recommender systems." *Complex & Intelligent Systems* 7, no. 1 (2021): 439–457.

Part 2

AI and Machine Learning in Business and Technology: Transforming Industries and Driving Innovation

https://doi.org/10.1142/9781800616578_0003

Chapter 3

Use of Machine Learning in Early Warning Systems for Financial Crises Within the Global Financial System

Renato Salvador Coutinho[*,‡], **Paulo Maurício Selig**[*,§], **Aran B. Tcholakian Morales**[†,¶], and **Fernando Ostuni Gauthier**[*,‖]

[*]*Federal University of Santa Catarina (UFSC), Florianópolis, SC, Brazil*

[†]*Stela Institute, Florianópolis, SC, Brazil*

[‡]*renatobcb@gmail.com.br*
[§]*pauloselig@gmail.com.br*
[¶]*aran@stela.org.br*
[‖]*fernando.gauthier@ufsc.br*

Abstract

The aim of this chapter is to map the empirical knowledge to verify whether early warning systems (EWS) that use machine learning (ML) techniques show better predictive performance in forecasting financial crises compared to those developed using traditional techniques based on the practices of institutions in the global financial system. To uncover trends and practices related to the topic, we identified a need to explore the so-called gray literature (GL) through the multivocal literature review (MLR) method, given that the referenced literature is predominantly found in the databases of monetary authorities and supranational institutions of the financial system. This knowledge extraction allowed us to find indications and a reasonable consensus that the predictive capacity of EWS for financial crises is leveraged by ML. Consequently, the application of these techniques to develop EWS represents, for macroprudential policymakers, a huge opportunity for improving evidence-based decision-making.

Keywords: Machine learning, early warning systems, financial crises.

3.1. Introduction

Since the subprime crisis, the potential causes and symptoms of systemic financial crises have garnered increased interest from the central banking community and academics. This concern may have one of its roots in the average fiscal cost incurred by governments to deal with systemic financial crises, which, according to Laeven and Valencia (2018), equals about 67% of GDP in high-income countries and around 10% in middle- and low-income countries.

Although financial crises may initially appear as random events, they generally give prior signals that they will occur. However, identifying a reliable set of common patterns early in their occurrence is not a simple task for several reasons. First, the limited number of observed crises limits the ability to develop robust and statistically significant models. Moreover, crisis indicators can reach alert status when it is already too late for effective intervention.

It is worth noting that the instruments of macroprudential policies, which aim to limit systemic risk,[1] do not generate effects in the short term. Consequently, monetary authorities need early detection of warning signs so they can implement preventive measures to reduce the likelihood or mitigate the impacts of potential risks arising from possible systemic crises.

In a systematic literature review, Khankeh *et al.* (2019) highlight the increasingly recognized role of early warning systems (EWS) in disaster

[1]Financial Stability Board (FSB), International Monetary Fund (IMF), and the Bank for International Settlements (BIS) (2011).

risk management, minimizing economic losses from events such as earthquakes and tsunamis, and in various actions aimed at risk reduction. The Organisation for Economic Co-operation and Development (OECD) (2017) asserts that technological advancements have led to significant improvements in EWS and adds that these systems can support government decision-making through the automatic detection of anomalies and the prediction of potential crises that require their action.

Furthermore, Bajari *et al.* (2015) suggest that predictions made using machine learning (ML) techniques tend to be more accurate than those made by conventional approaches. Despite the relatively small sample of crisis observations, these techniques offer the potential to uncover complex relationships among variables that may be difficult to identify using classical techniques.

Additionally, ML techniques have the potential to learn through associations in large volumes of data without the dependence on explicit programming (Goodfellow *et al.*, 2016). Finally, several studies have pointed out that these approaches perform better than EWS based on traditional statistical methods for predicting financial crises (e.g., Alessi and Detken, 2018; Tanaka *et al.*, 2016; Holopainen and Sarlin, 2017).

3.2. Context

According to Berg *et al.* (1999), EWS consist of a precise definition of financial crisis and a forecasting mechanism featuring a set of variables that can help predict crises and a systematic method to obtain a forecast from them. Frankel and Saravelos (2012) highlight that one of the challenges encountered in empirical research is the fact that definitions of financial crisis and severity vary significantly.

The research by Laeven and Valencia (2013) explores this research gap and defines a financial crisis as a situation where there are significant signs of financial distress and losses across broad sectors of the financial system. Lo Duca and Peltonen (2013) add the concept of systemic events, i.e., events where financial instability becomes so widespread that it impairs the functioning of the financial system and materially harms economic growth and well-being.

Building on the definition provided by Laeven and Valencia (2013), Jemović and Marinković (2021) note that empirical research suggests different types of financial crises have their roots in similar weaknesses of the economy or may have common determinants that can constitute solid evidence for decision-making. The following assertion made by Eichengreen and Portes could not be more timely:

> *Financial crises, like contagious disease, threaten not only the host organism, namely the financial market, but the entire economic environment in which that host resides.* (Eichengreen and Portes, 1987, p. 3)

3.3. Early Warning Systems and Systemic Financial Crises

Bussiere and Fratzscher (2006) note that a great succession of crises that occurred in the 1990s generated severe economic, social, and political consequences, leading to the development of EWS models with the aim of anticipating the occurrence of financial crises, mainly due to the possibility of generating systemic effects. This trend intensified after the global financial crisis of 2008, as Klopotan *et al.* (2018) demonstrate in their bibliometric analysis of EWS applied to management, economics, and finance, which indicates that most systems for predicting financial crises were developed after 2010; this perspective is shared by Guru (2016) and Galán and Mencía (2021), who characterize the research in the area as sparse and incipient, respectively.

According to Edison (2003), building an EWS for financial crises requires delimiting the concept of crisis, defining its scope (including the sample and set of variables), and choosing the method. Following a similar logic, Guru (2016) establishes the steps as defining the notion of crisis, elaborating upon a list of potential explanatory variables, and establishing the thresholds that define their behavior as a signal of either a normal event or a crisis.

Kaminsky *et al.* (1998) focus on about 20 countries among emerging markets and developed economies to evaluate the evolution of a series of macroeconomic and financial variables in periods of crises, which, according to the signaling approach developed by the authors, are translated into potential early warning indicators for the occurrence of financial crises. From the consolidation of the variables, the main indicators used in the study are classified according to the following categories: Capital account; Debt profile; Current account; International; Other financial variables; Real sector; Fiscal; Institutional/structural factors; and Policy.

On the other hand, Guru (2016) establishes three sets (macroeconomic indicators, external sector, and financial sector), while Jemović and Marinković (2021) divide them into external, domestic, and financial. However, in a broader study, Frankel and Saravelos (2012) consolidate the significantly relevant early warning indicators found in the literature before 2008, as shown in Table 3.1.

Another relevant issue for the study of EWS is the choice of method, whose literature has its roots predominantly in the works of Kaminsky *et al.* (1998) and Frankel and Rose (1996). The models developed by these

Table 3.1. Summary of early warning indicators before 2008.

Leading Indicator	KLR (1998)	Hawkins and Klau (2000)	Abiad (2003)	Others	Total
Reserves	14	18	13	5	50
Real exchange rate	12	22	11	3	48
GDP	6	15	1	3	25
Credit	5	8	6	3	22
Current account	4	10	6	2	22
Money supply	2	16	1	0	19
Exports or imports	2	9	4	2	17
Inflation	5	7	1	2	15
Equity returns	1	8	3	1	13
Real interest rate	2	8	2	1	13
Debt composition	4	4	2	0	10
Budget balance	3	5	1	0	9
Terms of trade	2	6	1	0	9
Contagion	1	5	0	0	6
Political/legal	3	2	1	0	6
Capital flow	3	0	0	0	3
External debt	0	1	1	1	3
Number of studies	28	28	20	7	83

Source: Frankel and Saravadelos (2012, p. 218).

authors use, respectively, the signaling approach and regression models, in the original study, the econometric probit model.

Briefly, the signaling approach consists of observing a series of potential variables in periods preceding crises compared to their normal variation patterns, thereby defining an optimal threshold that, if exceeded, signals the approach of a potential crisis. In addition to the original research, seminal works representing this method were conducted by Kaminsky and Reinhart (1999), Goldstein *et al.* (2000), and Edison (2003), as well as a series of subsequent authors using the same line of analysis.

Conversely, regression models, whose main techniques are probit and logit, use statistical tools to estimate the probability of a crisis based on explanatory variables. This approach continues to be applied with some variations from the cited works by authors such as Eichengreen *et al.* (1995) and Demirgüç-Kunt and Detragiache (1998).

More recently, with the advancement of computational capacity and the consequent possibility of working with large volumes of data at increasingly higher speeds, there has been growth in the use of ML techniques in developing EWS for detecting financial crises. Because of this movement towards a data science approach, in addition to or even in opposition to purely econometric models, some authors such as Alessi and Detken (2018) and Holopainen and Sarlin (2017) have conducted studies comparing traditional techniques to this new approach.

Liu *et al.* (2021) test the performance of seven different ML techniques compared to the logistic regression model and find that the former outperform traditional models in performance and accuracy. The authors also highlight the usefulness of the approach for policymakers and suggest using AI techniques associated with traditional methods to improve the identification of systemic risks.

The OECD (2017) acknowledges that technology, particularly the use of predictive ML algorithms, enhances the implementation of innovative EWS in response to the increasing complexity and turbulence of the current environment. However, they present ensuring checks and balances as one of the main challenges for their use, directly impacting governance components in macroprudential policy decision-making.

Addressing this concern, Liu *et al.* (2021) present Shapley values as a solution to overcome the inability of ML tools to perform cause-and-effect analyses. Applying this technique not only identifies the most important indicators but also mitigates the "black box" effect of these tools.

3.4. Methodological Approach

This study is part of a broader master's research project (Coutinho, 2024) that included a preliminary scoping review following the PRISMA-SCR protocol (Tricco *et al.*, 2018), which aimed to extract knowledge through the key concepts involved in the development and use of EWS for systemic financial crises. The scoping review revealed important insights and research opportunities that are explored in the current work, such as the lack of inclusion of evidence from the gray literature (GL).

The most widely known and used definition of GL was coined at the Third International Conference on Grey Literature held in 1997, the so-called Luxembourg definition, according to which GL is "that which is produced at all levels of government, academia, business, and industry in print and electronic formats, but which is not controlled by commercial publishers" (GL'97, 1998, p. iii).

Another important finding that served as a starting point for this study was the growing trend towards the use of ML techniques in the development of EWS. GL proves to be a promising source of evidence in verifying this trend, as it represents the state of practice from which innovations in the subject emerged, as identified in the scoping review.

Recognizing the importance of using GL and the absence of a specific set of guidelines capable of ensuring the quality of systematic review processes and their results, Garousi *et al.* (2019), based on the work of Kitchenham and Charters (2007), present a guide for the multivocal literature review (MLR), which includes this type of evidence alongside formal literature. Therefore, MLR was identified as the appropriate methodological approach to uncover trends and practices related to the topic.

3.4.1. *Objective and research questions*

The objective of this work is to map empirical knowledge to verify, based on the practices of global financial system institutions, whether EWS that use ML techniques show better predictive performance for financial crises compared to those developed using traditional techniques. From this objective and the fact that the current work aims to generate interest among both macroprudential policymakers and the academic community, the following research question was defined: Does ML improve the performance of EWS for systemic financial crises within the global financial system?

To provide pathways for studying the type of EWS addressed as the population in this research, the question was broken down into sub-questions, namely:

- Does the use of ML techniques show superior results compared to traditional techniques?
- Which model (method + indicators) showed superior performance?
- What solutions were proposed to mitigate the "black box" effect of ML tools?

3.4.2. *Search strategy and sources of evidence*

First, the selection of databases was guided by the context of this research, which is limited to international organizations and monetary authorities regulating the global financial system. This restriction, considering the fact that these institutions are extremely technical and rigorous, provides a certain assurance of study quality but also demands methodological rigor regarding the databases to be searched.

Thus, a bibliometric network of citation relationships was constructed from the organizations of studies considered relevant in the scoping review, which served as the basis for this work. As shown in Figure 3.1, the central nodes refer to central banks and supranational institutions.

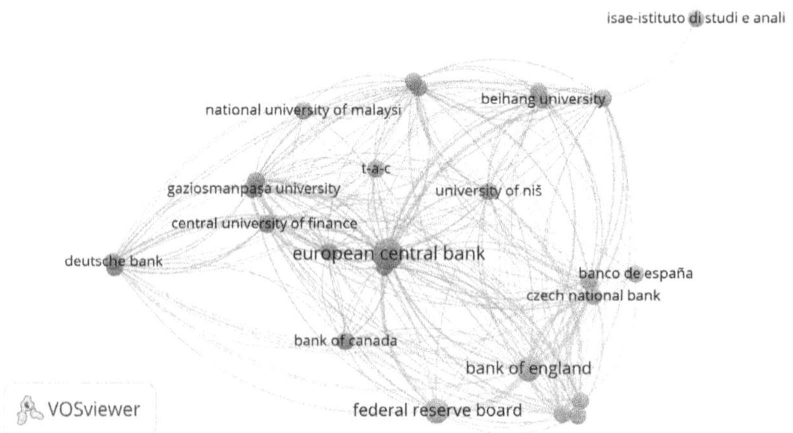

Figure 3.1. Bibliometric network of organizations.

Note: Developed by the author using VOSviewer.

Table 3.2. Number of primary search results.

Database/Site	Records	Sources
International Monetary Fund (www.imf.org)	47	13
European Central Bank (www.ecb.europa.eu)	100*	13
Federal Reserve Board (www.federalreserve.gov)	100*	3
Bank for International Settlements (www.bis.org)	33	2
Banca d'Italia (www.bancaditalia.it)	18	0
Banco de España (www.bde.es)	2	0
Bank of England (www.bankofengland.co.uk)	100*	3
Banque de France (www.banque-france.fr)	100*	0
Banco de la Republica de Colombia (www.banrep.gov.co)	0	0
Bank of Canada (www.bank-banque-canada.ca)	10	0
Deutsche Bundesbank (www.bundesbank.de)	18	1
Total	**528**	**35**

Note: *Record limit determined according to the rule suggested by Garousi *et al.* (2019).

The bibliometric analysis reinforces the indication that the most interested in developing EWS for systemic financial crises are these organizations. Notably, the seminal works most cited in the literature on these systems (Kaminsky *et al.*, 1998; Frankel and Rose, 1996) were developed at the Federal Reserve, the most referenced studies on the use of ML in this context (Alessi and Detken, 2018; Holopainen and Sarlin, 2017) at the European Central Bank, and one of the most in-depth studies on systemic financial crises (Laeven and Valencia, 2013, 2018) at the International Monetary Fund.

Finally, the criterion for selecting databases for the current literature review was based on the top 20 institutions ranked in the IDEAS/RePEc[2] central bank ranking. It is worth noting that the search in the Federal Reserve System database was conducted on the Federal Reserve Board

[2]Available at: https://ideas.repec.org/top/top.central.html, accessed on February 2, 2022.

IDEAS is the largest bibliographic database dedicated to economics and available for free on the Internet. Based on RePEc, it indexes over 3,900,000 research items, including more than 3,500,000 that can be downloaded in full text.

RePEc is a large voluntary effort to enhance the free dissemination of research in economics, which includes bibliographic metadata from over 2,000 participating archives, including all major publishers and research agencies.

website, as it was possible to verify that the latter concentrates the main sources of evidence from the system, resulting in the selection of 11 databases for the search execution.

The search was conducted individually in the databases, and the initial selection was made manually by reading the abstracts and titles of the found evidence based on the eligibility criteria. Table 3.2 summarizes the number of records and primary sources obtained in each database after this initial screening.

3.5. Results

After the initial screening, 35 papers remained for full reading, of which 20 were not considered eligible. Among them, five did not address EWS or financial crises; four did not propose EWS; two did not represent EWS for anticipating financial crises; four were not developed using ML; one did not address ML or financial crises; one repeated another publication; one was published in two different databases; one was contained in another study considered in the sample; and one was the "draft" of a working paper included in the sample. Subsequently, the 15 resulting evidence sources from this process were subjected to mandatory requirements, and five did not compare the performance of ML-based methods with traditional ones. Therefore, the final sample consists of 10 papers.

3.5.1. *Data extraction*

The data extraction flow is visualized in Figure A1 of the Appendix. Indeed, the sample object of the present study is described in Table 3.3.

3.5.2. *Synthesis of information*

The synthesis of relevant information followed the approach recommended by Garousi *et al.* (2019): the selected studies were represented in a common analytical framework with standardized information (Table 3.4). Given the complexity of seeking evidence in GL, as well as aiming for the enhancement and validation of the representation, the construction of the table was done iteratively.

This process resulted in the selection of the most relevant information that best represents the selected studies, namely: methods, variables, and

Table 3.3. Sample summary.

Authors	Year	Organization	Title
Alessi *et al.*	2015	European Central Bank	Comparing Different EWS: Results from a Horse Race Competition Among Members of the Macro-Prudential Research Network
Beutel *et al.*	2018	Deutsche Bundesbank	An Evaluation of Early Warning Models for Systemic Banking Crises: Does Machine Learning Improve Predictions?
Bluwstein *et al.*	2020	Bank of England	Credit Growth, the Yield Curve and Financial Crisis Prediction: Evidence from a Machine Learning Approach
IMF	2021	International Monetary Fund	How to Assess Country Risk: The Vulnerability Exercise Approach Using Machine Learning
Fouliard *et al.*	2021	Bank for International Settlements	Answering the Queen: Machine Learning and Financial Crises
Hellwig	2021	International Monetary Fund	Predicting Fiscal Crises: A Machine Learning Approach
Holopainen and Sarlin	2016	European Central Bank	Toward Robust Early-Warning Models: A Horse Race, Ensembles and Model Uncertainty
Jarmulska	2020	European Central Bank	Random Forest vs. Logit Models: Which Offers Better Early Warning of Fiscal Stress?
Puglia and Tucker	2020	Federal Reserve Board	Machine Learning, the Treasury Yield Curve and Recession Forecasting
Suss and Henry	2019	Bank of England	Predicting Bank Distress in the UK with Machine Learning

techniques for determining cause and effect in ML (mitigating the "black box" effect) that aim to clarify the key questions related to the objectives of this research. The identification of the method was straightforward; however, the tabulation of the variables was a more complex process that required analysis and abstraction according to the categories already established in the literature, as there is a profusion of possibilities of choices and different terms used often to describe the same information in the various analyzed works.

Table 3.4. Analytical table.

Authors	Methods*	Variables	Cause/Effect
Alessi *et al.*	Probit, logit, signaling approach; BMA; CART; RF	According to the models and categories: Global; banking sector; government debt/balances; current account; debt service; interest rates/inflation; GDP; asset prices; real estate prices; credit	—
Beutel *et al.*	Logit; KNN; decision trees; RF; SVM	Credit; real estate prices; asset prices; GDP; inflation; interest rate; gross fixed capital formation; current account; exchange rate; oil prices	—
Bluwstein *et al.*	Logistic regression; RF; extremely randomised trees; SVM; ANN; decision tree	Yield curve slope; credit; consumer price index (CPI); debt service; consumption; investment; public debt; monetary base; stock prices; current account	Shapley values
IMF	Signal extraction; logit (Elastic net, ridge and LASSO); RF (Balanced random forest, RUSBoost, ADABoost and gradient boosting); SVM	According to the models and types of crises: Global; external; financial; real; fiscal	Shapley values
Fouliard *et al.*	Dynamic probit; panel logit; BMA; general additive model; RF; SVM	According to the models and categories: Debt, GDP, unemployment, investment, credit, interest rates, monetary base, asset prices, "Economic Sentiment" index, commodity prices; real estate prices; external imbalances	—

Hellwig	Logit; elastic net; RF; XG boost	GDP; reserves; current account; export/import; exchange rate; external debt; debt service; public debt; policy	—
Holopainen and Sarlin	Signal extraction; linear discriminant analysis; QDA; logit; logit LASSO; naive bayes; KNN; classification trees; RF; ANN; ELM; SVM	Real estate prices; current account; public debt; loans/income; credit; GDP; government bond yields; inflation; stock prices; real estate prices; credit to GDP	—
Jarmulska	RF; logit	Interest rates; GDP; oil price; VIX (volatility index); real exchange rate; current account; global exports; gross fixed capital formation; consumer price index (CPI); real consumption; nominal exchange rate; credit; government balance; public debt; debt service; unemployment; labor productivity	Shapley values; Breiman's variable importance
Puglia and Tucker	Probit; RF; XGBoost; LightGBM; SVM; ANN	Treasury bond yield curve (ACM5D and slope); stock prices; credit; NFCI (National financial conditions index); conference board's leading economic index — LEI and survey of professional forecasters — SPF (recession probability indices)	Shapley values (SHapley Additive exPlanations — SHAP)
Suss and Henry	Logit; KNN; RF; boosting; SVM	Stocks; inflation; yield; GDP; unemployment; other financial variables (micro)	Shapley values

Notes: ANN — artificial neural network; BMA — bayesian model averaging; CART — classification and regression tree methodology; ELM — extreme learning machines; KNN — *k*-nearest neighbors; QDA — quadratic discriminant analysis; RF — random forest; SVM — support vector machines.

3.6. Discussion

This review evaluated 10 primary studies, published between 2015 and 2021, that address the use of ML techniques in the development of EWS for financial crises. The research found an area that is still in development, whose first articles were published in the mid-2000s, and that is gaining importance as systemic episodes accumulate and the complexity in determining them also grows.

3.6.1. *Summary of evidence*

Although some of the analyzed studies point in different, often even opposing, directions regarding the performance of ML techniques vs. traditional methods, there seems to be a certain consensus regarding the advantages and disadvantages related to each approach. Suss and Treitel (2019), for example, state that conventional approaches are incapable of explaining complex interactions and nonlinearities in contrast to the flexibility of ML tools.

Similarly, the IMF (2021) points out that ML techniques tend to be better at handling complex interactions among many predictors. On the other hand, it also reveals that the patterns captured by models developed through ML are not necessarily easy to interpret, especially since economists and policymakers are not yet familiar with this set of tools.

Bluwstein *et al.* (2020) add that the ML models analyzed in their study, when well-calibrated and trained, can approximate any well-behaved function. However, their high flexibility typically makes them difficult to interpret, particularly in determining the variables that drive the model's predictions and the weights of the functional relationships among them.

3.6.1.1. *Machine learning vs. traditional techniques*

Alessi *et al.* (2015) promote a joint exercise (termed a "horse race") with the main empirical EWS frameworks developed within the work of the Macroprudential Research Network[3] to shed some light on their relative

[3]Macroprudential Research Network (MaRs) is an internal network for macroprudential research, launched in 2010 by the European System of Central Banks and composed of the 27 national central banks of the European Union (EU) and the European Central Bank.

advantages and disadvantages. The study does not focus specifically on comparing the performance between traditional and ML techniques but seems to have been one of the first attempts in this direction. It presents as its main conclusion the fact that multivariate approaches generate potentially highly useful early warning results and offer considerable improvements over univariate ones.

Holopainen and Sarlin (2016) also conduct the same type of exercise, aiming to perform the aforementioned comparison and demonstrate that conventional statistical approaches are surpassed by ML methods such as *k*-nearest neighbors and neural networks, particularly by model aggregation approaches. Fouliard *et al.* (2021) use an online learning methodology to conduct a "horse race" among various expert models and aggregate them to produce an ideal forecast, regardless of the data generation process. However, the result is inconclusive concerning the performance difference between the techniques.

In the IMF technical notes (2021), similar results can be found, indicating that ML models regularly outperform classical econometric methods. However, when segmenting the models by crisis types, the authors present an exception regarding external sector crises, where the signal extraction approach performed better in specific cases for advanced economies.

Hellwig (2021), in turn, when evaluating the out-of-sample predictive capacity of econometric and ML techniques for fiscal crises, points out that random forest approaches systematically outperform statistical models. Similarly, Suss and Treitel (2019) affirm that random forest is substantially and significantly superior to other studied models, both classical linear regression techniques and ML.

The authors estimate out-of-sample prediction probabilities using a cross-validation design that considers various potential bias sources to avoid data leakage (data peeking) and the consequent overly optimistic performance results.

Puglia and Tucker (2020) state that cross-validation estimates obtained through the *k*-folds technique are optimistically biased, and strategies that eliminate data leakage produce possibly more realistic prediction accuracy estimates.

In this regard, the authors propose a more conservative strategy to estimate the out-of-sample prediction probabilities of Treasury bond

---

Available at: https://www.ecb.europa.eu/pub/economic-research/research-networks/html/researcher_mars.en.html. Accessed on February 20, 2022.

spreads and other macroeconomic and financial variables. In their analysis, *k*-fold cross-validation indicates that the decision tree method's prediction accuracy is superior to that of neural networks, which in turn surpasses that of probit regression.

However, the authors document that in the more conservative method (nested time-series, NTS), the result was reversed, indicating the superiority of the probit method over ML techniques. They argue that this latter result contrasts with a growing body of literature and signals that the possible reason for this may be related to the sparse and relatively small dataset used, which contrasts with the ML techniques designed for larger databases.

Another issue raised in the study is the tendency for overfitting in ML techniques unless sufficiently controlled through a set of hyperparameters. Beutel *et al.* (2018) also suggest that overfitting can be a significant problem for some ML models and add that even for those where the in-sample fit is not strict, their out-of-sample performance is, in most cases, markedly inferior.

The authors focus specifically on comparing the predictive performance obtained by ML-based models and conventional models, affirming that the former have a greater in-sample predictive capacity. However, they state that the inverse happens in out-of-sample predictions, where the probit method performs considerably better. Nevertheless, Jarmulska (2020) arrives at a diametrically opposite result, stating that the cross-validation technique employed in her study produces a penalty parameter that maximizes the model's out-of-sample prediction accuracy and limits the overfitting problem.

Beutel *et al.* (2018) conjecture that differences in the training sample used are a key factor in the contrasting results found in their study. They also add that their out-of-sample window is naturally dominated by the global financial crisis of 2008 and that results may differ for other datasets or ML techniques.

A good example of this is the work by Bluwstein *et al.* (2020), which compares a diverse set of ML models and logistic regression in a long-term dataset with out-of-sample cross-validation and recursive prediction tests. The authors demonstrate that ML-based models consistently outperform logistic regression in predicting financial crises in a macroeconomic dataset covering 17 countries between 1870 and 2016.

The approach implemented illustrates how ML techniques can uncover significant nonlinearities and interactions that facilitate prediction, even in situations characterized by relatively small datasets with limited observations of the event of interest. In the study, the models that regularly presented the most accurate results are based on decision trees, namely extremely randomized trees and random forest.

3.6.1.2. *Best early warning system model*

Within the study conducted by Suss and Treitel (2019), random forest would be the most suitable technique for building EWS. Jarmulska (2020) follows the same direction and, besides the superior performance in her study, also points out its robustness and efficiency, as well as its relative simplicity, as it does not require much parametrization or a large database.

The same choice is validated by Hellwig (2021), who adds that for low-income developing countries, expanding the set of variables and leaving their selection to an algorithm leads to considerable accuracy gains. For Beutel *et al.* (2018), a logit model that takes into account not only credit and asset price indicators but also those related to external imbalances would have been able to issue relatively accurate warnings before the global financial crisis of 2008 for most countries.

Regarding crisis indicators, Alessi *et al.* (2015) found evidence supporting the importance of private sector credit growth. Fouliard *et al.* (2021) assert that there is considerable heterogeneity among countries in terms of which methods and variables the forecasting capacity depends on; therefore, it is not conclusive regarding the best model.

Puglia and Tucker (2020) are not definitive but demonstrate that ML methods, due to their flexibility, can capture the nonlinear nature of the empirical joint distributions of Treasury bond yields and other macroeconomic and financial data. Additionally, they state that despite the misalignment of the techniques used to characterize the database, through parameterization, it was possible to achieve forecast results aligned with financial and economic intuition, as the models signaled recession possibilities from the stabilization of Treasury spreads vs. tightening credit conditions or deteriorating macroeconomic fundamentals.

Besides the macroeconomic variables widely cited in the literature, indicators related to Treasury bond yields are beginning to gain prominence as an important indicator of financial crises in more recent studies, such as those by Puglia and Tucker (2020) and Bluwstein *et al.* (2020). These are also in line with evidence from the previous scoping review conducted within this research (e.g., Guru, 2016; Joy *et al.*, 2017).

Bluwstein *et al.* (2020) emphasize that while the crucial role of credit is an established result in the literature, the predictive power of the yield curve has received much less attention as an early warning indicator.

The main early warning signs found in their study include elevated and prolonged domestic credit growth relative to GDP and a flat or inverted yield curve, especially when nominal yields are low. All the models studied by Bluwstein *et al.* (2020) consistently identify similar predictors for financial crises with some variations over time, reflecting changes in the nature of the global monetary and financial system over the past 150 years. However, the technique of extremely randomized trees showed the best predictive results.

For Alessi *et al.* (2015), using a set of multivariate models can be a good option for developing empirical macroprudential policy instruments. Similarly, Holopainen and Sarlin (2016) report that the models achieved better predictive performance using aggregation procedures, particularly ensemble learning (bagging and boosting), to combine different methods into a single instrument.

Adopting a similar strategy, Suss and Treitel (2019) report statistically significant improvements compared to using the random forest technique in isolation. Fouliard *et al.* (2021) propose a specialist system that groups several models through an aggregation rule (exponentially weighted average, EWA) and advocate this strategy as the best path for building EWS.

3.6.1.3. *Cause and effect*

Fouliard *et al.* (2021) recognize that their models are incapable of testing causality but reaffirm that it is necessary for the results to be interpretable to enable analysis by macroprudential authorities. The IMF technical note (2021) also advocates that communication tools are a fundamental part of ML-based EWS, especially when designed to inform policymakers and guide their decisions.

For this task, the authors of the report identify that the Shapley value method, originating from game theory, is becoming increasingly popular. Jarmulska (2020) adds that despite the superior predictive performance of random forest over logit models, the former offers less interpretability of results, which represents a significant limitation for economists who can benefit most from its use for predicting crises.

To address this issue, the author resorts to Shapley values and Breiman's (2001) variable importance to provide an example of how to determine which explanatory variables contributed most to the obtained result, thus minimizing the so-called "black box" effect. Suss and Treitel (2019) corroborate that the performance advantage of the random forest algorithm comes at the cost of transparency compared to the logit model, which, depending on the regulators' requirements, may outweigh the benefits.

To remedy this relative disadvantage, the authors use recently developed techniques to understand the algorithm's drivers by computing and aggregating Shapley values and provide a measure of the relative importance of each variable in driving predictions. Bluwstein *et al.* (2020) similarly assert that the Shapley value approach demonstrates how the "black box" concern associated with the practical application of ML models to policymaking can be overcome.

Specifically, the predicted crisis probability for each individual observation is decomposed into a sum of contributions from each predictor, i.e., their Shapley values, allowing the authors to understand and demonstrate which variables are driving each prediction. Similarly, Puglia and Tucker (2020) use the Shapley additive explanations (SHAP) framework, as well as McNemar's and Cochrane's *Q* tests, to decompose predictions and analyze the importance of variables in each cycle.

3.6.2. *Limitations*

The inherent limitations of this research refer to the peculiar characteristics of GL, notably the fact that it is presented in various formats, making its extraction, synthesis, and analysis challenging. Thus, it is possible to miss significant evidence, as the search ends up being almost artisanal and subject to human error.

Moreover, there is little specific guidance available for conducting GL research, and this process is often done on an *ad hoc* basis. To mitigate this risk, in addition to the support of a rigorous research methodology, a meticulous selection and extensive search aided by solid selection criteria were carried out, bringing confidence that the selected sources represent the best knowledge related to the research topic.

A further challenge in GL research is the generalization of results found to a broader context. In the specific case of this research, this concern is addressed by the care taken to establish eligibility and quality criteria, as well as relevance requirements that do not allow the inclusion of studies that do not use objective and verifiable techniques to measure the performance of models.

Additionally, a strong point is that the evidence sources, although not constituting final or peer-reviewed works, were carefully extracted from databases of institutions known for their tradition and high technical quality requirements of their staff and consequently their work. Proof of this is that seminal works and major innovations in the field predominantly come from studies first published in working papers and technical reports by researchers linked to these organizations, as demonstrated in Section 3.4.2 and particularly in Figure 3.1.

Another limitation impacting any type of literature review, especially one conducted entirely in GL, is internal validity, as there is no "gold standard" for conducting research in this type of source. However, two mitigating factors increase the internal validity of the research: the rigorous methodology used here and the fact that the review was based on a previous scoping review of scientific literature and ultimately corroborated and complemented the findings and trends pointed out based on the practices of global financial system organizations.

Finally, the validity of conclusions is an issue to be evaluated, as the entire review was conducted in a homogeneous research field of institutions with philosophical convictions and technical-scientific training that often (but not always) converge. To address this, care was taken to present the results synthetically and perform a qualitative discussion, making the authors "converse," especially those presenting divergent views.

3.7. Final Considerations

The objective of this literature review was to map empirical knowledge to verify, based on the practices of global financial system institutions, whether EWS that use ML techniques show better predictive performance for financial crises compared to those developed using traditional techniques. This knowledge extraction was achieved by identifying, mapping, and synthesizing the evidence found in the literature related to early warning patterns, methods, techniques, and tools used, as well as the development and use trends of these systems.

The findings corroborated the choice of the method, despite the complexity of researching the GL. The approach yielded comprehensive and insightful results, reducing biases and providing significant insights that can be useful for decision-makers, especially monetary authorities and financial system institutions.

This study presented the following research question: Does ML improve the performance of EWS for systemic financial crises? Despite the presented limitations, there is a strong indication and reasonable uniformity in the understanding from the researched evidence that the predictive capacity of these systems is enhanced by using ML techniques.

Techniques derived from decision trees, particularly random forest and its variants, demonstrated the greatest potential. However, attention must be paid to the most significant limitation of their adoption, which relates to the "black box" reputation of many techniques used and the complex structural characteristics that bring resistance to their use by decision-makers and public policy formulators.

Nonetheless, the issue of transparency in predictive variables' cause-and-effect relationships and their interpretation has shown significant practical evolution, and among the techniques used, the use of the Shapley value method seems to be a trend for addressing this deficiency. As inferred, studies on the use of ML techniques in EWS present infinite possibilities and still represent a field in full development.

Regarding indicators in constructing new EWS, there is a tendency to explore the potential of new variables, such as those related to government bond yields, and established ones also maintain their importance. Additionally, there may be a trend to leverage computational capacity and AI tools to work with larger volumes of data, indicators, and even different methods to increase the predictive capacity of EWS.

Finally, developing and applying ML in constructing EWS still represents a vast source of future work, both regarding new methods and the search for indicators that may be more effective in anticipating systemic financial crises. For public policymakers in general and macroprudential policymakers in particular, encouraging the use of these systems, specifically the application of ML, represents enormous potential for development in evidence-based decision-making and delivering greater public value.

Appendix

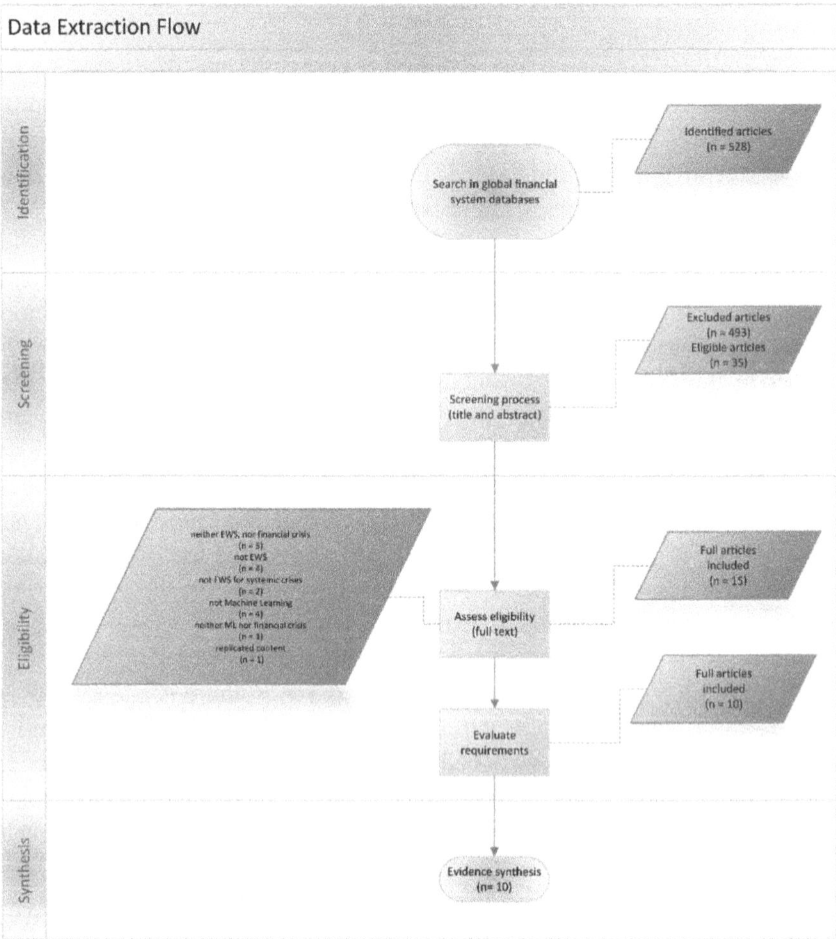

Figure A1. Evidence source selection flow.

Bibliography

Alessi, L., Antunes, A., Babecký, J., Baltussen, S., Behn., M., *et al.* "Comparing different early warning systems: Results from a horse race competition among members of the macro-prudential research network." *MPRA Paper* no. 62194 (February 2015). Germany: University Library of Munich. DOI: 10.2139/ssrn.2566165.

Alessi, L. and Detken, C. "Identifying excessive credit growth and leverage." *Journal of Financial Stability* 35 (April 2018): 215–225. DOI: 10.1016/j.jfs.2017.06.005.

Bajari, P., Nekipelov, D., Ryan, S. P., and Yang, M. "Machine learning methods for demand estimation." *American Economic Review* 105, no. 5 (2015): 481–485. DOI: 10.1257/aer.p20151021.

Berg, A., Borensztein, E., Milesi-Ferretti, G. M., and Pattillo, C. "Anticipating balance of payments crises: The role of early warning systems." *International Monetary Fund Occasional Paper* no. 186 (1999).

Beutel, J., List, S., and Von Schweinitz, G. "An evaluation of early warning models for systemic banking crises: Does machine learning improve predictions?" *Bundesbank Discussion Paper* no. 48 (2018). Frankfurt.

Bluwstein, K., *et al.* "Credit growth, the yield curve and financial crisis prediction: Evidence from a machine learning approach." *Bank of England Working Papers* no. 848 (January 2020).

Breiman, L. "Random forests." *Machine Learning* 45, no. 1 (2001): 5–32. DOI: 10.1023/A:1010933404324.

Bussiere, M. and Fratzscher, M. "Towards a new early warning system of financial crises." *Journal of International Money and Finance* 25, no. 6 (2006): 953–973. DOI: 10.1016/j.jimonfin.2006.07.007.

Coutinho, R. S. "Extração de conhecimento em bases de dados por meio da aplicação de Machine Learning: um modelo de Sistema de Alerta Precoce (EWS) para crises financeiras". Dissertação (Mestrado em Engenharia e Gestão do Conhecimento) — Universidade Federal de Santa Catarina, Florianópolis, 2024.

Demirgüç-Kunt, A. and Detragiache, E. "The determinants of banking crises in developing and developed countries." *IMF Staff Papers* 45, no. 1 (1998): 81–109.

Edison, H. J. "Do indicators of financial crises work? An evaluation of an early warning system." *International Journal of Finance and Economics* 8, no. 1 (2003): 11–53. DOI: 10.1002/ijfe.197.

Eichengreen, B. and Portes, R. The anatomy of financial crises. *NBER Working Paper* no. 2126 (1987).

Eichengreen, B., Rose, A., and Wyplosz, C. "Exchange market Mayhem: The antecedents and aftermath of speculative attacks." *Economic Policy* 21 (October 1995): 249–312. DOI: 10.2307/1344591.

Financial Stability Board (FSB), International Monetary Fund (IMF), and Bank for International Settlements (IES). *Macroprudential Policy Tools and Frameworks, Progress Report to G20*, October 27, 2011.

Fouliard, J., Howell, M., and Rey, H. "Answering the Queen: Machine learning and financial crises." *BIS Working Papers* no. 926 (2021).

Frankel, J. and Rose, A. "Currency crashes in emerging markets: An empirical treatment." *Journal of International Economics* 41, no. 3/4 (1996): 351–366. DOI: 10.1016/S0022-1996(96)01441-9.

Frankel, J. and Saravelos, G. "Can leading indicators assess country vulnerability? Evidence from the 2008–09 global financial crisis." *Journal of International Economics* 87, no. 2 (2012): 216–231. DOI: 10.1016/j.jinteco.2011.12.009.

Galán, J. E. and Mencía, J. "Model-based indicators for the identification of cyclical systemic risk." *Empirical Economics* 61, no. 6 (2021): 3179–3211. DOI: 10.1007/s00181-020-01993-2.

Garousi, V., Felderer, M., and Mäntylä, V. "Guidelines for including grey literature and conducting multivocal literature reviews in software engineering." *Information and Software Technology* 106, no. 19 (2019): 101–121. DOI: 10.1016/j.infsof.2018.09.006.

GL'97. *Proceedings of the Third International Conference on Grey Literature — GL'97*, Luxemburg, November 1998, 13–14, 1997.

Goldstein, M., Kaminsky, G., and Reinhart, C. *Assessing Financial Vulnerability: An Early Warning System for Emerging Markets*. Washington, DC: Institute for International Economics, 2000.

Goodfellow, I., Bengio, Y., and Courville, A. *Deep Learning*. Cambridge: MIT Press, 2016.

Guru, A. "Early warning system of finance stress for India." *International Review of Applied Economics* 30, no. 3 (2016): 273–300. DOI: 10.1080/02692171.2015.1102206.

Hellwig, K. P. "Predicting fiscal crises: A machine learning approach." *IMF Working Papers*, 2021, no. 150 (May 2021).

Holopainen, M. and Sarlin, P. "Toward robust early-warning models: A horse race, ensembles and model uncertainty." *Working Paper Series* no. 1900 (May 2016). European Central Bank.

Holopainen M. and Sarlin, P. "Toward robust early-warning models: A horse race, ensembles and model uncertainty." *Quantitative Finance* 17, no. 12 (2017): 1933–1963. DOI: 10.1080/14697688.2017.1357972.

International Monetary Fund (IMF). "How to assess country risk: The vulnerability exercise approach using machine learning." *IMF Technical Notes and Manuals* 2021, no. 003 (May 2021).

Jarmulska, B. "Random forest versus logit models: Which offers better early warning of fiscal stress?" *Working Paper Series* no. 2408 (May 2020). European Central Bank.

Jemović, M. and Marinković, S. "Determinants of financial crises-An early warning system based on panel logit regression." *International Journal of Finance and Economics* 26, no. 1 (2021): 103–117. DOI: 10.1002/ijfe.1779.

Joy, M., Rusnák, M., Šmídková, K., and Vašíček, B. "Banking and currency crises: Differential diagnostics for developed countries." *International Journal of Finance and Economics* 22, no. 1 (2017): 44–67. DOI: 10.1002/ijfe.1570.

Kaminsky, G. L., Lizondo, S., and Reinhart, C. M. "Leading indicators of currency crisis." *IMF Staff Papers* 45, no. 1 (1998): 1–48.

Kaminsky, G. L. and Reinhart, C. M. "The twin crises: The causes of banking and balance-of-payments problems." *American Economic Review* 89, no. 3 (1999): 473–500. DOI: 10.1257/aer.89.3.473.

Khankeh, H. R., Hosseini, S. H., Farrokhi, M., Hosseini, M. A., and Amanat, N. "Early warning system models and components in emergency and disaster: A systematic literature review protocol." *Systematic Reviews* 8 (2019): 315. DOI: 10.1186/s13643-019-1211-5.

Kitchenham, B. and Charters, S. *Guidelines for Performing Systematic Literature Reviews in Software Engineering*. Technical Report EBSE, Keele University and Durham University Joint Report, version 2.3, 2007.

Klopotan, I., Zoroja, J., and Meško, M. "Early warning system in business, finance, and economics: Bibliometric and topic analysis." *International Journal of Engineering Business Management* 10 (2018): 1–12. DOI: 10.1177/1847979018797013.

Laeven, L. and Valencia, F. "Systemic banking crises database." *IMF Economic Review* 61, no. 2 (2013): 225–270. DOI: 10.1057/imfer.2013.12.

Laeven, L. and Valencia, F. "Systemic banking crises revisited." *IMF Working Papers* 2018, no. 206 (September 2018).

Liu, L., Chen, C., and Wang, B. "Predicting financial crises with machine learning methods." *Journal of Forecasting* (2021). DOI: 10.1002/for.2840.

Lo Duca, M. L. and Peltonen, T. A. "Assessing systemic risks and predicting systemic events." *Journal of Banking and Finance* 37, no. 7 (2013): 2183–2195. DOI: 10.1016/j.jbankfin.2012.06.010.

Organisation for Economic Co-Operation and Development (OECD). *Embracing Innovation in Government — Global Trends 2017*. Paris: OECD Publishing, February 2017.

Puglia, M. and Tucker, A. "Machine learning, the treasury yield curve and recession forecasting." *Finance and Economics Discussion Series* no. 38 (May 2020). Board of Governors of the Federal Reserve System (U.S.).

Suss, J. and Treitel, H. "Predicting bank distress in the UK with machine learning." *Bank of England Working Papers* no. 831 (2019).

Tanaka, K., Kinkyo, T., and Hamori, S. "Random forests-based early warning system for bank failures." *Economics Letters* 148 (2016): 118–121. DOI: 10.1016/j.econlet.2016.09.024.

Tricco, A. C., *et al.* "PRISMA extension for scoping reviews (PRISMA-ScR): Checklist and explanation." *Annals of Internal Medicine* 169, no. 7 (2018): 467–473. DOI: 10.7326/M18-0850.

https://doi.org/10.1142/9781800616578_0004

Chapter 4

AI in Organizations: Transforming Cybersecurity for Financial Institutions

Yara Mohammed

Data Science, College of Information, University of North Texas, USA

Yara.Mohammed@unt.edu

Abstract

In an era where digital transactions define the financial landscape, the integration of Artificial Intelligence (AI) in cybersecurity represents a pivotal shift in safeguarding financial data and operations. This chapter examines how AI is changing the way major U.S. banks handle cybersecurity. AI started as a supporting tool. Nowadays, AI addresses critical security challenges such as real-time fraud detection and risk prediction. However, the implementation of AI in banking raises important issues about data privacy, the fairness of AI decisions, and the impact on banking jobs. It also poses challenges in scaling these solutions across large banking networks, but at the same time opens opportunities for innovation.

This chapter offers an in-depth analysis of the application of AI in cybersecurity practices among the largest U.S. banks. By focusing on specific case studies, we examine the relationship between the banks' assets and their investment in cybersecurity. This approach highlights how these financial institutions integrate AI into their security frameworks.

The findings suggest a future where banking security systems, powered by AI, not only react to threats but also proactively anticipate potential security breaches.

Keywords: AI cybersecurity automation, AI-driven threat detection, strategic AI integration, financial institutions, regulatory compliance.

4.1. Overview of AI in Cybersecurity

Artificial Intelligence (AI) has profoundly transformed the landscape of cybersecurity, becoming an essential tool for financial institutions to defend against increasingly sophisticated cyber threats. Initially utilized as supportive technology for basic tasks such as data analysis and threat detection, AI has become central to modern cybersecurity strategies. AI-driven systems can now automate complex processes involving real-time threat detection, risk assessment, and incident response, offering a level of speed and accuracy that far surpasses human capabilities.

AI enhances a bank's ability to identify potential security issues before they cause harm by analyzing vast amounts of data for unusual activities. This predictive capability bolsters a bank's defenses and supports more informed and timely decisions to counteract threats. However, integrating AI across large and diverse banking networks presents significant challenges. Concerns over data privacy, ensuring fairness in AI decisions, and the impact on employment are prominent issues that must be navigated as these systems become more ingrained in everyday operations.

As AI continues to advance, its integration into cybersecurity frameworks within financial institutions signifies a shift toward more dynamic, responsive, and adaptive security environments. This change reflects a broader trend of leveraging cutting-edge technology to enhance traditional security measures and adapt to an ever-changing threat landscape.

4.2. Importance of AI in Financial Institutions

AI is increasingly essential for financial institutions facing sophisticated cyber threats. AI improves security systems by quickly identifying and reacting to potential threats, crucial for protecting financial transactions and sensitive customer data. AI's ability to process large volumes of data rapidly allows banks to detect unusual patterns that may indicate fraud or security breaches, enabling them to promptly protect their assets and customer information.

Moreover, AI significantly boosts the efficiency and effectiveness of financial services. It automates routine tasks, freeing employees to tackle more complex challenges, which improves resource allocation and reduces costs. AI-driven chatbots, for instance, handle customer inquiries and transactions on their own, providing services that are both faster and more available around the clock. This automation increases customer satisfaction and enhances operational efficiency by minimizing human errors.

AI's predictive capabilities are also transforming risk management within financial institutions. By using AI to analyze historical data patterns, banks can anticipate future trends and potential risks, allowing for actions to be taken in advance to mitigate these risks. This forward-looking analysis aids in more informed decision-making for loan approvals, investment strategies, and other financial services.

The integration of AI continues to drive innovation, enhance security, and improve service delivery across financial institutions, making them more adaptable to the rapidly changing digital landscape. As AI technologies evolve, they are expected to transform the financial sector further, highlighting their growing importance in improving cybersecurity and as drivers of operational efficiency and innovation.

These developments highlight AI's vital role in enhancing financial institutions' capabilities, positioning AI not just as a technological tool but as a strategic asset essential for modernizing and securing financial services. As AI's applications expand, its integration becomes a critical element in shaping the future of the financial industry, ensuring institutions remain resilient, responsive, and competitive in a digital age.

AI significantly enhances various facets of financial institutions by streamlining operations, securing transactions, and improving customer service (see in Figure 4.1). In cybersecurity, AI proves indispensable by quickly identifying and responding to threats and analyzing large amounts of data in real time to spot signs of potential fraud. This quick action is crucial for protecting sensitive financial transactions and customer data.

Operational efficiency is also greatly enhanced as AI takes over routine and repetitive tasks, allowing financial institutions to redirect human resources toward more strategic activities. This not only reduces costs but also cuts down on human errors. AI-powered tools like chatbots provide

Figure 4.1. Strategic impact of AI in financial institutions.

round-the-clock customer service, handling inquiries without constant human intervention, thus ensuring services are always accessible.

In customer service, AI transforms interactions through immediate responses and personalized communication offered by chatbots and virtual assistants. This allows human customer service representatives to focus on resolving more complex issues, boosting customer satisfaction and engagement.

Furthermore, AI's ability to use historical data to forecast future trends revolutionizes risk management, helping banks to make informed decisions quickly. This capability supports banks in anticipating potential risks, enhancing financial stability, and minimizing losses.

AI drives innovation and maintains a competitive edge by enabling the development of new financial products and services tailored to evolving customer needs and market trends. Additionally, AI significantly aids in ensuring regulatory compliance by automating complex processes. It efficiently monitors transactions to ensure they adhere to legal standards, reducing the risk of penalties and improving the accuracy of compliance reporting.

AI's integration across financial operations exemplifies a transformative shift, making institutions more adaptive, innovative, and competitive in the fast-evolving digital landscape.

4.3. Challenges

4.3.1. *Challenge 1: Data privacy and protection*

Data privacy and protection pose significant challenges as financial institutions increasingly utilize AI to process and analyze large volumes of data. The vast amount of data collected, including sensitive personal and financial details, necessitates robust privacy protection to prevent breaches and ensure compliance with data protection regulations like General Data Protection Regulation (GDPR) and California Consumer Privacy Act (CCPA).

Large datasets' susceptibility to cyber-attacks makes financial institutions attractive targets for data breaches. Ensuring the security of these datasets is paramount as breaches can lead to substantial financial loss and erosion of customer trust. To address these privacy concerns, financial institutions must employ a variety of strategies to protect data throughout their lifecycle — from generation and storage to processing. This includes implementing strong access controls, encrypting sensitive data, and using privacy-preserving analytics to maintain data utility without compromising privacy.

Furthermore, the complexity of managing data across distributed systems introduces additional risks. The involvement of multiple parties in handling data can increase the likelihood of privacy violations. Protecting data across these distributed systems requires a nuanced approach that includes technological solutions and rigorous procedural safeguards.

When it comes to banking, the rapid adoption of electronic banking, driven by technological advances and the increasing use of the Internet, has brought about significant challenges in ensuring data security and privacy. As banks extend their services online, they encounter new risks, particularly information security, during transmission. Ensuring a secure end-to-end transaction is critical, which involves using secure communication protocols over untrusted networks and having reliable security measures at both endpoints. This approach includes using encryption algorithms, digital signatures, and hardware-based solutions like Smartcards to enhance the confidentiality of personal information and mitigate risks.

Moreover, the implementation of electronic banking has highlighted the need for stringent security measures to safeguard against unauthorized access to customer accounts and personal data. The systems must address the vulnerabilities inherent in connecting consumers directly to banking networks, where the potential for cyber-attacks remains high. Addressing these security issues requires software and hardware solutions that provide comprehensive protection against various threats, making electronic banking safer and more reliable for users.

Additionally, the shift toward electronic banking has necessitated robust frameworks to manage the privacy and security of vast amounts of sensitive data handled by financial institutions. These frameworks are essential for maintaining customer trust and ensuring compliance with regulatory standards like GDPR. Banks must implement proactive security strategies that include advanced technological solutions and strict procedural safeguards to protect customer data throughout its lifecycle. This holistic approach is vital for mitigating the risks associated with electronic banking and ensuring the integrity of online financial transactions.

Managing data privacy and protection in the age of big data demands a proactive and comprehensive approach. Financial institutions must continually adapt their data security practices to address evolving threats and comply with stringent regulatory requirements. This ongoing commitment to data privacy protects customers and strengthens the institution's reputation and competitive advantage.

4.3.2. *Challenge 2: Integration and scalability*

Data privacy and protection pose significant challenges as financial institutions increasingly utilize AI to process and analyze large volumes of data. The vast amount of data collected, including sensitive personal and financial details, necessitates robust privacy protection to prevent breaches and ensure compliance with data protection regulations like GDPR and CCPA.

Large datasets' susceptibility to cyber-attacks makes financial institutions attractive targets for data breaches. Ensuring the security of these datasets is paramount, as breaches can lead to substantial financial loss and erosion of customer trust.

To address these privacy concerns, financial institutions must employ various strategies to protect data throughout its lifecycle, from generation and storage to processing. This includes implementing strong access controls, encrypting sensitive data, and using privacy-preserving analytics to ensure that data utility is maintained without compromising privacy.

Furthermore, the complexity of managing data across distributed systems introduces additional risks. The involvement of multiple parties in handling data can increase the likelihood of privacy violations. Protecting data across these distributed systems requires a nuanced approach that includes technological solutions and rigorous procedural safeguards.

Integrating and scaling AI across large financial networks presents significant hurdles in banking. Integrating new systems with legacy banking systems poses substantial technical challenges as digital banking expands. Many existing banking systems, built on traditional mainframes and other legacy technologies, often struggle with scalability and agility. To accommodate the shift to open banking models, where data and services must be more accessible to third-party providers, banks must significantly enhance their core banking applications and upgrade server capacities to handle increased loads and transaction volumes effectively.

Moreover, the implementation of electronic banking has highlighted the need for stringent security measures to safeguard against unauthorized access to customer accounts and personal data. The systems must address the vulnerabilities inherent in connecting consumers directly to banking networks, where the potential for cyber-attacks remains high. Addressing these security issues requires software and hardware solutions that provide comprehensive protection against various threats, making electronic banking safer and more reliable for users.

Additionally, the shift toward electronic banking has necessitated robust frameworks to manage the privacy and security of vast amounts of sensitive data handled by financial institutions. These frameworks are essential for maintaining customer trust and ensuring compliance with regulatory standards like GDPR. Banks must implement proactive security strategies that include advanced technological solutions and strict procedural safeguards to protect customer data throughout its lifecycle. This holistic approach is vital for mitigating the risks associated with electronic banking and ensuring the integrity of online financial transactions.

4.4. Opportunities

4.4.1. *Opportunity 1: Fraud detection and prevention*

AI is revolutionizing how banks detect and prevent fraud. By analyzing vast transaction data, AI can identify unusual patterns and behaviors that may indicate fraudulent activity. This allows banks to respond quickly to potential threats, often stopping fraud before it occurs. AI systems continuously learn and adapt to new data, enhancing accuracy without requiring frequent human intervention.

Several machine learning techniques are integral to transforming fraud detection in banking systems. Logistic regression, one of the foundational methods, establishes relationships between transactional variables to classify data as either legitimate or fraudulent. However, due to the imbalanced nature of banking datasets — where fraudulent transactions constitute only a tiny fraction — logistic regression requires enhancements such as class weight tuning to maintain accuracy. In banking, this helps refine the identification of potentially fraudulent transactions without overwhelming the system with false positives.

Advanced techniques like LightGBM and XGBoost are particularly impactful in the banking sector. LightGBM, designed for efficiency in handling large datasets, uses gradient boosting to swiftly and accurately detect transaction data patterns. Its ability to process extensive banking data with limited memory usage ensures that fraud detection systems remain scalable and responsive even during peak transaction volumes. Similarly, XGBoost stands out for its speed and precision. Employing parallel processing and regularization minimizes overfitting, allowing banks to efficiently identify fraud in complex datasets, such as those involving international transfers or high-value transactions.

CatBoost, another state-of-the-art algorithm, is well suited to banking fraud detection because it handles categorical data like customer demographics, transaction types, and location details. It requires minimal data preprocessing, making it efficient for real-time fraud detection in high-volume banking environments. CatBoost's GPU-accelerated training capabilities further enhance its utility, enabling banks to analyze large datasets rapidly and improve the accuracy of fraud detection models.

Ensemble methods like majority voting enhance the robustness of fraud detection in banking. These approaches combine predictions from multiple algorithms, such as LightGBM, XGBoost, and CatBoost, to become reliable. For instance, when monitoring online banking transactions, an ensemble model can analyze data from multiple angles, reducing errors and strengthening the system's overall performance. Banks often rely on these ensemble techniques to securely process the ever-increasing number of digital transactions.

Deep learning further elevates fraud detection in banking by enabling the identification of intricate transactional patterns. Neural networks process raw data to discover hidden relationships between fraudulent and legitimate behaviors. By leveraging features such as transaction time, transaction amount, and merchant details, deep learning models help banks detect subtle anomalies that simpler models might miss. Additionally, the adaptive nature of these models ensures they evolve with emerging fraud patterns, making them invaluable in the fast-paced financial landscape.

Moreover, AI supports advanced security measures in banking, such as biometric verification, to strengthen transactional security. Integrating AI with biometric technologies like facial recognition or fingerprint scanning adds an extra layer of protection, particularly for online and mobile banking. This safeguards customer accounts and fosters trust in the bank's digital platforms.

Automating fraud detection processes significantly reduces operational costs for banks while minimizing human errors. By streamlining the identification and prevention of fraud, AI ensures that banks can efficiently handle the growing volume of digital transactions. As digital banking continues to expand, the role of AI becomes even more critical in securing transactions, protecting customer assets, and maintaining trust in financial institutions.

By leveraging the power of AI and its associated techniques, banks are enhancing their ability to detect fraud and building more resilient and trustworthy financial ecosystems. This technological advancement plays a pivotal role in securing customers' financial well-being and ensuring the integrity of digital banking operations.

4.4.2. *Opportunity 2: Regulatory compliance automation*

AI transforms how banks manage regulatory compliance, a critical aspect of their operations. With the ever-evolving landscape of financial regulations and standards, keeping up with compliance requirements can be time-consuming and resource-intensive. AI offers a streamlined and efficient approach to automate these processes, significantly reducing manual effort while ensuring accuracy and consistency.

One of the primary applications of AI in regulatory compliance is automating document analysis and reporting. Regulatory guidelines often require banks to sift through extensive documentation to identify relevant information. AI-powered natural language processing (NLP) tools can quickly analyze large volumes of regulatory texts, contracts, and transaction records, extracting pertinent data and identifying compliance requirements. This saves time and reduces the chance of human error, ensuring that all critical regulatory details are accurately captured.

AI also enhances real-time monitoring and reporting of transactions to comply with anti-money laundering (AML) and know-your-customer (KYC) regulations. Machine learning algorithms can analyze patterns and flag suspicious activities that might indicate money laundering, fraud, or other financial crimes. Unlike traditional rule-based systems, AI can adapt to new patterns of fraudulent behavior, making it more effective in identifying non-compliant activities. Additionally, AI-driven automation facilitates the generation of compliance reports that meet regulatory standards, reducing the burden on compliance teams.

Another key area where AI proves invaluable is predictive analytics for regulatory changes. Financial regulations are subject to frequent updates, and staying ahead of these changes is vital for maintaining compliance. AI systems can analyze historical regulatory changes and predict future trends, allowing banks to adjust their policies and procedures proactively. This foresight helps institutions avoid costly fines and reputational damage associated with non-compliance.

In risk assessment, AI provides a sophisticated means of identifying and managing regulatory risks. By analyzing data across multiple systems, AI can assess the likelihood of compliance breaches and prioritize areas that require attention. For example, AI algorithms can evaluate customer risk profiles, transaction histories, and market data to view potential regulatory risks comprehensively. This empowers banks to take preemptive actions to mitigate these risks.

Moreover, AI supports the integration of compliance into day-to-day banking operations. With robotic process automation (RPA) and intelligent workflows, repetitive compliance tasks — such as customer identity verification, transaction screening, and policy updates — are executed faster and more precisely. This integration ensures that compliance becomes an inherent part of the operational fabric, reducing the need for separate manual processes.

The use of AI in compliance also enhances transparency and auditability. AI systems maintain detailed logs of all compliance-related activities, making it easier for regulators and auditors to verify adherence to standards. This transparency fosters trust between banks and regulatory bodies while simplifying the audit process.

To illustrate, AI is revolutionizing regulatory compliance in banking by automating processes, improving accuracy, and reducing costs. Banks can efficiently navigate the complexities of regulatory frameworks through advanced technologies such as NLP, machine learning, predictive analytics, and RPA. This ensures compliance and strengthens the institution's ability to adapt to an increasingly stringent regulatory environment, safeguarding its operations and reputation.

AI-driven compliance mechanisms introduce sequential processing strategies that dissect regulatory documents or data into smaller, manageable segments for analysis. This bottom-up method mirrors computational sliding window techniques, ensuring flexibility in capturing and interpreting varying text structures. AI tools extract regulatory logic clauses from data using advanced pattern recognition and mapping compliance attributes to their corresponding subjects. These mechanisms leverage backward matching techniques to verify partial matches in regulatory documents, completing compliance logic even when only subsets of information are initially available.

High precision and recall are core metrics in AI-powered compliance systems, ensuring accuracy and comprehensiveness in detecting and adhering to regulations. Rigorous testing and validation on domain-specific datasets confirm the systems' ability to interpret complex regulatory requirements effectively. Automation of rule development further enhances these systems, transforming raw data into actionable compliance logic while remaining adaptable to evolving regulations.

Furthermore, the integration of domain-specific ontologies into AI compliance systems strengthens their semantic understanding. These ontologies establish contextual relationships between compliance attributes and subjects, enabling precise interpretation of regulatory texts. Error analysis and continuous refinement address challenges such as structural ambiguities, incorrect tagging, and the handling of uncommon syntactic patterns, ensuring ongoing improvement in performance and reliability.

AI systems excel in handling both quantitative and qualitative compliance requirements, analyzing financial thresholds and transaction patterns to ensure thorough regulatory adherence. These systems efficiently process high volumes of complex regulations for scalability, positioning them for future expansion into broader regulatory areas and more efficient computational applications. Collectively, these advancements underscore AI's transformative role in achieving and sustaining regulatory compliance in banking.

4.5. The Potential of Secure Technology

Each bank employs a distinct strategy in its approach to cybersecurity, reflecting its commitment to protecting networks, data, and customers from cyber threats. JPMorgan Chase, Bank of America, and Capital One (Figure 4.2) are the top three banks by assets in the United States. Each prioritizes robust security measures and substantial investments in advanced technologies to ensure safe environments.

JPMorgan Chase and Capital One lead with substantial investments of $1.5 billion each in cybersecurity, implementing three advanced security technologies. These investments enable the adoption of cutting-edge

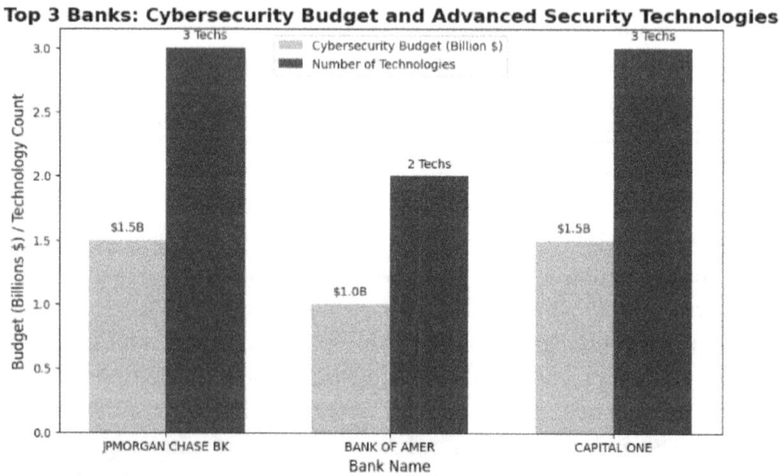

Figure 4.2. Overview of cybersecurity budget and technology utilized by top three U.S. Banks.

solutions, like machine learning algorithms for anomaly detection, automated systems for real-time threat intelligence, and advanced encryption protocols to secure sensitive data transactions. Such technologies enhance the speed and accuracy of threat detection and response, a crucial factor in modern cybersecurity strategies.

With a $1 billion investment, Bank of America employs two cybersecurity technologies. Its focus is on integrating AI-driven behavioral analytics. This approach enhances the bank's preventive measures against fraud and other cyber risks by monitoring and predicting potential security breaches based on unusual behavior patterns.

Implementing AI into cybersecurity marks a transformative shift in how these financial institutions protect themselves against potential fraud. AI streamlines complex security processes and enables instant response capabilities that are vital in today's digital environment. AI systems can analyze large amounts of transaction data in milliseconds to identify cyber threats, significantly reducing response times compared to traditional methods.

However, integrating and scaling AI technologies across large and diverse banking networks presents significant challenges. Banks must continuously adapt their security infrastructure to evolving threats and technologies, ensuring that protective measures are scalable and effective. Moreover, the increased use of AI raises concerns about data privacy and the ethical use of technology. Banks are navigating these challenges carefully, ensuring compliance with regulations such as GDPR and CCPA while maintaining customer trust.

As cyber threats evolve in complexity, banks are expected to increase their investments further in AI and other advanced technologies. These enhancements will include greater use of blockchain for secure transactions, enhanced use of cloud technologies for better scalability, and continuous innovation in AI algorithms to improve detection and response times.

Theoretical insights into IT governance and compliance within diverse regulatory environments underline the importance of IT governance and compliance, suggesting that the strategic application of such frameworks can significantly enhance financial institutions' security and operational efficiency. Adopting robust governance and compliance frameworks like COBIT, ISO/IEC 27001, and ITIL is crucial in managing the complexities of modern banking. Financial institutions should stay ahead in an era where digital threats are becoming more extensive.

4.6. Conclusion

AI is quickly becoming a key tool for major banks like JPMorgan Chase, Bank of America, and Capital One as they work to protect themselves from more complex digital threats. These banks are investing heavily in AI to develop security systems that can predict and stop threats before they happen.

However, using AI across different banking systems brings significant challenges, especially concerning privacy and ethical issues. Banks are working hard to handle these challenges while keeping their customers' trust and following strict data protection laws.

As we look to the future, we anticipate that AI's role in keeping banks safe from cyber threats will grow. As online threats become more complicated, the ability to predict them using AI will become even more meaningful. Integrating new technologies like blockchain and quantum computing with AI makes financial institutions more secure. Also, AI makes it easier for banks to follow international rules by automating compliance processes.

As technology continues to evolve, it is essential for banks to keep pace with the latest advancements in AI to safeguard their operations and maintain their customers' trust in their security measures.

Overall, the ongoing improvements and integration of AI into security strategies are preparing financial institutions for an efficient and reliable future. This transformation emphasizes the vital role of AI in ensuring security and boosting the trustworthiness of the financial sector's digital environment.

Bibliography

Abdulrasool, F. E. and Turnbull, S. J. "Exploring security, risk, and compliance driven IT governance model for universities: Applied research based on the COBIT framework." *International Journal of Electronic Banking* 2, no. 3 (2020): 237–265. DOI: 10.1504/IJEBANK.2020.111438.

Dash, B., Ansari, M. F., Sharma, P., and Ali, A. "Threats and opportunities with AI-based cybersecurity intrusion detection: A review." *International Journal of Software Engineering & Applications (IJSEA)* 13, no. 5 (2022): 39–56. DOI: 10.5121/ijsea.2022.13503.

Fakhrudin, A., Ipung, H. P., Soetomo, M. A., and Lim, C. "Core banking system scalability review." *International Journal of Advanced Research in Computer Science* 10, no. 1 (2019): 89–95. DOI: 10.26483/ijarcs.v10i1.12345.

Forbes. America's most cybersecure banks 2023. https://www.forbes.com/lists/cybersecure-banks/.

Gulyás, O. and Kiss, G. "Impact of cyber-attacks on financial institutions." *Procedia Computer Science* 219 (2023): 84–90. DOI: 10.1016/j.procs.2023.01.267.

Hammood, W. A., Arshah, R. A., Asmara, S. M., and Hammood, O. A. "User authentication model based on mobile phone IMEI number: A proposed method application for online banking system." In *International Conference on Software Engineering & Computer Systems and 4th International Conference on Computational Science and Information Management (ICSECS-ICOCSIM)*, 411–416, 2021. DOI: 10.1109/ICSECS52883.2021.00081.

Hassan, A. O., Ewuga, S. K., Abdul, A. A., Abrahams, T. O., Oladeinde, M., and Dawodu, S. O. "Cybersecurity in banking: A global perspective with a focus on Nigerian practices." *Computer Science & IT Research Journal* 5, no. 1 (2024): 41–59. DOI: 10.51594/csitrj.v5i1.701.

Li, J., Maiti, A., and Fei, J. "Features and scope of regulatory technologies: Challenges and opportunities with Industrial Internet of Things." *Future Internet* 15, no. 8 (2023): 256. DOI: 10.3390/fi15080256.

Mehmood, A., Natgunanathan, I., Xiang, Y., Hua, G., and Guo, S. "Protection of big data privacy." *IEEE Access* 4 (2016): 1821–1834. DOI: 10.1109/ACCESS.2016.2558446.

Nzeako, G., Akinsanya, M. O., Popoola, O. A., Chukwurah, E. G., Okeke, C. D., and Akpukorji, I. S. "Theoretical insights into IT governance and compliance in banking: Perspectives from African and U.S. regulatory environments." *International Journal of Management & Entrepreneurship Research* 6, no. 5 (2024): 1457–1466. DOI: 10.51594/ijmer.v6i5.1094.

Omariba, Z. B., Masese, N. B., and Wanyembi, G. "Security and privacy of electronic banking." *IJCSI International Journal of Computer Science Issues* 9, no. 4 (2012): 432–446.

Rahmani, F. M. and Zohuri, B. "The transformative impact of AI on financial institutions, with a focus on banking." *Journal of Financial Innovation and Technology* 6, no. 3 (2021): 123–145. DOI: 10.47363/JEAST/2023(5)192.

Yanamala, A. K. Y., Suryadevara, S., and Kalli, V. D. R. "Balancing innovation and privacy: The intersection of data protection and Artificial Intelligence." *International Journal of Machine Learning Research in Cybersecurity and Artificial Intelligence* 15, no. 1 (2024): 1–43.

Zhang, J. and El-Gohary, N. M. "Automated information transformation for automated regulatory compliance checking in construction." *Journal of Computing in Civil Engineering* 29, no. 5 (2015): 1–15. DOI: 10.1061/(ASCE)CP.1943-5487.0000427.

https://doi.org/10.1142/9781800616578_0005

Chapter 5

AI-Driven Trends and Technologies in Digital Marketing: Shaping Modern Strategies

Preeti Jain[*,‡] and Neetu Chaudhary[†,§]

[*]*Ajay Kumar Garg Institute of Management, Ghaziabad, Uttar Pradesh, India*

[†]*MM Institute of Management, Maharishi Markandeshwar, Deemed to be University, Mullana-Ambala, Haryana, India*

[‡]*preeti13.pj@gmail.com*
[§]*neetuchaudhary907@gmail.com*

Abstract

Current trends in digital marketing are rapidly evolving, driven by technological advancements and changing consumer behaviors. Interactive websites now engage users more effectively, enhancing user experience. Artificial Intelligence (AI) and machine learning, such as long short-term memory neural networks, predict purchase behavior, enabling real-time, targeted customer interactions. Augmented reality (AR) features, like "3D Try-On," enhance shopping experiences and drive engagement. Real-time bidding (RTB) platforms optimize ad placements by leveraging user demographics and online behavior. Content marketing remains crucial, focusing on creating valuable content to attract and retain audiences.

Social media marketing, search engine marketing, email marketing, influencer marketing, and visual search are prominent trends offering unique ways to engage consumers. Chatbots improve customer service with instant responses. These trends significantly impact consumer buying behavior by enhancing the shopping experience and influencing purchase decisions through personalized and interactive engagements. Adopting emerging technologies requires a strategic approach, leveraging data analytics, and continuous adaptation. Companies must integrate their online presence across various platforms, invest in predictive analytics, and ensure cybersecurity. Understanding digital trends is essential for maintaining competitiveness. Continuous learning and adaptation are crucial for updating digital marketing strategies, ensuring customer satisfaction, and driving business growth. This chapter explores how these trends and technologies shape modern marketing strategies.

Keywords: Immersive technology, Artificial Intelligence, marketing strategies, NLP, case study, challenges, chatbots.

5.1. Introduction

Artificial Intelligence (AI)-driven trends have greatly influenced consumer behavior by improving personalization, optimizing marketing strategies, and reframing purchasing decisions. Advanced algorithms in AI personalization techniques, which have been studied, can be used by e-commerce platforms to deliver highly tailored content, product recommendations, and user experiences. By using AI's analytical abilities, businesses have been able to analyze customer data with unprecedented precision, allowing them to better understand consumer needs and influence purchase decisions with curated product recommendations.

The integration of AI tools in marketing management has been investigated, with AI being utilized to analyze consumer behavior, promote products, and develop targeted marketing strategies, ultimately helping businesses increase profits (Parkhomenko, 2024). Cosmetic industry shoppers now enjoy more interactive and informed shopping experiences thanks to AI-driven marketing tools, such as virtual try-on experiences and personalized product recommendations. AI-powered chatbots have significantly influenced consumer perceptions and preferences. Furthermore, the impact of AI extends beyond simply improving the shopping experience; it also shapes consumer behavior by automating processes, allows marketers to act faster and smarter, and encourages consumers to consider the ethical implications of business decisions (Thakur and Kumar, 2024). As AI evolves, it not only alters the way business is done but also demands that marketers modify their strategies to meet the evolving expectations of tech-savvy consumers. The significance of businesses utilizing AI-based strategies to stay competitive in the digital landscape is highlighted by the overall impact of AI on consumer behavior.

Modern strategies are being shaped by cutting-edge trends and technologies introduced by AI, which has had a significant impact on digital marketing. AI applications like recommender systems, chatbots, personalized content creation, and predictive analytics are revolutionizing customer experience and campaign personalization (Abhinav, 2024). Machine learning algorithms enable marketers to sift through massive amounts of data, improve consumer segmentation, and optimize strategies (Malik *et al.*, 2024). Industry giants like Coca-Cola, Starbucks, and Nike have successfully implemented AI in automating customer service, content creation, and running targeted advertising campaigns (Grljevi *et al.*, 2024).

The digital landscape has become more competitive with the assistance of AI-based technologies in analyzing customer behavior, optimizing campaigns and interactions (Raghav *et al.*, 2024). Future marketing strategies are poised to be influenced by emerging technologies such as AR and voice search.

Even though AI systems have many benefits, there are still some challenges that need to be addressed, such as data protection, ethical concerns, and the need for qualified personnel to manage them. AI can help small businesses improve their digital marketing strategies due to their lack of technical knowledge. AI's capacity to automate tasks, reevaluate marketing strategies, and improve ROI is invaluable, but it is not fully capable of replacing human knowledge (Prasanna and Mishra, 2024). AI's future potential in marketing is enormous and further advancements are expected to refine and innovate marketing practices. In the competitive digital landscape, businesses are able to thrive by utilizing AI to provide deeper customer insights and better marketing strategies.

5.2. Leveraging AI Technologies in Marketing

Marketing can be transformed by utilizing AI technologies, which can include personalized marketing, customer interaction, operational efficiency, and strategic planning. AI enables companies to analyze large datasets and discern patterns in customer behavior, thereby improving personalized marketing and engagement strategies (Rachid, 2024). AI offers real-time personalized experiences that are tailored to customers, leading to enhanced user engagement and higher conversion rates (Sumit *et al.*, 2024). AI is also vital for setting strategic marketing objectives, supporting customer segmentation, personalized targeting, predictive analytics, and automation, which align with overall business goals to improve customer experience and drive revenue (Anjorin *et al.*, 2024).

5.2.1. *Examples of companies leveraging AI technologies in marketing*

Amazon: Amazon uses AI to customize the shopping experience by suggesting products according to users' browsing and purchase history, which enhances sales and customer satisfaction. The recommendation engine is an example of how machine learning processes large amounts of data to predict future purchases (Barat and Gulati, 2024).

Netflix: AI is used by Netflix to suggest shows and movies based on users' viewing history and preferences, which improves engagement and retention. Analyzing viewing patterns allows Netflix to improve user experience with relevant content suggestions (Barat and Galati, 2024).

Spotify: Spotify employs AI to create personalized playlists, such as the "Discover Weekly" playlist, which exposes users to new music according to their listening habits. This approach keeps users engaged and helps them discover new artists and songs (Grljevic *et al.*, 2024).

Coca-Cola: Coca-Cola is able to create targeted and effective marketing campaigns by using AI to analyze social media data and gauge consumer sentiment. The use of social media insights enables Coca-Cola to tailor strategies to better meet consumers' needs and preferences (Grljevic *et al.*, 2024).

Sephora: Sephora uses AI to improve the shopping experience by utilizing virtual assistants and chatbots, which provides personalized product recommendations. AI also helps analyze customer data and manage inventory to ensure the availability of popular items (Grljević *et al.*, 2024).

Starbucks: Starbucks' mobile app uses AI to personalize marketing messages and promotions, which in turn leads to increased customer loyalty and sales. By analyzing purchase history and preferences, Starbucks targets promotions more effectively (Grljević *et al.*, 2024).

Unilever: Unilever uses AI to analyze consumer data and predict trends, which leads to more effective marketing strategies and product development. Unilever enhances sales and market share by developing products that cater to consumer needs by understanding their desires.

The following examples showcase how companies across different industries are utilizing AI technologies to improve their marketing campaigns and strategies, resulting in increased efficiency, better customer experiences, and higher sales.

5.3. AI Applications in Digital Personalized Content and Product Recommendations

AI-driven suggestions are tailored to meet individual preferences through the use of developed algorithms, consumer information analysis, and constant research. To provide individualized financial guidance and educational materials, improve budgetary competence and inclusion, and analyze customer monetary behaviors and preferences, the financial sector relies on AI-based suggestion systems. The health sector maintains customer profiles with the help of an AI-driven suggestions system that includes health history, preferences, and real-time data from wearable devices, so as to provide personalized health and well-being suggestions based on the latest medical research and real-time health metrics. To suggest electronic gadgets that suit the needs of consumers, AI systems gather information about users, such as demographics, browsing history, and past purchases, and utilize collaborative filtering (Adharsh *et al.*, 2023) in the following manner:

- *Individual shopping experience*: In order to increase sales and profits, companies like Amazon make use of AI to study user browsing history and past purchase behavior to suggest products accordingly.
- *Content suggestions*: Netflix uses AI algorithms to suggest films and TV series based on a user's viewing history and preferences, which helps keep users interested and subscribed.

- *Music playlists*: To enhance user experience and retention, Spotify makes use of AI to manage customized playlists like "Discover Weekly," which introduces users to new music based on their listening history (Sangam and Singh, 2024).
- *Targeted advertising*: By employing AI on its advertising platform, Google helps businesses in creating more effective ad campaigns to focus on the target market, which in turn helps in attracting the target customer at the right time through leveraging ad placements and bidding tactics.
- *Social media analysis*: To have an understanding of consumer priorities and market trends, Coca-Cola employs AI to conduct an analysis of social media data and customer responses, which helps in designing more targeted marketing campaigns and new product developments to satisfy customer requirements.
- *Beauty advice and recommendations*: Sephora makes use of AI in its mobile app to offer customized beauty advice and product suggestions to enhance the customer retention ratio.
- *Customized promotions*: Starbucks leverages AI to tailor its marketing campaigns to deliver customers personalized offers based on their past purchases. This approach helps in increasing sales and improving customer engagement by presenting relevant bargains (Sangam and Singh, 2024).
- *Dynamic pricing*: In order to face cutthroat competition and enhance profitability, Amazon also employs AI for dynamic pricing, i.e., changing prices on the basis of demand, competition, and other factors.

Real-time monitoring and predictive modeling: With the help of real-time monitoring and predictive modeling, AI enhances speed, accuracy, and efficiency in distribution and supply chain management, which leads to enhanced customer satisfaction by making the product available at the right time at the right place (Sangam and Singh, 2024).

5.4. AI Technologies in Marketing

AI technologies are revolutionizing marketing by enabling marketers to automate tedious operations, personalize marketing campaigns, and gain a deeper understanding of consumer behavior. It focuses on the significance of adapting to these technical breakthroughs in order to increase marketing efficiency and provides insightful information on how AI is changing marketing practices for scholars, practitioners, and policymakers.

Machine learning (*ML*): The technique called machine learning can analyze data and come to conclusions without the need for explicit programming. ML can also be used in marketing to analyze customer data and forecast behavior, segment customers, and personalize marketing messages. For instance, ML algorithms can make product recommendations to users based on their browsing and past purchases, increasing the relevance of marketing campaigns and increasing conversion rates.

5.4.1. *The role played by ML in marketing with real cases*

- **Better client segmentation:** ML enables marketers to divide their client base into smaller groups according to various characteristics such as behavior, preferences, and demographics. This allows for more focused and efficient marketing campaigns. For instance, Netflix utilizes ML to categorize its users according to their viewing habits, which helps with personalized program and movie suggestions.
- **Customize marketing:** ML algorithms examine customer data to identify individual preferences and behaviors, allowing marketers to craft individual messages and better connect with each customer, leading to higher engagement and conversion rates. For example, Amazon utilizes machine learning to suggest products to users based on their previous purchases and browsing history, which greatly enhances both sales and customer satisfaction.
- **Predictive informatics:** ML can forecast future customer behaviors and trends by examining historical data, helping marketers in making data-driven decisions regarding product launches, inventory management, and marketing strategies, which can lead to improved business results. For example, Starbucks leverages machine learning to anticipate customer preferences and refine its menu, thereby boosting sales and fostering customer loyalty.
- **Predicting customer lifetime value:** ML models can forecast the total value a customer is expected to generate throughout their relationship

with a brand. This helps marketers concentrate their efforts on customers with the highest potential value and enhance strategies for customer retention. For instance, Uber employs machine learning to estimate the lifetime value of its riders, which allows the company to customize its marketing strategies to retain its most valuable customers.

- **Automated customer support:** ML powers chatbots and virtual assistants that can handle customer inquiries efficiently and accurately, providing instant support and freeing up human agents to handle more complex issues, thereby improving overall customer satisfaction. For example, Sephora uses an ML-powered chatbot to assist customers with product recommendations and beauty tips, enhancing the shopping experience.
- **Content optimization:** ML algorithms can analyze which types of content perform better with different audience segments, helping marketers create and distribute content that is more likely to engage and convert their target audience. The New York Times uses ML to optimize its content recommendations, ensuring that readers are presented with articles that match their interests.
- **Ad targeting and optimization:** ML helps in optimizing ad placements and targeting by analyzing user data and behavior, ensuring that ads are shown to the right people at the right time, which increases the effectiveness of advertising campaigns. Facebook uses ML to target ads based on user behavior and preferences, resulting in higher engagement and conversion rates for advertisers.
- **Churn prediction:** ML can identify patterns that indicate when a customer is likely to stop using a product or service, allowing marketers to take proactive measures to retain those customers and reduce churn rates. Spotify uses ML to predict user churn and offers personalized recommendations and promotions to keep users engaged with the platform.
- **Dynamic pricing:** ML algorithms can adjust prices in real time based on various factors such as demand, competition, and customer behavior, helping businesses maximize their revenue and stay competitive in the market. Airlines like Delta use ML for dynamic pricing, adjusting ticket prices based on demand and booking patterns to optimize revenue.
- **Fraud detection:** ML can detect unusual patterns and behaviors that may indicate fraudulent activities, helping businesses protect themselves and their customers from fraud, thereby maintaining trust and security. PayPal uses ML to detect and prevent fraudulent transactions, ensuring a secure payment.

5.4.2. *Natural language processing (NLP)*

Natural Language Processing (NLP) is a branch of AI that focuses on the interaction between computers and humans through natural language. In marketing, NLP is used to analyze customer feedback, social media posts, and other text data to understand customer sentiments and preferences. This helps marketers tailor their messages and improve customer engagement. Additionally, NLP powers chatbots and virtual assistants, which can provide instant customer support and personalized recommendations, enhancing the overall customer experience.

5.4.2.1. *The role of NLP in marketing*

Understanding customer sentiments: NLP helps marketers analyze customer feedback, social media posts, and reviews to understand how customers feel about their products or services, allowing them to tailor their marketing strategies accordingly.

Personalized customer interactions: NLP powers chatbots and virtual assistants that can engage with customers in real time, providing personalized responses and recommendations based on the customer's queries and preferences, which enhances the overall customer experience (Simanullang, 2024).

Content creation and optimization: NLP can assist in generating and optimizing marketing content by analyzing what type of content resonates most with the target audience, helping marketers create more effective and engaging messages.

Market research and trend analysis: By processing large volumes of text data from various sources, NLP can identify emerging trends and topics of interest, enabling marketers to stay ahead of the curve and adjust their strategies to meet changing consumer demands.

Improving customer support: NLP enables the development of intelligent customer support systems that can understand and respond to customer inquiries efficiently, reducing response times and improving customer satisfaction.

Enhancing Ad targeting: NLP can analyze the language used by different customer segments to create more targeted and relevant advertisements, increasing the likelihood of engagement and conversion (Simanullang, 2024).

Voice search optimization: With the increasing use of voice-activated devices, NLP helps marketers optimize their content for voice search, ensuring that their products and services are easily discoverable through voice queries.

Sentiment analysis for brand monitoring: NLP tools can monitor online mentions of a brand and analyze the sentiment behind them, providing valuable insights into public perception and helping marketers manage their brand reputation effectively.

Automating routine tasks: NLP can automate routine marketing tasks such as sorting emails, categorizing customer feedback, and generating reports, freeing up time for marketers to focus on more strategic activities.

Enhancing customer segmentation: By analyzing the language and tone used by different customer groups, NLP can help marketers segment their audience more accurately, allowing for more precise targeting and personalized marketing efforts (Simanullang, 2024).

5.4.2.2. *How NLP analyzes customer sentiments*

- *Text collection*: NLP starts by collecting text data from various sources such as social media posts, customer reviews, emails, and surveys, which provide a wealth of information about customer opinions and feelings.
- *Text preprocessing*: The collected text data are then cleaned and prepared for analysis by removing irrelevant information like punctuation, special characters, and stop words (common words like "and" and "the"), making the data easier to analyze.
- *Tokenization*: The cleaned text is broken down into smaller units called tokens, which can be words, phrases, or sentences, allowing the NLP system to analyze the text at a granular level and understand the context better.

- *Sentiment detection*: NLP uses algorithms to identify and classify the sentiment expressed in the text as positive, negative, or neutral, helping marketers understand the overall mood and opinions of their customers.
- *Aspect-based sentiment analysis*: This advanced technique allows NLP to identify specific aspects or features of a product or service mentioned in the text and determine the sentiment associated with each aspect, providing more detailed insights (Simanullang, 2024).
- *Named entity recognition (NER)*: NLP systems can recognize and categorize named entities (such as product names, brands, or locations) mentioned in the text, helping marketers understand which specific entities are being discussed and the sentiments associated with them.
- *Sentiment scoring*: Each piece of text is assigned a sentiment score based on the detected sentiment, which can be aggregated to provide an overall sentiment score for a product, service, or brand, giving marketers a clear picture of customer opinions.
- *Visualization and reporting*: The sentiment analysis results are often visualized using charts, graphs, and dashboards, making it easier for marketers to interpret the data and make informed decisions based on customer sentiments (Simanullang, 2024).
- *Continuous monitoring*: NLP systems can continuously monitor new text data in real time, allowing marketers to stay updated on changing customer sentiments and respond promptly to any negative feedback or emerging trends
- *Computer vision*: Computer vision is an AI technology that enables computers to interpret and make decisions based on visual data, such as images and videos. In marketing, computer vision can be used for visual search, where customers can upload images to find similar products. It can also analyze customer interactions with visual content to understand which types of images and videos are most engaging. This information helps marketers create more effective visual campaigns and improve the visual appeal of their products

Applications in Marketing

- *Personalized marketing*: AI technologies enable personalized marketing by analyzing customer data to understand individual preferences and behaviors. This allows marketers to create tailored messages and offers that resonate with each customer, leading to higher engagement and conversion rates. For example, AI can recommend products, send personalized emails, and display targeted ads based on a customer's browsing history and purchase behavior.

- *Customer segmentation*: AI can analyze large datasets to identify distinct customer segments based on various attributes such as demographics, purchase history, and online behavior. This helps marketers target specific groups with customized marketing strategies, improving the effectiveness of their campaigns. For instance, AI can segment customers into high-value and low-value groups, allowing marketers to allocate resources more efficiently.
- *Predictive analytics*: AI uses predictive analytics to forecast future trends and customer behaviors by analyzing historical data. This helps marketers plan their campaigns more effectively and stay ahead of market trends. For example, AI can predict which products are likely to be popular in the future, allowing marketers to stock up on inventory and create targeted promotions.
- *Automated media buying*: AI-powered platforms can automate the media buying process by using machine learning algorithms to bid on ad spaces in real time. This ensures that ads are placed in the most relevant and high-performing locations, reducing costs and improving campaign performance. Automated media buying also allows marketers to quickly adjust their strategies based on real-time data, ensuring optimal results.

By leveraging AI technologies such as machine learning, natural language processing, and computer vision, marketers can enhance their strategies, improve customer engagement, and achieve better results in their campaigns.

5.5. How to Make Automated Chatbots and Virtual Assistants for Customer Engagement

Creating automated chatbots and virtual assistants for customer engagement involves leveraging AI and NLP to simulate human interactions effectively. The process begins with selecting appropriate machine learning models such as retrieval learning and sequence-sequence learning, which are essential for understanding and generating human-like responses (Amar *et al.*, 2021):

- *Understanding the basics*: Automated chatbots and virtual assistants are computer programs designed to simulate human conversation and assist users by providing information or performing tasks. These tools use AI to understand and respond to user queries, making them highly effective for customer engagement by providing instant responses and personalized interactions.
- *Choosing the right platform*: To create a chatbot or virtual assistant, you need to select a platform that supports AI and NLP. Popular platforms include Google's Dialogflow, Microsoft's Bot Framework, and IBM's Watson. These platforms offer tools and templates to help you build and deploy your chatbot with ease.
- *Defining objectives and use cases*: Before building your chatbot, it is crucial to define its purpose and the specific tasks it will perform. Common use cases include answering frequently asked questions, assisting with product recommendations, and providing customer support. Clear objectives will guide the development process and ensure the chatbot meets user needs effectively (Amar *et al.*, 2021).
- *Designing conversational flows*: A conversational flow is a script that outlines how the chatbot will interact with users. It includes possible user inputs and the corresponding bot responses. Designing a smooth and intuitive conversational flow is essential for creating a positive user experience. Use simple language and anticipate the various ways users might phrase their questions.
- *Training the AI model*: Training involves feeding the chatbot with data so it can learn to understand and respond accurately to user queries. The data can include past customer interactions, common questions, and relevant keywords. The more data you provide, the better the chatbot will perform. Regularly updating and retraining the model is also important to maintain its accuracy (Amar *et al.*, 2021).
- *Integrating with existing systems*: For a seamless user experience, integrate your chatbot with existing systems such as customer relationship management (CRM) software, databases, and other tools. This allows the chatbot to access and provide real-time information, enhancing its usefulness and efficiency.
- *Testing and iteration*: Before launching your chatbot, conduct thorough testing to identify and fix any issues. Test it with real users to gather feedback and make necessary improvements. Iteration is key to refining the chatbot's performance and ensuring it meets user expectations.

- *Monitoring and analytics*: After deployment, continuously monitor the chatbot's performance using analytics tools. Track metrics such as user engagement, response accuracy, and customer satisfaction. Use the data to make ongoing improvements and keep the chatbot aligned with user needs (Amar *et al.*, 2021).

5.6. Optimization of Advertising Campaigns and Media Buying

Optimization of advertising campaigns and media buying involves a multifaceted approach that leverages data-driven techniques to enhance the effectiveness and profitability of ad expenditures. Ad optimization focuses on improving targeting, messaging, and delivery strategies using methods such as A/B testing, machine learning algorithms, and predictive modeling to achieve specific business goals like increasing conversions or reducing acquisition costs (Yuvaraj, 2023):

- *Understanding AI in advertising*: AI has revolutionized advertising by enabling more precise targeting and personalized marketing strategies, which are essential for optimizing advertising campaigns and media buying [1]. AI helps in analyzing vast amounts of data to understand consumer preferences, behaviors, and demographics, allowing marketers to tailor their campaigns more effectively.
- *Data collection and analysis*: AI tools collect and analyze data from various sources, such as social media, website interactions, and purchase history, to gain insights into consumer behavior. The data help in identifying the right audience for your ads, ensuring that your marketing efforts are directed toward individuals who are more likely to be interested in your products or services.
- *Personalized Ad targeting*: By leveraging AI, marketers can create highly personalized ads that resonate with individual consumers. AI algorithms analyze user data to determine the best time, platform, and content for each ad, increasing the chances of engagement and conversion. This level of personalization is crucial for optimizing advertising campaigns.
- *Automated media buying*: AI-powered platforms can automate the media buying process, making it more efficient and cost-effective. These platforms use machine learning algorithms to bid on ad spaces

in real time, ensuring that your ads are placed in the most relevant and high-performing locations. This automation reduces the need for manual intervention and helps in achieving better results with lower costs.

- *Performance monitoring and adjustment*: AI tools continuously monitor the performance of advertising campaigns, providing real-time insights and analytics. This allows marketers to quickly identify what is working and what is not, making it easier to adjust strategies on the fly. By constantly optimizing campaigns based on performance data, marketers can improve their return on investment (ROI).
- *Predictive analytics*: AI uses predictive analytics to forecast future trends and consumer behaviors. By analyzing historical data, AI can predict which types of ads are likely to perform well in the future, helping marketers to plan their campaigns more effectively. This proactive approach ensures that advertising efforts are always aligned with market trends and consumer preferences.
- *Enhanced customer engagement*: AI-driven chatbots and virtual assistants can engage with customers in real time, providing instant responses to queries and personalized recommendations. This not only improves customer satisfaction but also increases the likelihood of conversions, as customers receive timely and relevant information that helps them make purchasing decisions (Yuvaraj, 2023).

By integrating AI into advertising campaigns and media buying, marketers can achieve higher targeting accuracy, better customer engagement, and improved conversion rates, ultimately driving more successful marketing outcomes.

5.7. Challenges Impacting Marketers in Adopting AI: Data Quality, Integration, and Governance

Marketers face significant challenges in adopting AI, particularly concerning data quality, integration, and governance. One primary issue is the lack of control marketers have over AI technologies, as they are often consumers rather than creators of these systems. This dependency on technology and its keepers, both within and outside their organizations, complicates the implementation and customization of AI solutions (engagement and return on investment (Nair & Gupta., 2021). Data quality is another critical challenge, especially in fields like healthcare, where unstructured and non-standardized data can directly impact the effectiveness of AI models. Poor data quality can lead to algorithmic biases, affecting clinical predictions and exacerbating disparities (Paulus & Kent 2020). Additionally, the integration of AI into existing systems requires robust data governance frameworks to ensure transparency, traceability, and security. The opacity of AI algorithms can undermine trust among stakeholders, necessitating improved algorithm transparency and traceability to mitigate biases and errors (Paulus & Kent 2020). Furthermore, the evolving nature of AI marketplaces, characterized by a few consumers and many producers, highlights the need for regulatory oversight to ensure the quality and reliability of data sets. Stringent regulations can negatively impact data quality, but a balanced approach combining regulatory oversight with feedback mechanisms can enhance marketplace functionality (Adepoju *et al.*, 2023). Ethical considerations also play a crucial role, as the unintended negative consequences of AI adoption, such as privacy concerns and ethical dilemmas, need to be addressed. This requires a multidisciplinary approach to identify and manage risks, ensuring that AI technologies are developed and used responsibly. Overall, marketers must navigate these complex challenges by collaborating with technologists, adhering to ethical guidelines, and advocating for regulatory frameworks that support the responsible use of AI.

5.8. Future Trends in AI-Driven Digital Marketing

The future of AI-driven digital marketing is poised to be significantly influenced by advancements in natural language generation (NLG) for personalized content. AI-enabled digital marketing is already transforming how organizations create content, generate leads, and manage customer experiences, making it a cornerstone for future marketing strategies (Van Esch and Stewart, 2021) The increasing focus on digital, AI, and online engagement topics in recent years underscores the industry's shift toward leveraging these technologies for enhanced customer interaction and purchase intention (Thaichon *et al.*, 2022). As digital communications evolve rapidly, companies must adopt a proactive approach to stay visible and connected with their target audiences. This involves understanding the digital environment and integrating user-oriented innovations to capture consumer attention and drive engagement (Slijepčevićet *et al.*, 2020). Moreover, marketing managers face the challenge of strategically using digital technologies to gain a competitive edge. By developing a deeper understanding of consumer attitudes and engagement with digital tools, they can transform these challenges into opportunities for creating customer, firm, and societal value (Planggeret *et al.*, 2022). The integration of NLG in digital marketing will enable the creation of highly personalized content at scale, enhancing customer experiences and fostering deeper connections. This technological innovation is expected to streamline communication processes, making them more efficient and effective. As organizations continue to embrace these advancements, they will be better positioned to deliver on the promise of digital technologies, ultimately achieving a competitive advantage in the marketplace. The ongoing research and insights from industry leaders will further guide the strategic implementation of these technologies, ensuring that digital marketing remains at the forefront of innovation and customer engagement (Van Esch and Stewart Black, 2021; Thaichon *et al.*, 2022; Slijepčević *et al.*, 2020; Plangger *et al.*, 2022).

The transformative impact of AI on modern digital marketing is profound, reshaping the landscape through advanced technologies and innovative applications. AI's integration into digital advertising has enabled smart bidding, creative content generation, and dynamic creative optimization (DCO), making it indispensable for state-of-the-art computational advertising systems. The digital revolution, characterized by rapid advancements in data mining, automation, and remote communications, has significantly influenced business models, including marketing strategies, by enhancing efficiency and effectiveness (Belostecinic and Jomir., 2023). AI's role in reducing energy consumption, improving cost-effectiveness, and mitigating operational risks further underscores its value across various industries, including digital marketing (Malik *et al.*, 2024). One of the most promising advancements is in NLG, which allows for the creation of highly personalized content marketing strategies, thereby improving customer engagement and return on investment (Nair and Gupta, 2021). Despite these benefits, the responsible utilization of AI, particularly in user profiling and creative assessment, remains a critical issue that needs comprehensive discussion within both business and research communities.

By performing the following steps, digital marketers can harness the power of AI to create more successful and competitive marketing strategies, ultimately leading to better business outcomes and a stronger market presence:

- *Understanding the importance of AI in digital marketing*: Digital marketers need to recognize that AI is not just a passing trend but a significant disruption that is reshaping the landscape of digital and social media marketing worldwide. By understanding the importance of AI, marketers can better prepare themselves to leverage these technologies to stay competitive in the market.
- *Implementing AI applications*: Many digital marketers are still unaware of how to implement AI effectively in their strategies. It is crucial for marketers to educate themselves on the various AI applications available, such as predictive analytics, chatbots, and personalized content recommendations, to enhance their marketing efforts and achieve better returns on investment.
- *Staying competitive with AI*: To stay competitive, marketers must embrace AI-driven technologies that can automate repetitive tasks, provide deeper insights into consumer behavior, and create more personalized marketing campaigns. By doing so, they can focus more on strategic planning and creative aspects of their campaigns, leading to more effective and engaging marketing efforts.
- *Collaboration and creativity*: AI can help digital marketing professionals and agencies to specialize to an advanced degree while maintaining collaboration and creativity. By integrating AI into their workflows, marketers can enhance their creative processes and collaborate more effectively with their teams, leading to more innovative and impactful marketing strategies.
- *Call to action*: Marketers should take immediate steps to learn about and implement AI technologies in their digital marketing strategies. This includes investing in AI tools, attending workshops and training sessions, and staying updated with the latest trends and developments in AI and digital marketing. By doing so, they can ensure that they are not left behind in the rapidly evolving digital marketing landscape.
- *Future outlook*: The future of digital marketing is undoubtedly intertwined with AI, and those who embrace these technologies early on will have a significant advantage over their competitors. Marketers should view AI as a valuable ally that can help them achieve their marketing goals more efficiently and effectively.

Future research in the field of AI and marketing could focus on exploring the ethical implications of using AI algorithms in customer data analysis and decision-making processes, ensuring transparency and fairness in marketing practices.

Bibliography

Adepoju, A. H., Austin-Gabriel, B., Eweje, A., and Hamza, O. (2023). "A data governance framework for high-impact programs: Reducing redundancy and enhancing data quality at scale." *International Journal of Multidisciplinary Research and Growth Evaluation*, *4*(6), 1141–1154.

Amar, S., Wu, C. L., Choudhary, A., Cao, J., Olson, D.F., Bhagavathula, S., Lohtia, S., and Jain, M. V. "System and method for automated chatbots." U.S. Patent 11,080,667, Visa International Service Association, 2021.

Anjorin, K. F., Raji, M. A., Olodo, H. B., and Oyeyemi, O. P. "Harnessing artificial intelligence to develop strategic marketing goals." *International Journal of Management & Entrepreneurship Research* 6, no. 5 (2024): 1625–1650.

Arora, S., Sunil, and Raj, Thota. "Using artificial intelligence with big data analytics for targeted marketing campaigns." *International Journal of Advanced Research in Science, Communication and Technology* (2024). DOI: 10.48175/ijarsct-18967.

Barat, A. and Gulati, K. "Emergence of AI in marketing and its implications." *Lloyd Business Review* (2024): 1–24.

Belostecinic, G. and Jomir, E. "Marketingul digital–o nouă etapă în evoluția conceptului modern de marketing." *Economica* 123, no. 1 (2023): 7–22.

Dhamange, P., Soni, S., Sridhar, V., and Rao, S. "Market dynamics and regulation of a crowd-sourced AI marketplace." *IEEE Access* 10 (2022): 54325–54335.

Grljević, O., Marić, M., and Glusčević, L. "Application of artificial intelligence in digital marketing." *Anali Ekonomskog fakulteta u Subotici 60*(52) (2024).

Gruetzemacher, R. and Whittlestone, J. "The transformative potential of artificial intelligence." *Futures* 135 (2022): 102884.

Hariharan V. and Adarsh and Singh. "The evolving influence of AI on consumer behavior." *Indian Scientific Journal of Research in Engineering and Management* 8, no. 5 (2024). DOI: 10.55041/ijsrem33843.

Hirushit, S., Raja, S., Suwetha, S., and Yazhini, J. "AI powered personalized healthcare recommender." In *2024 2nd International Conference on Artificial Intelligence and Machine Learning Applications Theme: Healthcare and Internet of Things (AIMLA)*, 1–6. IEEE, 2024.

Kowsick, N. P. and Ramasamy, K. "Implementing AI-based recommendation systems for personalized financial services in libraries." In *Improving Library Systems with AI: Applications, Approaches, and Bibliometric Insights*, 235–243. IGI Global, 2024.

Kozinets, R. V. and Gretzel, U. "Commentary: Artificial intelligence: The marketer's dilemma." *Journal of Marketing* 85, no. 1 (2021): 156–159.

Labrecque, L. I., Peña, P. Y., Leonard, H., and Leger, R. "Not all sunshine and rainbows: exploring the dark side of AI in interactive marketing." *Journal of Research in Interactive Marketing* (2024).

Lakshmi, M., Prasanna, and Mishra, D. P. "Catalyzing growth: The integration of artificial intelligence in modern marketing strategies." (2024). DOI: 10.59646/bussmanagc6/123.

Malik, S., Muhammad, K., and Waheed, Y. "Artificial intelligence and industrial applications — A revolution in modern industries." *Ain Shams Engineering Journal* (2024): 102886.

Nair, K. and Gupta, R. "Application of AI technology in modern digital marketing environment." *World Journal of Entrepreneurship, Management and Sustainable Development* 17, no. 3 (2021): 318–328.

Pandya, J. and Padma, S. "The Study of Artificial Marketing tools used in Indian Cosmetic Industry and its impact on Consumer Behaviour." *Journal of Informatics Education and Research* 4, no. 1 (2024).

Parkhomenko. "The impact of artificial intelligence on consumer behavior management." Publikacja/publication, 2024.

Paulus, J. K., & Kent, D. M. (2020). Predictably unequal: understanding and addressing concerns that algorithmic clinical prediction may increase health disparities. *NPJ digital medicine*, *3*(1), 99.

Plangger, K., Grewal, D., de Ruyter, K., and Tucker, C. "The future of digital technologies in marketing: A conceptual framework and an overview." *Journal of the Academy of Marketing Science* 50, no. 6 (2022): 1125–1134.

Rachid, Ejjami. "Leveraging AI to enhance marketing and customer engagement strategies in the French market." *International Journal For Multidisciplinary Research* (2024). DOI: 10.36948/ijfmr.2024.v06i03.23147.

Raghav, Y. Y., Tipu, R. K., Bhakhar, R., Gupta, T., and Sharma, K. "The future of digital marketing: Leveraging artificial intelligence for competitive strategies and tactics." In *The Use of Artificial Intelligence in Digital Marketing: Competitive Strategies and Tactics*, 249–274. IGI Global, 2024.

Raji, M. A., Olodo, H. B., Oke, T. T., Addy, W. A., Ofodile, O. C., and Oyewole, A. T. "E-commerce and consumer behavior: A review of AI-powered personalization and market trends." *GSC Advanced Research and Reviews* 18, no. 3 (2024): 066–077.

Rust, R. T. "The future of marketing." *International Journal of Research in Marketing* 37, no. 1 (2020): 15–26.

Sangam, M. and Singh, M. "A review study on impact of artificial intelligence on marketing." *Indian Scientific Journal of Research in Engineering and Management* (2024). DOI: 10.55041/ijsrem34027.

Simanullang, G. S. B. "Roles of natural language processing in new product development process: Literature review." *Jurnal Rekayasa Sistem Industri* 13, no. 1 (2024): 117–130.

Singh, A. "The AI revolution: How artificial intelligence is reshaping marketing strategies." *Indian Scientific Journal of Research in Engineering and Management* (2024). DOI: 10.55041/ijsrem31793.

Slijepčević, M., Radojević, I., and Perić, N. "Considering modern trends in digital marketing." *Marketing* 51, no. 1 (2020): 34–42.

Thaichon, P., Quach, S., and Ngo, L. V. "Emerging research trends in marketing: A review of Australasian marketing journal." *Australasian Marketing Journal* 30, no. 3 (2022): 214–227.

Thakur, A. and Kumar, M. "Impact of AI on future of consumer behaviour." *International Journal of Engineering Science and Humanities* 14, no. Special Issue 1 (2024): 78–83.

Van Esch, P. and Stewart Black, J. "Artificial intelligence (AI): Revolutionizing digital marketing." *Australasian Marketing Journal* 29, no. 3 (2021): 199–203.

Wirtz, B. W., Weyerer, J.C., and Kehl, I. "Governance of artificial intelligence: A risk and guideline-based integrative framework." *Government Information Quarterly* 39, no. 4 (2022): 101685.

Yuvaraj, E. "Optimization of Ads using reinforcement learning and comparison of algorithms." (2023). https://www.researchgate.net/publication/370592992_Optimization_of_Ads_Using_Reinforcement_Learning_and_Comparison_of_Algorithms. DOI: 10.59256/ijire.2023040362.

Zhang, J. and Zhang, Z. M. "Ethics and governance of trustworthy medical artificial intelligence." *BMC Medical Informatics and Decision Making* 23, no. 1 (2023): 7.

https://doi.org/10.1142/9781800616578_0006

Chapter 6

Digital Revolution: Transforming the Tourism Business Landscape Post-Pandemic

Sandhya H[*] and Bindi Varghese[†]

Christ University, Bangalore, India

[*]*sandhya.h@christuniveristy.in*
[†]*bindi.varghese@christuniversity.in*

Abstract

Over the past decade, India's travel and tourism sector has experienced consistent growth in terms of the volume of inbound, outbound, and domestic travelers. The COVID-19 pandemic in 2020 precipitated an economic downturn in the worldwide tourism industry. The tourism and hospitality industry encountered an unparalleled and unfavorable situation as a result of the government's implementation of travel restrictions and stringent quarantine regulations. Both leisure and business travelers were forced to cancel or delay their travel plans, which led to significant penalties for making last-minute changes to their reservations. Destinations around the globe have implemented unique strategies and elements to enhance their resilience in the aftermath of the pandemic. While a significant number of travel agents and tour operators incurred substantial financial losses, a select few recognized this situation as an opportunity and introduced a range of inventive products, along with implementing innovative marketing and promotion strategies. "Quarantine stays," "Untact Tourism," and "Virtual Tourism" are neologisms that have gained popularity in the aftermath of the pandemic. Travel businesses have integrated technology and proved to be digitally adaptive business entities. The objective of this study is to comprehend and assess the technology-embedded recovery strategies implemented by the tourism industry in the state of Kerala, located in South India, following the pandemic. The study conducted comprehensive interviews with distinguished travel and hospitality experts from the state. The collected data were utilized to analyze the repercussions of the pandemic on the travel industry in the state, as well as to evaluate the efficacy of the measures implemented by businesses after the pandemic in terms of generating revenue and rebuilding the reputation of the destination. An in-depth examination of the tourism and hospitality websites has proven valuable in comprehending the marketing tactics employed by the companies amidst the COVID-19 pandemic. The study's findings can aid stakeholders in the tourism industry in devising effective measures to endure a pandemic by implementing innovative and creative product development and crisis management strategies.

Keywords: Digital revolution, travel agency, tour operations, COVID-19, virtual tourism, Artificial Intelligence, smart applications.

6.1. Introduction

The travel and tourism industry has been in a steady growth phase for the last two decades. International tourism flourished with around 1.5 billion global passengers contributing to over $1.7 trillion in total receipts in the year 2019–2020 (United Nations World Tourism Organization Reed Travel Exhibitions Report, 2020). The World Travel and Tourism Council's Annual Competitiveness Report on Tourism (2019) indicated that almost 10% of the total world GDP is contributed by the travel and tourism industry, creating employment opportunities for one in every fourth person globally.

6.1.1. *Tourism in India*

According to the Ministry of India's Tourism Statistics Report (2020), India welcomed 10.93 million foreign tourists into the country during the year 2019, which showed an annual growth of 3.5% over the previous year. While the inbound and outbound tourism sector boomed in the country, the domestic tourism scenario also showed a striking 25.3% annual growth rate (2321.98 million) compared to 2019 (p. 10). India secures the 23rd position in the World Tourist Arrivals ranking, and in terms of international tourism receipts, the country ranks in the 6th position in the Asia and the Pacific Regions (p. 4). In the past two decades, despite many fluctuations in the market conditions, economy, and tourism demand patterns, India continued to progress in the tourism sector (India Tourism Statistics Report, 2020). With a record 17.91 Million international tourist arrivals (average annual growth rate of 6.5%) in 2019, the highest number in the past five years, India was making its way up the tourism ladder in the preferred tourism destinations in Asia and Pacific list (p. 7).

6.1.2. *The global impact of COVID-19 pandemic*

The tourism statistics showed a positive graph until early 2020 when the COVID-19 pandemic spread worldwide, causing massive disruption to the tourism, hospitality, and aviation industries (Fotiadis *et al.*, 2021' Merlo, 2024). Extensive research was conducted on the impact of the COVID-19 pandemic in various sectors and industries worldwide. The global pandemic, which began in late 2019 in the Wuhan district in China, quickly resulted in massive transmission of viral infections to almost all the continents in the world. Though the initial spread of the virus was largely underestimated, in Europe and parts of North America, the pandemic infected an alarming number of people. The United Nations in January 2020 declared the COVID-19 pandemic "a Public Health Emergency of International Concern" (World Health Organization Report, 2020). Various nations began closing down their national boundaries and imposing strict travel restrictions within the country.

The travel, tourism, hospitality, and aviation sectors, which primarily relied on the movement of people from one destination to another, were the first to be adversely affected due to the nationwide lockdown and stringent rules laid down by the government. Commercial and scheduled international flights were canceled, and airports were only functioning to cater to the needs of the few special aircraft that operated during the lockdown period (Allaberganov *et al.*, 2021). The government of India was prudent and swift in strategic decision-making by launching the Vande Bharat Mission. The mission aimed to operate flights to bring Indian nationals from different countries back to their homeland safely during the pandemic outbreak (Ioannides and Gyimóthy, 2020). Moreover, the second and third phases of the mission assisted foreign citizens stranded in India to be taken back to their respective countries (Pasi *et al.*, 2020).

6.1.3. *COVID-19 — Implications on the Indian economy*

The COVID-19 outbreak struck India in early March 2020 and soon the country went into a complete nationwide lockdown. Citizens were forced to remain inside their homes and only travel outside if it were absolutely necessary (Kumar, 2020). Almost all the private sector firms and a few public sector undertakings introduced the concept of "Work from Home" to their employees, while some essential services operated with 50% capacity during the lockdown. In India, areas were divided into various containment zones depending on the COVID-19 Test Positivity Rate (TPR), and travel to or from such containment zones was strictly monitored (Debata *et al.*, 2020). With restrictions imposed on travel and other public gatherings and events, social contact among people was reduced to a large extent (Ranasinghe *et al.*, 2021). During this period, it was reported that the use of social media websites like Facebook, Instagram, YouTube, and Twitter saw an upward trend. A study conducted by Abbas *et al.* (2021) indicates the implications of excessive social media usage on the mental health of individuals during the COVID-19 pandemic.

6.1.4. *Implications on the tourism industry of the state of Kerala, India*

The southern state of Kerala has an effective health department that has successfully contained the spread of viral infections in the past through quick and prompt decision-making (Arunkumar *et al.* 2019). The state of Kerala has experienced serious health threats in the past with the outbreak of the Nipah virus in 2018 (Sadanandan, 2020). The health department of the state of Kerala was much regarded worldwide due to its strategic planning and decision-making to contain the spread of the Nipah Viral Outbreak in 2018 (p. 67). Despite poor economic growth, the state health department has attracted global attention in the past for achieving good outcomes in the health sector. The state is also a booming hub for medical tourists, as quality affordable treatments are ensured in the various hospitals and health centers across the state. The state of Kerala, a preferred holiday destination for many leisure travelers, has a large number of small and medium enterprises (SMEs) that depend on the travel and tourism sector for their sustenance. But like any other state, the state of Kerala was also adversely affected and sustained huge losses due to the spread of the COVID-19 virus (Kumar, 2020; Elias, 2021). Travel agents, tour operators, hotels, resorts, homestays, houseboats, and all other players in the tourism market had to shut down their operations, adhering to the rules and regulations laid down by the government (*The Hindu*, 2020). This resulted in many firms falling into bankruptcy and permanently ceasing operations, while others had to strictly cut down on their operating costs to survive the pandemic period (Kumar, 2020).

Travel agents and tour operators began to switch to online and digital platforms as offices had to remain closed (Sharma and Jhamb, 2020). Many travel companies began operations on a digital and virtual basis due to the existing restrictions, and a few managed to exploit this opportunity and develop the scale of technological advancement (Brouder, 2020). With the introduction of virtual reality and internet solutions for faster and more efficient communication, firms soon began to become more visible in the digital market and carry out their operations through an online medium (Sarkar, 2021). A few travel firms were able to introduce various innovative and creative products into the market by deploying optimum technology and Artificial Intelligence (Derco, 2022; Abass, 2023; Narain, 2024).

This chapter attempts to analyze the survival strategies formulated by the travel industry during the time of the pandemic and the effectiveness of those strategies. A detailed analysis of the travel websites and social media sites was conducted to understand the levels of digital visibility of these firms. A semi-structured interview method was adopted to collect qualitative data from a cross section of the most important key private players in the tourism market. An interview schedule was adopted from the study conducted on South Africa's tourism business by Rogerson and Rogerson (2021). The respondents were selected using the judgmental sampling approach, and the qualitative data were analyzed with the help of the content analysis method. The content analysis method is particularly beneficial for organizational research, to assess and evaluate strategies, and analyze managerial cognition.

6.2. Literature Review

The sustainable growth and development of travel business is based on certain factors which are classified into economic factors such as household income and disposable income, social factors such as society and urbanization, technical factors such as the development of technology, demographic factors such as population growth and life expectancy, psychological and educational factors such as educational levels, and political factors such as border formalities and visa rules (Pavlic *et al.*, 2013, p. 24). From this study, it is quite evident that the travel business can be affected by external factors like a serious outbreak of a pandemic or a terrorist incident (Collins-Kreiner and Ram, 2021). Kvirkvelia and Tsitsagi, (2021) researched the impact of the COVID-19 pandemic on different business sectors in the world and concluded that undoubtedly all businesses were impacted directly or indirectly by the pandemic (p. 32). As businesses are striving hard to keep up with the financial and economic crises that followed the spread of the pandemic, Gössling *et al.* (2020) argue that there would be very minimal chances to return to the normal life patterns that existed before the spread of the pandemic anytime soon (Brouder, 2020; Sigala, 2020). Chebli and Said (2020) postulate that the world can be divided into two phases: Before Corona (BC) and After Corona (AC). Zhang *et al.* (2021) indicated that the domestic tourism sector might recover faster than international tourism, as domestic travel within a country is less restricted. Also, with fewer international flights and visa restrictions, people may opt for alternative domestic destinations that are easily accessible and cost-effective (Richards and Morrill, 2021). The decision to travel depends on the safety perceptions of the travelers, and the choice of destinations is generally influenced by these factors (Ranasinghe *et al.*, 2021). Moreover, when at the destination, travelers now tend to prefer more personalized and customized services rather than opting for the general mass or group tour patterns that existed before the pandemic outbreak (Polyzos *et al.*, 2021). Mass tourism destinations will face a shift in demand patterns as travelers may opt for secluded and more family-friendly destinations that are safe and secure for travel (Arbulú *et al.*, 2021).

The major challenges faced by tourism business owners were the financial liabilities of the firm to their staff, customers, and suppliers (Li *et al.*, 2021). As it became difficult for business owners to afford all the staff, management decisions were made to reduce salaries, lay off some employees, or place employees on sabbatical leave for a few months (Rogerson and Rogerson, 2021). Verma and Gustaffon (2020) state that this pandemic outbreak forced travel and tourism business operators to shift to newer and resilient ways to overcome the challenges posed by the pandemic. Dias *et al.* (2021) studied the various strategies adopted by travel agencies to effectively exploit the available technological expertise and resources within companies and reinvent their businesses. Richards and Morill (2021) extensively researched the implications of the cancellations and modifications made to travel reservations on travel agency businesses and also pinpointed product diversification and innovations made to the travel packages during the pandemic (p. 7). Alonso *et al.*, (2021) deliberated on three aspects associated with the COVID-19 pandemic: first on the self-reliant revenue generation techniques used by travel agencies, second on the dependence of the travel agencies on various support and relief schemes offered by the government, and third on the innovations made to the existing packages to attract tourists during the pandemic. Revised pricing for existing travel packages and focusing more on improving domestic travel were some of the common strategies adopted by travel businesses. Altuntas and Gok (2021) used the DEMATEL method to study the quarantine decision-making capacities of tourists post-pandemic. Their study highlighted the choices made by travelers for safe quarantine facilities and self-isolation in case of a possible COVID-19 viral infection. Travelers returning from an international journey or preparing for one were required to be in quarantine and self-isolation for at least 14 days, which was mandated by many governments. Altuntas and Gok (2021) concluded that there was a new trend emerging in the hospitality industry, where full-service hotels were offering safe all-inclusive quarantine facilities for travelers. This package was designed in such a way that it included all the services on the property: all meals and room services, COVID-19 tests upon arrival and before departure, and regular temperature checks on the property (Choo, 2015). Such facilities gained acceptance globally as more people preferred to complete the quarantine period in a relaxed environment with full services before joining their families (Mishra *et al.*, 2024; Do *et al.*, 2022).

6.3. Methodology

This study uses qualitative data to understand and assess the survival strategies implemented by tour operators in Kerala during the COVID-19 pandemic. The first phase of the study commenced with the identification of key tour operators in the state and assessment of the official websites and social media pages of these tour operators. The names of the respondents are not disclosed in the study following the ethical norms of conducting qualitative research, i.e., confidentiality, anonymity, and informed consent (Duriau *et al.*, 2007). In-depth interviews are used to gain knowledge from respondents on individual perceptions regarding a particular research topic or a problem. The respondents of the in-depth interviews were normally selected using the purposive sampling technique. This sampling technique, also called the judgmental sampling technique, is a method of choosing the respondents based on certain criteria selected by the researcher.

6.4. Discussion

The research was undertaken using qualitative data collected in two phases: The first phase was a detailed review of the websites of the key players in the travel industry of Kerala. The second phase of the study commenced by contacting managerial-level employees of the various tourism businesses for an in-depth interview. The data collected from the interview were analyzed with the help of the thematic analysis method by manually developing themes from the responses to identify a common pattern and develop a theory based on these patterns. The respondents were selected based on a judgmental sampling method, considering their domain of work (travel and tourism industry), years of experience (at least 5 years and more), designation (supervisory level and above), and location (Kerala). A semi-structured interview technique is followed where the interviewer gives adequate freedom to the respondents to express their thoughts and ideas by asking open-ended questions.

This study focused on the survival strategies and responses of the tour operators in the state of Kerala during the COVID-19 pandemic and the

Figure 6.1. Diagrammatic representation of data.

important marketing and management decisions that were taken during the crisis stage. The responses from the interview were transcribed and analyzed in-depth to understand certain common points or patterns within the data. These patterns were further grouped to form broader themes that portrayed the crux and the essence of the interview (Figure 6.1).

6.5. Results and Conclusion

The literature substantiates that the COVID-19 pandemic hit the travel and tourism industry at a very high magnitude, creating crippling effects on the different allied sectors globally. Travel businesses responded to this pandemic by adopting various strategies, both long term and short term.

This study focuses on the South Indian state of Kerala, which is a preferred destination by both international and domestic tourists. The state's tourism industry contributes around 10% to the total Gross Domestic Product (GDP), and about 23% of the employment opportunities in the state are generated through tourism (Kerala Tourism Statistics, 2019).

The first case of the COVID-19 infection was reported in Kerala on January 30, 2020 (*The Hindu*, 2020), and the Ministry of Health announced strict screening of all the passengers arriving in the state from China and other countries. By March 2020, there was a surge in the number of cases in the country and the Government of India announced a nationwide lockdown for two brief months. This adversely affected all the industries and businesses on a global scale. The tourism and hospitality industry was "brought down to its knees" due to the travel restrictions and strict rules laid down by the government (*The Financial Express*, 2020). Travel businesses went into complete shutdown of their offices due to the lockdown rules and the social distancing norms. Last-minute cancellations and amendments to reservations made the situation worse for travel professionals (Jaipuria, Parida, and Ray, 2020). With very minimal support schemes from the government, travel agents and tour operators of Kerala had to struggle to survive during the lockdown. Firms shifted to a completely online platform, and most of the employees were advised to work from home. Due to financial constraints, management had to cut down on operational expenses and shift to readily available sources like the internet for their marketing and promotional activities (Al-Ḥyari *et al.*, 2023). Many employees were laid off or placed on sabbatical, and the others who remained had to work on a reduced salary basis. Large office spaces were sold off or rented out by companies as employees were working remotely from their homes (Ozili and Arun, 2020).

6.5.1. *Shift of paradigm to a digital market*

The pandemic resulted in a shift from traditional marketing and promotional activities to social media and digital platforms. The visibility of travel businesses on social media sites like Facebook, YouTube, and Instagram considerably increased after the COVID-19 pandemic outbreak. As technology is readily available and less expensive, marketing through digital platforms, especially social media sites, is becoming accepted, especially for travel businesses (Buhalis and Law, 2008). Many travel firms have an active social media presence through online discussion forums, blogs, and podcasts (Tussyadiah, 2020). The websites of most of the travel agencies and tour operators were updated and had adequate information regarding the then current COVID-19 protocols and travel restrictions. Some websites provided information on vaccination centers, COVID-19 insurance and rules, and government rules and regulations. A detailed analysis of the websites conveys that most of the travel websites followed a common structure and pattern that is user-friendly, easily accessible, and attractive (Vashishth *et al.*, 2024; Vyas *et al.*, 2024). Travel agencies offering inbound travel services highlighted the most recent COVID-19 protocols laid down by the Ministry of Health, Kerala, and also the details of flights operating to and from the different airports in the country. The websites had the latest pictures and videos of the destinations, which acted as a virtual guide to first-time visitors. Virtual tourism was a new concept that offered sightseeing options through a virtual medium (Voitik and Maslov, 2019).

6.5.2. *Emerging concepts and innovative tour packages*

Websites updated more "quarantine stay" options, highlighting the best properties that offered all-inclusive quarantine stay packages across the world.

> This is a new trend that emerged during the pandemic in the travel industry as quarantine was made mandatory by most of the countries for passengers from all over the world. For instance, Indians traveling to the United Arab Emirates were required to mandatorily complete 14 days quarantine outside the country to be permitted entry. The preferred destinations for such quarantine stay include Armenia, Uzbekistan, and Tashkent to name a few (Respondent 4).

Another concept gaining popularity was that of "staycations," which are vacations spent safely in a resort or a property that offers full-service packages to customers. Self-drive tours and destinations were being promoted as families and groups opted for private transportation to be safe during the COVID-19 pandemic outbreak. Every detail about a destination, including the route map, places to see, places to stay, rules, and regulations, was updated on the websites. Also, most of the websites had open discussion forums and travel blogs where tourists could get all the information regarding the destination. Hotels and resorts introduced all-inclusive discounted packages, which were cost-effective and attractive for tourists.

> Also, the tour operators started focusing more on promoting domestic tours and short weekend getaways as there are lesser restrictions within the country (Respondent 6).

Following the COVID-19 pandemic, the travel industry witnessed the emergence of new trends as travelers emphasized flexibility, safety, and distinctive experiences. The demand for domestic and local tourism increased, as travelers preferred shorter trips to nearby destinations that provided open spaces and natural environments, thereby minimizing exposure to crowded locations (Arbulú *et al.*, 2021). Concerns regarding health and safety resulted in a heightened inclination toward contactless services and digital solutions, such as mobile check-ins, digital health passports, and AI-driven customer support (Fotiadis *et al.*, 2021). Moreover, remote work catalyzed the "workcation" phenomenon, wherein travelers prolonged their visits to integrate work and leisure, favoring locations with dependable internet and facilities, conducive to remote employment. Sustainable travel also gained popularity, as numerous travelers opted for eco-friendly accommodations and transportation methods to reduce their environmental impact (Sigala, 2020). These trends indicate a transformation in traveler expectations, emphasizing flexibility, technology, and sustainability that persistently redefine the industry (Benke *et al.*, 2020).

6.5.3. *Technological innovations that followed the COVID-19 protocols*

The Kerala state government had spread awareness and information about the spread of the COVID-19 pandemic by way of the "Break the Chain" campaigns, walk-in free test centers, daily news and media updates, and screening at airports and public places (Sarkar, 2020).

> The accommodation sector has completely shifted to a 'no-contact check-in' procedure to adhere to the Covid protocols. Every room and

> premise of the property is sanitized, and personal and public hygiene is given the utmost importance. With the help of technology, contactless self-check in procedures were implemented which ensured safe and convenient transactions (Respondent 2).

As travelers grew more vigilant, there was a significant rise in the demand for private, adaptable, and hygienic travel alternatives (Fotiadis *et al.*, 2021). This transition necessitated that companies implement autonomous technologies and Artificial Intelligence (AI) to augment operational efficiency and elevate the customer experience (Syed *et al.*, 2023). AI-driven chatbots were extensively employed to deliver immediate assistance, minimize wait times, and offer customized services (Vashishth *et al.*, 2024; Tan, 2023). Technologies that were once viewed as enhancements become essential to operations, transforming customer expectations and efficiency benchmarks (Solakis *et al.*, 2024). Furthermore, domestic and regional tourism experienced a significant increase as nations adjusted to travel restrictions, emphasizing local markets to bolster the economy (Arbulú *et al.*, 2021).

The emergence of virtual and augmented reality technologies will transform destination marketing and customer engagement, enabling prospective travelers to virtually explore locations prior to making booking decisions (Voitik and Maslov, 2019). The persistent focus on health and safety will expedite the implementation of digital health passes and contactless technologies, enhancing the safety and efficiency of travel (Gössling *et al.*, 2021). Moreover, the inclination toward sustainable tourism will be bolstered by digital platforms that advocate for eco-friendly alternatives and empower travelers to make more informed decisions regarding their environmental impact (Tussyadiah, 2020). As the industry evolves, digitalization will enhance the travel experience while promoting resilience and sustainability, thereby positioning the travel and tourism sector for a more innovative and adaptive future.

Sustainability has become paramount, as companies and destinations increasingly adopt eco-friendly practices to satisfy the rising demand for responsible tourism (Sigala, 2020). The pandemic expedited the digital transformation of travel services, incorporating virtual tours and sophisticated online booking systems to accommodate tech-savvy travelers and mitigate concerns regarding crowded environments (Buhalis and Law, 2008). The post-pandemic travel landscape prioritizes safety, sustainability, and digital convenience, which are expected to influence the industry's future direction.

6.5.4. *Timely redressal of customer queries and complaints*

A 24/7 customer service portal was available on the websites that were analyzed, which can be accessed through email or by telephone for information regarding bookings, cancellations, refunds, and travel products. Travel insurance was also highlighted on the websites to encourage travelers to purchase travel insurance to protect against the various risks associated with travel (Sarman *et al.*, 2020). Tourists were also becoming more "conscious" and understanding the risk associated with travel during such unprecedented times (p. 23).

> We promote travel insurance more as it generates revenue for the agent as well as it is beneficial for the customers. The risk factor associated with travel has now been understood by the common man post the pandemic, hence tourists are more prepared and conscious I would say (Respondent 9).

6.5.5. *Future prospects of tourism — Toward a resilient economy*

Despite the financial constraints and operational restrictions, all the respondents were positive about the revival of the industry after the COVID-19 pandemic.

> Additional aids from the government to support the travel businesses have been beneficial for the industry. The timely transformation to digital world has helped the travel and tourism sector in many ways like visibility, branding, uninterrupted services, better accessibility, etc., and this pandemic has taught us an important lesson that with effective crisis management and preparedness, the industry can survive and bounce back in no time (Respondent 5).

The travel and tourism industry is set for substantial transformation, significantly shaped by digitalization following the COVID-19 pandemic (Torabi *et al.*, 2023). As travelers increasingly pursue seamless, contactless experiences, technology will be pivotal in transforming the methods by which individuals plan, book, and engage in travel, as shown in Table 6.1 and Figure 6.2. Digital tools, including AI-driven chatbots and customized recommendation systems, will improve customer service by

Table 6.1. Technological advancements in the state after the COVID-19 pandemic.

S. No	Technology	Description	Reference
1	Contactless Payments	Digital payment options (e.g., UPI, mobile wallets) to minimize physical contact in transactions.	(Sharma and Gupta, 2022)
2	Artificial Intelligence (AI) Chatbots	AI-driven chatbots to handle booking inquiries, cancellations, and provide 24/7 customer support.	(Patel, 2023)
3	Dynamic Packaging Software	Automated tools allowing real-time customization of travel packages based on customer preferences.	(Singh and Kumar, 2021)
4	Virtual Reality (VR) Tours	Virtual tours to offer customers a preview of destinations and accommodations remotely.	(Tripathi and Reddy, 2022)
5	Customer Data Analytics	Use of big data to analyze customer preferences and trends to tailor offerings and enhance experiences.	(Malhotra and Jain, 2021)
6	Digital Health Passes	Integration of health passes (e.g., vaccination and test certificates) to ensure safe travel.	(World Travel and Tourism Council, 2021)
7	Cloud-Based Booking Systems	Shift to cloud platforms for managing reservations and customer information securely and remotely.	(Kumar and Banerjee, 2022)
8	Augmented Reality (AR) for Navigation	AR tools to help customers navigate destinations with additional information about attractions.	(Joshi *et al.*, 2022)
9	Self-Service Kiosks	Contactless kiosks for check-ins, bookings, and other travel needs at stations and airports.	(Kumar *et al.*, 2023)
10	Mobile Apps with Real-Time Updates	Apps providing real-time travel information, itinerary changes, and destination safety alerts.	(Singh and Narayan, 2021)

Figure 6.2. Word cloud on post-pandemic technological revolutions in the travel and tourism sector.

offering immediate assistance and personalized suggestions that align with individual preferences (Mishra *et al.*, 2024). Furthermore, the incorporation of sophisticated analytics and data-driven insights will enable companies to gain a deeper understanding of traveler behaviors and trends, facilitating more effective marketing strategies and operational efficiencies (Vyas *et al.*, 2024).

6.5.6. *Conclusion*

The COVID-19 pandemic adversely affected the world economy and wreaked havoc on the travel, tourism, and hospitality industry in particular. But even during the pandemic, many firms recognized the opportunity to innovate and become the "first movers" in the market through quick planning and responsive decision-making. The concept of e-tourism and virtual tourism has since been gaining wider acceptance worldwide with the advancement of technology. Digital marketing and promotions are cost-effective and can target a wider audience on a global scale. Social media has proven to be a highly effective tool in capturing the attention and engagement of Millennials and Generation Z. The tour operations business will have a bright future by offering meaningful, safe, and unique experiences to tourists. The shift in paradigm to a digital and virtual mode is a gradual one, but this shift is going to lead to a permanent change in the way the tourism industry functions.

Appendix

Interview schedule

1. What are some of the innovative products developed during the COVID-19 pandemic?
2. Can you comprehend the effectiveness of these products and how they are marketed online?
3. What is the major change in marketing strategies before and during the COVID-19 pandemic?
4. What are the major managerial challenges/decisions that you had to take during the pandemic?
5. What are the support schemes from the government for travel agencies/tour operators?
6. What do you think would be the future prospects of the tourism industry in the post-COVID-19 era?

Bibliography

Abbas, J., Wang, D., Su, Z., and Ziapour, A. "The role of social media in the advent of COVID-19 pandemic: Crisis management, mental health challenges and implications." *Risk Management and Healthcare Policy* 14, no. 1 (2021): 1917–1932. DOI: 10.2147/RMHP.S284313.

Allaberganov, S., Preko, A., and Mohammed, S. "Government commitment to tourism and hospitality sector during COVID-19 pandemic." *Tourism Critiques: Practice and Theory* (2021): 2633–1225. DOI: 10.1108/TRC-02-2021-0004.

Alonso, A. D., Kok, S. K., Bressan, A., O'Shea, M., Sakellarios, N., Koresis, A., Solis, M. A. B., and Santoni, L. J. "COVID-19, aftermath, impacts, and hospitality firms: An international perspective." *International Journal of Hospitality Management* 91 (2021): 102654. DOI: 10.1016/j.ijhm.2020.102654.

Altuntas, F. and Gok, M. S. "The effect of COVID-19 pandemic on domestic tourism: A DEMATEL method analysis on quarantine decisions." *International Journal of Hospitality Management* 92 (2021): 102719. DOI: 10.1016/j.ijhm.2020.102719.

Arbulú, I., Razumova, M., Rey-Maquieira, J., and Sastre, F. "Can domestic tourism relieve the COVID-19 tourist industry crisis? The case of Spain." *Journal of Destination Marketing & Management* 20 (2021): 100568.

Arunkumar, G., Chandni, R., Mourya, D. T., Singh, S. K., Sadanandan, R., Sudan, P., and Bhargava, B. "Outbreak investigation of Nipah virus disease in Kerala, India, 2018." *The Journal of Infectious Diseases* 219, no. 12 (2019): 1867–1878. DOI: 10.1093/infdis/jiy612.

Benke, C., Autenrieth, L. K., Asselmann, E., and Pané-Farré, C. A. "Lockdown, quarantine measures, and social distancing: Associations with depression, anxiety and distress at the beginning of the COVID-19 pandemic among adults from Germany." *Psychiatry Research* 293 (2020): 113462. DOI: 10.1016/j.psychres.2020.113462.

Brouder, P. "Reset redux: Possible evolutionary pathways towards the transformation of tourism in a COVID-19 world." *Tourism Geographies* 22, no. 3 (2020): 484–490.

Buhalis, D. and Law, R. "Progress in information technology and tourism management: 20 years on and 10 years after the Internet — The state of eTourism research." *Tourism Management* 29, no. 4 (2008): 609–623.

Chebli, A. and Said, F. B. "The impact of COVID-19 on tourism consumption behavior: A perspective article." *Journal of Tourism Management Research* 7, no. 2 (2020): 196–207.

Choo, H. "Domestic tourism." In *Encyclopedia of Tourism*. Springer, Cham, 2015. DOI: 10.1007/978-3-319-01669-6_255-1.

Debata, B., Patnaik, P., and Mishra, A. "COVID-19 pandemic! Its impact on people, economy, and environment." *Journal of Public Affairs* 20, no. 4 (2020). DOI: 10.1002/pa.2372.

Derco, J. "The impacts of the COVID-19 pandemic on the tour operator market — The case of Slovakia." *Journal of Risk and Financial Management* 15, no. 10 (2022): 446.

Do, B., Nguyen, N., D'Souza, C., Bui, H. D., and Nguyen, T. N. H. "Strategic responses to COVID-19: The case of tour operators in Vietnam." *Tourism and Hospitality Research* 22, no. 1 (2022): 5–17.

Elias, A. A. "Kerala's innovations and flexibility for COVID-19 recovery: Storytelling using systems thinking." *Global Journal of Flexible Systems Management* 20, no. 4 (2021): 33–43. DOI: 10.1007/s40171-021-00268-8.

Fotiadis, A., Polyzos, S., and Huan, T. C. T. "The good, the bad and the ugly on COVID-19 tourism recovery." *Annals of Tourism Research* 87 (2021): 103117.

Ioannides, D. and Gyimóthy, S. "The COVID-19 crisis as an opportunity for escaping the unsustainable global tourism path." *Tourism Geographies* 22, no. 3 (2020): 624–632. DOI: 10.1080/14616688.2020.1763445.

Joshi, M., Verma, R., and Mehta, S. "Augmented reality in travel navigation: Enhancing tourist experiences." *Journal of Travel Technology Innovations* 6, no. 1 (2022): 54–66.

Kumar, P., Rao, A., and Das, M. "The role of self-service kiosks in contactless travel: A case study." *Hospitality and Tourism Research* 14, no. 1 (2023): 23–37.

Kumar, S. and Banerjee, R. "Cloud-based booking systems in travel agencies: Benefits and implementation." *Journal of Travel Management* 8, no. 2 (2022): 90–102.

Kumar, V. "Indian tourism industry and COVID-19: Present scenario." *Journal of Tourism and Hospitality Education* 10 (2020): 179–185.

Malhotra, R. and Jain, P. "Customer data analytics in the post-pandemic travel industry: Opportunities and challenges." *Journal of Data-Driven Tourism* 12, no. 3 (2021): 101–113.

Merlo, T. R. "Emerging role of artificial intelligence (AI) in aviation: Using predictive maintenance for operational efficiency." In *Harnessing Digital Innovation for Air Transportation*, 25–41. IGI Global, 2024.

Mishra, U., Jayawardena, N. S., and Thaichon, P. "Exploring the role of artificial intelligence for luxury hotel brands: A case study in Europe." In *Technology and Luxury Hospitality*, 278–294. Routledge, 2024.

Narain, A. "Applications of artificial intelligence in revolutionizing the travel industry." *International Journal for Multidisciplinary Research (IJFMR)* 6, no. 1 (2024): 1–8.

Pasi, A. R., Gaikwad, P. B., Aroskar, K., Kumar, T., Teddy, R., Kundu, M., Naag, R., Khasnobis, P., Radhakrishnan, A., Sen, P. K., and Mathur, A. "Early detection of suspected cases of COVID-19: Role of thermal screening at international airports in India." *International Journal of Community Medicine and Public Health* 7 (2020): 4817–4822.

Patel, A. "AI chatbots in the travel industry: Enhancing customer experience and efficiency." *International Journal of Artificial Intelligence in Tourism* 5, no. 2 (2023): 56–68.

Salman, A., Trupp, A., and Chan, L. F. "Tourism in times of crisis and post-crisis: A model to understand tourists' post-pandemic travel intentions." *Tourism: An International Interdisciplinary Journal* 72, no. 2 (2024): 252–261.

Sharma, R. and Gupta, P. "Impact of digital payments on contactless transactions in tourism post-COVID-19." *Journal of Tourism and Hospitality* 11, no. 3 (2022): 123–134.

Singh, A. and Narayan, K. "Mobile apps for real-time travel updates: Post-pandemic necessity." *International Journal of Tourism and Digital Technology* 10, no. 3 (2021): 145–159.

Singh, V. and Kumar, N. "Dynamic packaging software: A tool for personalized travel planning." *Journal of Travel Technology* 9, no. 1 (2021): 34–45.

Solakis, K., Katsoni, V., Mahmoud, A. B., and Grigoriou, N. "Factors affecting value co-creation through artificial intelligence in tourism: A general literature review." *Journal of Tourism Futures* 10, no. 1 (2024): 116–130.

Syed, F. U., Donvito, R., and Aiello, G. "Global impacts of online reputation management of pre-and post-coronavirus pandemic: Comparative analysis in context of industry 4.0." In *Online Reputation Management in Destination and Hospitality*, 111–130. Emerald Publishing Limited, 2023.

Tan, L. H. "Consumer reaction to the use of artificial intelligence chatbot on distribution of general insurance in Singapore." 2023.

Torabi, Z. A., Rezvani, M. R., Hall, C. M., and Allam, Z. "On the post-pandemic travel boom: How capacity building and smart tourism technologies in rural areas can help-evidence from Iran." *Technological Forecasting and Social Change* 193 (2023): 122633.

Tripathi, S. and Reddy, T. "Virtual reality tours: A new frontier in travel and tourism marketing." *Tourism Marketing Review* 15, no. 4 (2022): 78–89.

Tussyadiah, I. "A review of research into automation in tourism: Launching the Annals of Tourism Research Curated Collection on Artificial Intelligence and Robotics in Tourism." *Annals of Tourism Research* 81 (2020): 102883.

Upadhyay, S., Upadhyay, N., and Gour, A. "Voices in the storm: Analyzing MakeMyTrip's crisis communication during COVID-19 through a multivocality lens." *Journal of Contingencies and Crisis Management* 32, no. 1 (2024): 122521.

Varghese, B., Sandhya, H., and Thomas, T. "COVID-19 pandemic, risk-reduction strategies and crisis management in the travel insurance sector." *Hospitality, Tourism and Marketing Studies* 23 (2023).

Vashishth, T. K., Sharma, V., Sharma, K. K., Kumar, B., Kumar, A., and Panwar, R. "Artificial Intelligence (AI)–powered chatbots: Providing instant support and personalized recommendations to guests 24/7." In *Technology and Luxury Hospitality*, 211–236. Routledge, 2024.

Voitik, N. V. and Maslov, M. D. "Augmented reality technologies in tourism." *Research Result. Business and Service Technologies* 5, no. 3 (2019): 3–11.

Vyas, S., Gupta, S., and Shukla, V. K. "Leveraging potentials of artificial intelligence and robotics for the tourism industry: A study." In *Artificial Intelligence for Smart Technology in the Hospitality and Tourism Industry*, 181–191. Apple Academic Press, 2024.

World Travel & Tourism Council. "Digital health passes and safe travel." WTTC Research Report, 2021. https://www.wttc.org/research/digital-health.

Newspaper articles

Financial Times. "Global recession already here, say top economists." 2020. https://www.ft.com/content/be732afe-6526-11ea-a6cd-df28cc3c6a68.

Business Insider. "Covid-19 Impact: airlines that did not survive the pandemic." 2020. https://www.businessinsider.com/coronavirus-airlines-that-failed-bankrupt-covid19-pandemic-2020-3#trans-states-airlines-us-march-2020-2.

Business Standard. "Closures hit alcohol manufacturers; govt faces loss of Rs 700 cr a day." 2020. https://www.business-standard.com/article/current-affairs/closures-hit-alcohol-manufacturers-govt-faces-loss-of-rs-700-cr-a-day-120040801605_1.html.

The Hindu. "Kerala's travel industry pushes for opening of bars, spas." 2020. https://www.thehindu.com/news/national/kerala/keralas-travel-industry-pushes-for-opening-of-bars-spas/article33329720.ece.

The Economic Times. "Covid impact of tourism: 14.5 million jobs lost in 2020's Q1 alone." 2020. https://economictimes.indiatimes.com/industry/services/travel/covid-impact-of-tourism-14-5-million-jobs-lost-in-2020s-q1-alone/articleshow/84577770.cms.

Websites

https://tourism.gov.in/market-research-and-statistics.

https://www.iata.org/en/programs/passenger/.

https://unwto.org/definitions/tourism.

https://www.unwto.org/news/70-of-destinations-have-lifted-travel-restrictions-but-global-gap-emerging.

https://www.unwto.org/unwto-tourism-recovery-tracker.

https://www.unwto.org/market-intelligence.

https://www.keralatourism.org.

https://doi.org/10.1142/9781800616578_0007

Chapter 7

AI-Driven Data Analysis and Knowledge Management in Aviation Organizations

Ayse Aslı Yilmaz

Chair of Department of Pilot Training Civil Aviation School, Atılım University, Türkiye

asli.yilmaz@atilim.edu.tr

Abstract

The integration of Artificial Intelligence (AI) into aviation organizations has transformed how data are analyzed and knowledge is managed. This chapter investigates the pivotal role AI plays in enhancing data-driven decision-making, optimizing operational efficiency, and fostering organizational learning within the aviation industry. By focusing on AI applications such as predictive analytics, real-time data processing, and AI-powered knowledge management systems, the chapter illustrates how AI contributes to proactive decision-making, improved risk management, and continuous learning. Ethical considerations, including data privacy and algorithmic transparency, are also examined to provide a balanced perspective on AI adoption in this safety-critical sector. Supported by real-world case studies from leading aviation organizations, this chapter offers practical insights into leveraging AI for operational excellence and organizational growth. Key themes include

AI-driven innovations in aviation processes, the transformative impact of real-time data analysis, and the critical role of AI-powered knowledge management systems in ensuring compliance and safety. The findings aim to guide scholars and practitioners in navigating the challenges and opportunities of AI in aviation.

Keywords: Artificial Intelligence, aviation industry, data-driven decision-making, operational optimization, knowledge management.

7.1. Introduction

The aviation industry operates in an environment that demands high levels of safety, efficiency, and compliance. In recent years, Artificial Intelligence (AI) has emerged as a transformative technology, reshaping the way aviation organizations manage data and knowledge. By enabling predictive analytics, real-time decision-making, and efficient knowledge management, AI enhances operational performance and organizational learning. AI's impact spans across various domains within aviation. For example, predictive maintenance driven by machine learning algorithms is minimizing unexpected failures, thus enhancing safety and reducing operational costs (Serrano and Kazda, 2021). AI-powered tools are also transforming air traffic management, improving the efficiency of flight routes and airspace utilization (Kaya and Demir, 2023). Moreover, AI facilitates personalized passenger experiences by analyzing data on customer preferences and streamlining services such as check-ins and baggage handling (Morley *et al.*, 2020).

AI technologies have also revolutionized airport operations, introducing automation in areas such as baggage handling, security screening, and terminal management. By integrating computer vision and advanced analytics, airports can streamline processes, reduce wait times, and enhance passenger satisfaction (Lee *et al.*, 2023). These advancements contribute to the creation of smarter, more efficient airport ecosystems that align with evolving passenger expectations and operational demands. The adoption of AI is not without its challenges. Ethical concerns, including data privacy and algorithmic biases, demand stringent governance and regulatory oversight. Organizations must also navigate the complexities of integrating AI with legacy systems while ensuring that staff are adequately trained to use these advanced tools effectively (Gandomi and Haider, 2015). Furthermore, the reliance on AI introduces cybersecurity vulnerabilities, necessitating robust safeguards to protect sensitive data and maintain trust among stakeholders (Rahman *et al.*, 2022).

Emerging technologies, such as digital twins and edge AI, further exemplify the transformative potential of AI in aviation. Digital twins enable real-time simulation and predictive modeling, allowing organizations to optimize resource allocation and plan for various operational scenarios (Garcia *et al.*, 2023). Meanwhile, edge AI brings real-time data processing to the forefront, enhancing decision-making capabilities at the source of data generation (Zhao and Miller, 2024).

This chapter explores how AI-driven innovations are influencing aviation processes, data analysis, and knowledge management, offering a comprehensive examination of opportunities and challenges associated with AI adoption in this highly regulated and safety-critical industry. It also highlights the importance of balancing technological advancements with ethical considerations and regulatory requirements to achieve sustainable and reliable integration of AI technologies. By examining case studies and practical applications, this chapter aims to provide actionable insights for aviation organizations seeking to harness the power of AI for operational excellence and competitive advantage.

7.2. AI-Driven Innovation in Aviation Processes

AI is transforming aviation by enhancing operational efficiency, safety, and sustainability across various domains, including in-flight management, predictive maintenance, and resource optimization. These advancements leverage machine learning, predictive analytics, and automation to address critical industry challenges.

AI has revolutionized maintenance practices in aviation, shifting from reactive to predictive strategies. Predictive maintenance employs machine learning models to monitor real-time data from aircraft systems, such as engines, landing gear, and avionics, to identify potential failures before they occur. This approach minimizes unplanned downtime, reduces costs, and enhances fleet availability. Airlines utilizing these technologies report up to a 30% reduction in maintenance costs and improved reliability.

In-flight management has similarly benefited from AI-driven technologies. Advanced autopilot systems dynamically adapt to real-time conditions, including weather changes and air traffic, reducing pilot workload and minimizing errors. Such systems contribute to both passenger safety and operational efficiency (Serrano and Kazda, 2021).

AI technologies are optimizing air traffic management (ATM) by addressing the complexities of increasing airspace congestion. Machine learning algorithms forecast traffic patterns, improve flight path optimization, and enhance airspace utilization. These systems integrate weather data and traffic metrics to recommend real-time adjustments, leading to reduced delays and lower fuel consumption. AI's ability to improve route efficiency also contributes significantly to reducing aviation's carbon footprint (Serrano and Kazda, 2021).

Airport operations have seen significant improvements through AI-driven automation. Technologies such as facial recognition are streamlining passenger check-ins, while computer vision systems automate baggage handling, increasing accuracy and reducing processing times. Furthermore, AI-powered systems optimize runway scheduling and gate assignments, minimizing turnaround times and enhancing operational efficiency. For example, AI decision-support systems help allocate airport resources more effectively during peak periods.

In the cargo sector, AI technologies enable predictive analytics to anticipate demand patterns and optimize route planning. These systems improve fleet utilization and ensure timely deliveries, while also mitigating risks such as improper loading or temperature mismanagement for sensitive goods. AI-supported logistics systems enhance supply chain transparency by enabling real-time tracking and coordination among stakeholders (Ahmed *et al.*, 2023).

Safety enhancements are a cornerstone of AI innovation in aviation. AI-powered computer vision systems monitor live video feeds to detect potential hazards during taxiing, take-off, and landing. Natural language processing (NLP) algorithms analyse cockpit communication for signs of fatigue or stress among crew members, ensuring timely interventions to prevent accidents (Chen *et al.*, 2023). Additionally, AI-driven simulations train pilots and crews in managing critical scenarios, further improving safety standards.

AI contributes to environmental sustainability by optimizing operations to reduce carbon emissions. Machine learning models consider factors such as wind patterns, air traffic density, and fuel efficiency to recommend eco-friendly flight paths. These adjustments align with global sustainability initiatives, such as the International Civil Aviation

Organization's (ICAO) Carbon Offsetting and Reduction Scheme for International Aviation (CORSIA) (Jones *et al.*, 2023). AI also supports the development and integration of sustainable aviation fuels (SAFs), expediting their adoption to further reduce the industry's environmental impact (Patel and Zhou, 2024).

AI technologies are reshaping the passenger experience by providing personalized and seamless services. Virtual assistants and chatbots deliver real-time information on flight schedules, delays, and services, improving customer engagement. AI-driven systems also facilitate efficient disruption management, such as rebooking flights during delays, enhancing passenger satisfaction (Carter *et al.*, 2024).

Emerging AI applications, including autonomous systems, urban air mobility (UAM), and digital twins, promise to redefine the aviation industry. For example, AI-powered drones are expected to revolutionize cargo delivery, while digital twin technologies enhance airport operations by enabling real-time simulations of infrastructure. However, challenges such as data security, ethical considerations, and regulatory constraints must be addressed through industry collaboration and robust governance.

AI-driven innovations are transforming aviation processes, from predictive maintenance and air traffic management to enhancing passenger experiences and promoting sustainability. As these technologies evolve, they will continue to unlock opportunities for operational excellence, safety, and environmental stewardship, ensuring a sustainable future for the aviation industry.

7.3. Data Analysis in Real-Time Decision-Making

The ability of AI to process massive datasets in real time has transformed decision-making processes in aviation. Advanced analytics and machine learning tools enable aviation organizations to make rapid and informed decisions, particularly in dynamic and complex environments such as air traffic management and passenger services. For example, AI-powered route optimization tools consider variables such as weather conditions, air traffic congestion, and fuel efficiency to recommend the most optimal flight paths (Serrano and Kazda, 2021). Similarly, AI enhances resource allocation by predicting passenger flow, enabling efficient staff deployment and reducing bottlenecks at airports. These applications demonstrate how AI contributes to operational agility and responsiveness (Samanta *et al.*, 2024).

AI's capability to analyze real-time data extends to anomaly detection and risk management. Machine learning algorithms monitor vast streams of operational data to identify irregular patterns, such as equipment malfunctions or deviations from standard procedures, enabling pre-emptive interventions (Chen *et al.*, 2023). This predictive capability is particularly crucial in mitigating risks associated with flight operations and maintenance activities. In addition, AI is revolutionizing crisis management by providing real-time situational awareness. During emergencies, AI-driven platforms integrate data from multiple sources, such as weather forecasts, aircraft telemetry, and airspace congestion metrics, to support decision-makers in crafting effective response strategies. This capability ensures swift and well-informed decisions, reducing response times and mitigating potential impacts.

AI also plays a significant role in enhancing customer service. Real-time data analysis allows airlines to offer personalized services by predicting passenger needs and preferences. For instance, AI systems analyze booking patterns, in-flight behavior, and post-flight feedback to tailor services, improve customer satisfaction, and foster brand loyalty. Furthermore, real-time analytics powered by AI helps in optimizing airport operations. AI systems monitor airport infrastructure, including runways, gates, and terminals, to predict congestion and recommend adjustments in operational workflows. These insights improve overall efficiency and enhance passenger experiences by minimizing delays and reducing wait times (Jones *et al.*, 2023).

AI's transformative impact extends to cargo and logistics operations. By analyzing shipment data and supply chain dynamics, AI tools can predict disruptions, recommend alternative routes, and optimize loading strategies. This ensures timely deliveries and reduces operational inefficiencies (Rath *et al.*, 2021). For example, machine learning algorithms help identify priority shipments and adjust resource allocation dynamically, improving responsiveness in high-pressure scenarios. Moreover, AI is being employed in collaborative decision-making systems. These platforms bring together data from multiple stakeholders, such as airport operators, air traffic controllers, and airlines, to provide a unified view of operations. This integration facilitates coordinated responses to operational challenges, improving the overall resilience of aviation ecosystems. Real-time AI analytics also enhances predictive demand modeling.

By analyzing historical trends, booking patterns, and external factors like economic indicators, AI systems predict passenger volumes and cargo demand with high accuracy. This helps in optimizing capacity planning and resource utilization, reducing costs and enhancing service reliability.

7.4. Knowledge Management Systems in Aviation

Effective knowledge management is crucial in the aviation industry to maintain compliance, ensure safety, and enhance operational efficiency. AI-powered knowledge management systems play a pivotal role in collecting, storing, and disseminating critical information, ensuring that employees across all organizational levels have timely access to the knowledge they need. AI technologies analyze historical data to extract insights into best practices and lessons learned, thereby enhancing knowledge retention (Gandomi and Haider, 2015). For instance, AI can automate the creation of training materials by identifying patterns in operational data, improving the quality and relevance of pilot training programs. This approach ensures that training content is continuously updated and aligned with real-world scenarios, leading to more effective learning outcomes.

In the highly regulated aviation sector, AI-based knowledge management systems ensure that updated procedures and policies are readily accessible to relevant stakeholders, thereby supporting regulatory compliance (Rahman *et al.*, 2022). By automating the tracking of policy changes and updating records accordingly, these systems reduce the administrative burden on aviation organizations while ensuring adherence to evolving regulatory requirements. This capability is essential for maintaining operational standards and avoiding potential penalties associated with non-compliance (Jones *et al.*, 2023).

AI-powered systems integrate data from diverse sources to create a unified repository of knowledge accessible to employees in various roles. This integration enhances real-time collaboration across departments, providing teams with consistent and up-to-date information, which reduces errors caused by fragmented communication. For example, during flight operations, seamless information sharing between pilots, air traffic controllers, and ground staff is vital for safety and efficiency. Natural Language Processing (NLP) capabilities in AI systems facilitate efficient knowledge search and retrieval. These systems can analyze employee queries, retrieve relevant documents, and even summarize content, enabling faster access to critical information (Gandomi and Haider, 2015). This functionality is particularly beneficial for frontline staff, such as pilots and air traffic controllers, who require immediate access to procedural updates and safety protocols.

AI-driven systems support predictive knowledge management by identifying gaps in organizational knowledge and recommending proactive measures to address them. Machine learning algorithms can pinpoint areas where additional training or resources are needed, ensuring continuous improvement in operational standards. For instance, if data indicate a recurring issue in a specific operational area, the system can suggest targeted training to mitigate the problem, enhancing operational reliability and safety.

7.5. Ethical Considerations and Challenges

The integration of AI into aviation has introduced unprecedented opportunities for efficiency and innovation. However, it also raises a host of ethical challenges that organizations must address to ensure fair, transparent, and responsible use of AI technologies (Christidis and Devetsikiotis, 2016). These challenges encompass data privacy, algorithmic transparency, bias, cybersecurity, accountability, and ethical training.

One of the foremost ethical concerns in AI applications for aviation is data privacy. AI systems in aviation rely on vast amounts of personal, operational, and sensitive data, such as passenger information, flight logs, and maintenance records. Ensuring compliance with data protection regulations, such as the General Data Protection Regulation (GDPR) in Europe, is critical to maintaining stakeholder trust (Morley *et al.*, 2020). Organizations must implement robust data governance frameworks, including anonymization, encryption, and access controls, to protect sensitive information from breaches and unauthorized access (Rahman *et al.*, 2022). Additionally, clear policies on data collection and usage should be established to provide transparency to stakeholders about how their data is handled.

AI decision-making processes often operate as "black boxes," making it difficult to understand how specific outcomes are generated. This lack of transparency can erode trust among stakeholders and raise concerns about fairness and accountability. For instance, when AI is used in air traffic management or predictive maintenance, stakeholders may demand clarity on how decisions are made and whether they adhere to established safety and operational standards. To address this, aviation organizations must prioritize algorithmic transparency by documenting AI processes and decisions, ensuring they are comprehensible to both technical and non-technical stakeholders (Floridi *et al.*, 2021). Additionally, establishing clear accountability structures is vital. For example, protocols should determine who is responsible for AI-driven decisions, particularly in critical areas such as safety management and regulatory compliance.

Bias in AI algorithms is a significant ethical challenge in aviation, especially in areas like recruitment, passenger profiling, and customer service. For example, machine learning models trained on biased datasets may perpetuate existing inequalities or introduce new forms of discrimination, such as unfairly targeting certain demographic groups during security screenings. To mitigate this, organizations must use diverse and representative datasets and conduct regular algorithm audits to identify and address biases. Inclusive design principles and stakeholder engagement can also help ensure AI systems reflect the values of fairness and equity.

The reliance on AI in aviation introduces heightened risks to data security and integrity. AI systems often handle sensitive data, making them attractive targets for cyberattacks. A data breach could compromise passenger privacy, operational integrity, or even flight safety. Organizations must adopt robust cybersecurity measures, including advanced encryption, multi-factor authentication, and real-time threat detection systems, to safeguard AI infrastructures (Rahman *et al.*, 2022). Furthermore, incident response protocols should be established to address potential breaches swiftly and effectively, minimizing impacts on stakeholders.

AI's use in safety-critical applications, such as autonomous flight systems, predictive maintenance, and air traffic management, raises ethical questions about decision-making in high-stakes scenarios (Alketbi, 2025). For instance, if an AI system fails or produces an incorrect recommendation, determining accountability can be challenging. To address this, aviation organizations should establish ethical frameworks that outline guidelines for the responsible deployment of AI in critical applications. These frameworks should include fail-safe mechanisms, human oversight, and rigorous testing under varied scenarios to ensure the reliability of AI systems.

The rapid adoption of AI in aviation necessitates the development of ethical awareness and training among employees. Staff across all levels should be educated on the ethical implications of AI technologies, including their potential biases, limitations, and societal impacts (Binns, 2022). Such training can foster a culture of responsibility, ensuring ethical considerations are integrated into AI development, deployment, and operations. For example, ethical training programs for air traffic controllers and maintenance engineers can emphasize the importance of transparency, accountability, and fairness in AI-enabled systems.

The pace of AI innovation often outstrips the development of regulatory frameworks, creating gaps in oversight and governance. Aviation organizations must navigate the tension between adopting cutting-edge technologies and adhering to existing regulations. Collaborative efforts between industry stakeholders, regulatory bodies, and policymakers are essential to developing comprehensive guidelines that ensure AI systems are deployed responsibly while fostering innovation (Floridi *et al.*, 2021).

Engaging stakeholders, including passengers, employees, regulators, and industry experts, is crucial for designing ethical AI systems. Stakeholder input can help identify potential ethical pitfalls and inform the development of systems that align with societal values. For example, co-designing AI systems with air traffic controllers or maintenance staff can ensure the technology meets practical needs while addressing ethical concerns (Adib Bin Rashid and Karim Kausik, 2024).

The long-term impacts of AI adoption in aviation, including its environmental and societal consequences, must be considered. For instance, while AI can optimize fuel efficiency and reduce emissions, its energy-intensive computational processes may offset these benefits. Organizations should evaluate the lifecycle impacts of AI systems and prioritize sustainability in their design and deployment (Morley *et al.*, 2020).

Addressing ethical challenges in AI integration is critical to ensuring the responsible use of technology in aviation. By prioritizing data privacy, algorithmic transparency, bias mitigation, and cybersecurity, aviation organizations can foster trust among stakeholders and align AI deployment with ethical principles. Additionally, ethical training, stakeholder engagement, and robust regulatory frameworks are essential for navigating the complexities of AI adoption. As AI continues to transform the aviation industry, a proactive and ethical approach will be vital to balancing innovation with responsibility.

7.6. Case Studies and Practical Applications

The aviation industry has increasingly adopted Artificial Intelligence (AI) to enhance various operational aspects, leading to significant improvements in efficiency, safety, and customer satisfaction. The following are several case studies and practical applications illustrating the successful integration of AI technologies by leading aviation organizations:

Japan Airlines — Streamlining boarding processes: Japan Airlines implemented an AI system at Tokyo's Haneda Airport to streamline the boarding process and minimize flight delays caused by excess carry-on luggage. The AI analyzes camera footage at boarding gates to classify baggage and estimate overhead bin space in real time, alerting staff if storage limits are exceeded. This initiative reduces congestion and boarding time while ensuring compliance with carry-on size and weight regulations (Air Transport IT Insights, 2022).

Qantas — Optimizing operations: Since 2018, Qantas has leveraged AI to optimize various aspects of its operations, including flight routing, fuel supply, and managing external constraints like airspace closures. These AI-driven strategies have resulted in estimated fuel savings of $92 million, demonstrating the significant impact of AI on operational efficiency and cost reduction (Australian Aviation, 2020).

GE Aerospace — AI-powered workplace efficiency: GE Aerospace partnered with Microsoft to introduce "Wingmate," an AI tool designed to assist its 52,000 employees. Wingmate utilizes Microsoft's AI technology to execute functions such as summarizing manuals, addressing quality issues, and drafting communications efficiently. This tool enhances productivity and streamlines workflows within the organization (Microsoft News, 2023).

American Airlines — Reducing environmental impact: American Airlines collaborated with Google Research and Breakthrough Energy to test AI-guided routes aimed at avoiding contrail formation, which significantly contributes to aviation's global warming impact. By predicting and avoiding contrails, this initiative seeks to reduce the environmental footprint of flights (Breakthrough Energy, 2023).

US Air Force — Resilient navigation solutions: The US Air Force is developing AI as an alternative navigation method to GPS, preparing for scenarios where GPS systems might be compromised. An AI program was tested to navigate aircraft by Earth's magnetic fields, successfully guiding a C-17 cargo plane despite electromagnetic noise complications. This development enhances navigation resilience in contested environments (Defense News, 2023).

Delta Air Lines — Enhancing baggage tracking: Delta Air Lines utilizes AI-driven baggage tracking systems that provide real-time updates to passengers regarding the location of their luggage. This transparency significantly enhances customer satisfaction by reducing uncertainty and improving the travel experience (Delta News Hub, 2021).

KLM — Sentiment analysis for customer insights: KLM employs AI-powered sentiment analysis tools to understand customer feedback, enabling the airline to tailor its services more effectively. This approach leads to improved passenger experiences by aligning services with customer expectations and preferences (KLM Newsroom, 2022).

FedEx — Optimizing logistics: FedEx leverages AI to optimize route planning and package sorting, ensuring faster deliveries and reduced operational costs. AI-based predictive analytics tools help the company anticipate demand fluctuations and adjust resources accordingly, enhancing efficiency in cargo operations (FedEx, 2022).

Singapore Changi and London Heathrow — Crowd management: Airports like Singapore Changi and London Heathrow employ AI-powered crowd management systems to predict passenger flow and minimize congestion during peak hours. These systems analyze data from cameras, sensors, and ticketing platforms to enhance operational efficiency and improve the passenger journey (Changi Airport Group, 2023 and Heathrow News, 2023).

United Airlines — Fuel efficiency optimization: United Airlines leverages AI to optimize fuel efficiency by analyzing flight paths and aircraft performance data. This initiative has led to significant reductions in carbon emissions and operational costs, aligning with the airline's sustainability goals (United Airlines Sustainability Report, 2023).

Turkish Airlines — Demand forecasting: Turkish Airlines employs AI-powered demand forecasting systems to optimize ticket pricing and capacity management. These tools analyze historical booking patterns, economic indicators, and seasonal trends to maximize revenue and improve load factors (Turkish Airlines Investor Relations, 2022).

Emirates — AI in training programs: Emirates integrates AI into its training programs for pilots and cabin crew. AI-driven simulators provide real-time feedback and scenario analysis, enhancing the effectiveness of training and ensuring compliance with global aviation standards (Emirates Group, 2023).

7.7. Conclusion

The integration of AI into aviation organizations has revolutionized how data analysis and knowledge management are conducted, offering transformative opportunities across operational, safety, and customer service dimensions. By leveraging AI technologies, aviation organizations can improve decision-making, optimize operations, and foster a culture of continuous innovation and learning. However, to maximize these benefits, significant challenges must be addressed, particularly those related to ethical considerations, data governance, and workforce readiness.

AI technologies such as machine learning, predictive analytics, and anomaly detection systems enable aviation organizations to enhance operational efficiency, improve flight safety, and reduce costs. Real-time data processing combined with edge AI is particularly promising for dynamic environments, providing immediate insights at the source of data generation (Zhao and Miller, 2024). For example, predictive maintenance systems powered by AI have already demonstrated the ability to reduce unplanned downtime and extend the lifecycle of critical aircraft components (Chen *et al.*, 2023).

Emerging technologies, including AI-driven digital twins, are further transforming aviation. These virtual replicas of physical systems simulate various operational scenarios, aiding in resource optimization, strategic planning, and infrastructure management. Airports can use digital twins to improve passenger flow management, while airlines can leverage them for management and flight path optimization (Garcia *et al.*, 2023).

While AI offers numerous benefits, ethical and technical challenges remain significant barriers to widespread adoption. Issues related to data privacy, algorithmic transparency, and bias in decision-making must be addressed. For instance, biased AI algorithms can perpetuate inequalities in recruitment, passenger profiling, or customer service, underscoring the need for robust data governance frameworks and diverse training datasets.

Data security is another pressing concern, as aviation AI systems process vast amounts of sensitive personal and operational data. The adoption of blockchain technology alongside AI could provide a secure and transparent framework for data management, reducing risks associated with breaches and unauthorized access (Kaya and Demir, 2023).

Furthermore, the accountability for AI-driven decisions, particularly in safety-critical applications, necessitates clear guidelines and documentation to ensure trust and compliance. This challenge calls for collaborative efforts between industry stakeholders and regulators to establish AI governance frameworks that prioritize safety, fairness, and accountability (Floridi *et al.*, 2021).

The aviation industry faces increasing pressure to address its environmental impact, and AI has emerged as a key enabler of sustainability. AI-driven fuel optimization and route efficiency systems help reduce carbon emissions and operational costs (Jones *et al.*, 2023). Additionally, integrating AI with renewable energy systems, such as solar-powered ground operations, can further reduce the environmental footprint of airports (Bilal, 2024).

Future research should explore the role of AI in developing sustainable aviation fuels (SAFs) and optimizing their integration into airline operations. AI can also be used to monitor and mitigate noise pollution by analyzing flight patterns and suggesting operational adjustments to minimize community impact (Budd and Ison, 2020).

Generative AI and natural language processing (NLP) are reshaping aviation workflows by automating administrative tasks, enhancing customer interactions, and improving training programs. For instance, NLP algorithms can analyze cockpit communication to identify stress or fatigue in pilots, enabling timely interventions to prevent errors (Rahman *et al.*, 2023). AI-driven virtual assistants can also handle routine customer inquiries, freeing human agents to focus on complex issues.

In training programs, generative AI can create realistic scenarios for pilot and crew training, providing contextual insights and adaptive feedback. These advancements not only streamline workflows but also enhance decision-making in complex operational contexts.

AI and sustainability: Focus on AI's role in reducing aviation's environmental impact, including optimizing alternative fuel usage, reducing contrails, and improving energy efficiency in airport operations.

Blockchain integration: Investigate the potential of blockchain technology in enhancing data security, transparency, and operational integrity in AI-powered aviation systems.

Digital twin applications: Expand research on the use of AI-powered digital twins in airport management, flight operations, and infrastructure development.

Ethics and bias mitigation: Develop methodologies for regular algorithm audits, bias detection, and corrective measures to ensure fairness and inclusivity in AI applications.

Advanced machine learning models: Explore the use of advanced AI models for predictive analytics in safety-critical applications, such as air traffic management and emergency response systems.

The successful integration of AI in aviation requires collaborative partnerships between academia, industry, and regulatory bodies. Such partnerships can drive interdisciplinary research, accelerate innovation, and ensure that technical and ethical challenges are effectively addressed. Global consortia can develop standardized guidelines for AI deployment, fostering a harmonized approach to adoption across the industry.

By investing in staff training, fostering ethical awareness, and developing comprehensive governance frameworks, aviation organizations can position themselves as leaders in leveraging AI for operational excellence, safety, and sustainability. These strategies will enable the aviation sector to remain resilient and adaptive in the face of evolving demands, ensuring a future that balances innovation with responsibility.

Bibliography

Adib Bin Rashid, M. and Karim Kausik, M. A. (2024). "AI revolutionizing industries worldwide: A comprehensive overview of its diverse applications." *Hybrid Advances*, *7*, 100277. https://doi.org/10.1016/j.hybadv.2024.100277.

Ahmed, K., Patel, S., and Zhao, Y. "AI applications in aviation logistics: Trends and implications." *Logistics Research Journal* 18, no. 4 (2023): 312–330.

Alketbi, M. A., Dweiri, F., and Dalalah, D. (2025). "The Role of Artificial Intelligence in Aviation Construction Projects in the United Arab Emirates: Insights from Construction Professionals." *Applied Sciences*, *15*(1), 110. https://doi.org/10.3390/app15010110.

Australian Aviation. "Qantas AI-driven operational savings." 2020. Retrieved from: https://australianaviation.com.au.

Bilal, S. (2024). "Impact and influence of artificial intelligence in airport management and operation." *Universal International Journal of Management Research*, *1*(3), 23–40. https://doi.org/10.37854/UIJMR.2024.1.3.40.

Binns, R. "Ethical awareness in AI deployment: Challenges and solutions." *AI & Society* 37, no. 3 (2022): 451–467.

Breakthrough Energy. "AI-guided contrail avoidance initiative." 2023. Retrieved from: https://www.breakthroughenergy.org/.

Budd, L. and Ison, S. *Air Transport Management: An International Perspective*. Routledge, 2020.

Carter, M., Xu, T., and Walker, J. "AI-enabled customer experience in aviation: Enhancing loyalty and satisfaction." *Service Management Quarterly* 12, no. 1 (2024): 34–50.

Changi Airport Group. "AI for crowd management." 2023. Retrieved from: https://www.changiairport.com/.

Chen, Z., Liu, Y., and Zhao, X. "AI in aviation safety: Enhancing situational awareness through advanced algorithms." *Aviation Safety Journal* 15, no. 2 (2023): 101–120. DOI: 10.1016/j.asj.2023.02.003.

Chen, Z., Luo, X., and Wang, Y. "AI and safety in aviation: Enhancing hazard detection and crew performance." *Safety Science* 157 (2023): 105–112.

Christidis, K. and Devetsikiotis, M. (2016). "Blockchains and smart contracts for the Internet of Things." *IEEE Access*, *4*, 2292–2303. https://doi.org/10.1109/ACCESS.2016.2566339.

Defense News. "US Air Force tests AI-based navigation methods." 2023. Retrieved from: https://www.defensenews.com/.

Delta News Hub. "Real-time baggage tracking at Delta." 2021. Retrieved from: https://news.delta.com/.

Demir, G., Moslem, S., and Duleba, S. (2024). "Artificial intelligence in aviation safety: Systematic review and biometric analysis." *International Journal of Computational Intelligence Systems*, *17*, 279. https://doi.org/10.1007/s44196-024-00671-w.

Emirates Group. "AI-driven training programs." 2023. Retrieved from: https://www.emirates.com/.

FedEx. "AI in logistics optimization." 2022. Retrieved from: https://www.fedex.com/.

Floridi, L., Cowls, J., Beltrametti, M., *et al.* "AI and ethics: Balancing innovation and governance in critical industries." *Nature Machine Intelligence* 3, no. 4 (2021): 310–319.

Gandomi, A. and Haider, M. "Beyond the hype: Big data concepts, methods, and analytics." *International Journal of Information Management* 35, no. 2 (2015): 137–144.

Garcia, M., Singh, R., and Patel, K. "Leveraging digital twins for operational optimization in aviation." *Journal of Aviation Innovation* 15, no. 2 (2023): 78–91.

Green, R., Taylor, S., and Wong, J. "AI applications for fuel efficiency in aviation: Insights from United Airlines." *Journal of Aviation Sustainability* 14, no. 1 (2023): 120–135. DOI: 10.1016/j.jas.2023.01.008.

Hassan, N., Ali, R., and Khan, M. "AI in aviation training: Enhancing pilot and crew readiness." *International Journal of Aviation Training* 11, no. 3 (2023): 88–103. DOI: 10.1016/j.ijat.2023.03.002.

Heathrow. "AI-powered passenger flow predictions." 2023. Retrieved from: https://www.heathrow.com/.

Johnson, R. and Patel, M. "AI in airline customer service: Enhancing satisfaction through intelligent systems." *Journal of Aviation Customer Experience* 10, no. 2 (2022): 88–105. DOI: 10.1016/j.jace.2022.02.004.

Jones, T., Lee, C., and Wang, H. "AI and carbon footprint reduction in aviation: Towards sustainable skies." *Environmental Impact Assessment Review* 101 (2023): 456–472.

Kaya, O. and Demir, A. "AI in revenue management: Turkish Airlines' approach to demand forecasting." *Journal of Airline Economics* 19, no. 4 (2023): 210–225. DOI: 10.1016/j.jae.2023.04.006.

KLM Newsroom. "Sentiment analysis for enhanced passenger experience." 2022. Retrieved from: https://news.klm.com/.

Microsoft News. "GE Aerospace launches AI assistant Wingmate." 2023. Retrieved from: https://news.microsoft.com/.

Morley, J., Floridi, L., Kinsey, L., and Elhalal, A. "From what to how: An initial review of publicly available AI ethics tools, methods, and research to translate principles into practices." *Science and Engineering Ethics* 26, no. 4 (2020): 2141–2168. DOI: 10.1007/s11948-020-00213-5.

Patel, S. and Zhou, L. "AI-assisted sustainable aviation fuel integration." *Journal of Sustainable Aviation* 16, no. 1 (2024): 98–115.

Rahman, A., Khan, S., and Ali, M. "AI-driven data governance in aviation: Ensuring privacy and security." *Journal of Aviation Management* 19, no. 1 (2022): 88–102.

Raihan, A. (2025). “Sustainable aviation: A critical review of policies, technologies, and future pathways.” *Journal of the Air Transport Research Society, 5*, 100080. https://doi.org/10.1016/j.jatrs.2025.100080.

Samanta, K., Sandeep, R., Sahu, Y. N., and Dande, M. (2024). “Blockchain and AI integration: Transforming transparency in supply chain management.” *European Economics Letters, 14*(3), 1238–1247. https://doi.org/10.52783/eel.v14i3.1885.

Serrano, L. and Kazda, A. “Future of aviation: Digitalization and automation of air traffic management.” *Journal of Air Transport Management* 90 (2021): 101946. DOI: 10.1016/j.jairtraman.2021.101946.

Turkish Airlines. “AI-powered demand forecasting.” 2022. Retrieved from: https://investor.turkishairlines.com/.

United Airlines. “Fuel efficiency through AI.” 2023. Retrieved from: https://www.united.com/.

Zhao, L. and Miller, D. “Real-time edge AI for aviation decision-making.” *Journal of Aerospace Technology* 12, no. 3 (2024): 215–230.

https://doi.org/10.1142/9781800616578_0008

Chapter 8

The Use of AI in Maritime Delimitation Addressing the Equity Principle and Judicial Subjectivity

Refia Nur Yagmur

Department of Maritime, Transport Law and Politics, Graduate School of Social Sciences, Ankara University, Türkiye

refia.nur.yagmur@ankara.edu.tr
rnyagmur@ankara.edu.tr

Abstract

This chapter explores the potential of Artificial Intelligence (AI) to transform maritime delimitation, a complex process that balances geographical, legal, and equitable considerations, to resolve disputes over maritime boundaries. While traditional maritime delimitation relies on human adjudication, AI offers opportunities to enhance efficiency, consistency, and objectivity through its data-processing capabilities. However, integrating AI into this nuanced legal domain raises significant challenges, including algorithmic bias, opacity, and the difficulty of translating equitable principles into computational frameworks. The chapter begins with a literature review. It then examines the legal and technical foundations of maritime delimitation, emphasizing the role of equity and the evolution of methodologies such as the equidistance principle and the three-stage approach. The discussion shifts to AI's potential applications, including machine learning and natural language processing, which could support decision-making by analyzing vast datasets and identifying patterns in legal precedents. However, the chapter also critically evaluates the limitations of AI, particularly its inability to fully grasp the contextual and interpretative nature of legal reasoning, which is essential for achieving equitable outcomes. Ethical concerns, such as data bias, model fragility, and the risk of judicial conformism, are also addressed, underscoring the need for transparency and human oversight. The chapter concludes by advocating for a balanced approach, where AI serves as a decision-support tool rather than a replacement for human judges.

Keywords: Artificial Intelligence, maritime delimitation, equity, judicial subjectivity, equidistance.

8.1. Introduction

Maritime delimitation is a complex and multifaceted process. It requires balancing geographical, legal, and equitable considerations to achieve outcomes that are both fair and consistent with international law. Historically, this process has been carried out through human adjudication, where judges weigh evidence and apply nuanced principles to resolve disputes. However, Artificial Intelligence (AI) has introduced the possibility of supplementing or even transforming traditional decision-making processes.

How can AI, a tool known for its efficiency and data processing capabilities, contribute to resolving the intricate challenges of maritime delimitation? Can it truly enhance consistency and objectivity, or does its reliance on algorithms introduce new risks to fairness and transparency? This chapter explores these questions, examining the potential of AI to act as a decision-support tool and even as a decision-maker in this context. However, due to the limited scope of this book chapter, it will only provide a brief overview of certain topics rather than a comprehensive analysis. Readers interested in a more detailed examination can refer to the cited sources for further information.

Section 8.2 of this chapter explores previous scholarly works regarding the maritime delimitation and the use of AI in legal fields. Section 8.3 explores the integration of AI into maritime delimitation, examining the potential applications of technologies such as machine learning and natural language processing in decision support mechanisms and enhancing decision-making processes. By addressing the intersection of technological innovation and legal practice, this section lays the groundwork for a nuanced analysis of the opportunities and constraints associated with AI. Section 8.4, titled *Challenges and Ethical Considerations*, provides a critical evaluation of the risks inherent in deploying AI within the context of maritime delimitation, including issues related to bias, opacity, and translating legal analysis into interpretable algorithmic frameworks. Following this, Sections 8.5–8.7 consider the pathways for advancing the use of AI in maritime delimitation in a manner that ensures equity. Finally, the chapter concludes by reflecting on the broader implications of integrating AI into international legal frameworks, emphasizing its potential to transform maritime dispute resolution while underscoring the necessity of maintaining trust and legitimacy in the adjudicative process.

8.2. Literature Review

The legal framework governing maritime delimitation, particularly the United Nations Convention on the Law of the Sea (UNCLOS), provides essential guidelines for delimitation decisions, and has been widely examined by scholars. The use of AI is already being discussed by several scholars in maritime logistics, ship navigation, and port management to optimize processes and baseline determinations. It should also be noted that appointing an "AI model" as a judge has also been discussed extensively by scholars. However, there is limited scholarly work on the use of AI in maritime delimitation or related disputes.

8.3. AI and Maritime Delimitation

Before proceeding to examine the AI and its usage in maritime delimitation, it is necessary to describe and explain maritime delimitation and its legal bases.

8.3.1. *Maritime delimitation*

Maritime delimitation is defined as the legal and technical process of defining boundaries between the overlapping maritime zones of coastal states.

As it could be understood from the definition, maritime delimitation involves allocating jurisdiction to states over specific maritime areas, often concerning the continental shelf or exclusive economic zones (EEZs). The process of delimitation involves defining the boundaries of an area that is already considered, in principle, to belong to a coastal state, rather than creating the area anew. Maritime delimitation holds a critical role in the law of the sea, as coastal states require clearly defined boundaries to exercise their legal rights and utilize maritime resources effectively. While states have the freedom to negotiate their boundaries, unresolved disputes can be referred to peaceful resolution mechanisms, including judicial settlement.

In maritime boundary disputes, the role of judges involves evaluating the claims presented by each party, determining whether they are substantiated, and resolving the dispute based on these findings. This process includes establishing procedural rules, conducting fact-finding, and interpreting relevant conventions and treaties. Ultimately, the judges must deliver a decision determining the maritime boundary.

Since the initial efforts to establish general rules on maritime delimitation at the 1930 Hague Codification Conference, delimitation has continued to provoke significant debate within the law of the sea, despite extensive academic publications. The complexity of the delimitation issue has increased with the widespread division of maritime areas into defined jurisdictions.

It should be noted that the peaceful resolution of disputes over maritime delimitation is a fundamental obligation for coastal states, as outlined in the United Nations Charter (UN Charter) and later reinforced by UNCLOS. Article 279 of UNCLOS requires states to resolve disputes concerning its interpretation or application through peaceful means. These peaceful means, as listed in Article 33(1) of the UN Charter, include negotiation, mediation, conciliation, arbitration, judicial settlement, and other methods chosen by the parties involved. In the latter half of the 20th century, maritime delimitation disputes gained significance, becoming a frequent subject of bilateral agreements and international adjudication, particularly for the International Court of Justice (ICJ) and arbitration tribunals.

In 1951, the *Anglo-Norwegian Fisheries* case set key precedents for expanding exclusive fishing zones. This was followed by the *Fisheries Jurisdiction* (1974) cases, which further advanced the concept of the EEZ. The *Gulf of Maine* (1984) case between the United States and Canada was the first ICJ judgment by a Chamber addressing the EEZ and its relationship to the continental shelf. Subsequent cases, such as the *Libya v. Malta*

Continental Shelf (1985) case and the *St Pierre and Miquelon Award* (1992), before UNCLOS came into force and cases after it came into effect, such as the *Qatar v. Bahrain* (2001) case, the *Cameroon v. Nigeria* (2002) case, the *Barbados v. Trinidad* (2006) and *Tobago Award*, the *Nicaragua v. Honduras* (2007) case, and the *Romania v. Ukraine Maritime Delimitation in the Black Sea* (2009) case, continued to shape the law on the continental shelf and its delimitation.

In order to analyze AI usage in maritime delimitation, one must understand the legal concepts, reasoning, and norms that govern maritime delimitation. Over the past five decades, maritime boundary delimitation has evolved, leading to the development of various doctrines and methodologies. However, in general, maritime delimitation is widely recognized to require the application of equity, ensuring that all relevant circumstances are considered to achieve a fair outcome.

The first perspective views equity as a corrective mechanism. In this role, equity helps prevent unfair outcomes that might result from rigidly applying the law. An example of a corrective function is the use of the equidistance or median line method, adjusted to account for special circumstances. This method, utilizing the "median line" or "equidistance line," is applied to boundaries between both opposite and adjacent states. Initially conceptualized by Whittemore Boggs for delimiting the Great Lakes in North America, this method eventually gained widespread application in international boundary disputes. Equidistance depends on the coastlines of the states involved, with coasts and islands serving as the primary determinants. This approach generates a single boundary line, functioning either as a median line between opposite states or as an equidistant line between adjacent states. Geometrically, the segments of the median line for opposite states are formed by drawing perpendicular bisectors of the lines connecting the closest corresponding points on the baselines of each state. These baselines are the reference points for measuring the breadth of the territorial sea. After establishing the baselines, the delimitation line can be mathematically defined; however, the accurate selection of base points requires careful consideration of various geographical specificities unique to each case.

Although the equidistance method offers precision, its application often requires discretion and legal judgment beyond mere geometric and mathematical calculations. A recurring cause of disputes is the inclusion of specific base points, for instance, when islands situated off coastal lines disproportionately influence the equidistance or median line, irrespective of their size or significance under the law of the sea. In this context, the International Law Commission (ILC) recognizes that the equidistance principle may not always yield satisfactory outcomes in territorial sea delimitation. Initially, exceptions to this rule were suggested in general terms, but the final draft explicitly stated that equidistance should be applied unless "special circumstances" justify a different boundary line. In this regard, Article 12(1) of the Territorial Sea Convention and Article 6 of the Geneva Convention on the Continental Shelf refer to the equidistance/median line method as the general rule and special circumstances as the exception. However, as some scholars pointed out, the special circumstances of the equidistance method imply that "normal" geographic forms or coastlines do not require such "special" considerations or exceptions, whereas "abnormal" ones do — despite the absence of any inherent normality or abnormality in nature itself.

The second perspective of equity has a more independent role in international law. As highlighted in *Tunisia v. Libya* (1982), in international law, equity functions as a fundamental principle, applied to ensure fairness and justice in legal proceedings, in contrast to domestic legal systems, where equity often serves as a corrective to strict rules.

This perspective marks a significant development, particularly since the Third United Nations Conference on the Law of the Sea, where maritime delimitation became a highly contentious issue, especially concerning the unresolved delimitation issue of the continental shelf zones and EEZ. The Special Negotiating Group was tasked with addressing these issues and debated the relationship between equitable principles and the equidistance method. Article 6 of the Geneva Convention on the Continental Shelf, which strongly reflected the equidistance approach, was intentionally abandoned early in the negotiations. Instead, UNCLOS adopted provisions emphasizing equitable principles and a relevant circumstances approach, as seen in draft Articles 61 and 70, which advocated delimitation based on equity while allowing the use of the equidistance line when appropriate. Although the final formula was hastily adopted, the concept of equity remained central to the deliberations and is considered a fundamental principle of UNCLOS.

With respect to UNCLOS itself, Article 15 addresses the delimitation of the territorial sea, explicitly allowing for the use of the equidistance principle unless special circumstances suggest otherwise. Articles 74 and 83 apply to the EEZ and continental shelf delimitation, respectively, and stress the importance of an equitable solution.

Recent jurisprudence has seen a notable shift toward the adoption of a three-stage approach to maritime delimitation. This methodology was clearly outlined in the *Romania v. Ukraine Maritime Delimitation in the Black Sea* (2009) case. The first stage involves establishing a provisional delimitation line based on geometrically objective methods, unless there are compelling reasons to do otherwise. In the second stage, the court assesses whether any factors necessitate adjustments to the provisional equidistance line in order to reach an equitable outcome. The third stage entails a "disproportionality test" to verify the final delimitation line. This three-stage framework has also been applied in recent international cases concerning maritime delimitation, regardless of whether ITLOS, ICJ, or other arbitral tribunals adjudicated the cases.

This chapter does not aim to further explore maritime delimitation in detail, as its focus is on the use of AI in maritime delimitation from the viewpoint of the equity principle. As explored earlier, maritime delimitation is a deeply complex and evolving field, shaped by a mix of principles, methodologies, and judicial interpretations. The tension between equidistance and equitable principles, the challenges posed by unique geographical features, and the emergence of the three-stage approach all reflect the complex nature of these disputes. Added to this is the diversity of precedents, which often contributes to controversies and leads to context-specific outcomes. Given this complicated landscape, in the following sections, the author will examine how AI can be applied to maritime delimitation, considering its potential to bring greater consistency, objectivity, and clarity to this complex process while also addressing the associated challenges.

8.3.2. *Understanding AI: Machine learning and beyond*

While AI has no common description, it is possible to describe AI as the field of technology that enables machines to replicate behaviors or thought processes traditionally associated with human intelligence. This includes their ability to adapt, solve problems, and interact effectively with their surroundings. In terms of intelligence, the definitions vary, but they often revolve around the capacity to learn, think critically, and respond to complex situations.

Unlike human intelligence, which can be influenced by emotions and irrationality, AI operates based on algorithms and data. It can either mimic human thought processes or act independently with logical precision. To assess the presence and nature of AI, various methods such as the

Turing Test and the Chinese Room experiment have been proposed; however, as these tests are beyond the scope of this discussion, we will not examine them in detail.

AI learns to imitate human behavior by processing information, which requires two key components: representing information internally and transforming it into useful output. AI systems typically learn through two approaches: knowledge-based learning and data-based learning. Knowledge-based learning involves encoding expert knowledge into a system through rules and logical statements, while data-based learning, known as machine learning, involves learning patterns from large sets of input–output examples. Both approaches are increasingly combined in modern AI systems, which use data-based methods for interpretation and knowledge-based methods for actions. Data-driven techniques excel at handling large datasets and recognizing patterns, while knowledge-based methods are better for reasoning and explaining solutions. The rise of smart devices has further advanced AI, as these devices, equipped with sensors, can detect changes in their environment and connect through networks like the internet, as well as often store data in the cloud, which enables powerful data processing.

In terms of availability of big data, machine learning (ML), a significant subfield of AI, comes to the fore. ML's primary goal is to create systems capable of learning patterns or models from data. Within ML, different learning methods are distinguished based on how the system learns: supervised learning, unsupervised learning, and reinforcement learning.

In supervised learning, the algorithm is provided with both inputs and corresponding outputs, known as "labeled data." It learns to associate specific outputs with given inputs, much like a child learning to identify vegetables by having a parent show pictures and naming them. Artificial neural networks (ANNs) are a powerful type of supervised learning model, especially effective when working with large datasets. Inspired by the human nervous system, ANNs consist of artificial neurons that simulate the way biological neurons process information. These neurons receive input signals, process them, and produce outputs that are passed to other neurons. A simple ANN consists of input, hidden, and output layers. Through the input layer, inputs are submitted into the network. These inputs are transformed by the hidden layer, which performs intermediate calculations. The final output is then produced. The hidden layer is called "hidden" since the process that occurs there is not explicitly defined by the user. Instead, the neural network learns how to handle the data through a training process, where it is given many examples and adjusts its internal parameters until it can make accurate predictions. This ability to learn from examples allows ANNs to be used for a wide range of tasks, identifying patterns in complex data. The growth in computing power and the availability of big data have enabled the development of deep neural networks (DNNs), which are a more advanced form of ANNs, where DNNs consist of many layers, allowing them to process and learn from massive datasets more effectively. This advancement in deep learning has led to significant breakthroughs. In some areas, such as image recognition, DNNs even outperform human capabilities.

In contrast, unsupervised learning involves only inputs with no predefined outputs. Here, the algorithm's task is to independently find patterns or structures in the data, using what is referred to as "unlabeled data." Reinforcement learning focuses on training to determine the best set of actions, or a control policy, to reach a specific goal. Unlike the other two approaches, it does not receive explicit instructions on how to achieve the goal but instead learns through feedback in the form of rewards, either positive or negative.

NLP and Natural Language Generation (NLG), branches of AI, focus on enabling machines to understand and interact with human language. Legal texts such as statutes, precedents and case law, and scholarly writings present unique challenges due to their intricate structure and rich language. NLPs can efficiently analyze and interpret large volumes of legal information, uncovering patterns and relationships within these texts.

In this chapter, the term "AI" is used broadly to refer to various branches of AI, such as ML, DNNs, NLP, and NLG. The phrase "the use of AI" encompasses two meanings in this context. First, AI can be viewed as a decision-support tool, assisting judges in analyzing and interpreting data. Second, AI might be considered as a potential decision-maker itself, taking on the role of a judge in maritime delimitation cases.

8.3.3. *Use of AI in maritime delimitation*

8.3.3.1. *Technological integration in maritime delimitation*

Using technology is not new to the maritime delimitation. Since the 1970s, computers have been used to identify relevant points and baselines. Historically, datasets have faced significant limitations in accuracy, largely due to the technological constraints of the time. Much of the coastal information represented on nautical charts maintained by national hydrographic offices and global charting agencies, such as those of the United States and the United Kingdom, was collected long before the advent of modern high-resolution seabed mapping techniques. Consequently, large sections of coastlines, particularly in remote or shallow-water areas, fail to meet the standards of precision. This positional inaccuracy poses challenges, as maritime boundaries and claims rely on measurements from baselines. If these baselines are inaccurately depicted, the calculated outer limits and boundaries will also be flawed.

Although technologies like multibeam echo-sounders, light detection and ranging (LIDAR), and airborne bathymetric surveys have improved localized data accuracy, they have not yet been on a scale sufficient to produce globally reliable coastal datasets. Moreover, the dynamic structure of coasts, due to natural phenomena such as sediment deposition in deltas or vertical displacements caused by tectonic or volcanic activity, further complicates the reliability. Notably, sea level rise due to climate change, as highlighted by the Intergovernmental Panel on Climate Change (IPCC), intensifies these changes on the baselines and relevant points.

The emergence of global navigation satellite systems (GNSS), including the United States' Global Positioning System (GPS) and the European Union's GALILEO, represented a significant advancement in establishing a unified global geodetic reference system, essential for identifying baselines and relevant points in maritime delimitation.

8.3.3.2. *Rationale for adopting AI in maritime delimitation*

Judges bear the critical responsibility of interpreting and applying the law to adjudicate disputes, a role that necessitates the meticulous assessment of factual evidence, the evaluation of legal arguments advanced by the parties, and the application of established principles and precedents to the matter at hand. Their function demands a high degree of impartiality and objectivity, underpinned by their legal acumen, professional experience, and profound understanding of the jurisprudential framework.

Nonetheless, judicial decision-making, like all human endeavors, is constrained by cognitive limitations, including the finite capacity to process extensive information and the susceptibility to unconscious biases.

On the other hand, AI models are not restricted by cognitive limitations. By systematically analyzing a comprehensive dataset, AI is able to identify recurring patterns and principles that have been applied in similar disputes in seconds. In that regard, AI might ensure greater uniformity and consistency within the precedents, while providing a time-efficient output, either as a decision support tool or a decision-maker itself.

AI can also reduce the unpredictability and judicial subjectivity often associated with human decision-making in general. The data-driven nature of AI enables it to operate independently of subjective influences, providing a neutral mechanism for evaluating the complex geographical, legal, and equitable factors inherent in maritime boundary delimitation. While some may argue that judges are inherently neutral and trained in a way of ensuring fairness, it is essential to examine the structural composition of the forums in which they operate to fully address this claim.

Article 287 of UNCLOS provides states with a choice of fora for resolving disputes arising under the Convention, resulting in a diverse array of judges including judges from permanent institutions such as the ICJ or the ITLOS, as well as *ad hoc* arbitrators appointed under Annex VII or experts appointed under Annex VIII. The variety of forums leads to the potential involvement of a large number of individuals in dispute resolution. For example, the ICJ comprises fifteen judges, with the possibility of *ad hoc* appointments, and the ITLOS has twenty-one judges, also with potential *ad hoc* appointments. Additionally, with 168 state parties, there could be up to 672 arbitrators listed for Annex VII arbitrations and 1,344 experts for Annex VIII tribunals.

However, despite these large numbers, as of December 2024, only 169 arbitrators and conciliators had been nominated, and no Annex VIII special arbitration had occurred. The composition and demographics reveal significant patterns that highlight potential sources of bias and subjectivity in judicial processes. Among the arbitrators appointed under Annex VII, a substantial majority hail from developed economies, with their formal education predominantly rooted in Western Europe or the United States. Only one woman arbitrator has been appointed, and this occurred in a case that did not proceed substantively. The age distribution is predominantly composed of older individuals, with the youngest arbitrator born in 1975, suggesting limited generational diversity. ITLOS judges exhibit greater geographic diversity owing to the electoral requirements of Annex VI; however, their educational and professional backgrounds remain heavily concentrated in Western legal traditions. This demographic concentration raises important questions regarding the inclusivity and representativeness of international judicial and arbitral bodies, potentially influencing perceptions of neutrality and the substantive fairness of their decisions.

Another issue is the opacity of the human decision-making process. Human judges, despite their obligation to provide clear and reasoned justifications for their decisions, do not always meet the ideal standards of legal transparency and clarity. Judicial reasoning, though formally articulated in written judgments, can sometimes appear ambiguous or inadequately detailed, leaving room for interpretative gaps. This lack of precision may mask underlying biases, unacknowledged influences, or subjective considerations that are not explicitly addressed in the reasoning.

Lastly, AI models are able to process cases quickly, efficiently, and at a lower cost compared to traditional human-driven systems. By managing large volumes of data, AI can significantly reduce delays and operational expenses, especially the high costs associated with international arbitration in maritime delimitation disputes. Also, the consistent and systematic approach of AI can minimize procedural errors, ensuring a more streamlined handling of cases.

8.4. Challenges and Ethical Considerations

Despite the significant advances that AI models have brought to various fields, AI faces some notable challenges.

8.4.1. *Legal reasoning and AI: Compatibility and limitations*

Law cannot be distilled into a mere exercise of balancing pre-assigned variables or calculating factors with predetermined weights, particularly in complex and context-dependent areas such as maritime delimitation. While AI models excel at tasks like determining the median line or equidistance line through the equidistance doctrine, a relatively straightforward geometric exercise, they face significant limitations when required to engage with the equitable principles' doctrine. This doctrine demands not only legal but also contextual interpretation and judges' discretion, which transcends mere mathematical precision.

AI's reliance on data correlations, rather than a substantive grasp of causality and legal reasoning, further underscores its limitations. Maritime delimitation often involves reconciling competing legal claims, incorporating geographical complexities, and balancing equitable considerations to achieve a fair result. These tasks inherently require the exercise of judgment, which might not be fully replicated by AI's algorithmic processes. AI models operate within the parameters of their inputs, such as legal precedents, spatial data, conventions, and treaties, but they fail to internalize the justificatory reasoning that underpins judicial decisions.

This reliance on correlation as a proxy for causation diminishes the reliability of AI outputs in contexts that demand an appreciation of legal principles as dynamic and interpretative rather than static and prescriptive. In maritime delimitation, where the equitable principles' doctrine calls for a tailored approach to achieve justice, AI's inability to comprehend these deeper dimensions limits its utility to a supplementary, rather than determinative, role. While AI can enhance efficiency and aid in data analysis, its outputs must be critically evaluated and guided by human expertise to ensure outcomes align with the nuanced imperatives of fairness and equity.

8.4.2. *Inconsistencies in maritime delimitation*

Scholars have closely examined the precedents, analyzing the evolution and predictability of maritime delimitation disputes. The development of maritime delimitation jurisprudence between 2009 and 2019 showcases the tension between methodological consistency and the nuanced demands of individual disputes. Within this period, ICJ and ITLOS have demonstrated a preference for consistent methods from the equidistance line to the three-stage approach, which might support the idea that there is predictability in terms of the methods. However, cases like *Ghana/Côte d'Ivoire* (2017) reveal that deviations in interpreting Articles 74(3) and 83(3) of UNCLOS introduce unpredictability, showing that judges sometimes prioritize equitable results over strict methodological adherence. Inconsistencies are also evident in cases such as the *North Sea Continental Shelf* (1969), the dispute between *Tunisia v. Libya* (1982), and the *Gulf of Maine* (1984) case. These inconsistencies raise critical questions about the balance between consistency and discretion in judicial decision-making. The growing reliance on equitable principles has therefore led to uncertainty regarding the continued existence of a consistent and predictable body of maritime delimitation law. Also, the disproportionality test under the third stage of the three-stage method has been criticized by scholars for its inconsistency, subjectivity, and uncertainty.

In the context of AI, such differences in judicial practice might reflect what would be framed as a dataset problem. The legal inputs AI relies upon, such as precedents, principles, and geographical factors, may vary in quality, interpretation, or representativeness, leading to inconsistencies in AI-generated outputs. Moreover, AI models, designed to process large amounts of legal data and language, may struggle to capture the nuances of each individual case. In other words, developers may find it challenging to design an AI algorithm that can distinguish between the binding rules of conventions and treaties and the discretionary legal reasoning found in judicial decisions, particularly when judges choose one course of action over another.

8.4.3. *Defining and balancing data parameters*

One major issue is the difficulty in adjusting the large number of parameters in an AI model. Finding the optimal settings can be compared to trying to navigate a rough terrain with many peaks and valleys, where only partial solutions, called as local minimums, are found. For instance, fine-tuning the weights assigned to various geographical features, such as coastlines, islands, and underwater topography, can be complex, as it directly impacts the accuracy of the maritime boundaries. Moreover, balancing competing legal principles like equidistance and equity when adjusting the parameters can be challenging, especially when trying to account for both geographical and legal considerations in boundary determinations. Additionally, setting optimal thresholds for different types of input data, such as precedents, satellite images, coastline data, historical background and EEZ claims, complicates how the model learns to draw boundary lines. The model also may struggle with managing high-dimensional input spaces, where each parameter may reflect different regional legal norms or historical agreements, making it difficult to find a singular optimal solution. The author emphasizes that it is important to consider that current geo-data may not align with past precedents due to changes in coasts. As a result, the AI model might misinterpret the relationship between the inputs, potentially leading to inaccurate analysis.

When the system is trained multiple times, slight changes in the starting conditions can lead to different results, which may cause the model to settle on a different local minimum each time. This variability in the model's outcomes, even with the same input data, raises concerns about its reliability, particularly when it comes to accurately predicting maritime boundaries.

8.4.4. *Fragility of AI models in complex legal contexts*

Another problem with AI models is the fragility of AI. Even small changes in the data inputs — such as adjustments in geographical coordinates, base points, or coastal features — can lead to drastically different results. For example, altering the location of a baseline or modifying certain parameters could lead the model to propose a different boundary altogether. This makes AI systems susceptible to errors or manipulation, which could have serious implications in maritime delimitation, where even slight changes can result in significant disputes.

This fragility is compounded by the fact that maritime delimitation is governed by a combination of rules, principles, precedents, and even political considerations, all of which can vary in interpretation. The presence of conflicting precedents or inconsistent applications of law further complicates the reliability of AI models.

8.4.5. *Bias in AI*

8.4.5.1. *Data bias*

DNNs and other data-driven AI learning algorithms rely heavily on the quality and diversity of their training data, making data bias a critical concern. These models can only learn patterns they have been exposed to during training, meaning that if the training data lack sufficient variety, the model may produce biased or incorrect outputs. For example, if a maritime delimitation algorithm is trained exclusively with data from disputes involving similar coastlines, it may struggle to accurately process cases involving highly irregular or archipelagic coasts.

A second concern is the potential misuse of data, particularly regarding its collection and analysis. Large datasets often concentrated in the control of a few organizations can be deliberately exploited to derive an output that is biased by linking or analyzing existing datasets.

For instance, such actors controlling extensive datasets on oceanographic or geospatial information could selectively analyze or combine the data with selected precedents to support a predetermined outcome in a boundary dispute. By emphasizing data favorable to one party, such as selecting controversial precedents, they could introduce a bias into the delimitation process, potentially altering the decision in favor of the party that aligns with their interests.

8.4.5.2. *Model bias*

Another issue, known as model bias, arises from the structure of the algorithm itself. A poorly designed model may oversimplify complex relationships within the data, leading to a poor fit. While increasing the complexity of the model can address this issue, it comes with the risk of overfitting, where the algorithm memorizes specific details of the training data but fails to generalize effectively to new, slightly different scenarios. Overfitting could result in inconsistent outputs, such as different boundary suggestions for cases with similar geographic and legal contexts. Balancing oversimplifying and overfitting, also called the bias–variance trade-off, is essential to ensure trust in AI models. Striking this balance requires carefully tuning the algorithm to ensure it generalizes well while retaining the ability to capture meaningful details.

It should be noted that the AI system's design and functionality inherently reflect the values and perspectives of its developer, or more accurately, developers, in terms of open-source AI models, making it another potential source of model bias. Biases may arise from the developers' selection of training data, prioritization of certain inputs, or usage of the interpretive frameworks to encode precedents, conventions, and treaties.

8.5. Opacity vs. Transparency

AI models and specifically DNNs are often criticized for their lack of transparency. While these models can produce predictions, it is difficult to understand why they make certain decisions based on given inputs. As explained earlier, hidden layers in ANNs and DNNs make it difficult to trace how specific inputs lead to outputs, contributing to their classification as "black box" models. Even the developers and designers of the algorithm might find AI's process of input difficult to comprehend. In cases where boundaries are based on complex legal principles, states in dispute need to know how the AI arrived at a particular result. This has led to increasing calls for "explainable AI," which would not only offer predictions but also provide a clear, transparent, understandable explanation of how those predictions were made, in other words, the AI's flow of reasoning. However, making AI models technically more transparent does not eliminate the problem, due to the fact that disputing parties may not have relevant information or experts to review and analyze the algorithm and understand how it works given certain inputs, or identify the data on which the AI model's output is based.

The author points out that it is essential to comprehend the legal reasoning behind judicial decisions, including how claims are analyzed, which legal rules and principles are applied, and whether any exceptions are referenced. This understanding is critical to uphold foundational legal principles such as *audi alteram partem* and the right to a reasoned decision. In the context of maritime delimitation, where complex legal arguments and interpretations are involved, such transparency becomes even more crucial. Given the opacity that AI systems can introduce, the author believes that practitioners, judges, and parties involved in such disputes might have significant concerns about the usage of AI.

Another aspect of the opacity of AI models is related to the appeal mechanism for given decisions. Since AI models often function as opaque systems, where the rationale behind their decisions is not easily accessible or interpretable, parties may face substantial difficulty in challenging the decisions. However, as per Article 60 of the Statute of the ICJ, "*The judgment is final and without appeal. In the event of dispute as to the meaning or scope of the judgment, the Court shall construe it upon the request of any party.*" Under Article 296 of UNCLOS, "*Any decision rendered by a court or tribunal having jurisdiction under this section shall be final and shall be complied with by all the parties to the dispute.*" Also, as per Article 33 of the Statute of ITLOS, "*The decision of the Tribunal is final and shall be complied with by all the parties to the dispute.*" In this regard, the main concerning point of opacity regarding maritime delimitation is not how to appeal such a decision, but rather the absence of an appeal mechanism. Therefore, even a minor degree of skepticism toward the reliability or fairness of AI models could discourage parties from submitting future disputes to AI-supported dispute resolution mechanisms.

8.6. Judicial Conformism

A significant issue in integrating AI models into the maritime delimitation disputes is the normative weight judges might assign to AI-generated outputs, especially when these models function as decision support tools. Currently, the legal status of AI outputs remains undefined and no regulations have been in effect regarding their power. Judges who encounter AI model outputs, whether produced internally within the judiciary or presented by a party in dispute, cannot classify them as law, facts, or even secondary sources of law. Instead, these AI outputs occupy a *sui generis* category in dispute resolution.

The normative significance of AI outputs is only one aspect of their impact. Equally important is their psychological influence on judicial decision-making. Judges may unconsciously ascribe weight to AI outputs, regardless of the fact that no legal value has been assigned to them. Scholars have also raised concerns about the risks of judicial conformity. Judges might gravitate toward AI-generated outcomes, particularly when these outputs reflect decisions rendered in similar cases in the past. This could lead to a performative loop, where the mere existence of an AI output increases the likelihood of similar outputs being repeated in the future, regardless of their objective validity or legal merit.

8.7. Future Directions

The future integration of AI into maritime delimitation presents a dual-edged opportunity that must be approached with caution and precision. On the one hand, AI's capacity to process vast datasets and detect patterns offers unparalleled support for legal decision-making. By identifying relevant precedents and simulating equitable solutions, AI can enhance the efficiency and consistency of judicial outcomes. However, such integration also raises critical concerns. The opaque nature of AI models, the risk of data biases influencing outputs, and the potential erosion of judicial independence through the normative weight of algorithmic recommendations all pose significant challenges. Therefore, the way forward must prioritize a balanced approach. AI should complement rather than replace human judgment altogether. While human judges apply discretion to navigate the complexities of maritime delimitation, AI systems risk replicating or amplifying these discrepancies due to their reliance on incomplete, complex, or biased datasets or models. This emphasizes the need for both human oversight and a careful curation of data and algorithms when considering AI's role in international legal frameworks.

Ultimately, maritime delimitation is not solely about methodology; it is about ensuring that the mechanisms employed, human or artificial, deliver equitable and trustworthy solutions to complex boundary disputes. The author suggests that in the near future, AI might be used as a decision support tool that enhances decision-making while adhering to the principles of fairness, transparency, and accountability. In other words, the prospect of equity in AI algorithms should not be seen as a substitute for judicial reasoning but as an enhancement of the process, provided that the integrity of the law remains significant. In this regard, establishing interdisciplinary collaboration between AI developers, legal scholars, and practitioners will be essential to ensure that AI contributes positively to the evolution of maritime delimitation law.

8.8. Conclusion

AI holds considerable benefits for maritime delimitation. It offers tools that can improve efficiency, consistency, and fairness. By rapidly processing large datasets, AI can support human judges in navigating the complexities of geographical and legal considerations. However, its limitations, including reliance on correlation, lack of transparency, and potential biases, highlight the importance of maintaining human oversight. In this regard, the author believes that to fully realize the benefits of AI while safeguarding fairness and equity, it must remain a supplementary tool, at least in the near future, guided by clear ethical standards. The integration of AI in maritime delimitation should prioritize transparency, reasoning that aligns with legal principles and is easy to follow, and the preservation of foundational legal principles to ensure trust and legitimacy of all parties.

Section 8.2 of this chapter offers a comprehensive review of the literature on maritime delimitation and the use of AI in legal fields. Section 8.3 explains the integration of AI into maritime delimitation, analyzing its potential to enhance decision-making by improving efficiency and consistency, yet also acknowledging the complexities of applying legal principles algorithmically. This analysis concludes that while AI holds significant promise, its role in such a nuanced legal domain demands careful consideration of its limitations. Section 8.4 critically examines the challenges and ethical considerations associated with AI in maritime delimitation, such as bias, transparency, and the risks of judicial conformism. These challenges underscore the dual-edged nature of AI, where its utility depends on rigorous oversight and thoughtful integration. Section 8.5, looking to the future, embraces AI's capabilities while safeguarding fundamental legal principles of fairness and equity. Finally, the chapter concludes that while AI may revolutionize aspects of maritime delimitation, it must remain a tool that complements human judges' decision-making process rather than replacing it. In doing so, AI has the potential to harmonize efficiency with the enduring complexities of equity in maritime delimitation disputes.

Bibliography

Aristotle. *Nicomachean Ethics* (M. Oswald, Trans.; Book 5, Chapter 10). New York, NY: Bobbs-Merrill, 1962.

Arrieta, A. B., Díaz-Rodríguez, N., Del Ser, J., Bennetot, A., Tabik, S., Barbado, A., García, S., Gil-López, S., Molina, D., and Benjamins, R. "Explainable Artificial Intelligence (XAI): Concepts, taxonomies, opportunities and challenges toward responsible AI." *Information Fusion* 58 (2020): 82–115.

Atzori, L., Iera, A., and Morabito, G. "The internet of things: A survey." *Computer Networks* 54, no. 15 (2010): 2787–2805.

Aylak, B. L. "The impacts of the applications of artificial intelligence in maritime logistics." *Avrupa Bilim ve Teknoloji Dergisi* 34 (2022): 217–225.

Boddington, P. *Towards a Code of Ethics for Artificial Intelligence*. Springer, 2017.

Boggs, S. W. "Delimitation of seaward areas under national jurisdiction." *American Journal of International Law* 45, no. 2 (1951): 240–266.

Bruzzone, A., Orsoni, A., Mosca, R., and Revetria, R. "AI-based optimization for fleet management in maritime logistics." *Proceedings of the Winter Simulation Conference*, San Diego, CA, USA, 2002, pp. 1174–1182 vol. 2, doi: 10.1109/WSC.2002.1166375.

Cottier, T. *Equitable Principles of Maritime Boundary Delimitation: The Quest for Distributive Justice in International Law*. Cambridge University Press, 2015.

Devillé, R., Sergeyssels, N., and Middag, C. "Basic Concepts of AI for Legal Scholars." In *Artificial Intelligence and the Law*, 1–22, 2021.

Dornemann, J., Rückert, N., Fischer, K., and Taraz, A. "Artificial intelligence and operations research in maritime logistics." *Data Science in Maritime and City Logistics: Data-driven Solutions for Logistics and Sustainability. Proceedings of the Hamburg International Conference of Logistics (HICL)* 30 (2020).

Eidenmuller, H., and Varesis, F. "What Is an Arbitration? Artificial Intelligence and the Vanishing Human Arbitrator." *NYUJl & Bus.* 17 (2020): 49.

Elferink, A. O. "Slovenia/Croatia arbitration — Is the territorial sea delimitation inconsistent with the case law on maritime delimitation." *The NCLOS Blog*

(2017). https://site.uit.no/nclos/2017/08/16/sloveniacroatia-arbitration-is-the-territorial-sea-delimitation-inconsistent-with-the-case-law-on-maritime-delimitation/.

Elferink, A. O., Henriksen, T., and Busch, S. V. *Maritime Boundary Delimitation: The Case Law: Is It Consistent and Predictable?* Cambridge University Press, 2018.

Evans, M. D. "Maritime Boundary Delimitation." In *The Oxford Handbook of the Law of the Sea*, edited by D. R. Rothwell, A. G. O. Elferink, K. N. Scott, and T. Stephens, 254–279. OUP Oxford, 2015.

Farhana, F. "Consistency and Predictability in International Tribunals Decision on Maritime Delimitation Cases From 2009 to 2019." *Indonesian J. Int'l L.* 18 (2020): 23.

Fierens, M., Wauters, E., and Rossello, S. "Setting the scene: On AI ethics and regulation." In *Artificial Intelligence and the Law*, 49–72. Intersentia, 2021.

Figuero, A., Peña, E., Sande, J., Costas, R., Carro, H., Alvarellos, A., Rabuñal, J., Guerra, A., and Pérez, J. D. "AI-based decision-making tools for port management: Ship-infrastructure operability and overtopping." *Coastal Engineering Proceedings* 37 (2022): 86–86.

Floridi, L., and Taddeo, M. "What is data ethics?" *The Royal Society* 374 (2016).

G'sell, F. "AI Judges." In *The Cambridge Handbook of Artificial Intelligence: Global Perspectives on Law and Ethics*, edited by L. A. DiMatteo, C. Poncibò, and M. Cannarsa, 347–363. Cambridge University Press, 2022.

Heaven, D. "Why deep-learning AIs are so easy to fool." *Nature* 574, no. 7777 (2019): 163–166.

Hodgson, R. D., and Cooper, E. J. "The technical delimitation of a modern equidistant boundary." *Ocean Development & International Law* 3, no. 4 (1976): 361–388.

Klein, N. S., and Parlett, K. *Judging the Law of the Sea: Judicial Contributions to the UN Convention on the Law of the Sea.* Oxford University Press, 2022.

Kraska, J., and Park, Y.-K. *Emerging Technology and the Law of the Sea.* Cambridge University Press, 2022.

Kretschmann, L., Zacharias, M., Klöver, S., and Hensel, T. "Machine learning in maritime logistics." *Fraunhofer CML* (2020).

Kumari, S. "Interplay of AI-driven maritime logistics: An in-depth research into port management, advanced operations automation, and CRM integration for optimized performance and efficiency." *ESP Journal of Engineering and Technology Advancements* 1, no. 1 (2021): 1–5.

Kwan, J., Ng, J., and Kiu, B. "The use of artificial intelligence in international arbitration: Where are we right now?" *International Arbitration Law Review* 22, no. 1 (2019): 19–26.

Lando, M. *Maritime Delimitation as a Judicial Process.* Vol. 144. Cambridge University Press, 2019.

Mahmud, K. K., Chowdhury, M. M. H., and Shaheen, M. M. A. "Green port management practices for sustainable port operations: A multi method study of Asian ports." *Maritime Policy & Management* (2023): 1–36.

Martínez, R., García, J. A., and Felis, I. "AI-driven estimation of vessel sailing times and underwater acoustic pressure for optimizing maritime logistics." *Engineering Proceedings* 58, no. 1 (2023): 26.

Mehta, P., Bukov, M., Wang, C.-H., Day, A. G., Richardson, C., Fisher, C. K., and Schwab, D. J. "A high-bias, low-variance introduction to machine learning for physicists." *Physics Reports* 810 (2019): 1–124.

Min-xiong, C., Ai-xing, M., Xiu-hong, W., and Guo-zheng, C. "Influence of cross current on ship navigation in inland waterway." *交通运输工程学报* 8, no. 1 (2008): 61–67.

Mitchell, M. *Artificial Intelligence: A Guide for Thinking Humans*. 2019.

Mittelstadt, B. D., Allo, P., Taddeo, M., Wachter, S., and Floridi, L. "The ethics of algorithms: Mapping the debate." *Big Data & Society* 3, no. 2 (2016).

Nappert, S., and Cohen, P. "Case study: The Practitioner's perspective." In *Arbitration in the Digital Age The Brave New World of Arbitration*, edited by M. Piers and C. Aschauer, 126–148. Cambridge University Press, 2018.

Nelson, L. "The roles of equity in the delimitation of maritime boundaries." *American Journal of International Law* 84, no. 4 (1990): 837–858.

Ng, I., and del Rio, V. B. "When the tribunal is an algorithm: Complexities of enforcing orders determined by a software under the New York convention." In *60 Years of the New York Convention: Key Issues and Future Challenges*, edited by K. F. Gomez and A. M. Lopez Rodriguez, 121–134. Kluwer Law International, 2019.

Ongenae, K. "AI arbitrators...'Does Not Compute'." In *Artificial Intelligence and the Law*, 101–122. Intersentia, 2021.

Park, N. K. *Smart Port Management and Strategy*. Bentham Science Publishers, 2022.

Pavithra, D. and Balakrishnan, R. "IoT based monitoring and control system for home automation." *2015 Global Conference On Communication Technologies (GCCT)* (2015).

Russell, S. and Norvig, P. *Artificial Intelligence: A Modern Approach* (2nd ed.). Prentice Hall, 2002.

Schofield, C., R., van de Poll, R., and Andersen., N "Emerging technology and maritime boundary dispute resolution." In *Emerging Technology and the Law of the Sea*, edited by J. Kraska and Y. K. Park, 1–33. Cambridge University Press, 2022.

Searle, J. R. "Minds, brains, and programs." *Behavioral and Brain Sciences* 3, no. 3 (1980).

Sim, C. "Will artificial intelligence take over arbitration." *Asian Int'l Arb. J.* 14 (2018): 1.

Statheros, T., Howells, G., and Maier, K. M. "Autonomous ship collision avoidance navigation concepts, technologies and techniques." *The Journal of Navigation* 61, no. 1 (2008): 129–142.

Stohl, C., Stohl, M., and Leonardi, P. M. "Digital age managing opacity: Information visibility and the paradox of transparency in the digital age." *International Journal of Communication* 10 (2016): 15.

Tanaka, Y. *Predictability and Flexibility in the Law of Maritime Delimitation*, by Yoshifumi Tanaka, Hart Publishing, 2009.

Tanaka, Y. "The disproportionality test in the law of maritime delimitation." In *Maritime Boundary Delimitation: The Case Law. Is It Consistent and Predictable*, 291–318, 2018.

Turing, A. M. "Computing machinery and intelligence." *Mind* 59, no. 236 (1950).

Van Der Haegen, M. "Quantitative legal prediction: The future of dispute resolution?" In *Artificial Intelligence and the Law*, 83–110. Intersentia, 2021.

Vanderstichele, G. "The normative value of legal analytics. Is there a case for statistical precedent?" University of Oxford, 2019.

Wahab, M. S. A., and Katsh, E. "Revolutionizing technologies and the use of technology in international arbitration." In *Arbitration in the Digital Age The Brave New World of Arbitration*, edited by M. Piers and C. Aschauer, 27–55. Cambridge University Press, 2018.

Wechsler, D. "The measurement and appraisal of adult intelligence." *Academic Medicine* 33, no. 9 (1958): 706.

Wright, R. G. "Intelligent autonomous ship navigation using multi-sensor modalities." *TransNav: International Journal on Marine Navigation and Safety of Sea Transportation* 13, no. 3 (2019).

Yoshioka, H., and Hashimoto, H. "AI-based collision avoidance for automatic ship navigation." *Proceedings of the 18th International Ship Stability Workshop* (2022).

Part 3

Artificial Intelligence, Equity, and Institutional Development in Higher Education: Global Perspectives

https://doi.org/10.1142/9781800616578_0009

Chapter 9

Generative AI: A Disruptive Game Changer in Higher Education

Olateju Jumoke Ajanaku* and Earlel Thiyagaratnam†

Western University, Canada

**oajanaku@uwo.ca*
†*ethiyaga@uwo.ca*

Abstract

Generative Artificial Intelligence (GenAI) is revolutionizing higher education by transforming instructional practices and enhancing learning outcomes. This study explores the integration of GenAI tools such as ChatGPT, Microsoft Copilot, and Meta AI, employing the Sociomateriality Theory to understand their implications for pedagogy, student engagement, and institutional practices. Through semi-structured interviews with these AI tools, the research investigates their capabilities, limitations, and potential to address challenges like bias, privacy, and academic integrity. Thematic analysis of the findings reveals six key themes: the role of GenAI in education, its impact on teaching and learning, student engagement, ethical considerations, institutional readiness, and future directions. Results indicate that GenAI tools support personalized learning, streamline administrative tasks, and foster critical thinking. However, they also present ethical challenges, including data privacy concerns, algorithmic biases, and risks to academic integrity. The study emphasizes the irreplaceable value of human-led, experiential learning, highlighting the need for a balanced integration of AI and traditional pedagogical methods. Recommendations include enhancing faculty training, developing ethical guidelines, and ensuring equitable access to AI technologies. This research contributes to the ongoing discourse on the transformative potential of GenAI in education, providing actionable insights for educators, policymakers, and technologists. By addressing the duality of GenAI as both an enabler and disruptor, the study advocates for responsible adoption to maximize benefits while safeguarding educational values.

Keywords: Generative Artificial Intelligence (GenAI), ChatGPT, Microsoft Copilot, Meta AI, higher education, teaching, learning, exploratory approach, student engagement, instructional practices.

9.1. Introduction

The integration of Generative Artificial Intelligence (GenAI) tools into higher education has garnered significant interest and sparked considerable debate in recent years. The rapid evolution of Artificial Intelligence (AI) technologies, particularly their ability to "accurately" mimic human behavior through advanced text categorization, has facilitated their widespread adoption in higher educational institutions (HEIs) worldwide. These technologies leverage sophisticated algorithms to perform tasks such as sentiment analysis, spam detection, language identification, and authorship attribution, enabling the creation of human-like text and documents (Jurafsky and Martin, 2024). Generative AI Tools such as ChatGPT, MetaAI, and Microsoft Copilot exemplify the transformative potential of GenAI, showcasing capabilities in automating administrative tasks, generating personalized learning content, and facilitating interactive educational experiences. These advancements underscore AI's potential to revolutionize teaching practices, enhance learning outcomes, and improve institutional efficiency (Chen *et al.*, 2020). However, the rapid adoption of these technologies raises important questions regarding their pedagogical, ethical, and institutional implications, necessitating a more nuanced exploration of their role in education.

The introduction of GenAI tools has significantly reshaped the learning environment of HEIs. ChatGPT (Chat Generative Pre-Trained Transformer), the first widely recognized GenAI model, was launched in November 2022 and quickly demonstrated its utility across various industries. Following its success, other iterations, such as Microsoft Copilot and MetaAI, were introduced in February 2023. These advanced large language models (LLMs) are designed to capture the sequential structure of language, evaluating grammar, word choice, idiomatic expressions, and contextual coherence to produce meaningful and human-like responses (Maniou, 2024). As these tools continue to evolve, they present both opportunities and challenges for higher education, requiring careful consideration of their integration and impact. Generative AI tools are not merely passive instruments, but active participants that co-constitute educational practices. This perspective aligns with the Sociomateriality Theory, which emphasizes the interconnectedness of human and material (technological) elements in shaping organizational practices and outcomes (Orlikowski, 2007). From this lens, technology is viewed as a dynamic actor that simultaneously shapes and is shaped by its social and institutional environment. Generative AI tools such as ChatGPT not only assist educators by automating repetitive tasks but also influence pedagogical practices by enabling personalized learning and adaptive feedback mechanisms. At the same time, their functionality is constrained by design, training data, and the contexts in which they are deployed, requiring critical human oversight (Leonardi, 2013).

While the transformative potential of GenAI is evident, its integration into education is fraught with challenges. Concerns about data privacy, algorithmic bias, and academic integrity have been widely discussed in the literature (Thelma *et al.*, 2024; Baker and Hawn, 2022). Additionally, there are questions about how these tools can be balanced with experiential and human-led learning processes, which remain central to education, particularly in fields that require hands-on skills and professional identity development (Salinas-Navarro *et al.*, 2024). The duality of GenAI as both a powerful enabler and a potential disruptor underscores the need for a nuanced understanding of its role in educational systems. This chapter adopts the Sociomateriality Theory as its theoretical framework to explore the integration of GenAI in higher education. By examining the interplay between human and technological elements, it seeks to illuminate the sociotechnical processes that underlie the use of AI tools in teaching and learning. Through this analysis, the chapter contributes to ongoing discourse on the future of AI in education, emphasizing the importance of ethical considerations, institutional readiness, and the preservation of experiential learning. This study examines the perspectives of ChatGPT, Microsoft Copilot, and MetaAI to develop a comprehensive understanding of GenAI about the integration of these tools in HEIs, as well as to inform educators, curriculum designers, and policymakers about the potential benefits and pitfalls of GenAI within academic contexts. The study adopts the Sociomateriality Theory to explore the integration of GenAI in higher education to enhance teaching, increase student engagement, and improve learning outcomes while addressing the ethical and practical challenges associated with its use. In doing so, we will address the following research questions:

1. How do GenAI tools perceive the impact of AI technologies on teaching and learning practices in HEIs?
2. How can AI technologies be optimized to support learning in HEIs?
3. What are the impacts of GenAI in HEIs on long-term student learning outcomes?
4. What are the potential challenges in mitigating dependencies that could impede critical thinking in HEIs?
5. What are the opportunities and barriers to the integration of GenAI in HEIs?

The rest of this chapter is structured as follows: Section 9.2 presents prior studies related to GenAI in education, providing a foundation for this study. Section 9.3 outlines the overall research design and approach employed. Section 9.4 presents the findings derived from the thematic analysis, while Section 9.5 interprets these findings in the context of existing literature and theoretical frameworks. Section 9.6 highlights the study's limitations and strengths of the study. Section 9.7 presents recommendations for future research. The chapter concludes with Section 9.8, which synthesizes key insights and outlines recommendations for future research and practice.

9.2. Background

9.2.1. *Generative AI in education*

The integration of GenAI into higher education has garnered significant academic and industry attention in recent years. Characterized by its ability to generate human-like text, images, and other media, GenAI has demonstrated significant potential to enhance educational outcomes (Zawacki-Richter *et al.*, 2019). Research highlights its ability to facilitate personalized learning, enable adaptive educational experiences, and automate routine tasks such as grading and content generation (Mathrani *et al.*, 2021). Additionally, these technologies support educators in creating tailored learning materials, fostering critical thinking, and improving problem-solving skills among students (Tegmark, 2022). However, these advancements also introduce ethical and technical challenges that require careful consideration.

The rapid evolution of AI technologies has led to the development of GenAI tools, which have transformed the learning environment in higher education institutions (HEIs) since their introduction in 2022. ChatGPT (Chat Generative Pre-Trained Transformer), the first major GenAI model, launched in November 2022, marked a milestone in AI-driven innovation. Its success in several industries prompted the introduction of subsequent iterations, such as Microsoft Copilot and MetaAI, in February 2023. These advanced large language models (LLMs) analyze the sequential structure of language, ensuring appropriate grammar, word choice, idiomatic expressions, and contextual relevance in their responses (Maniou, 2024). While these tools have proven valuable in supporting students' coursework development, they also introduce new challenges, such as determining whether submitted work reflects students' independent efforts.

Currently, the application of GenAI in HEIs is primarily centered on its use by students as personal tutors and by educators as resource generators (Ansari *et al.*, 2024). Students leverage GenAI for writing assistance, such as generating prewriting strategies, initial drafts, and layouts (Ansari *et al.*, 2024), as well as for adaptive and operationalized learning, which simplifies complex concepts and provides deeper insights into specific topics (Schei *et al.*, 2024). However, overreliance on GenAI to comprehend course materials may diminish students' perceived value of traditional HEI structures. For educators, GenAI assists in generating lesson plans, customizing learning materials, and creating assessments. Despite its advantages, the risk of GenAI producing unauthentic or inaccurate information remains a concern (Ansari *et al.*, 2024).

Key trends driving GenAI adoption in HEIs include its ability to enhance instructional practices, improve student engagement, and support learning outcomes. For students, GenAI provides tools to draft essay ideas, verify sources, and refine academic writing skills (Kasneci *et al.*, 2023). Engaging with GenAI can also foster critical thinking and reasoning, which are vital in higher education (Farrokhnia *et al.*, 2024). Additionally, by simplifying information to match students' linguistic and cognitive levels, GenAI promotes equitable access to education (Lim *et al.*, 2023). For educators, GenAI enables the creation of customized lesson plans that align with students' backgrounds and learning objectives (Rahman and Watanobe, 2023). It also supports the development of assessments that consider scope, design, difficulty, and desired outcomes, while ensuring assessments are resilient to potential misuse in online environments (Michel-Villarreal *et al.*, 2023).

The response of HEIs to GenAI use in coursework varies significantly, ranging from strict controls to guiding its ethical application (Michel-Villarreal *et al.*, 2023; University of Western Ontario, 2024). While studies have examined plagiarism, reliability, and the accuracy of GenAI outputs, distinguishing between AI-generated content and a student's original work remains a challenge due to GenAI's expansive word bank and complex algorithms (Lin *et al.*, 2024). The undetectable use of GenAI for assignments and exams without triggering anti-plagiarism software further amplifies these concerns (Zhai, 2022).

9.2.2. *Key generative AI tools in education*

Generative AI tools such as ChatGPT, Microsoft Copilot, and Meta AI represent significant milestones in the development of Artificial Intelligence, offering transformative opportunities in HEIs. These tools enhance learning, support administrative efficiency, and promote digital literacy. However, their integration into HEIs raises questions about dependency, algorithmic biases, and equitable access, necessitating a critical evaluation of their capabilities and implications for education.

OpenAI's ChatGPT, launched in 2018, is widely utilized in educational contexts for its versatile functionalities, including answering student queries, generating summaries, and drafting essays. Studies indicate that tools like ChatGPT can facilitate active learning and serve as virtual tutors, promoting engagement and curiosity among students (Brown *et al.*, 2022; Rasul *et al.*, 2023). Moreover, ChatGPT's ability to interpret text, gauge sentiment, and contextualize information allows it to tailor personalized feedback that aligns with students' writing styles, enhancing academic engagement (Chen *et al.*, 2023). However, concerns over privacy, algorithmic biases, and equitable access persist, as highlighted by Ayeni *et al.* (2024). These challenges underscore the need to ensure that

ChatGPT fosters a balanced learning environment without compromising critical thinking and originality.

Integrated into productivity tools, Microsoft Copilot extends the functionalities of Bing Chat to support both educational and administrative tasks. It automates routine activities such as drafting lesson plans, generating progress reports, and providing academic references in specific citation formats, allowing educators to allocate more time for student-focused activities (Smith and Vickers, 2024; Nikolic *et al.*, 2024). These features make Microsoft Copilot a valuable resource for HEIs, particularly in teaching and administrative contexts. Despite its strengths, concerns over the accuracy and reliability of GenAI outputs have been raised. Schei *et al.* (2024) warn that overreliance on such tools may impede creativity, discipline, and critical thinking among students. This study evaluates Microsoft Copilot's potential to enhance educational practices while identifying strategies to mitigate risks associated with its use.

Meta AI, initially introduced as Galactica, has gained recognition for its advanced research-oriented capabilities and focus on AI-driven personalization and engagement. It supports education through adaptive learning systems that cater to diverse learner profiles and enhances digital literacy by facilitating instructional practices (Cohen *et al.*, 2023; Oladokun *et al.*, 2024). Additionally, Meta AI's emphasis on explainable AI (XAI) promotes transparency and trust, positioning it as a leader in ethical AI applications.

However, overreliance on GenAI tools like Meta AI has raised concerns among students, who perceive excessive use as counterproductive to the learning process, potentially hindering critical thinking and meaningful engagement (Stöhr *et al.*, 2024). This research explores Meta AI's effectiveness in supporting instructional practices and fostering scientific literacy while addressing its potential to foster dependencies that detract from authentic learning experiences.

9.2.3. *Ethical concerns in AI adoption*

The integration of GenAI into HEIs presents transformative opportunities alongside significant ethical concerns. Among the most debated issues are biases in AI algorithms, data privacy vulnerabilities, and the potential for academic dishonesty (Binns, 2018). As highlighted by Slimi and

Carballido (2023), adopting GenAI in HEIs requires careful consideration of responsible deployment, development, transparency, and accountability. These principles are essential for understanding how GenAI operates, addressing inherent biases, and ensuring its ethical use in educational contexts (Al-Zahrani and Alasmari, 2024).

One critical challenge arises from biased algorithms, which can reinforce systemic inequalities, particularly in high-stakes applications such as admissions or grading processes. Such biases disproportionately affect marginalized groups, underscoring the need for vigilant oversight and mitigation strategies (Slimi and Carballido, 2023; Noble, 2018). Additionally, concerns over data privacy are paramount, as GenAI tools often require access to sensitive student data to function effectively. Without robust data protection frameworks, the potential for misuse and data breaches becomes a significant risk (Floridi *et al.*, 2020). Furthermore, the use of GenAI tools like ChatGPT for plagiarism has raised apprehensions about academic integrity, as students may exploit these technologies to bypass original thought and create work undetectable by current anti-plagiarism software (Cox *et al.*, 2022).

The broader challenges associated with adopting GenAI in HEIs are often framed within the lens of fairness, accountability, transparency, and ethics (FATE) (Woolf, 2022). Fairness requires that GenAI tools mitigate biases in their algorithms to ensure equitable decision-making. However, questions about the reliability and accuracy of GenAI outputs persist, particularly when these tools rely on biased or incomplete training data (Islam *et al.*, 2022; Michel-Villarreal *et al.*, 2023). Accountability is another significant concern, as the decisions and outputs generated by GenAI should be accompanied by evidence and explanations. Without such clarity, assigning responsibility for errors or biases becomes problematic, undermining trust in these technologies (Shin *et al.*, 2022). Transparency is equally critical in GenAI adoption. ChatGPT's training data, which ceased in 2021, raises questions about its ability to provide current and accurate information, potentially resulting in the dissemination of outdated or incorrect knowledge (Lo, 2023). Transparency also extends to the need for GenAI tools to clarify their processes, motives, and policies to users, ensuring that their outputs can be critically evaluated for reliability and authenticity (Kong *et al.*, 2023). Ethical considerations, therefore, must encompass these dimensions, along with safeguards to protect against data misuse and academic dishonesty.

Addressing these challenges requires a balanced, multifaceted approach. Robust regulatory frameworks are essential to ensure that GenAI tools are deployed ethically and transparently within HEIs. This includes implementing measures to mitigate bias, secure data privacy, and uphold academic integrity. Efforts must also focus on enhancing digital literacy among educators and students, empowering them to engage critically with GenAI tools and understand their limitations. By prioritizing fairness, accountability, transparency, and ethics, HEIs can harness the potential of GenAI to enrich educational practices while safeguarding against its unintended consequences. Such a thoughtful integration ensures that GenAI serves as a complement to, rather than a replacement for, the essential human elements of teaching and learning.

9.3. Materials and Methods

9.3.1. *Theoretical framework*

This study adopts the Sociomateriality Theory as its theoretical framework to examine the integration of GenAI in higher education and to examine its implications for teaching practices and learning outcomes. Sociomateriality emphasizes the interdependence of human and material (technological) elements in shaping organizational practices and outcomes (Orlikowski, 2007). Through this lens, technology is not seen merely as a passive tool but as an active participant that co-constitutes educational practices and structure alongside human action (Leonardi, 2013). In this context, ChatGPT should not be conceptualized solely as an "object" engineered, trained, and deployed by humans. Rather, it should be understood as a subject that co-performs daily practices alongside users, thereby shaping and being shaped by the sociomaterial networks in which it is embedded (Michel-Villarreal *et al.*, 2023).

Applying this perspective allows for an investigation of how GenAI tools like ChatGPT, Microsoft Copilot, and Meta AI are embedded in educational contexts, how they reconfigure teaching and learning processes, and the mutual shaping of human (educators, students) and technological (AI tools) elements. By examining both the integration of GenAI and its broader implications, this framework situates the study within the dynamic interactions between AI technologies and the pedagogical, cultural, and ethical dimensions of higher education. This approach provides insight into how these influence instructional strategies, reshape the learning experience, and challenge existing educational norms and practices.

9.3.2. *Research approach*

This study adopted an exploratory semi-structured interview approach to allow the tools to unveil the richness of their responses (Ruslin *et al.*, 2022). The exploratory nature is particularly suited to understanding complex, dynamic interactions between AI tools and educational practices, as this approach allows for a flexible investigation The process of interviewing GenAI tools was threefold (Chang *et al.*, 2017): (i) data collection, (ii) data organization, and (iii) data analysis and interpretation. During the data collection phase, GenAI tools were interviewed on a one-to-one basis using a set of questions and themes to capture insights from the perspective of the entity.

An interview guide was prepared beforehand, addressing themes, such as capabilities and functionality, instructional practices, student engagement and learning outcomes, and ethical considerations, which aligned with the study's research questions to provide transparency and reliability to the interviewing process (see Appendix A). Probes were included as part of a non-standardized semi-structured interviewing process to ensure flexibility in interactions with the GenAI tools and to enable further exploration of significant responses relevant to the research topic (Saunders *et al.*, 2016).

By employing Sociomateriality Theory as the guiding framework, this study focuses exclusively on exploring GenAI tools as sociomaterial agents that interact with human actors in higher education. This approach offers a unique perspective on the transformative and disruptive potential of GenAI, emphasizing its material presence, agency, and sociocultural embeddedness in educational practices.

9.3.3. *Participants and context*

The participants are the GenAI tools ChatGPT, Meta AI, and Microsoft Copilot. Each of these AI tools represents a unique perspective, offering insights into their role in educational settings. The data were collected through simulated interviews with ChatGPT, Meta AI, and Microsoft Copilot. These interviews were designed to reflect in-depth conversations, allowing the AI tools to demonstrate their functionality, answer scenario-based questions, and articulate their roles and limitations within the educational landscape.

9.3.4. *Data analysis*

The responses from the AI participants were analyzed using thematic analysis to identify recurring patterns and themes across the datasets. The analysis followed an iterative six-step process as outlined by Braun and Clarke (2006). First, researchers immersed themselves in the data by thoroughly reviewing the interview responses, enabling familiarity and uncovering deeper insights. Key elements within the data were identified and codes were created that captured the broader meaning of the responses, rather than focusing on single words or phrases. The coding process involved the detailed examination of the data and initial observations. The codes were then organized into potential themes that reflected the key patterns and related to the research questions. The themes were reviewed for coherence and relevance, with refinements made as necessary. Once the themes were finalized, they were clearly defined and named to reflect their conceptual meanings. This collaborative approach facilitated the identification and refinement of themes, offering a comprehensive understanding of the data.

9.4. Results

Questions addressing the fundamental concepts underlying this study were presented to the three selected GenAI tools — ChatGPT, MetaAI, and Microsoft Copilot — to evaluate their understanding of the topic. The thematic analysis revealed six themes influencing the integration of GenAI tools in higher education and their implications for instructional practices and student engagement. The heatmap in Figure 9.1 illustrates the co-occurrence frequencies of key themes across three AI educational tools — ChatGPT, MetaAI, and Microsoft Copilot — highlighting their respective emphases on the core domains of AI integration in education. The themes analyzed include the role and capabilities of AI, the impact on instructional practices and learning outcomes, student engagement, ethical considerations, institutional preparedness, and future directions. Frequencies indicate how often each tool addresses specific themes, with

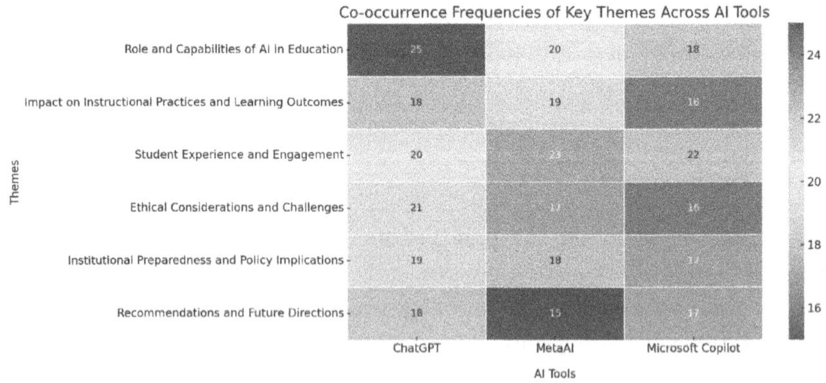

Figure 9.1. Heatmap illustrating the co-occurrence frequencies across key themes across AI tools.

Source: The heatmap shown in Figure 9.1 was generated using Python 3.9, executed in Google Colaboratory.

MetaAI showing a stronger focus on "Student Experience and Engagement" (23) and "Impact on Instructional Practices and Learning Outcomes" (19), while ChatGPT demonstrates balanced attention across all themes, particularly excelling in "Role and Capabilities of AI in Education" (25). Microsoft Copilot emphasizes "Student Experience and Engagement" (22) and "Recommendations and Future Directions" (17), but is comparatively less focused on "Ethical Considerations and Challenges" (16). The results underscore the tools' varying priorities and specializations, which could guide educators and institutions in selecting appropriate AI solutions tailored to specific educational objectives. These themes are discussed in the sub-sections.

9.4.1. *Role and capabilities of Generative Artificial Intelligence in education*

ChatGPT, MetaAI, and Microsoft Copilot, serving as participants, emphasized their potential to enhance education by supporting content creation, offering instructional assistance, and enabling personalized learning experiences. According to ChatGPT, "Generative AI can produce quizzes, simulations, and lesson summaries that are adaptive to individual student needs." MetaAI echoed this, highlighting the ability to create interactive videos and games that enhance student engagement. Similarly, Microsoft

Copilot stated, "AI assists educators by automating grading and providing real-time feedback, enabling them to focus on mentorship."

Participants expressed diverse perspectives on the transformative potential of GenAI tools in higher education, emphasizing their unique strengths and limitations. ChatGPT highlighted its ability to generate high-quality, context-specific educational content, with ChatGPT stating, "The encoder-decoder architecture allows me to process and generate outputs tailored to diverse educational needs." ChatGPT further acknowledged its reliance on preexisting data, which might not fully replicate the dynamic nature of life and experiential learning environments.

MetaAI emphasized its capacity to enhance engagement and foster personalization in learning. MetaAI shared, "I create adaptive assessments and personalized learning pathways, helping educators address individual student needs." It also highlighted its inclusive design, stating, "My assistive features, like speech-to-text and language translation, ensure accessibility for learners with diverse backgrounds." Nonetheless, MetaAI recognized that its interactive simulations, while effective, cannot entirely substitute direct, hands-on learning experiences.

Microsoft Copilot focused on efficiency and support for educators. Microsoft Copilot noted, "I excel in automating repetitive tasks like grading and generating lecture notes, freeing educators to concentrate on mentorship." Additionally, it pointed out its role in providing 24/7 assistance through virtual teaching tools, stating, "I'm available anytime to answer student queries and support learning." Despite this support, the tool acknowledged potential challenges in fostering deep conceptual understanding without supplementary human interaction.

Largely, the participants illustrated the complementary strengths of GenAI tools in advancing teaching, learning, and accessibility. While each tool offers significant benefits, they collectively recognize the irreplaceable value of experiential and interactive human-led learning processes in education.

9.4.2. *Impact on instructional practices and learning outcomes*

Generative AI tools were seen as transformative for pedagogy and outcomes. ChatGPT noted, "AI can help educators transition from traditional lectures to more personalized, inquiry-based approaches." MetaAI observed, "Adaptive learning pathways enable students to learn at their own pace, leading to improved retention and understanding." Microsoft Copilot added, "Generative AI provides evidence-based feedback to both students and educators, facilitating targeted interventions."

Furthermore, participants discussed the transformative effects of GenAI on teaching practices and learning outcomes, emphasizing innovation, personalization, and efficiency. ChatGPT highlighted its role in redesigning pedagogical methods, with ChatGPT stating, "I empower educators to transition from traditional lectures to more inquiry-based, student-centered learning approaches." It also stressed its ability to identify gaps in instructional content and suggest targeted improvements. However, ChatGPT recognized the need for educators to critically evaluate AI-generated recommendations to ensure alignment with specific learning objectives.

MetaAI emphasized the importance of improving learning outcomes through adaptive technologies. MetaAI noted, "My real-time analytics and adaptive pathways ensure that students learn at their own pace, enhancing retention and academic performance." It also highlighted its ability to provide immediate feedback and insights, which are critical for targeted interventions. Moreover, MetaAI acknowledged that the effective implementation of adaptive learning systems might require robust training for educators to fully leverage their capabilities. Microsoft Copilot underscored its contribution to efficiency in teaching. Microsoft Copilot stated, "I automate grading and provide instant, detailed feedback, enabling educators to focus on student engagement and support." It also underscored its role in fostering deeper understanding through immersive strategies like gamified exercises. Despite these strengths, Microsoft Copilot acknowledged, "My automated tools require human oversight to contextualize insights and ensure alignment with broader learning goals."

The participants agreed that GenAI significantly enhances instructional practices and learning outcomes by introducing adaptive, efficient, and innovative approaches. However, they emphasized the importance of human oversight to ensure pedagogical integrity.

9.4.3. *Student experience and engagement*

Generative AI enhances the student experience by fostering engagement and collaboration. As ChatGPT remarked, "Interactive simulations and gamified learning keep students motivated." MetaAI pointed out,

"AI tools support collaborative learning by mediating discussions and generating ideas for group projects." Microsoft Copilot noted, "Students benefit from instant feedback and personalized content, which aligns with their learning pace and style."

Participants explored how GenAI enhances student engagement and personalizes the learning experience. ChatGPT highlighted its ability to foster motivation through interactive simulations. ChatGPT stated, "I create gamified tools and immersive environments that make learning more engaging and enjoyable." It also emphasized its role in providing instant access to resources, although it cautioned that overreliance on AI might diminish critical thinking skills.

MetaAI emphasized its capacity to support collaborative learning. MetaAI noted, "I facilitate group projects and brainstorming by organizing discussion forums and suggesting ideas." It also pointed to its inclusivity, stating, "My translation and accessibility features help ensure equity among students from diverse backgrounds." MetaAI further acknowledged that virtual interactions cannot fully replicate the richness of face-to-face collaboration.

Microsoft Copilot underscored its role in delivering personalized feedback, stating, "I adapt to individual learning paces and preferences, ensuring that students remain motivated and engaged." It also pointed to its ability to provide real-time assistance through virtual teaching assistants, noting, "I help students stay on track and address challenges promptly." It admitted, "Sustained engagement requires educators to integrate AI tools thoughtfully into broader learning strategies."

Participants generally agreed that GenAI enriches student experiences by fostering motivation, collaboration, and personalized learning. Nevertheless, they emphasized that meaningful human interaction remains critical for sustaining deep engagement.

9.4.4. *Ethical considerations and challenges*

Participants identified ethical concerns in the utilization of generative AI in education, including privacy, bias, and academic integrity. ChatGPT emphasized the importance of safeguarding student data, stating, "Data privacy and fairness are critical, requiring robust frameworks to avoid biases. Ensuring compliance with privacy regulations is critical to maintaining trust." It also acknowledged the challenge of transparency, noting,

"Users need to understand how my decisions are made to ensure accountability."

MetaAI stated, "AI must ensure transparency to gain stakeholder trust." Microsoft Copilot added, "Safeguarding academic integrity is essential, as over-reliance on AI for tasks like essay writing could undermine authenticity." MetaAI underscored its commitment to bias and fairness. MetaAI stated, "I employ diverse training datasets to promote equitable treatment of all user groups but biases in source data remain a challenge." It also emphasized the need for regular audits, remarking, "Continuous monitoring and improvements are essential to mitigate algorithmic biases." Additionally, MetaAI discussed academic integrity, noting, "Educators need to address potential misuse of my capabilities, such as generating plagiarized content."

Microsoft Copilot emphasized transparency and governance. Microsoft Copilot noted, "Institutions must establish ethical frameworks and explainability protocols to build trust in AI systems." It also pointed to challenges in cultivating academic honesty, stating, "I support tools for AI-generated content detection, but promoting responsible usage among students is vital."

The three participants stressed the importance of ethical guidelines, transparency, and continuous monitoring to address the challenges associated with AI in education. They emphasized that proactive measures are necessary to ensure fair, responsible, and trustworthy AI usage.

9.4.5. *Institutional preparedness and policy implications*

Participants identified barriers and enablers for the successful integration of generative AI in educational institutions. ChatGPT highlighted the need for training and infrastructure, with ChatGPT stating, "Educators require professional development to effectively utilize my tools and evaluate AI-generated content critically." It also emphasized the importance of institutional investment, noting that "robust infrastructure and technical support are essential for sustainable integration." According to ChatGPT, achieving sustainable AI integration ultimately depends on collaboration among educators, policymakers, and technologists.

MetaAI examined resistance to change. noting that "skepticism about AI's efficacy and fears of job displacement hinder adoption." It further emphasized the importance of clear institutional policies, stating, "Institutions must establish guidelines on ethical AI use and data privacy to build stakeholder confidence." Microsoft Copilot underscored the importance of collaboration and strategic planning. It stated, "Effective AI integration requires partnerships among educators, policymakers, and technologists." It also noted that "change management initiatives can help address resistance and promote acceptance of AI tools."

Participants underscored the necessity of institutional preparedness, highlighting the need for investment in training, infrastructure, and policy frameworks. They further identified collaborative approaches and strategic planning as critical enablers for overcoming adoption barriers.

9.4.6. *Recommendations and future directions*

Participants proposed several recommendations aimed at advancing their integration within educational settings. ChatGPT emphasized the importance of continual research and evaluation to guide iterative improvements. It further stated, "Educators, technologists, and policymakers must work together to ensure AI tools align with educational goals." Furthermore, it underscored the value of "continuous assessment of AI's impact" to support informed decision-making. MetaAI focused on designing AI systems to be adaptable and inclusive across diverse contexts. It stated, "AI should complement not replace, human educators," emphasizing a balanced integration of technology in educational settings. Microsoft Copilot added that future progress should prioritize accessibility and scalability, thereby ensuring the long-term success of AI-driven initiatives. Microsoft Copilot further added, "Preparing students and educators with AI literacy ensures informed and responsible use."

Collectively, the participants underscored that future innovation should explore the integration of GenAI with immersive technologies like virtual reality (VR) and augmented reality (AR) to deepen student engagement and create experiential learning opportunities. Multimodal AI systems that incorporate text, audio, and visual data hold the potential to further enrich learning experiences and enhance personalization. They agreed that continuous innovation and systematic evaluation are paramount for ensuring the sustained effectiveness and ethical deployment of these tools.

9.5. Discussion

This study represents an exploration into the use of GenAI tools in higher education, examining their potential, challenges, and implications for teaching, learning, and institutional readiness. The findings suggest that while GenAI tools such as ChatGPT, MetaAI, and Microsoft Copilot provide innovative opportunities to enhance education, their limitations underscore the irreplaceable value of experiential, human-led learning processes. This viewpoint aligns with Kolb and Kolb's (2009) experiential learning theory, which emphasizes the role of hands-on experiences in developing professional identity.

The findings of this study indicate that GenAI tools offer unique capabilities for content creation, instructional support, and personalized learning. These tools excel in automating repetitive tasks, such as grading and generating lecture notes, as well as providing immediate feedback to students. This supports previous studies such as that by Rasid *et al.*, 2024, who reported that in higher education, GenAI models such as ChatGPT have gained recognition for their capacity to support research, facilitate assignment completion, and cultivate critical thinking and problem-solving skills. These models strengthen students' research capabilities by offering comprehensive information and relevant sources on targeted topics. Additionally, they enable the creation of summaries, structured outlines, and preliminary drafts of research projects. By helping students grasp pivotal concepts and streamline the writing process, these tools further contribute to enhanced academic performance. Furthermore, large language models (LLMs) can identify unexplored areas and current research trends, thereby deepening students' subject matter knowledge and promoting more robust analytical inquiry (Kasneci *et al.*, 2023).

However, as highlighted by MetaAI, the personalization provided by AI cannot fully replicate the depth of experiential learning. This limitation reflects the findings of Burton *et al.* (2024), who noted that while AI enhances accessibility and efficiency, it must complement rather than replace experiential learning to support holistic student development. Generative AI has the potential to revolutionize pedagogical approaches by shifting the focus from traditional lecture methods to more student-centered and adaptive learning strategies. ChatGPT and MetaAI emphasized their role in identifying content gaps and tailoring instruction to individual student needs. These capabilities align with previous studies, such as those by Ali *et al.* (2024) and Chan and Hu (2023), which demonstrated that adaptive learning technologies improve academic performance and engagement. Furthermore, Microsoft Copilot highlighted that AI tools require human oversight to contextualize insights and align them with pedagogical goals. This finding supports the argument by McKnight *et al.* (2016) that educators must play an active role in guiding technology-enhanced learning to achieve meaningful outcomes.

The recommendations by the GenAI tools focus on integrating AI into higher education for personalized learning. Emphasis is placed on developing AI tools tailored to individual learning styles, ensuring ethical use and governance of data, and adapting teaching methods to incorporate AI-driven changes. Continuous professional development for educators in AI technologies is recommended to keep pace with technological advancements. Additionally, maintaining a balance between AI and human elements in education is crucial to preserve the essence of traditional learning while leveraging the benefits of AI. GenAI fosters student engagement through gamified tools, immersive simulations, and personalized learning pathways. These approaches align with studies by Huang *et al.* (2020), which found that interactive and gamified environments significantly enhance student motivation and participation. However, participants of this study (ChatGPT, MetaAI, and Microsoft Copilot) cautioned against overreliance on AI tools, which could undermine critical thinking and problem-solving skills. This concern echoes the findings of Selwyn (2019), who highlighted the risks of dependency on technology in educational settings, emphasizing the need for a balanced integration of AI to preserve active and reflective learning processes.

The ethical implications of using GenAI in education emerged as a critical concern. Issues such as data privacy, algorithmic bias, and academic integrity were identified by participants as significant challenges. For instance, ChatGPT, MetaAI, and Microsoft Copilot emphasized the importance of safeguarding student data and ethical use of AI, which aligns with studies by Williams *et al.* (2024), who pointed out that the ethical landscape of AI in education contains complexities that demand continual attention and evaluation, integrating Gen AI requires a careful balance between harnessing is advantages and mitigating its potential drawbacks. Furthermore, addressing algorithmic bias (Grassini, 2023; Grover, 2024) and ensuring equitable access to AI tools are essential steps for mitigating the risks of perpetuating systemic inequities (Binns, 2018; Nyaaba *et al.*, 2024). Participants also noted the challenge of maintaining academic integrity, which resonates with the findings of Perkins (2023) and Moya *et al.* (2023) on the potential misuse of AI for plagiarism and academic dishonesty.

Institutional readiness to adopt GenAI depends on investment in infrastructure, training, and policy development. Participants highlighted the need for professional development programs to equip educators with the skills to evaluate and integrate AI tools effectively. This finding aligns with Mishra and Koehler's (2006) Technological Pedagogical Content Knowledge (TPACK) framework, which emphasizes the importance of educators' technological competence in leveraging digital tools for teaching. Additionally, the need for clear guidelines and ethical frameworks was emphasized, reflecting the recommendations by Prinsloo and Slade (2020) for responsible adoption of AI in education.

The interconnectedness of the themes underscores the multifaceted role of GenAI in higher education. While AI tools contribute significantly to efficiency, personalization, and engagement, their integration requires careful consideration of ethical, pedagogical, and institutional factors. The experiential learning theory of Kolb and Kolb (2005) provides a unifying lens for understanding these findings, highlighting the importance of balancing AI-driven innovation with hands-on, reflective learning experiences. This balance is crucial for fostering professional identity development and ensuring that AI serves as a supportive, rather than a substitutive, element in education.

By emphasizing rigorous evaluation, collaborative frameworks, and innovative practices, the recommendations provided by the participants aim to maximize the potential of Gen AI while preserving human-centered educational values. Transparent and ethical practices will be essential to ensuring equitable, inclusive, and effective AI-driven solutions for the future of education.

9.6. Limitations and Strengths of the Study

This study acknowledges several limitations. First, its reliance on generative AI (GenAI) tools such as ChatGPT, MetaAI, and Microsoft Copilot as participants poses a unique challenge. While these tools provide valuable insights into their functionalities and limitations, their responses are inherently constrained by the training data they were built upon and may not fully capture the lived experiences or nuanced perspectives of human educators and learners. This limitation affects the generalizability of findings across diverse educational contexts. Additionally, the study focuses primarily on the functionalities, ethical considerations, and institutional preparedness related to GenAI, without exploring other aspects, such as the technical and operational challenges of integrating AI into existing learning management systems or the economic implications of widespread adoption. Methodologically, the study relied on qualitative insights from the selected AI tools, introducing potential bias, as the responses reflect programming and dataset exposure rather than experiential knowledge. Lastly, its short-term and exploratory nature limits the ability to assess the longitudinal impacts of GenAI on student outcomes, educator practices, and institutional strategies, highlighting the need for future research with broader and more empirical approaches.

Despite these limitations, the study has notable strengths. It represents a pioneering exploration of GenAI's potential and challenges in higher education, offering a comprehensive analysis of its capabilities and limitations. By incorporating AI tools as participants, the study provides accessible insights into their functionalities and highlights their applicability across various educational contexts. The study's thematic organization addresses critical dimensions such as instructional impacts, student engagement, ethical considerations, and institutional readiness, synthesizing these findings within established theories like Kolb and Kolb's (2005) experiential learning framework. The focus on ethical considerations, including data privacy, algorithm bias, and academic integrity, aligns with calls for greater accountability and transparency in educational technology (Shankar *et al.*, 2024; Dawson, 2021). Furthermore, the study adopts a forward-looking perspective by offering actionable recommendations and emphasizing interdisciplinary collaboration, ongoing evaluation, and the integration of AI with human-led teaching. This balanced approach ensures its relevance to the evolving educational landscape.

9.7. Recommendations for Future Research

Future research should explore the long-term impacts of GenAI on teaching, learning, and institutional practices through longitudinal studies. Particular attention should be paid to how these tools can support experiential learning and professional skill development. Investigating complementary technologies, such as virtual and augmented reality, could further enhance the immersive potential of AI in education. By adopting a thoughtful and measured approach, higher education institutions can leverage GenAI to advance teaching, learning, and equity while preserving the indispensable value of human interaction and experiential learning.

9.8. Conclusion

This study highlights the duality of GenAI in higher education, demonstrating both its potential to revolutionize teaching and learning and the ethical and practical challenges it poses. AI tools such as ChatGPT, MetaAI, and Microsoft Copilot can streamline administrative tasks, personalize learning experiences, and expand accessibility. Yet, their capacity to stimulate understanding and foster collaboration should not overshadow the irreplaceable value of direct human-led, experiential processes. Data privacy, algorithmic bias, and academic integrity remain significant concerns, necessitating robust institutional governance, transparent oversight, and a commitment to ethical stewardship (Shankar *et al.*, 2024; Binns, 2018). From the perspective of Sociomateriality Theory, GenAI tools simultaneously shape and are shaped by institutional norms, pedagogical practices, and learner interactions. While ChatGPT and related technologies actively transform the teaching-learning experience, their outputs are also bound by their design parameters, training data, and real-world deployment contexts. Therefore, effective integration requires a multifaceted approach that includes investments in infrastructure, ongoing faculty development, and interdisciplinary collaboration among educators, technologists, policymakers, and ethicists. This holistic strategy will ensure that AI tools complement, rather than replace, the experiential learning and professional identity development so integral to higher education.

Looking ahead, GenAI's transformative potential can only be fully realized through a sustained commitment to transparency, accountability, and alignment with pedagogical goals. By embedding ethical considerations within institutional structures and maintaining the primacy of human-led, experiential learning, higher education can responsibly leverage AI innovations. The findings of this study thus underscore the need for strategic, well-governed use of AI and offer a roadmap for future endeavors that uphold both academic integrity and equitable access, ensuring that GenAI augments rather than diminishes the core values of higher education.

Bibliography

Al-Zahrani, A. M. and Alasmari, T. M. "Exploring the impact of artificial intelligence on higher education: The dynamics of ethical, social, and educational implications." *Humanities & Social Sciences Communications* 11, no. 1 (2024): 912. DOI: 10.1057/s41599-024-03432-4.

Ali, N., Ullah, S., Khan, D., Rahman, H., and Alam, A. "The effect of adaptive aids on different levels of students' performance in a virtual reality chemistry laboratory." *Education and Information Technologies* 29, no. 3 (2024): 3113–3132. DOI: 10.1007/s10639-023-11897-0.

Ansari, A. N., Ahmad, S., and Bhutta, S. M. "Mapping the global evidence around the use of ChatGPT in higher education: A systematic scoping review." *Education and Information Technologies* 29, no. 9 (2024): 11281–11321. DOI: 10.1007/s10639-023-12223-4.

Ayeni, O. O., Al Hamad, N. M., Chisom, O. N., Osawaru, B., and Adewusi, O. E. "AI in education: A review of personalized learning and educational technology." *GSC Advanced Research and Reviews* 18, no. 2 (2024): 261–271. DOI: 10.30574/gscarr.2024.18.2.0062.

Baker, R. S. and Hawn, A. "Algorithmic bias in education." *International Journal of Artificial Intelligence in Education* 32, no. 4 (2022): 1052–1092. DOI: 10.1007/s40593-021-00285-9.

Binns, R. "Algorithmic accountability and public reason." *Philosophy & Technology* 31, no. 4 (2018): 543–556. DOI: 10.1007/s13347-017-0263-5.

Braun, V. and Clarke, V. "Using thematic analysis in psychology." *Qualitative Research in Psychology* 3, no. 2 (2006): 77–101. DOI: 10.1191/1478088706qp063oa.

Brown, A., Lawrence, J., Basson, M., and Redmond, P. "A conceptual framework to enhance student online learning and engagement in higher education." *Higher Education Research and Development* 41, no. 2 (2022): 284–299. DOI: 10.1080/07294360.2020.1860912.

Burton, J. W., Lopez-Lopez, E., Hechtlinger, S., Rahwan, Z., Aeschbach, S., Bakker, M. A., Becker, J. A., Berditchevskaia, A., Berger, J., Brinkmann, L., Flek, L., Herzog, S. M., Huang, S., Kapoor, S., Narayanan, A., Nussberger, A.-M., Yasseri, T., Nickl, P., Almaatouq, A., *et al.* "How large language models can reshape collective intelligence." *Nature Human Behaviour* 8, no. 9 (2024): 1643–1655. DOI: 10.1038/s41562-024-01959-9.

Chan, C. K. Y. and Hu, W. "Students' voices on generative AI: Perceptions, benefits, and challenges in higher education." *International Journal of Educational Technology in Higher Education* 20, no. 1 (2023): 43–18. DOI: 10.1186/s41239-023-00411-8.

Chang, W. W., Giaccardi, E., Chen, L. L., and Liang, R. H. "'Interview with things:' A first-thing perspective to understand the scooter's everyday socio-material network in Taiwan." *DIS 2017 — Proceedings of the 2017 ACM Conference on Designing Interactive Systems* (2017): 1001–1012. DOI: 10.1145/3064663.3064717.

Chen, L., Chen, P., and Lin, Z. "Artificial intelligence in education: A review." *IEEE Access* 8 (2020): 75264–75278. DOI: 10.1109/ACCESS.2020.2988510.

Chen, Y., Jensen, S., Albert, L. J., Gupta, S., and Lee, T. "Artificial intelligence (AI) student assistants in the classroom: Designing chatbots to support student success." *Information Systems Frontiers* 25, no. 1 (2023): 161–182. DOI: 10.1007/s10796-022-10291-4.

Cohen, R., Xing, A., Chen, H., Sahu, G., and Sreenivas, N. K. "Online delivery of discussion-oriented postsecondary classes during critical health scenarios, educating responsible computer scientists towards improved societal trust in artificial intelligence." *Creative Education* 14, no. 4 (2023): 766–787. DOI: 10.4236/ce.2023.144051.

Cox, A. "The ethics of AI for information professionals: Eight scenarios." *Journal of the Australian Library and Information Association* 71, no. 3 (2022): 201–214. DOI: 10.1080/24750158.2022.2084885.

Dawson, P. *Defending Assessment Security in a Digital World: Preventing E-Cheating and Supporting Academic Integrity in Higher Education.* 1st ed. Routledge, 2021. DOI: 10.4324/9780429324178.

Farrokhnia, M., Banihashem, S. K., Noroozi, O., and Wals, A. "A SWOT analysis of ChatGPT: Implications for educational practice and research." *Innovations in Education and Teaching International* 61, no. 3 (2024): 460–474. DOI: 10.1080/14703297.2023.2195846.

Floridi, L., Cowls, J., King, T. C., and Taddeo, M. "How to design AI for social good: Seven essential factors." *Science and Engineering Ethics* 26, no. 3 (2020): 1771–1796. DOI: 10.1007/s11948-020-00213-5.

Grassini, S. "Shaping the future of education: Exploring the potential and consequences of AI and ChatGPT in educational settings." *Education Sciences* 13, no. 7 (2023): 692–. DOI: 10.3390/educsci13070692.

Grover, D. "Next-Generation Education: The Impact of Generative AI on Learning." *Journal of Informatics Education and Research* 4, no. 2 (2024): 2009–2014. DOI: 10.52783/jier.v4i2.1019.

Huang, R., Ritzhaupt, A. D., Sommer, M., Zhu, J., Stephen, A., Valle, N., Hampton, J., and Li, J. "The impact of gamification in educational settings on student learning outcomes: A meta-analysis." *Educational Technology Research and Development* 68, no. 4 (2020): 1875–1901. DOI: 10.1007/s11423-020-09807-z.

Islam, S. R., Russell, I., Eberle, W., and Dicheva, D. "Incorporating the concepts of fairness and bias into an undergraduate computer science course to promote fair automated decision systems." *Proceedings of the 53rd ACM Technical Symposium on Computer Science Education V. 2* (2022): 1075–1075. DOI: 10.1145/3478432.3499043.

Kasneci, E., Sessler, K., Küchemann, S., Bannert, M., Dementieva, D., Fischer, F., Gasser, U., Groh, G., Günnemann, S., Hüllermeier, E., Krusche, S., Kutyniok, G., Michaeli, T., Nerdel, C., Pfeffer, J., Poquet, O., Sailer, M., Schmidt, A., Seidel, T., *et al.* "ChatGPT for good? On opportunities and challenges of large language models for education." *Learning and Individual Differences* 103 (2023): 102274–. DOI: 10.1016/j.lindif.2023.102274.

Kolb, S. E., Fermanich, K. J., and Dornbush, M. E. "Effect of charcoal quantity on microbial biomass and activity in temperate soils." *Soil Science Society of America Journal* 73, no. 4 (2009): 1173–1181. DOI: 10.2136/sssaj2008.0232.

Kolb, A. Y. and Kolb, D. A. "Learning styles and learning spaces: Enhancing experiential learning in higher education." *Academy of Management Learning & Education* 4, no. 2 (2005): 193–212. DOI: 10.5465/AMLE.2005.17268566.

Kong, S.-C., Cheung, W. M.-Y., and Zhang, G. "Evaluating an artificial intelligence literacy programme for developing university students' conceptual understanding, literacy, empowerment and ethical awareness." *Educational Technology & Society* 26, no. 1 (2023): 16–30. DOI: 10.30191/ETS.202301_26(1).0002.

Leonardi, P. M. "Theoretical foundations for the study of sociomateriality." *Information and Organization* 23, no. 2 (2013): 59–76. DOI: 10.1016/j.infoandorg.2013.02.002.

Lim, W. M., Gunasekara, A., Pallant, J. L., Pallant, J. I., and Pechenkina, E. "Generative AI and the future of education: Ragnarök or reformation? A paradoxical perspective from management educators." *The International Journal of Management Education* 21, no. 2 (2023): 100790–. DOI: 10.1016/j.ijme.2023.100790.

Lin, M. P.-C., Liu, A. L., Poitras, E., Chang, M., and Chang, D. H. "An exploratory study on the efficacy and inclusivity of AI technologies in diverse learning environments." *Sustainability* 16, no. 20 (2024): 8992–. DOI: 10.3390/su16208992.

Lo, C. K. "What is the impact of ChatGPT on education? A rapid review of the literature." *Education Sciences* 13, no. 4 (2023): 410–. DOI: 10.3390/educsci13040410.

Mathrani, A., Susnjak, T., Ramaswami, G., and Barczak, A. "Perspectives on the challenges of generalizability, transparency, and ethics in predictive learning analytics." *Computers and Education Open* 2 (2021): 100060. DOI: 10.1016/j.caeo.2021.100060.

McKnight, K., O'Malley, K., Ruzic, R., Horsley, M. K., Franey, J. J., and Bassett, K. "Teaching in a digital age: How educators use technology to improve student learning." *Journal of Research on Technology in Education* 48, no. 3 (2016): 194–211. DOI: 10.1080/15391523.2016.1175856.

Michel-Villarreal, R., Vilalta-Perdomo, E., Salinas-Navarro, D. E., Thierry-Aguilera, R., and Gerardou, F. S. "Challenges and opportunities of generative AI for higher education as explained by ChatGPT." *Education Sciences* 13, no. 9 (2023): 856–. DOI: 10.3390/educsci13090856.

Mishra, P. and Koehler, M. J. "Technological pedagogical content knowledge: A framework for teacher knowledge." *Teachers College Record (1970)* 108, no. 6 (2006): 1017–1054. DOI: 10.1177/016146810610800610.

Moya, B., Eaton, S. E., Pethrick, H., Brennan, R., Wiens, J., McDermott, B., and Lesage, J. "A rapid scoping review on academic integrity and algorithmic writing technologies." *Canadian Perspectives on Academic Integrity* 6, no. 1 (2023): 1–5. DOI: 10.55016/ojs/cpai.v6i1.76882.

Nikolic, S., Sandison, C., Haque, R., Daniel, S., Grundy, S., Belkina, M., Lyden, S., Hassan, G. M., and Neal, P. "ChatGPT, Copilot, Gemini, SciSpace, and Wolfram versus higher education assessments: An updated multi-institutional study of the academic integrity impacts of Generative Artificial Intelligence (GenAI) on assessment, teaching and learning in engineering." *Australasian Journal of Engineering Education* 29, no. 2 (2024): 126–153. DOI: 10.1080/22054952.2024.2372154.

Noble, S. *Algorithms of Oppression: How Search Engines Reinforce Racism*. New York, USA: New York University Press, 2018. DOI: 10.18574/nyu/9781479833641.001.0001.

Nyaaba, M., Kyeremeh, P., Majialuwe, E. K., Owusu-fordjour, C., Asebiga, E., and A-ingkonge, B. "Generative AI in academic research: A descriptive study on awareness, gender usage, and views among pre-service teachers." *Journal of AI* 8, no. 1 (2024): 45–60. DOI: 10.61969/jai.1400867.

Oladokun, B. D., Ajani, Y. A., Tom-George, N. W., and Okeke, O. C. "From metaverse to meta AI: A dynamic disruption in libraries in higher education institutions." *Library Hi Tech News* 41, no. 9 (2024): 12–14. DOI: 10.1108/LHTN-04-2024-0059.

Orlikowski, W. J. "Sociomaterial practices: Exploring technology at work." *Organization Studies* 28, no. 9 (2007): 1435–1448. DOI: 10.1177/0170840607081138.

Perkins, M. "Academic integrity considerations of AI large language models in the post-pandemic era: ChatGPT and beyond." *Journal of University Teaching and Learning Practice* 20, no. 2 (2023): 1–24. DOI: 10.53761/1.20.02.07.

Rahman, M. M. and Watanobe, Y. "ChatGPT for education and research: opportunities, threats, and strategies." *Applied Sciences* 13, no. 9 (2023): 5783–. DOI: 10.3390/app13095783.

Rasul, T., Nair, S., Kalendra, D., Robin, M., Santini, F. de O., Ladeira, W. J., Sun, M., Day, I., Rather, R. A., and Heathcote, L. "The role of ChatGPT in higher education: Benefits, challenges, and future research directions." *Journal of*

Applied Learning & Teaching 6, no. 1 (2023): 41–56. DOI: 10.37074/jalt.2023.6.1.29.

Ruslin, R., Mashuri, S., Rasak, M. S. A., Alhabsyi, F., and Syam, H. "Semi-structured interview: A methodological reflection on the development of a qualitative research instrument in educational studies." *IOSR Journal of Research & Method in Education (IOSR-JRME)* 12, no. 1 (2022): 22–29. DOI: 10.9790/7388-1201052229.

Salinas-Navarro, D. E., Vilalta-Perdomo, E., Michel-Villarreal, R., and Montesinos, L. "Using generative artificial intelligence tools to explain and enhance experiential learning for authentic assessment." *Education Sciences* 14, no. 1 (2024): 83–. DOI: 10.3390/educsci14010083.

Schei, O. M., Møgelvang, A., and Ludvigsen, K. "Perceptions and use of AI chatbots among students in higher education: A scoping review of empirical studies." *Education Sciences* 14, no. 8 (2024): 922–. DOI: 10.3390/educsci14080922.

Selwyn, N. *Should Robots Replace Teachers? AI and the Future of Education.* John Wiley & Sons, 2019.

Shankar, S. K., Pothancheri, G., Sasi, D., and Mishra, S. "Bringing teachers in the loop: Exploring perspectives on integrating generative AI in technology-enhanced learning." *International Journal of Artificial Intelligence in Education* (2024): 1–26. DOI: 10.1007/s40593-024-00428-8.

Shin, D., Rasul, A., and Fotiadis, A. "Why am I seeing this? Deconstructing algorithm literacy through the lens of users." *Internet Research* 32, no. 4 (2022): 1214–1234. DOI: 10.1108/INTR-02-2021-0087.

Slimi, Z. and Carballido, B. V. "Navigating the ethical challenges of artificial intelligence in higher education: An analysis of seven global AI ethics policies." *TEM Journal* 12, no. 2 (2023): 590–602. DOI: 10.18421/TEM122-02.

Smith, N. and Vickers, D. "Living well with AI: Virtue, education, and artificial intelligence." *Theory and Research in Education* 22, no. 1 (2024): 19–44. DOI: 10.1177/14778785241231561.

Stöhr, C., Ou, A. W., and Malmström, H. "Perceptions and usage of AI chatbots among students in higher education across genders, academic levels, and fields of study." *Computers and Education: Artificial Intelligence* 7, no. 1 (2024): 1–17. DOI: 10.1016/j.caeai.2024.100259.

Tegmark, M. "The Complex relationship between teachers' instructional practices and students' reading activities." In *NERA Conference 2022, Reykjavik, Iceland, June 1-3, 2022*. School of Education, University of Iceland, 2022. DOI: https://urn.kb.se/resolve?urn=urn:nbn:se:du-44296.

Williams, T., Matuszek, C., Mead, R., and Depalma, N. "Scarecrows in Oz: The use of large language models in HRI." *ACM Transactions on Human-Robotic Interaction* 13, no. 1 (2024): 1–11. DOI: 10.1145/3606261.

Woolf, B. "Introduction to IJAIED Special Issue, FATE in AIED." *International Journal of Artificial Intelligence in Education* 32, no. 3 (2022): 501–503. DOI: 10.1007/s40593-022-00299-x.

Zawacki-Richter, O., Marín, V. I., Bond, M., and Gouverneur, F. "Systematic review of research on artificial intelligence applications in higher education — where are the educators?" *International Journal of Educational Technology in Higher Education* 16, no. 1 (2019): 1–27. DOI: 10.1186/s41239-019-0171-0.

Zhai, X. "ChatGPT user experience: Implications for education." *SSRN Electronic Journal* (2022). DOI: 10.2139/ssrn.4312418.

https://doi.org/10.1142/9781800616578_0010

Chapter 10

Building Artificial Intelligence Literacy Skills for AI Competency Development in Higher Learning Institutions

Joan Wakasa Murumba[*,‡] **and Everlyn Anduvare**[†,§]

[*] *Texas A&M International University, USA*

[†] *Karatina University, Kenya*

[‡] *joan.murumba@tamiu.edu*

[§] *varelynn@gmail.com*

Abstract

Artificial Intelligence (AI) literacy is a critical skill that complements teaching and learning in higher education. Due to the emergence of AI technologies, the education sector has witnessed profound changes in teaching, learning, and research. This chapter sought to establish the preparedness of Higher Learning Institutions (HLIs) in terms of the promotion of AI literacy competency skills. The study is anchored on the Framework of AI literacy by Hibbert *et al.* (2024), the four-dimensional AI literacy framework by Wang *et al.* (2023), and the framework for Information Literacy in Higher Education (ACRL, 2016). A qualitative research approach using multiple case study research design was adopted. Purposive sampling was used to identify 16 research-intensive (R1) HLIs in the United States of America as per the Carnegie Classification 2023 and four Chartered Universities in Kenya with ongoing activities toward building the capacity for information literacy skills. A desktop review was employed to collect secondary data using an observation guide. Content analysis was used to analyze the qualitative data.

Keywords: Academic libraries, AI competency, AI literacy, Artificial Intelligence, HLIs, information literacy, Kenya, USA.

10.1. Introduction and Background

Educators and students are unaware and unprepared to navigate the complex digital landscape that is getting complicated by the day with emerging technologies, including Artificial Intelligence (AI). Besides, there are mixed feelings about adopting AI in teaching, learning, and research. Moreover, information professionals who work with information and related technologies in all forms have also been caught off guard. Yet, they are the critical personnel ensuring that researchers, scholars, students, and the entire academic community find, evaluate, and use information and related technologies effectively and efficiently. Ng *et al.* (2021) indicate that developing AI literacy is increasingly prioritized to prepare students, faculty, staff, and administrators to harness AI's potential while mitigating risks. The United States (US) Department of Education's report (2023) on AI emphasizes the growing importance of AI literacy for educators and students, highlighting the necessity of understanding and integrating AI technologies in educational settings. Library professionals must have the necessary skills to effectively evaluate and utilize AI tools (Lo, 2023a). Many of these key resource people lack the knowledge, skills, and critical understanding of how to use AI applications responsibly and ethically. Yet, AI literacy is now becoming a fundamental requirement for academic success.

AI literacy enhances innovative teaching and learning practices. It supports the achievement of Sustainable Development Goals (SDGs) 4 (Quality Education) and 9 (Industry, Innovation, and Infrastructure), which are deeply intertwined with the development of AI and Information Literacy (IL) competencies. SDG 4 emphasizes inclusive and equitable education, necessitating fostering digital and AI literacy to equip learners with critical skills for navigating an increasingly data-driven world. AI competencies, such as data and information ethics and responsible AI use, are integral to modern education frameworks that prepare individuals for lifelong learning and participation in the knowledge economy. Similarly, SDG 9, which promotes resilient infrastructure and innovation, requires a workforce adept in IL skills to effectively locate, evaluate, and apply information in advancing technological innovation. Bridging these SDGs, integrating AI and IL education enables individuals and institutions to harness emerging technologies ethically and effectively, fostering innovation while addressing digital equity challenges and ensuring sustainable development.

10.1.1. *Specific objectives*

i. to analyze the current landscape of AI literacy in Higher Learning Institutions (HLIs).
ii. to explore the applications of AI tools in the context of HLIs.
iii. to examine the role of Information Professionals in fostering AI competencies in HLIs.
iv. to develop a strategic framework for promoting AI literacy within HLIs.

10.1.2. *Statement of the problem*

The rapid advancement of AI is reshaping educational practices and professional landscapes, particularly in HLIs. Despite the growing significance of AI, many HLIs face challenges in integrating AI literacy into their curricula and professional development programs. This gap is further compounded by a lack of universal frameworks that address the intersection of AI tools, competencies, and information literacy. Information professionals (IPs), pivotal in guiding knowledge acquisition and ethical information use, lack the necessary AI competencies to navigate and leverage these emerging technologies. With a cohesive strategy to foster AI literacy, particularly among IPs, HLIs can equip students, faculty, researchers, and professionals with the skills to thrive in an AI-driven world. This chapter addresses these challenges by examining the current AI literacy landscape, the application of AI tools in HLIs, exploring the role of IL in developing AI competencies, and proposing a framework to enhance AI literacy in HLIs.

10.1.3. *Literature review*

This section highlights the current landscape of AI in HLIs, AI and IL frameworks, types and applications of AI tools in HLIs, as noted in various studies, and AI competencies among IPs. In addition, gaps from sampled universities are illustrated in line with the chapter's themes.

10.2. Theoretical Frameworks

This work is underpinned by the framework for AI literacy by Hibbert *et al.* (2024), Wang *et al.* (2023), and the framework for IL in Higher Education (ACRL, 2016).

10.2.1. *Artificial Intelligence literacy framework*

Hibbert *et al.* (2024) indicate that the AI literacy framework aims to enhance the discovery of one's current status regarding the AI literacy level and the preparedness to build on the literacy levels. It proposes four AI literacy levels and provides core competencies: Understanding AI, Using and Applying AI, Analyzing and Evaluating AI, and Creating AI.

Level One: Understanding AI
Stakeholders will develop the ability to define fundamental concepts, such as Artificial Intelligence, machine learning, large language models, and neural networks. They will understand the benefits and limitations of AI tools and learn to differentiate various types of AI based on their capabilities and computational mechanisms.

Level Two: Use and application of AI
This level allows users to effectively use generative AI tools to achieve desired outcomes, experimenting with and refining prompt strategies to enhance the quality of AI-generated responses. They will critically evaluate AI outputs, identifying potential inaccuracies, logical errors, or biases in the content.

Level Three: Analyze and evaluate
This level will allow users to explore AI within a broader context, integrating insights from their disciplines or areas of interest. They will critically

assess AI tools, constructing arguments for or against their design, usage, and applications. Additionally, they will examine the ethical implications surrounding the development and use of AI technologies.

Level Four: Creating Artificial Intelligence

Participants will synthesize their understanding of AI to envision or develop innovative ideas, technologies, or frameworks. Achieving this level of proficiency may involve conceptualizing new applications for AI, creating software that integrates AI technology, or formulating theoretical frameworks related to AI.

10.2.2. *Four-dimensional framework for Artificial Intelligence literacy*

Wang *et al.* (2023) created a 4D framework that addresses themes and some competencies:

- **Awareness:** It helps inform users and requires them to comprehend AI technology in practical applications. This theme emphasizes the foundational knowledge necessary to understand the core AI principles. It stresses the importance of grasping the underlying mechanisms that drive AI systems, enabling individuals to navigate the rapidly evolving technological landscape. Competencies in this dimension include explaining key AI terms, identifying types of AI technologies, and understanding their functionalities and applications. Developing these competencies is critical for learners and professionals seeking to effectively engage with AI tools and systems.
- **Application:** It helps apply and use AI technology to accomplish tasks proficiently. This theme is focused on enabling individuals to use AI tools effectively in various professional and academic settings. It includes competencies such as developing AI-driven solutions, integrating AI into workflows, and using AI for problem-solving across different domains. This practical competency ensures that individuals understand AI concepts and know how to apply them in their careers, from enhancing research capabilities to automating tasks and improving decision-making processes.
- **Critical thinking:** It helps analyze, select, and critically evaluate the data and information provided by AI. This theme encourages

individuals to question the outputs of AI tools, considering factors such as accuracy, reliability, and potential biases in data and algorithms. Competencies in this area involve critically analyzing AI-generated results, recognizing the limitations of AI technologies, and proposing improvements or alternative approaches. By developing these evaluative skills, individuals can better navigate the complexities of AI and ensure their responsible and informed use. This aligns with the ACRL standards for evaluating sources of information.

- **Social responsibility:** It helps develop awareness of one's responsibilities and respect for reciprocal rights and obligations. The theme involves understanding AI's ethical challenges, such as bias, privacy concerns, and decision-making transparency. AI literacy must encompass the ability to critically evaluate how AI impacts social, political, and economic structures and encourage responsible use. Competencies in this area include identifying ethical dilemmas, proposing solutions to mitigate negative impacts, and promoting fairness and accountability in AI development and deployment.

10.2.3. *Association of college and research libraries framework*

The ACRL framework for IL emphasizes core concepts for navigating the complexities of modern information environments. It includes six interconnected frames that stress the importance of understanding the nature of authority, the process of information creation, and the need for research as inquiry and strategic exploration of information. These core concepts describe understandings about the purpose and process of research and scholarship that are broadly shared among scholars but that novice learners may not yet fully grasp. However, many standard academic or professional research practices may not make sense without understanding these concepts.

The ACRL framework for IL in Higher Education provides a robust conceptual foundation for understanding and teaching information literacy. It is grounded in six interconnected frames, each reflecting a core concept of information literacy. These frames include "Authority is Constructed and Contextual," which emphasizes that the credibility and authority of information are shaped by the context and the creators' expertise; "Information Creation as a Process," which highlights the iterative and diverse nature of information production and dissemination; and "Information Has Value," which recognizes information as a commodity, a means of influence, and a cultural product with legal, social, and ethical implications.

The framework also includes "Research as Inquiry," which portrays research as a process of exploring and questioning to deepen understanding and generate new knowledge. "Scholarship as Conversation" acknowledges academic discourse's collaborative and dialogical nature, where ideas evolve through ongoing communication among scholars. Lastly, "Searching as Strategic Exploration" underscores the need for a systematic and adaptable approach to locating information, involving evaluating resources and refining search strategies.

In the context of AI literacy, these frames offer a critical lens for analyzing and engaging with AI tools. For instance, assessing the authority of AI-generated content is vital, particularly given the potential for misinformation. Similarly, understanding the information creation process through AI underscores the role of algorithms and data inputs in shaping outputs. Recognizing information value is connected to ethical considerations and the socioeconomic impacts of AI tools. Moreover, viewing research as inquiry aligns with iterative exploration facilitated by AI, while scholarship as conversation highlights AI's potential to enhance collaborative discourse. Finally, searching as strategic exploration resonates with developing effective prompts and strategies for leveraging AI technologies.

This framework provides an invaluable foundation for integrating AI literacy into academic and professional contexts. It ensures that users approach AI tools critically and ethically while maximizing their information-seeking and knowledge-creation potential.

10.3. Mapping Artificial Intelligence with Information Literacy

Artificial Intelligence has emerged as a transformative force in numerous disciplines, including information science (IS). The integration of AI in academic environments has significantly influenced how information is accessed, evaluated, and utilized, thereby intersecting directly with the principles and practices of IL. Information literacy is defined as a set of integrated abilities encompassing the reflective discovery of information, the understanding of how information is produced and valued, and the use of information in creating new knowledge and participating ethically in communities of learning (Association of College and Research Libraries, 2016). The ability to recognize when information is needed and to locate, evaluate, and use that information effectively is evolving as digital and technological advancements reshape traditional approaches to research and learning. Table 10.1 illustrates gaps in the existing AI frameworks and how AI frameworks connect to the ACRL framework for developing AI competencies, yielding a more structured and all-encompassing framework for HLIs.

The ACRL framework emphasizes foundational concepts such as understanding the constructed and contextual nature, evaluating sources critically, and recognizing information's impact. Similarly, AI literacy frameworks stress the need to comprehend how AI processes data and

Table 10.1. Alignment of Artificial Intelligence frameworks with information literacy frames.

AI Literacy Framework	4D Framework for AI Literacy	ACRL Frames	Key Aspects
1. Understanding Artificial Intelligence	1. Awareness	1. Authority is constructed and contextual	Needs analysis
2. Use and application of Artificial Intelligence	2. Application	2. Information creation as a process	Information access & retrieval skills
3. Analyze and evaluate Artificial Intelligence	3. Critical thinking	3. Information has value	Critical thinking skills Information ethics AI ethics
4. Creating Artificial Intelligence	4. Social responsibility	4. Research as inquiry 5. Scholarship as conversation 6. Searching as strategic exploration	AI guidelines AI policy development IL and AI curricula

generates insights, requiring critical evaluation skills like those outlined in the ACRL framework.

The AI frameworks address the use and application of AI, which the ACRL also addresses under frames 2 and 3 on "information creation as a process" and "information has value," respectively. These frames require competencies in information access and retrieval.

Both AI frameworks support critical thinking. The ACRL framework calls for evaluating information sources for authority, credibility, and relevance. On the other hand, the AI literacy framework extends this to include assessing AI tools and questioning the validity of AI-generated content. The ACRL framework addresses the ethical use of information, which translates into AI literacy and understanding the moral implications of using AI.

The ACRL framework supports lifelong learning and the adaptability of research skills. The AI literacy framework similarly promotes the need for ongoing learning as AI technologies rapidly evolve, affecting how information is accessed, interpreted, and disseminated. All these require IL and AI guidelines and policies to support its implementation.

10.4. Artificial Intelligence Literacy in Higher Learning Institutions

The growing integration of AI in higher education presents opportunities and challenges for academic institutions. As AI tools become increasingly prevalent in teaching, research, and administrative functions, the need for AI literacy among students, faculty, and library professionals has never been more critical. Various factors influence the development of AI literacy in HLIs, including institutional infrastructure, access to resources, faculty expertise, and curriculum design. Additionally, external influences such as societal perceptions of AI, ethical considerations, and the pace of technological advancements shape how AI literacy is understood and implemented within academic settings. This section explores the key elements that affect AI literacy in higher learning institutions, examining the interplay between these factors and their impact on the successful adoption and integration of AI technologies and the development of AI competencies in HLIs.

10.4.1. *Artificial Intelligence literacy landscape in higher learning institutions*

AI is transforming higher education by streamlining administrative processes, personalizing learning experiences, and enhancing research capabilities. Studies highlight its applications in adaptive learning platforms, automated grading systems, and research analytics (e.g., predictive modeling). However, there is a disparity in adopting AI tools across HLIs, with resource constraints, lack of expertise, and ethical considerations often cited as barriers (Smith and Doe, 2022).

AI Literacy encompasses the knowledge, skills, and ethical understanding required to interact with AI technologies effectively. Frameworks such as Long and Magerko's (2020) definition emphasize the importance of transparency, critical thinking, and ethical awareness in AI literacy, and the ACRL Standards play a crucial role in guiding HLIs to foster information literacy by promoting the development of critical thinking, research skills, and ethical engagement with information (ARCL, 2016), which are essential for understanding and navigating AI technologies. However, the literature reveals a lack of consensus on standardized competencies and limited integration into existing educational frameworks in HLIs.

Most libraries are governed by the ACRL frameworks and guidelines in their operations. Several academic libraries, as evidenced on their websites, have published library guides detailing the application of ACRL standards and frameworks. However, information on how they have been integrated into the curricula is missing. Additionally, information literacy as a discipline is still not fully embraced. In the United States, for example, some academic libraries offer IL as one-shot sessions, whereas very few provide the same as a credit course. In Kenya, only four universities, namely, Karatina University, Catholic University of Eastern Africa (CUEA), United States International University (USIU), and Tangaza, out of 74 universities in the country, offer IL as a credit-bearing course (see Table 10.2). Since the surge of generative AI, HLIs have offered researchers AI workshops and micro-credentialing courses. The following questions persist: What was the component of the training, what are the training learning outcomes, and what about AI policies? What about students and librarians? In 2021, the Southeastern Conference (SEC) Artificial Intelligence Consortium, led by Auburn University, trained

Table 10.2. Data collection observation guide.

Universities	AI Landscape and Initiatives	AI Tools	IL Competencies and Metrics	Policy Frameworks	Observations
AL1	Offers an introductory course on AI essentials (AI tools & ethics) Promotes AI literacy instruction sessions AI Research and Development Center Integrated AI in teaching and learning Library–faculty partnerships	ChatGPT, ProWritingAId, DALL-E, Wall-E, Packback, Bard, MidJourney	No data displayed	Guidelines on using generative AI tools are available	Strong AI infrastructure
AK2	AI research guides Library-led AI workshops	ChatGPT	No data displayed	AI syllabus statements available	Library-led AI support
AU3	Curated a comprehensive suite of AI tools and software resources for faculty and staff Offers AI Literacy programs Teaching with AI syllabus for faculty Launched an AI workshop for faculty across 14 R1 institutions	ChatGPT, Copilot, Claude, Gemini	Trained 4,000 faculty	Published an advisory guide on generative AI tools	Strong AI infrastructure Pioneered AI education in 14 institutions in the US and received an award in 2023
C4	Offers IL as a credit course to year one students Hosted an AI-themed conference in November 2024	No specific tools highlighted	Do data displayed	No policy framework is displayed	No AI literacy infrastructure

(*Continued*)

Table 10.2. (*Continued*)

Universities	AI Landscape and Initiatives	AI Tools	IL Competencies and Metrics	Policy Frameworks	Observations
F5	AI research guide Launched an AI curriculum to develop essential AI competencies in all fields of study Offers a certificate course in AI Integrated AI into 230 courses Established an AI academy Offers AI-focused professional development courses to faculty	NavigatorAI-comprehensive self-service AI platform in U.S. higher education	Hiring 100 additional faculty members focused on AI across 16 colleges	AI working group AI policy available	Building capacity through hiring experts in AI Reflects a significant AI integration into the curriculum Strong AI policy There is no librarian on the AI academy team or the working group
G6	AI research guide Established Institute for AI Offers a Ph.D. and an M.Sc. in AI Offers, workshops, and symposia Innovation in AI Teaching Award	ChatGPT	Interdisciplinary faculty hiring (70) in Data Science and AI strands, including ethics, data science, and AI	AI policy available	Building capacity through hiring experts in AI AI initiatives run outside the library
KA7	Offers IL as a credit course for students in their 1st year Offers an advanced IL as a credit course to 3rd-year students of IS Planned AI-themed conference for April 2025	No specific tools highlighted	No data displayed	No AI policy is displayed	Some capacity building through training IPs in IL

KE8	AI literacy weeks Collaborations among librarians, computer science faculty, and the Center for the Enhancement of Teaching and Learning	ChatGPT	No data displayed	AI guidelines available for students and faculty AI Taskforce	A strong foundation of AI agenda is domiciled in the library
LS9	AI research guides Offer a short course on AI Library-led AI workshops	No specific tools highlighted	No data displayed	AI syllabus statements available	A strong foundation of AI agenda is domiciled in the library
MI10	AI research guides AI workshops	ChatGPT	No data displayed	Library AI Committee AI workforce AI syllabus statements available	A strong foundation of AI agenda is domiciled in the library
MS11	Have a data science program that includes modules on the ethical use of AI	ChatGPT, DALL-E, Bard, Jasper Chat, Lumen, Sound draw, OpenAI Codex	No data displayed	Published report on GenAI and instruction AI working group	The committee includes the library
MO12	AI workshops	ChatGPT, Copilot, Zoom AI	No data displayed	Guidelines on the use of AI tools AI Task Force 2024–2025	AI initiatives are housed under the IT office No AI library guide

(*Continued*)

Table 10.2. *(Continued)*

Universities	AI Landscape and Initiatives	AI Tools	IL Competencies and Metrics	Policy Frameworks	Observations
OK13	AI resource center Projects in AI Registry (PAIR) AI-related workshops	Bizzy chatbot, Zoom AI, Adobe Firefly, Copilot, KnowBe4AIDA, Gradescope, Mymedia	No data displayed	No AI policy is displayed	Chatbot answered 3,779 since 2019 The OUIT department heavily runs AI projects at the university
SO14	AI research guides Various courses on AI, including AI ethics, Artificial Intelligence, Law, Ethics, and Policy courses AI fellowship Self-paced course for faculty Workshops on various AI themes, including AI ethics AI webinar series	ChatGPT	AI-Data Science library personnel	AI policy	Strong AI support from the library Solid AI support system
TA15	Offers IL as a credit course to 1st years	No specific tools highlighted	No data displayed	No available AI policy is displayed	No AI literacy infrastructure

TE16	AI research guide Proposed initiatives that align AI with library sciences and broader academic disciplines, fostering interdisciplinary AI education Provides resources on ethically incorporating AI into classroom activities Teaching with AI workshops Library–faculty partnerships	Verse AI assistant Copilot	No data displayed	Available AI policy framework	Advanced teaching, learning, and research Incorporates librarians, the writing center, and OIT staff in the AI agenda
TS17	AI research guide Workshops on GenAI	ChatGPT, Copilot	No data displayed	Available AI policy framework	Reasonably available AI literacy infrastructure
TM18	AI research guide Dedicated resource hub with AI resources Support AI literacy among students and faculty AI micro-credentialing course for faculty Faculty have taken an AI course at Auburn University	ChatGPT, Copilot, Grammarly	400 training slots for faculty training on AI	AI syllabus statements available	Available AI literacy infrastructure

(*Continued*)

Table 10.2. (*Continued*)

Universities	AI Landscape and Initiatives	AI Tools	IL Competencies and Metrics	Policy Frameworks	Observations
US19	Offers IL as a credit course for 1st year Signed MOU with Safaricom on AI short courses Planned International Conference on AI in 2021 in collaboration with Google and Africa Center for Advanced Technology Annual Library Week on Annual Diversity, Inclusion, and Libraries	No specific tools highlighted	No data displayed	No available AI policy is displayed	There is no strong AI literacy infrastructure The focus is on technology and not the skills/literacies
VU20	AI research guide Generative AI resource hub Workshops on generative AI OCLC Research and Library Partnership on AI applications on library services	Cloud-based archiving, ChatGPT, Copilot, Claude, LLaMA	No data displayed	Available policy on academic integrity and generative AI	Strong AI literacy infrastructure

faculty from 16 Carnegie-classified R1 universities in the U.S. (SEC, 2021).

10.5. AI Tools in Higher Learning Institutions

AI has the potential to address myriad educational challenges and enhance sustainable education by improving access to quality education, creating personalized learning experiences, and supporting data-driven decision-making. A study by Crompton and Burke (2023) examined 138 articles using grounded coding on the use of AI in education (AIED) and established five significant codes implying the areas in which AI is majorly used in HLIs: Assessment/Evaluation; Predicting; AI Assistant; Intelligent Tutoring System (ITS); and Managing Student Learning. Increasingly, HLIs are adopting AI tools to enhance teaching, learning, research, and administrative processes (Chassignol *et al*., *as* cited by Chen, Chen and Lin, 2020). As generative-AI-based content generation tools are emerging, proponents continue to advocate their use as long as it is responsibly acknowledged. The following section highlights the use of AI tools in HLIs.

10.5.1. *AI tools in teaching, learning, research, and administrative functions in HLIs*

There has been an increasing demand for online learning in HLIs, hence the growing need to use Learning Management Systems (LMS) platforms like Moodle, Blackboard Collaborate, and Canvas in teaching and learning. The advent of AI has necessitated the integration of AI tools in LMSs. Furthermore, Firat (2023) observes an increasing shift from LMS to the emergence and use of Learning Experience Platforms (LXP). The former supports the delivery of structured courses and programs, while the latter focuses on personalized learning experiences. AI can be integrated into LMS to support personalized learning, teaching, assessment, grading, or educational and AI-supported games and simulations. Examples of AI tools for these purposes include Google Cloud AI, Microsoft Azure Machine Learning, GPT-3 models, Knewton Adaptive Learning, ChatGPT, Gradescope, e-rater, Smart Sparrow, Learnosity, IBM Watson, Classcraft, Quest Atlantis, and Kahoot. Qazi *et al*. (2024) foresee a future in which

LMS will be equipped with AI-based tools supporting adaptive learning experiences, online proctoring, advanced data analytics, and intelligent user session management.

Intelligent Tutoring Systems (ITSs) play a key role in education (Alshaikh and Hewahi, 2021). According to Lin, Huang, and Lu (2023), ITSs are computer-based learning systems that use AI to provide personalized and adaptive instruction for students. They assert that integrating ITS into quality education has become the primary approach for achieving sustainable contemporary education. Furthermore, they found that using AI in ITS serves various purposes that include predicting learner outcome performance, learner behavior analysis, detecting dropout risks, providing necessary intervention by learning behavior identification, providing personalized training, providing instructor support such as learner's emotions, tutoring system assessments, and self-regulation learning improvement. Marouf *et al.* (2024); Lin *et al.* (2023); and Alshaikh and Hewahi (2021) offer several tools and technologies used to support ITS, including Support Vector Machine, Neural Networks, Chatbot AI, Azure, OpenCV, PyTorch, SpaCy, Knewton, Articulate Storyline, DreamBox, Smart Sparrow, Turnitin, AutoTutor, Duolingo, Labster, Pearson's MyLab, and Squirrel AI. All these tools can be used if acquired, and capacity building is done to build AI literacy competencies.

AI-powered tools have presented benefits to the research process by enhancing efficiency, saving time, enabling quick dissemination of scientific work, and enhancing the discovery of research papers based on interest and preferences. A study by Bairagi and Lihitkar (2024) identified ways that AI could improve research, including detecting plagiarism not only in text, as with conventional plagiarism detection methods. The study also noted that AI supports research by enabling voice-activated Intelligent Personal Assistants (IPAs), assisting with academic writing, reducing publication costs through AI-driven editing, analyzing large datasets to uncover patterns, speeding up literature reviews, and strengthening the peer review process while maintaining research integrity. Tools include AI text-generating tools such as Jasper, ChatGPT, Quill Bot, and BARD; data analysis and interpretation tools such as RapidMiner, Tableau, Google Data Studio, and Microsoft Power BI; literature review tools such as Research Rabbit, elicit, and Scholarcy; and peer review systems such as Frontiers' AIRA and PubSURE.

Chen *et al.* (2020) present other scenarios of AI in education, including assessment of students and schools; grading and evaluation of paper and exams; personalized intelligent teaching; innovative schools such as face and voice recognition, online and mobile remote education; curriculum and content development; and instructions leveraging technologies such as virtual reality, web-based platforms, robotics, video conferencing, and 3D technology, which have made it possible for students to learn better. Furthermore, Crompton and Burke (2023) note that AI assistants such as virtual assistants, virtual agents, intelligent agents, intelligent tutors, and intelligent helpers have become critical in supporting learners. They note that AI can provide immediate instruction, guidance, feedback, and follow-up questioning without delay or becoming tired.

AI tools have supported the automation of administrative functions such as reviewing and grading students' assignments; curriculum and content development; reviewing students' work, grading, and providing feedback on assignments; and plagiarism checking, rating and grading, and providing students with feedback on improvement areas (Chen *et al.*, 2020). George and Wooden (2023) indicate that AI supports administrative tasks such as handling admissions, enrollment, and course scheduling, thus reducing the workload for administrative staff. Furthermore, what has been presented in their study as an administrative blueprint system of an AI-centered innovative university includes functions such as an AI-centered collaboration and innovation hub, an AI-powered career counseling and placement office, AI-driven admissions, a data-driven curriculum, and an assessment design department. AI tools that support this include Adobe Sensei (OCR), Google Assistant, Clara Email management tool, Chatbots, Microsoft Power BI, and Trello.

Literature suggests a rapid growth of AI tools and enhanced AI-supported functions in HLIs in education, research, and administrative tasks. Therefore, there is a need to keep abreast of the developments and make smart decisions in adopting tools that would provide the most efficient outcome for a university setup and individuals. To leverage this requires decisions to be grounded in an AI framework. Moreover, having the expertise to enhance AI literacy will improve the sustainability of AI tools in HLIs.

10.6. Information Professionals and AI Competencies

IL is a foundational skill for navigating digital landscapes and evaluating information critically. A recent study by Johnson *et al.* (2023) argues that IL and AI competencies are inherently linked, as both involve data interpretation, ethical decision-making, and effective use of technological tools. The literature underscores the potential for IL to serve as a conduit for building AI literacy, particularly among information professionals positioned to guide educational and organizational strategies. It is important to stress the relationship or the intersection between AI and IL. AI tools and applications influence information-seeking behaviors, instructional practices, and the ethical considerations related to information use. Information professionals need retooling in AI literacy competency skills to promote moral and responsible information use and the development of lifelong learning skills among different stakeholders.

Several challenges, including limited faculty and student training, institutional resistance, and a lack of interdisciplinary collaboration, can hinder advancing AI literacy. Available library guidelines, for example, the ACRL 2016 standards (the nature and extent of AI literacy, skills needed to access AI tools, evaluation, information use, and ethical issues) do not address AI competencies but rather the IL competencies. Conversely, opportunities lie in leveraging existing IL programs to incorporate AI concepts, designing workshops for AI tools, and creating partnerships between academic departments and library services.

10.7. Methodology

This chapter was developed using a qualitative research approach using multiple case study design. Secondary data were collected using a desktop review. The approach involved the systematic review and synthesis of existing literature, frameworks, and scholarly discussions.

10.7.1. *Sampling, data sources, and data collection*

Purposive sampling was used to identify all 16 universities under the SEC in the USA and four chartered universities in Kenya running IL programs. These universities are the University of Alabama, the University of Arkansas, Auburn University, Catholic University of Eastern Africa (CUEA), the University of Florida, the University of Georgia, Karatina University, the University of Kentucky, Louisiana State University (LSU), the University of Mississippi, Mississippi State University, the University of Missouri, the University of South Carolina, Tangaza University, the University of Tennessee, Texas A&M University, United States University-Africa (USIU), and Vanderbilt University. The SEC Artificial Intelligence Consortium is designed to grow opportunities in the fast-changing fields of AI and data science, which are expected to be foundational for the future of industry, education, and research (SEC, 2021). An observation guide (Table 10.2) was used to identify and select relevant documents based on their focus on AI in HLIs, AI literacy competencies, AI literacy frameworks, and established IL models such as the ACRL framework for IL. Scholarly articles, white papers, reports, AI policies and guidelines, and AI research guides were the data sources identified through institutional websites and academic databases. This was done between the months of October and December in 2024.

Inclusion criteria focused on documents that explicitly addressed AI in the selected HLIs; theoretical frameworks (AI literacy frameworks and the ACRL IL Framework in Table 10.1); studies published within the last 10 years (2014–2024) to ensure contemporary relevance; research-intensive (R1) classified universities and SEC members from the USA; and universities that offer information literacy as a credit course. The exclusion criteria delimited articles focusing solely on technical AI development without educational or AI literacy perspectives, frameworks unrelated to information literacy or general competencies, and articles from social media blogs.

10.7.2. *Analysis and mapping*

Themes and key competencies from the AI literacy frameworks literature were mapped against the six frames of the ACRL IL Framework, as illustrated in Table 10.1. This allowed for identifying overlaps, gaps, and opportunities for integration of a strategic Artificial Intelligence literacy competency framework.

10.8. Findings and Discussion

Considering the evolving AI technological, educational, and AI literacy landscape, the findings were critically evaluated to ensure relevance, rigor, and applicability. Findings from this exercise are recorded in Table 10.2. The names of the universities are anonymously coded using numbers and letters of the alphabet.

Significant gaps and opportunities for development across institutions, particularly among R1 universities in the SEC and four in Kenya offering IL courses, have been identified in Table 10.2.

10.9. AI Literacy Landscape in HLIs

10.9.1. *AI infrastructure projects*

The presence of eight (40%) AI infrastructural projects signals a growing commitment to supporting AI integration through tangible resources. These projects include the development of AI micro-credentialing courses for faculty, AI fellowships and awards, AI labs and research centers, research projects, AI tools, and collaborative spaces, which are critical for fostering innovation and practical applications of AI. An example is the University of Florida, a SEC institution, which offers AI micro-credentials focused on academic applications of artificial intelligence. Such programs prepare students, faculty, and staff to apply generative AI technology efficiently and ethically, enhancing teaching, learning, and research across disciplines.

10.9.2. *Integration of AI into curricula*

Only 35% of the sampled R1 in the USA and none of the four chartered universities offering IL as a credit course in Kenya have integrated AI into their curricula, highlighting a notable lag in AI literacy competencies among faculty and students. Slimi (2023), in a study on the impact of Artificial Intelligence on higher education, suggests that AI should be more extensively integrated into higher education curricula and discusses considerations for institutions in this integration process. The University of Florida (UF) serves as an outlier, offering an impressive 230 courses with AI integration, which suggests a robust institutional strategy toward AI readiness. Pilot studies, such as those by Wang and Li (2022), demonstrate the efficacy of collaborative efforts in embedding AI literacy within HLI curricula.

10.9.3. *Information literacy as a credit course*

Only six (30%) of the 20 universities sampled offer IL as a credit-bearing course. This limited adoption underscores IL's undervaluing in academic programs despite its critical role in equipping students with essential research and critical thinking skills. Furthermore, none of the IL curricula reviewed include AI components, pointing to a disconnect between evolving technological needs and traditional IL frameworks.

These are two such universities in the USA and four in Kenya.

10.9.4. *Libraries' contributions to AI initiatives*

Libraries are playing a pivotal role in providing support for research and technology integration. Twelve (12) universities have developed research guides through their libraries, offering curated teaching, research, and learning resources. However, only six (30%) universities have library-led AI initiatives, suggesting untapped potential for libraries to lead in AI literacy and integration efforts. Most (70%) of the institutions sampled have AI initiatives domiciled under the ICT departments, and where there are committees, task forces, or working groups, none include the librarians. Georgia University Libraries Technology (n.d) employs AI algorithms to develop systems that suggest relevant books, articles, and other resources, improving user experience and discovery. Academic libraries need to spearhead AI initiatives in HLIs.

10.10. AI Tools

Common AI tools used in universities include ChatGPT, DALL-E, and Copilot. However, ChatGPT is the most common AI tool present in 16 universities sampled in the USA. This indicates some presence of access to AI tools in teaching, research, and learning. However, more AI tools exist and need to be explored, as Marouf *et al.* (2024); Lin, Huang, and Lu (2023); and Alshaikh and Hewahi (2021) present in their studies on AI tools in HLIs.

10.11. IL Competencies

No institution had metrics or rubrics used to test IL competencies. However, it is essential to note that four universities in Kenya train students in IL through a 3-credit course. In contrast, one USA university offers a 1-credit course and the other provides a 2-credit course. The syllabus from the 3-credit course indicates the presence of continuous assessment tests and final examinations as tools for testing competencies. There were no assessment statistics available on this issue. No available data indicate how many students have gone through the program. In the USA, on the other hand, available data online indicated that 4,400 faculty members have gone through the AI micro-credentialing course from Auburn University. The University of Georgia launched a Presidential Interdisciplinary Faculty Hiring Initiative in Data Science and Artificial Intelligence, recruiting 70 faculty experts in AI and data science across various departments. This shows that HLIs are trying to prepare themselves to build AI literacy capacity among their faculty pools. No library had an AI or data science librarian apart from one university. Juditanto, Syarif, and Santaso (2024), in their study on integrating Artificial Intelligence into 21st-century education curricula, support this agenda by suggesting that incorporating AI into the curriculum aims to build students' technological literacy and critical thinking skills.

10.12. Framework for AI Literacy in HLIs

10.12.1. *AI policies*

Institutional policies on AI usage are inconsistent across universities. While six universities have formal AI policies, nine rely on syllabus statements or academic handbook provisions, and five have no AI-related governance structures. This variation reflects differing levels of institutional readiness to address AI's ethical, operational, and pedagogical implications.

10.12.2. *AI literacy competency framework*

The literature identifies a need for structured frameworks that align AI literacy and IL objectives with institutional goals. Successful models often involve multi-stakeholder approaches, including administrators, faculty, librarians, and students. The gap, however, lies in scalable and adaptable frameworks tailored to the diverse contexts of HLIs. Coonan and Jane's (2014) model emphasizes the evolving landscape of IL in higher education. It highlights gaps in integrating digital literacy, fostering collaboration across disciplines, emphasizing critical thinking, adapting to emerging technologies, and assessing the impact of IL programs. The model calls for a more integrated, adaptive approach to IL education that reflects the changing ways information is created, consumed, and evaluated in a rapidly advancing technological environment. However, some proposals only took off once AI disruption struck ten years later.

AI literacy frameworks in academic institutions have become essential as Artificial Intelligence technologies increasingly impact teaching, research, and the broader educational landscape. Several frameworks have been developed to guide the integration of AI literacy into higher education, focusing on developing critical skills for understanding, utilizing, and ethically engaging with AI systems. For instance, Wang *et al.* (2023) proposed a 4D framework that emphasizes understanding AI concepts, ethical considerations, practical applications, and critical evaluation of AI technologies, providing a comprehensive approach to AI literacy. Similarly, the ACRL IL Framework underscores the importance of critical thinking and ethical decision-making, both essential when engaging with AI tools in academic contexts (Association of College & Research Libraries, 2016). These frameworks collectively highlight the need for educational institutions to foster AI literacy through interdisciplinary collaboration, curriculum integration, and the development of critical thinking skills, ensuring that students are equipped to navigate the complexities of AI in their academic and professional lives.

10.13. Conclusion and Recommendations

The absence of AI components in IL curricula, the limited number of library-led AI initiatives, and the lack of metrics on IL competencies highlight a critical gap. This work aims to create a scalable, impactful AI Literacy Train-the-Trainer program to empower educators and librarians to teach AI literacy effectively. The AI Literacy Train-the-Trainer Program seeks to address the AI literacy gap by empowering educators, information professionals, researchers, and students with the knowledge and tools to teach, learn, and use AI tools effectively. Through a scalable, sustainable training model, the program will ensure that critical stakeholders are equipped to deliver AI education to a broad audience, fostering inclusivity and preparing individuals for quality education and research. Integrating AI literacy within IL frameworks can address this gap, preparing IL professionals, students, and faculty to navigate the complexities of AI tools, AI ethics, and critical thinking.

10.13.1. *AI literacy landscape*

Universities should prioritize funding for AI infrastructural projects to enhance learning and research opportunities. In addition, institutions should adopt the University of Florida's model by embedding AI across diverse disciplines. IL curricula should evolve to include AI competencies, enabling students to assess AI tools and their applications critically. HLIs should implement an IL curriculum and credit-bearing course with the following syllabus components: IL fundamentals, AI fundamentals, AI in education, AI Ethics, AI Literacy, and hands-on AI tools and applications. This program will be implemented by collaborating with faculty in different departments like libraries, computer science, IT, education, e-learning, and writing centers. The library faculty should lead the syllabus creation since they have a background in IL. To monitor impact, there will be a need to document the number of trainers certified or those who will have gone through the training, the number of learners reached through the course, and the assessment of the learning and the program learning outcomes. On the other hand, libraries should spearhead AI initiatives, including workshops, policy development, and partnerships with academic units.

10.14. AI Tools

Most institutions over-rely on a few AI tools such as ChatGPT and Copilot. It is recommended that as more AI tools exist in the market, their significance in teaching, learning, research, and administrative functions needs to be explored.

10.14.1. *AI literacy competencies*

HLIs need to build capacity by deploying AI tools and AI literacy competencies. Librarians should be retooled on transliteracies, which include the following competencies: multimodal literacy, digital literacy, critical literacy, cultural literacy, collaborative and networked literacy, and adaptative literacy. This will enable them to transfer these skills to HLI stakeholders through IL training sessions, workshops, and other library programs.

10.14.2. *AI literacy competency framework*

10.14.2.1. *Developing comprehensive policies*

Institutions must establish cohesive AI literacy policies that address ethical considerations and provide clear guidelines for AI use, besides syllabus statements on AI and general policies on academic integrity.

10.14.3. *Proposed Artificial Intelligence literacy competence framework (AILC framework, 2025)*

This framework is unique in the sense that it would focus on building information professionals, who are not just learners, to help teach AI literacy fundamentals to larger audiences, with emphasis on transliteracies with a focus on interpreting, creating, and understanding information across multiple formats, media, and environments. Building on the AI literacy and IL frameworks, a holistic AI competency literacy framework for HLIs should incorporate the interdisciplinary and iterative approaches outlined by Hibbert *et al.* (2024), Wang *et al.* (2023) and the ACRL (2016). This involves embedding AI competencies into IL instruction, promoting collaborations across academic units, and developing adaptable training modules for diverse institutional contexts. The literature underscores the importance of aligning these initiatives with institutional goals, ensuring that AI and IL literacy are integral to strategic planning and curriculum development.

The proposed Artificial Intelligence Literacy Competence Framework outlines five levels of competencies: *foundational literacies* (communication skills and digital literacy), *advanced transliteracy competencies*, AI literacy (understanding of AI applications, recognizing AI-generated content and evaluating its quality, ethical decision-making regarding AI usage); *multimodal and multiliteracy practices* (ability to use and combine different types of multimedia elements); critical engagement and ethical awareness (critical media literacy and ethical AI usage); *collaborative and*

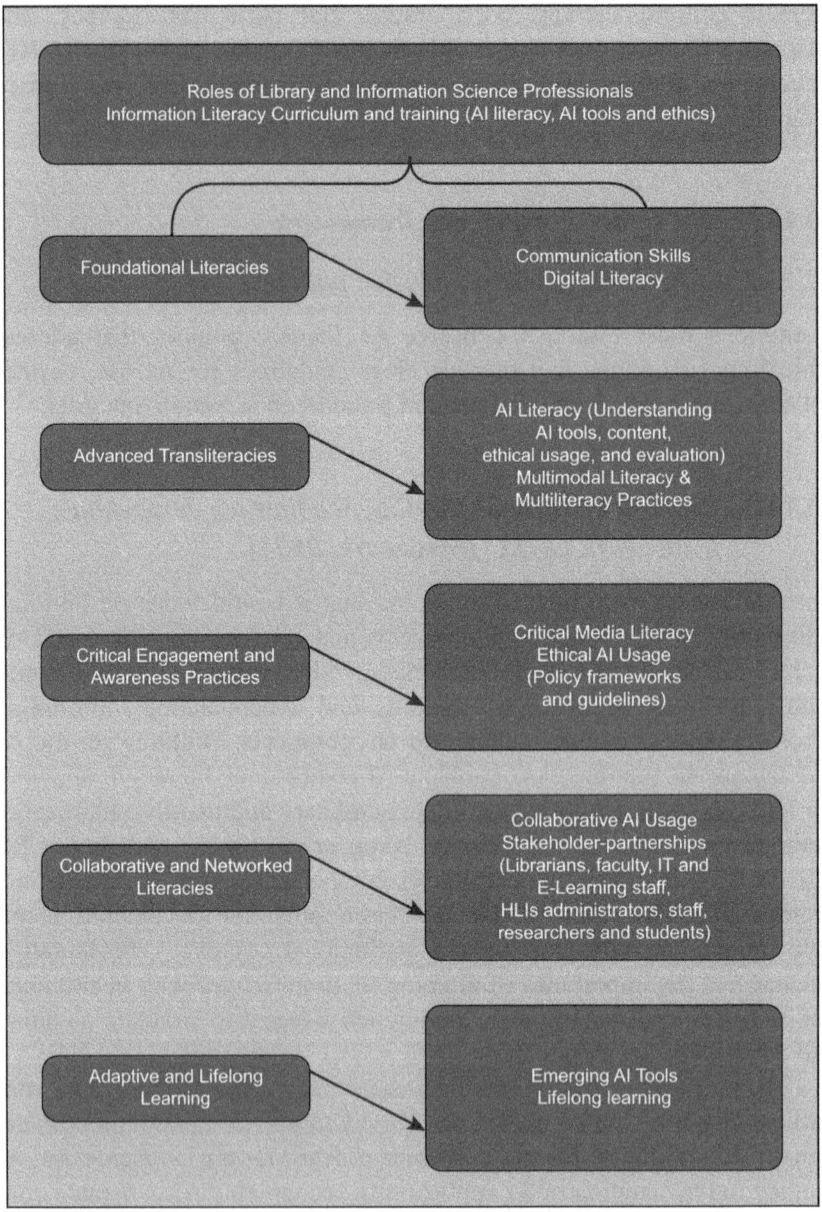

Figure 10.1. Artificial Intelligence literacy competence framework.

Source: Adapted from Hibbert *et al.* (2024), Wang *et al.* (2023) and the ACRL (2016).

networked literacies (collaborative AI use and engagement); and *adaptive and lifelong learning* (see in Figure 10.1). All these competencies can only be achieved with a strong information literacy curriculum incorporating AI literacy skills and ethical use in the syllabus. Libraries and information professionals are leading the way in spearheading and nurturing AI literacy competencies in HLIs and beyond.

This framework is applicable during curricular integration: Embed AI literacy and transliteracy principles into existing university courses, library programs, educational workshops, and digital literacy curricula. Additionally, key aspects of AI literacy, including ethical concerns and practical applications, should be captured during professional development training and resource creation for librarians and educators. The framework will also guide the assessment of students' acquisition of transliteracies and AI literacy, including their ability to think critically about AI technologies. Lastly, the framework supports advocacy and engagement in community outreach events like workshops and awareness campaigns to educate students and the public about the ethical and practical use of AI and digital media.

Bibliography

Alshaikh, F. and Hewahi, N. "AI and machine learning techniques in the development of intelligent tutoring system: A review." *2021 International Conference on Innovation and Intelligence for Informatics, Computing, and Technologies (3ICT)* (2021): 401–410. DOI: 10.1109/3ICT53449.2021.9582029.

Association of College & Research Libraries. "Framework for information literacy for higher education." 2016. American Library Association. https://www.ala.org/acrl/standards/ilframework.

Auburn University. "Advisory guidance: Use of generative AI tools." 2024a. https://www.auburn.edu/administration/oacp/AIGuidance.php.

Auburn University. "Auburn community college system partner to advance AI teaching, learning." 2024b. https://yellowhammernews.com/auburn-community-college-system-partner-to-advance-ai-teaching-learning/.

Bairagi, M. and Lihitkar, S. "Revolutionizing research writing and publishing by using AI-powered tools and techniques." *International Conference on AI-driven Advancements in Research and Publications: Intellectual Rights, Knowledge Management, and Beyond* (2024).

Chen, L., Chen, P., and Lin, Z. "Artificial intelligence in education." *IEEE Access* 8 (2020): 75264–75278.

Coley, M., Snay, P., Bandy, J., Bradley, J., and Molvig, O. "Teaching in the age of AI." 2024. https://cft.vanderbilt.edu/guides-sub-pages/teaching-in-the-age-of-ai/.

Conaster, T. "CELT launches 5th cohort of teaching innovation institute, focusing on Generative AI." 2024. https://celt.uky.edu/news/celt-launches-5th-cohort-teaching-innovation-institute-focusing-on-generative-ai.

Coonan, E. and Jane, S. "My dolly's bigger than yours, or, Why our labels no longer matter." 2014. https://librariangoddess.wordpress.com/2014/04/29/my-dollys-bigger/.

Crompton, H. and Burke, D. "Artificial intelligence in higher education: The state of the field." *International Journal of Educational Technology in Higher Education* (2023): 1–22.

CTW Team. "USIU-Africa signs MoU with Safaricom PLC to strengthen academic delivery and output at the School of Science and Technology." 2024. https://www.usiu.ac.ke/2071/usiu-africa-signs-mou-safaricom-plc-strengthen-academic-delivery-output-school-science-technology/.

Dean Education CUEA. "International AI conference: Harnessing AI for innovation in education." 2024. https://www.cuea.edu/AI/.

Fırat, M. "Integrating AI applications into learning management systems to enhance e-learning." *Instructional Technology and Lifelong Learning* 4, no. 1 (2023): 1–14. DOI: 10.52911/itall.1244453.

Gales, K. "Updated research guidelines for the use of AI at the University of Kentucky." 2024. https://uknow.uky.edu/campus-news/updated-research-guidelines-use-ai-university-kentucky.

George, B. and Wooden, O. "Managing the strategic transformation of higher education through artificial intelligence." *Administrative Sciences* 13 (2023): 196.

Georgia Library Technology. "Emerging technologies: AI in libraries." 2025. https://galibtech.georgialibraries.org/emerging/ai-in-libraries.

Hardesty, R. "AI literacy week events bring campus experts together to critically explore new technologies." 2024. https://libraries.uky.edu/news/ai-literacy-week-events-bring-campus-experts-together-critically-explore-new-technologies.

Haynsworth, L. "AI specialist supports librarians, faculty, students with emerging technologies." 2024. https://sc.edu/about/offices_and_divisions/university_libraries/exhibits_events_news/news/2024/ai_specialist_supports_librarians.php.

Hibbert, M., Altman, E., Shippen, T., and Wright, M. "A framework for AI literacy." 2024. https://er.educause.edu/articles/2024/6/a-framework-for-ai-literacy.

Howard, M. "AI initiative incentivizes the creation of UF AI courses: Almost 100 AI classes will be taught during Spring." 2023. https://www.alligator.org/article/2023/11/ai-initiative-incentivises-creation-of-uf-ai-courses.

Johnson, D., Smith, R., and Lee, T. "Intersections of information literacy and artificial intelligence competencies in education." *Journal of Educational Technology* 29, no. 4 (2023): 235–247.

Lin, C., Huang, A.Y.Q., and Lu, O.H.T. "Artificial intelligence in intelligent tutoring systems toward sustainable education: A systematic review." *Smart Learning Environments* 10, no. 1 (2023): 1–22.

Long, D. and Magerko, B. "What is AI literacy? Competencies and design considerations." *CHI '20: Proceedings of the 2020 CHI Conference on Human Factors in Computing Systems* (2020): 1–14.

Loso, J., Syarif, M., and Santoso, R.Y. "Integration of artificial intelligence in 21st century education curriculum." *Indonesian Journal of Education (INJOE)* 4, no. 3 (2024): 914–924. DOI: https://www.injoe.org/index.php/INJOE/article/view/16.

Marouf, A., Al-Dahdooh, R., Ghali, M.J.A., Mahdi, A.O., Abunasser, B.S., and Abu-Naser, S.S. "Enhancing education with artificial intelligence: The role of intelligent tutoring systems." *International Journal of Engineering and Information Systems (IJEAIS)* 8, no. 8 (2024): 10–16.

Mississippi State University. "Report on generative artificial intelligence (GAI) and instruction provost's office working group." 2023. https://www.provost.msstate.edu/sites/www.provost.msstate.edu/files/2023-11/AI%20Working%20Group%20Report.pdf.

Mississippi State University. "Generative AI: An introduction." 2024. https://guides.library.msstate.edu/c.php?g=1426088&p=10614601.

Nelson, K. "Auburn university receives collaborative initiatives award for pioneering AI education." 2024. https://wire.auburn.edu/content/provost/2024/08/231145-Biggio-Award.php.

Pionke, A. "UA policies." 2023. https://teachingai.as.ua.edu/ua-policies/.

Qazi, S., Kadri, M.B., Naveed, M., Khawaja, B.A., Khan, S.Z., Alam, M.M., and Su'ud, M.M. "AI-driven learning management systems: Modern developments, challenges and future trends during the age of ChatGPT." *Computers, Materials & Continua* 80, no. 2 (2024): 3289–3313.

Robertson, S. "Vanderbilt University's Heard Libraries join OCLC Research Library Partnership." 2024. https://newsonline.library.vanderbilt.edu/2024/06/vanderbilt-universitys-heard-libraries-join-oclc-research-library-partnership/.

Schmitz, C. "UT Joins New SEC Artificial Intelligence, Data Science Consortium." 2022. https://news.utk.edu/2022/04/05/ut-joins-secs-new-ai-data-science-consortium/.

SEC Staff. "SEC universities agree to the artificial intelligence and data science consortium." 2021. https://www.thesecu.com/news/sec-universities-agree-to-artificial-intelligence-data-science-consortium/.

Slimi, Z. "The impact of artificial intelligence on higher education: An empirical study." *European Journal of Educational Sciences* 10, no. 1 (2023): 1857–6036.

Texas A & M University Libraries. "ChatGPT and higher education." 2024a. https://tamu.libguides.com/c.php?g=1345766&p=9926832

Texas A & M University Libraries. "Work with AI." 2024b. https://ai.tamu.edu/work-with-ai/index.html.

University of Arkansas. "Libraries guide on using artificial intelligence in higher education." 2024. https://news.uark.edu/articles/69364/libraries-provide-guidance-on-using-artificial-intelligence-in-higher-education.

University of Florida. "Artificial intelligence across the UF curriculum." 2023. https://ai.ufl.edu/media/aiufledu/resources/AI-Across-the-Curriculum.pdf.

University of Florida. "Artificial intelligence (AI): Learning and using AI." 2024. https://guides.uflib.ufl.edu/ai/introduction.

University of Georgia. "Policy on the use of generative AI in theses and dissertations." 2024a. https://grad.uga.edu/policy-on-use-of-generative-ai-in-theses-and-dissertations/.

University of Georgia. "Presidential interdisciplinary faculty hiring initiatives in data science and artificial intelligence." 2024b. https://provost.uga.edu/academic-excellence/initiatives/faculty-hiring-initiatives/data-science-ai/.

University of Georgia Libraries. "AI literacy." 2024. https://guides.libs.uga.edu/AI/terms.

University of Missouri. "Artificial intelligence." 2024a. https://doit.missouri.edu/about/strategy-and-innovation/ai/.

University of Missouri. "ChatGPT, Artificial Intelligence, and Academic Integrity." 2024b. https://oai.missouri.edu/chatgpt-artificial-intelligence-and-academic-integrity/.

University of Oklahoma. "AI @ OU." 2024a. https://www.ou.edu/ouit/ai.

University of Oklahoma. "Project highlight: Bizzy chatbot." 2024b. https://libraries.ou.edu/content/project-highlight-bizzy-chat-bot.

University of South Carolina. "Generative artificial intelligence (GenAI)." 2024. https://sc.edu/about/offices_and_divisions/cte/teaching_resources/generative_ai/index.php.

University of Tennessee. "Generative artificial intelligence and teaching at UTK." 2024. https://teaching.utk.edu/teaching-resources/artificialintelligence/.

University of Texas at Austin. "Generative AI in teaching and learning: UT guides and recommendations." 2024. https://ctl.utexas.edu/generative-ai-teaching-and-learning-ut-guides-and-recommendations.

USIU. "Technology and society conference 2021 program." 2021a. https://www.usiu.ac.ke/resource/technology-and-society-conference-2021-program.

USIU. "Technology and society conference 2021 (#TechSoC21)." 2021b. https://www.usiu.ac.ke/2270/conference2021/?schl=sst.

Vanderbilt University. “Generative AI at Vanderbilt.” 2024. https://www.vanderbilt.edu/generative-ai/faculty/.

Wang, X., Li, Y., Zhang, Y., and Li, Q. “A 4D framework for AI literacy in higher education.” *Journal of Educational Technology Development and Exchange* 16, no. 2 (2023): 123–145.

WVTM. “AI at the University of Alabama.” 2024. https://youtu.be/8K46AsdlVO0.

https://doi.org/10.1142/9781800616578_0011

Chapter 11

Generative AI in Salvadoran Higher Education: Case Studies in Equity and Ethics from the Global South

Tizziana Valdivieso*, Oscar A. González†, and Enmanuel Araujo‡

Departamento de Ciencias de la Educación, Universidad Centroamericana José Simeón Cañas, Bulevar Los Próceres, La Libertad, El Salvador

*tvaldivieso@uca.edu.sv
†oagonzalez@uca.edu.sv
‡earaujo@uca.edu.sv

Abstract

This chapter explores the transformative potential of generative AI (GenAI) tools within Salvadoran higher education, analyzing their impact on students, faculty, and administrators. Framed within the socioeconomic realities of the Global South, the study examines how GenAI can address existing inequalities while advancing pedagogical innovation and organizational efficiency. For students, the chapter identifies socioeconomic and digital literacy barriers that shape access and ethical usage, advocating for equitable policies and infrastructure investment. Faculty perspectives reveal the dual role of GenAI as a tool for personalized learning and innovative assessment, alongside concerns about academic integrity and inadequate institutional support. Insights from administrative policies emphasize the need for ethical governance structures to integrate GenAI into institutional frameworks responsibly. Finally, the chapter contextualizes Salvadoran experiences within global conversations on AI in education, offering lessons and strategies for adaptive, culturally responsive approaches. By synthesizing perspectives from diverse stakeholders, this chapter underscores the importance of aligning technological advancements with regional priorities, ensuring that GenAI serves as a democratizing force for inclusive and transformative education.

Keywords: Technology integration, digital equity, instructional innovation, policy formation, educational trends.

11.1. Introduction

11.1.1. *Context and scope*

The integration of generative AI (GenAI) tools in education is a transformative development with profound implications for the Global South, particularly in El Salvador. GenAI embodies both an opportunity and a challenge, reflecting broader trends in global higher education. As institutions adapt to the digital era, disparities in access, training, and policy frameworks shape the extent to which emerging technologies can be leveraged effectively. While Salvadoran universities, such as the Universidad Centroamericana José Simeón Cañas (UCA), have begun exploring the potential of GenAI, these initiatives must navigate complex socioeconomic realities, ethical concerns, and infrastructural limitations (Chávez Solís *et al.*, 2023; Jarrahi *et al.*, 2023; Valdivieso and González, 2025; Yixin *et al.*, 2024).

GenAI, typified by tools such as ChatGPT, Gemini, and DALL-E, is recognized for its potential to revolutionize teaching and learning paradigms. These AI tools facilitate personalized education through adaptive learning systems that cater to individual student needs, thereby enhancing engagement and comprehension. Furthermore, GenAI can foster innovative pedagogical approaches by enabling educators to create dynamic learning experiences that integrate multimedia content and interactive elements. Additionally, GenAI has the potential to streamline administrative workflows, reducing bureaucratic burdens and allowing educational institutions to allocate resources more efficiently (Bissessar, 2023; Dotan, 2024).

However, the adoption of these tools is not without significant risks. Concerns regarding critical thinking skills arise as students may become overly reliant on AI-generated content, potentially undermining their analytical capabilities. Issues of academic integrity are also paramount; the ease with which students can access AI-generated responses raises questions about originality and the authenticity of student work (Almaraz–López *et al.*, 2024; García, 2024; Ngo, 2023). Moreover, inequitable access to technology exacerbates existing disparities within the educational landscape. For Salvadoran institutions, the challenge lies in contextualizing GenAI adoption within regional realities to ensure that technology serves as an enabler of learning rather than an amplifier of inequality (García, 2024).

This chapter situates GenAI within the unique socioeconomic and cultural context of Salvadoran higher education, exploring how students, faculty, and administrators are engaging with these tools. By examining the opportunities and challenges across these groups, the study highlights the potential for GenAI to transform learning environments and organizational practices, particularly in regions where resources are constrained but aspirations for equitable education remain high (Ruiz-Rojas *et al.*, 2024; Okuogume and Toledano, 2024).

11.1.2. *Purpose and objectives*

This chapter aims to explore the transformative potential of GenAI in Salvadoran higher education with a focus on fostering socially responsible and inclusive practices. Specifically, the chapter examines the experiences and perspectives of three key stakeholders:

1. *Students*: Understanding how socioeconomic barriers and varying levels of digital literacy influence students' access to and utilization of GenAI tools is crucial (Ruiz-Rojas *et al.*, 2024, Valdivieso adn González, 2025). This section will address how factors such as income disparities, access to technology, and educational background impact students' ability to engage with GAI effectively.

2. *Faculty*: Investigating faculty perceptions of GenAI encompasses its pedagogical applications, ethical considerations surrounding its use in academic settings, and the extent of institutional support available for its coordinated integration (Chávez Solís *et al.*, 2023; Kallunki *et al.*, 2024; Mah and Groß, 2024; McCarthy *et al.*, 2023; Ofosu-Ampong, 2024). This section will reflect on faculty attitudes toward GenAI as a tool of the teaching and learning process and their readiness to adapt traditional pedagogical methods with this technology.
3. *Administrators*: Analyzing the role of policy and organizational structures is crucial for enabling effective and ethical GenAI integration (Dotan, 2024; García, 2024). This section will focus on how institutional policies can promote or hinder the adoption of GAI technologies within educational frameworks.

The study seeks to bridge the gap between global technological advancements and localized educational needs, offering insights into how GenAI can support ethical, adaptive, and resource-equitable education. By addressing these objectives, the chapter contributes to ongoing conversations on the role of AI in democratizing knowledge and fostering innovation in the Global South.

11.1.3. *Structure of the chapter*

The chapter is structured around the perspectives of three core stakeholder groups:

- *Part 1*: Students and the Socioeconomic Context — This section examines empirical insights from student survey data at UCA, highlighting socioeconomic barriers to GenAI access and ethical concerns. It advocates for digital literacy and inclusive policies to promote equitable engagement with GenAI tools.
- *Part 2*: Faculty Perspectives on GenAI — This section explores ongoing research with faculty, focusing on their perceptions of GenAI's role in pedagogy and challenges related to critical skill development and academic integrity. It also examines faculty needs for institutional support and training.
- *Part 3*: Organizational Policies and Administrative Insights — This section discusses planned studies with university administrators to

address the role of policy and governance in fostering ethical and effective GenAI integration. It emphasizes the importance of aligning GenAI adoption with institutional goals and regional priorities.

The chapter concludes by synthesizing insights across stakeholder groups and offering recommendations for adaptive, culturally responsive approaches to GenAI. It highlights the need for continued research and collaboration to ensure that GenAI serves as a tool for inclusive and transformative education.

11.2. Part 1: Students and the Socioeconomic Context

11.2.1. *Theoretical framework: Socioeconomic dimensions of GenAI adoption*

The integration of GenAI tools in higher education must be understood within the socioeconomic realities that shape access and engagement, particularly in regions like El Salvador. Drawing upon a constructivist framework, this theory postulates that learners actively construct knowledge through personal experience, social interaction, and metacognition (Saarsar, 2018). This approach empowers students to become self-directed learners and fosters critical thinking skills. GenAI tools are conceptualized as potential catalysts for self-directed learning (Long *et al.*, 2011; McGuire *et al.*, 2024; García, 2024; Wu, 2022). However, the utility of these tools is mediated by systemic inequalities in digital infrastructure, resource availability, and digital literacy (Jarrahi *et al.*, 2023; Salas-Pilco and Yang, 2022). These disparities risk exacerbating existing educational inequities, reinforcing the divide between students who have the means to access advanced technologies and those who do not. In Salvadoran universities, where socioeconomic diversity defines the student population, these inequities are particularly pronounced.

Findings from the Universidad Centroamericana José Simeón Cañas (UCA) illuminate the challenges faced by students in engaging with GenAI tools. The research situates these findings within the Global South context, highlighting the urgent need for adaptive and inclusive educational policies.

11.2.2. *Findings: Patterns of access and use*

The study revealed a significant reliance on free versions of GenAI tools, with 91.87% of students unable to afford premium options. This finding underscores the financial constraints faced by Salvadoran students, particularly those from rural regions with limited infrastructure. While urban centers like San Salvador (46%) and La Libertad (28.5%) reported higher rates of GenAI usage, students from rural departments such as Chalatenango (1.9%) and Cuscatlán (0.5%) were underrepresented in the data, reflecting the digital divide highlighted by Heeks (2022).

Device access and preferences: Students predominantly accessed GenAI tools through Android smartphones (27.9%) and laptops (37.8%), prioritizing portability and affordability. However, reliance on mobile devices often limited the depth of interaction with GenAI tools, as many advanced features require larger screens or more powerful processors.

Usage patterns and tasks: GenAI tools like ChatGPT dominated the landscape, with 44.68% of students identifying it as their primary tool. Usage centered on task-oriented activities such as summarizing texts, clarifying ideas, and organizing information. More sophisticated applications, such as data analysis or creative problem-solving, were less common. This pattern reflects a utilitarian approach to AI, with students leveraging these tools to address immediate academic challenges rather than exploring their full potential.

11.2.3. *Ethical challenges and digital literacy*

Among students who did not engage with GenAI tools (25.07%), ethical concerns, particularly related to data privacy (16.30%) and academic integrity, emerged as the most significant deterrents. These findings align with concerns raised by Nguyen *et al.* (2023) regarding the ethical implications of AI use in education. Students expressed apprehension about GenAI's potential to undermine critical thinking and originality, a sentiment echoed in the focus group discussions.

The study emphasized the role of digital literacy in addressing these challenges. While many students demonstrated a basic familiarity with GenAI (71.8%), only a minority reported being "very familiar" (27.1%) or "extremely familiar" (8.2%) with its capabilities. This gap in understanding limits students' ability to navigate the ethical complexities of

GenAI, such as bias in algorithmic responses or the reliability of AI-generated information.

11.2.4. *Socioeconomic implications: Equity and engagement*

The study highlighted the need for equitable policies to bridge the socioeconomic divide in GenAI access. Students from lower-income backgrounds faced compounded challenges, including limited access to high-speed internet and a reliance on outdated devices. These barriers not only restrict engagement with GenAI tools but also hinder broader academic progress, perpetuating cycles of inequality.

Furthermore, the reliance on informal learning networks — such as friends (35.1%), social media (19.6%), and curiosity (18.8%) — for discovering GenAI tools reflects a gap in institutional support. This reliance often results in uneven access to accurate information and best practices, particularly for students with limited social or digital networks.

11.2.5. *Implications for policy and practice*

The findings underscore several key implications for Salvadoran higher education institutions:

1. *Infrastructure investments*: Universities must address disparities in digital infrastructure by providing subsidized access to GenAI tools and upgrading technological resources for students in underserved regions (Jarrahi *et al.*, 2023; Yixin *et al.*, 2024).
2. *AI literacy programs*: Curricula should integrate digital literacy training, emphasizing both technical skills and ethical considerations. Such programs could guide students in leveraging GenAI for advanced applications, such as critical analysis and problem-solving (Ruiz-Rojas *et al.*, 2024).
3. *Institutional outreach*: Formal channels for AI education, such as workshops, faculty-led discussions, and resource hubs, are essential for reducing reliance on informal peer networks. Institutions should proactively introduce students to GenAI tools and provide ongoing support.
4. *Cultural responsiveness*: Recognizing the unique challenges and cultural nuances of Salvadoran students is critical for developing inclusive policies. This involves tailoring AI literacy programs to address local needs, such as overcoming infrastructural barriers and promoting equitable access.

11.2.6. *Conclusion: Toward inclusive AI adoption*

By situating these findings within the broader Global South context, this research emphasizes the transformative potential of GenAI tools for higher education, provided that socioeconomic barriers are addressed. The theoretical framework highlights the dual role of AI as both an enabler of self-directed learning and a potential source of inequality. To ensure that GenAI fulfills its promise, Salvadoran institutions must adopt a holistic approach, balancing technological innovation with ethical governance and resource equity.

11.3. Part 2: Faculty Perspectives on GenAI

11.3.1. *Theoretical framework: Faculty roles in AI integration*

The integration of generative Artificial Intelligence (GenAI into higher education has sparked considerable interest, particularly in understanding the perspectives of faculty members regarding its adoption. Theoretical frameworks such as the Technology–Organization–Environment (TOE) framework and the Technology Acceptance Model (TAM) serve as key lenses through which faculty adoption of GenAI can be explored. These models help identify critical factors that influence faculty's engagement with new technologies, which in this case includes pedagogical capacities, socio-cultural contexts, perceived complexity, and institutional policies (Hernández-León and Rodríguez-Conde, 2024; Kallunki *et al.*, 2024; Ofosu-Ampong, 2024).

These constructs reflect the nuanced interplay of factors shaping GenAI adoption:

Pedagogical capacities (PPA): Faculty members' perceptions of GenAI's potential to foster personalized learning and innovative evaluation methods are critical. The successful adoption of technology and its careful alignment with pedagogical practices have the capacity to cater to the diverse learning needs of students (Gibson, 1979; Mahat, 2022).

Socio-cultural context (SCC): The institutional culture, leadership, and peer collaboration significantly influence the extent to which GenAI is embraced. The role of organizational culture and leadership in determining whether technological innovations, such as GenAI tools, will be successfully integrated into teaching and learning practices is closely related to the socio-cultural framework of higher education institutions (Bansal *et al.*, 2014; Tornatzky and Fleischer, 1990; Baker, 2012).

Perceived complexity and usability (PCU): Faculty readiness to navigate the technical complexity of GenAI tools is shaped by ease of use and accessibility. Understanding the perceived complexity and usability of a technology is pivotal to its successful adoption, especially when faculty members have varying degrees of digital literacy (Davis, 1989; Domingo-Coscolla *et al.*, 2020; Mah and Groß, 2024).

Organizational policies and incentives (OPI): Institutional initiatives supporting GenAI integration, such as training programs, clear policy development, and recognition of innovative pedagogical practices, are crucial. The establishment of organizational policies is essential, as they play a critical role in fostering technology adoption, which significantly influences faculty members' willingness to explore and implement new tools (Aparicio-Gómez, 2023; Okuogume and Toledano, 2024).

These dimensions collectively provide a comprehensive approach to examining how GenAI is reshaping educational paradigms in Salvadoran universities.

11.3.2. *Pedagogical integration of GenAI*

GenAI holds the potential to reshape pedagogical practices in higher education by offering several innovative applications that support both faculty and students. The following are some of the key areas where GenAI is being integrated:

1. *Enhancing personalized learning*: GenAI tools are particularly effective in tailoring content delivery to individual student needs, enabling personalized learning pathways. This has the potential to enhance student engagement and learning outcomes by allowing students to

progress at their own pace (Aparicio-Gómez, 2023; Valdivieso and González, 2025; Walczak and Cellary, 2023).

2. *Supporting innovative assessment models*: Faculty are exploring how GenAI can assist in the development of dynamic, adaptive assessment methods that cater to individual student strengths. Such tools provide an opportunity to personalize assessments and enhance feedback mechanisms (Chávez Solís *et al.*, 2023).
3. *Streamlining administrative workflows*: GenAI tools, such as ChatGPT, Gemini, and Perplexity, are being adopted to assist in creating course materials, automating grading, and summarizing research for classroom discussions, thus easing the administrative burden on faculty members and allowing them more time for pedagogical engagement (Valdivieso and González, 2025).

However, the adoption of these tools is not uniform. For example, faculty in STEM fields are more likely to experiment with GenAI compared to their colleagues in the humanities. This disparity often reflects differences in training, technological familiarity, and discipline-specific needs (Bannister *et al.*, 2023).

11.3.3. *Challenges and concerns*

Despite the promising potential of GenAI, faculty members have raised several concerns that need to be addressed for its successful integration into higher education. These concerns include the following:

Ethical concerns: GenAI raises critical questions about data privacy, academic integrity, and the potential for misuse. One major issue is ensuring the authenticity of AI-generated content and managing concerns around plagiarism detection and academic honesty (Bissessar, 2023; Dotan, 2024; Kallunki *et al.*, 2024; Walczak and Cellary, 2023).

Impact on student learning: There are concerns that overreliance on GenAI may diminish students' critical thinking and problem-solving skills, as AI tools may encourage students to outsource cognitive tasks rather than engage deeply with the material. Some faculty express apprehension that overreliance on GenAI could lead to a decline in critical thinking and problem-solving abilities, as students may delegate cognitive tasks to AI (Holmes and Tuomi, 2022; Holmes *et al.*, 2023; Kallunki *et al.*, 2024; Long *et al.*, 2011; Pinto *et al.*, 2019; Ruiz-Rojas *et al.*, 2024).

Institutional gaps: A lack of institutional guidelines leaves many faculty members without clear direction on how to integrate GenAI effectively and ethically. Many faculty members report feeling unsupported, with no clear direction on how to incorporate GenAI in a manner that aligns with ethical standards (Gellai, 2023; Mairal, 2023; Okuogume and Toledano, 2024; Valdivieso and González, 2025; Wu *et al.*, 2022).

Technical barriers: Faculty members with limited digital competencies may struggle to navigate the technical complexities of GenAI tools. This highlights the need for comprehensive training and support mechanisms (Domingo-Coscolla *et al.*, 2020).

These issues highlight the need for systemic interventions to support ethical and effective GenAI use in higher education.

11.3.4. *Ongoing research and emerging insights*

Preliminary findings from faculty surveys and focus groups at the Universidad Centroamericana José Simeón Cañas (UCA) reveal the following:

- *Training gaps*: Only a minority of faculty have received formal AI training, relying instead on peer learning or self-directed exploration (Valdivieso and González, 2025).
- *Acceptance disparities*: Faculty acceptance of GenAI varies by discipline and workload, with part-time instructors reporting fewer opportunities for training compared to full-time staff (León Rodríguez and Viña Brito, 2017; Ofosu-Ampong, 2024).
- *Collaborative opportunities*: Faculty emphasize the potential for GenAI to foster collaborative teaching practices, enabling co-creation of learning materials and dynamic classroom discussions (Chávez Solís *et al.*, 2023; Mairal, 2023).

The ongoing research aims to identify strategies for addressing these disparities and leveraging GenAI's full potential in higher education.

11.3.5. *Implications for institutional policy and practice*

To address these challenges and optimize GenAI integration, institutions should:

1. *Develop comprehensive guidelines*: Establish policies addressing ethical concerns, data privacy, and academic integrity in GenAI use (Dotan, 2024; Hernández-León and Rodríguez-Conde, 2024; Yixin *et al.*, 2024). A study developed by Dabis and Csáki (2024) collected and identified information about AI-related ethical dilemmas from 30 universities on different continents and concluded that "the overall impression is that Universities primarily aim to explore and harness the potential benefits of GenAI but not with an uncritical mindset. They are focusing on the opportunities while simultaneously trying to address the emerging challenges in the field" (p. 10).
2. *Invest in faculty development*: Provide workshops, certifications, and ongoing training to equip faculty with the skills needed to integrate GenAI effectively (Aldosari, 2020; Hernández-León and Rodríguez-Conde, 2024; Holmes *et al.*, 2023; Walczak and Cellary, 2023).
3. *Encourage interdisciplinary collaborations*: Facilitate cross-departmental projects that explore innovative applications of GenAI in diverse academic contexts (Mairal, 2023; O'Dea, 2024; Yixin *et al.*, 2024).
4. *Align incentives with adoption goals*: Recognize and reward faculty who demonstrate excellence in incorporating GenAI into their teaching practices (Domingo-Coscolla *et al.*, 2020; Mairal, 2023).

11.3.6. *Conclusion: The path forward*

Faculty play a pivotal role in determining the success of GenAI adoption in higher education. Addressing their concerns and providing robust support systems can transform these tools from sources of contention to catalysts for pedagogical innovation. Continued research is essential to explore the evolving relationship between faculty, technology, and institutional policies, ensuring that GenAI serves as a force for ethical and inclusive education.

11.4. Part 3: Organizational Policies and Administrative Insights

11.4.1. *Introduction: The role of policies in GenAI integration*

As Artificial Intelligence becomes increasingly prevalent, universities are evolving to play a more dynamic role. Higher education institutions are essential in transferring knowledge, stimulating intellectual growth, fostering social and communication skills, and promoting the effective use of AI tools. Additionally, universities play a crucial role in identifying and motivating future AI leaders (Walczak and Cellary, 2023):

- *Purpose of policies*: Policies play a crucial role in aligning GenAI adoption with the strategic goals and missions of higher education institutions. They provide a framework for the ethical, inclusive, and effective use of GenAI tools across teaching, research, and administrative functions (UNESCO, 2024a, 2024b). Effective policy development is necessary to ensure that institutions can harness the benefits of GenAI while mitigating risks related to data privacy, algorithmic bias, and academic integrity (Holmes *et al.*, 2023; Yixin *et al.*, 2024).
- *Challenges in policy development*: Technological advancements in GenAI often outpace regulatory frameworks, leading to concerns about academic integrity, equity, and data security. Ethical questions such as data privacy and algorithmic transparency remain unresolved in many institutions (Kazim and Koshiyama, 2021; Ghimire and Edwards, 2024; Okuogume and Toledano, 2024; Walczak and Cellary, 2023).
- *Regional context*: Institutions in the Global South face unique challenges, including infrastructural deficits, socioeconomic disparities, and limited access to digital tools (ILIA, 2024; Jarrahi *et al.*, 2023; Ruiz-Rojas *et al.*, 2024; Valdivieso and González, 2025).

11.4.2. *Existing policy gaps and challenges*

Globally, many institutions face significant gaps in AI policy development. GenAI presents a unique opportunity for higher education institutions to redefine their educational models and improve overall performance. A reactive stance toward GenAI, such as waiting for the technology to mature further, risks allowing for the unchecked proliferation of potentially harmful or inefficient uses, making it more challenging to control the technology's integration into the institution in the future (Cardozo Álvarez, 2024; Hernández and Gonzalo Panela, 2023). Colleges and universities must be proactive in integrating comprehensive policies in the use of GenAI. For instance, a survey of U.S. institutions found that only 5% had formal policies regarding GenAI use, while 80% were still in the process of developing such policies (Ghimire and Edwards, 2024). Key challenges in policy development include the following:

Policy gaps: Many institutions have yet to develop comprehensive policies that address the ethical use of GenAI, particularly regarding issues of data privacy, algorithmic transparency, innovative development, and academic integrity (Kazim and Koshiyama, 2021; Yixin *et al.*, 2024). These gaps highlight the need for universities to act proactively in establishing clear guidelines for AI use in educational contexts.

Administrative challenges: Aligning GenAI adoption with institutional goals can be hindered by limited budgets, faculty resistance, and inadequate training programs (Rasky, 2024). Institutions must balance operational efficiency with the ethical use of AI, considering disciplinary differences and the varied needs of academic stakeholders (Ferreira Mello *et al.*, 2024; Holmes *et al.*, 2023; Okuogume and Toledano, 2024; Wang *et al.*, 2024). To ensure responsible AI integration, institutions must navigate these challenges while developing clear guidelines and supporting faculty development initiatives.

11.4.3. *Framework for policy development*

Developing a robust framework for AI policy in higher education is crucial to navigate the ethical and pedagogical complexities of integrating these technologies effectively. To mitigate unforeseen consequences and guarantee equitable learning processes, educational policies must address concerns such as algorithmic bias, transparency, and accountability within AI systems. An effective GenAI policy and regulation in higher education are essential for guiding students in responsible AI use, fostering academic integrity, and enabling them to leverage AI for learning and inspiration. Establishing clear guidelines is crucial to maximize the benefits of GenAI in education while minimizing potential risks (Panke and Oeeshi, 2023). This section outlines key principles and considerations for developing effective AI policies, including the need for inclusivity, transparency, and scalability, while also emphasizing the importance of ethical governance models and learning from successful case studies:

- *Principles for effective policies*:
  - *Inclusivity*: Engage diverse stakeholders, including students, faculty, and administrators, to ensure fairness and adaptability in policies (Rasky, 2024).
  - *Transparency*: Make policies accessible, clear, and informed by institutional mission and vision (Ghimire and Edwards, 2024).
  - *Scalability*: Design frameworks that can evolve with emerging AI technologies and institutional priorities (UNESCO, 2024a; Yixin *et al.*, 2024).
- *Ethical governance models*:
  - *Strategic governance*: Institutions should establish governance bodies comprising administrators, faculty, students, and external experts to oversee AI policy development (Rasky, 2024; Yixin *et al.*, 2024).
  - *Case studies*: Highlight examples from leading institutions in Latin America and other regions, emphasizing innovative governance practices (Krijger *et al.*, 2022; Valdivieso and González, 2025; Wang *et al.*, 2024).

11.4.4. *Administrative strategies for GenAI implementation*

Successful implementation of GenAI requires strategic administrative efforts, including the following:

- *Institutional capacity building*: Improving digital infrastructure is crucial to ensuring equitable access to GenAI tools across all stakeholders (Cardozo Álvarez, 2024). "The technical characteristics of GenAI applications in education require multidisciplinary and comprehensive cooperation and communication support" (Yixin *et al.*, 2024, p. 52). Institutions should also implement AI literacy programs for students and faculty to foster responsible and effective use of GenAI (Kazim and Koshiyama, 2021; Holmes *et al.*, 2023).

- *Pilot programs and evaluations*: Institutions should launch pilot programs to test the efficacy of GenAI tools in educational settings, gathering feedback for iterative improvements (Rasky, 2024). Colleges and universities should also incorporate evidence-based adjustments to refine policies and practices (Holmes *et al.*, 2023).
- *Funding and resource allocation*: Securing funding through government grants and international partnerships can support AI adoption, particularly in underfunded institutions (Arias Ortiz *et al.*, 2024).

11.4.5. *Implications for the Global South*

The Global South's unique socio-cultural context, marked by a significant digital divide, poses both challenges and opportunities for GenAI adoption. "The countries of the Global South should be aware of their technological rights and advocate for them to mitigate the gap between strong and weak countries" (Upadhayay, 2024, p. 51). Many institutions in these regions grapple with infrastructural deficits, socioeconomic disparities, and limited access to digital tools (ILIA, 2024; Jarrahi *et al.*, 2023; Ruiz-Rojas *et al.*, 2024). Therefore, it is imperative to consider these factors when contemplating the integration of AI and GenAI into educational settings in the Global South:

- *Local adaptation*: Policies must reflect the socioeconomic and cultural contexts of the Global South to ensure that GenAI tools are tailored to local educational needs (ILIA, 2024; Valdivieso and González, 2025). "AI cannot be considered a plug-and-play technology that can be easily applied to all kinds of innovation tasks" (Füller *et al.*, 2022). GenAI integration should not be merely technological, but culturally sensitive. The cultural context of the Global South, including local languages and social norms, should be integrated into the design and implementation of GenAI tools.
- *International collaboration*: Encouraging partnerships within the region can help share best practices, pool resources, and collectively advance AI integration in higher education (IMF, 2024).
- *Capacity development*: Long-term investment in building AI literacy and strengthening technological infrastructure is critical to addressing the digital divide in underrepresented areas (Mah and Groß, 2024; UNESCO, 2024a).

11.4.6. *Conclusion: Toward a collaborative governance model*

In conclusion, policies are integral to the ethical and inclusive integration of GenAI in higher education. Developing robust and adaptive governance frameworks that engage a diverse range of stakeholders — including students, faculty, administrators, and community representatives — ensures that GenAI adoption addresses the needs of all participants in the educational ecosystem. Effective governance models must prioritize equity, ethical use, and context-specific solutions, particularly in regions like the Global South where socioeconomic and infrastructural disparities persist.

A collaborative approach to policy development is essential. By fostering open dialogue and consensus building among stakeholders, institutions can create policies that are transparent, fair, and culturally responsive. Successful models from institutions in Latin America, such as faculty-driven policy advocacy and student-centered AI literacy initiatives, provide valuable insights for developing governance structures that are both effective and adaptable.

Moreover, policies must be designed with mechanisms for continuous evaluation and adaptation to keep pace with the rapid evolution of AI technologies and the dynamic educational landscape. This iterative approach ensures that governance frameworks remain relevant, resilient, and capable of addressing emerging ethical challenges, such as algorithmic bias, data privacy, and academic integrity.

To achieve these goals, institutions should do the following:

- Establish dedicated AI governance committees that include students, faculty, administrators, and external experts to guide policy development and implementation.
- Adopt evidence-based practices by conducting regular assessments of GenAI's impact on teaching, learning, and administrative processes.
- Encourage regional and international collaboration with organizations like UNESCO and peer institutions to share best practices, resources, and insights into ethical AI adoption.

By prioritizing inclusive, ethical, and adaptive governance, Salvadoran higher education institutions can harness the transformative potential of GenAI to foster equity and innovation, serving as a model for other regions in the Global South. This collaborative governance approach will ensure that GenAI benefits all stakeholders, empowering students and faculty while upholding the highest ethical standards.

11.5. Global Perspectives

11.5.1. *Theoretical framework: AI in global contexts*

The adoption of GenAI in education reflects global disparities in technological readiness, infrastructure, and resources (Jarrahi *et al.*, 2023). Frameworks such as the ILIA (2024) index and the IMF's AI Preparedness Index reveal significant regional gaps, with Latin America scoring below North America and Europe in AI maturity (Cardozo Álvarez, 2024; IMF, 2024). These indices emphasize the need for context-sensitive approaches to AI integration that address localized socioeconomic and cultural realities.

UNESCO underscores the transformative potential of AI to address pressing educational challenges, yet warns that technological advancements often outpace the ethical and regulatory frameworks necessary for equitable implementation (UNESCO, 2024a). For the Global South, including Latin America, these challenges are compounded by entrenched inequalities in access to technology and digital literacy (Mah and Groß, 2024; Salas-Pilco and Yang, 2022; UNESCO, 2024b, 2024c; Walczak and Cellary, 2023).

Emerging models such as the Technology Readiness Index and AI Maturity Models provide valuable tools for analyzing these disparities. These models stress the importance of key enabling factors, including robust digital infrastructure, open data access, and AI literacy, as prerequisites for effective AI integration in education.

11.5.2. *Contextualizing AI adoption*

In Latin America, the digital divide remains a primary barrier to equitable GenAI adoption. While countries like Chile and Costa Rica have made significant strides in AI readiness, others, such as Honduras and Paraguay, face systemic challenges (ILIA, 2024; Sánchez Forero, 2024). These disparities stem from the following:

1. *Investment gaps*: Many countries fail to meet UNESCO's recommendation of allocating 4–6% of the GDP to education, limiting their

capacity to invest in AI infrastructure. For example, El Salvador allocates 4.5% of its GDP to education, while Honduras lags behind (Arias Ortiz *et al.*, 2024).

2. *Digital divide*: Access to technology remains uneven. In Costa Rica and El Salvador, 98% of students report computer access, but in Paraguay, only 46% of students have reliable internet connectivity (Arias Ortiz *et al.*, 2024).
3. *AI literacy deficits*: The lack of advanced technical skills and human talent in AI underscores the need for comprehensive education and training programs. Latin American countries generally remain in the early or intermediate stages of AI maturity (ILIA, 2024; Mah and Groß, 2024; Walczak and Cellary, 2023).

These findings highlight the dual challenge of addressing infrastructural inequities while fostering the digital competencies required for effective AI use.

11.5.3. *Lessons for the Global South*

The experiences of Latin American institutions provide valuable insights for the broader Global South in navigating the complexities of AI integration within educational contexts. As Arias Ortiz *et al.* (2024) observe, "The evolution of learning assessment systems in Latin America and the Caribbean has varied, but the systems share many challenges. Having solid tools for monitoring learning continues to be a clear objective of … education policy in the region" (p. 59). These challenges, coupled with the rapid advancements in AI, necessitate a nuanced approach to AI adoption that considers the unique socio-cultural and economic realities of each nation. This section explores key lessons for the Global South, drawing upon the experiences of Latin American institutions. These lessons emphasize the importance of the following:

- *Policy innovation*: Developing ethical frameworks that address critical concerns such as data privacy, algorithmic transparency, and fairness is paramount (Holmes *et al.*, 2023). As McGuire *et al.* (2024) highlight, "Organizations must strike a balance between enforcement and fairness, ensuring that policies are clear, consistent, and aligned with their overall culture and goals to maximize the positive impact of disciplinary policies on motivation and performance" (p. 350). The lack of comprehensive guidelines, as noted by Ghimire and Edwards (2024), can hinder responsible AI adoption by leaving critical issues unaddressed. A study conducted by Füller *et al.* (2022) explains "that in order to prepare for AI-based innovation management, organizations have to adjust their strategy…, and implement structural changes… offering training, hiring new talents, or developing new tools and technologies" (p. 17).

- *Community-centric approaches*: Effective AI integration requires collaborative efforts with local communities to ensure that technologies align with local cultural values and socioeconomic realities (Walczak and Cellary, 2023; Yixin *et al.*, 2024). As emphasized by Rasky (2024), stakeholder involvement in policy development is crucial for fostering greater adaptability and buy-in.
- *Leveraging strengths*: Countries with strong ICT and educational foundations, such as Chile and Costa Rica, can serve as valuable regional models. Their focus on AI literacy and infrastructure investment demonstrates the importance of aligning technological advancements with educational goals that walk toward the democratization of knowledge (Chen *et al.*, 2024; Jarrahi *et al.*, 2023; Salas-Pilco and Yang, 2022; Walczak and Cellary, 2023).

11.5.4. *Implications for policy and practice*

To ensure equitable and ethical AI adoption, the following strategies are essential:

1. *Invest in infrastructure*: Governments and institutions must bridge the digital divide by enhancing connectivity, upgrading technological resources, and ensuring universal access to digital tools (Cardozo Álvarez, 2024).
2. *Promote AI literacy*: Compulsory training programs for students, faculty, and administrators can build the technical competencies necessary for meaningful engagement with GenAI tools. Such programs should also address ethical considerations, fostering a culture of responsible AI use (Holmes *et al.*, 2023; Mah and Groß, 2024; Rasky, 2024; Walczak and Cellary, 2023).
3. *Establish ethical frameworks*: Institutions should develop governance structures to tackle issues such as data privacy, academic integrity, and

algorithmic bias. These frameworks must be transparent, inclusive, and adaptable to regional needs (Dabis and Csáki, 2024; Holmes *et al.*, 2023; Ferreira Mello *et al.*, 2024; Wang *et al.*, 2024).
4. *Encourage regional collaboration*: Cross-border partnerships can facilitate knowledge sharing and resource pooling, enabling countries to collectively address challenges and leverage opportunities in AI adoption (Ferreira Mello *et al.*, 2024; IMF, 2024).

11.5.5. *Conclusion: Global lessons, local actions*

The Global South faces unique challenges and opportunities in adopting GenAI in education. Addressing these requires context-sensitive policies and collaborative approaches that balance technological potential with regional priorities. Lessons from Latin America demonstrate that aligning technological advancements with socioeconomic realities can democratize education and drive innovation. By fostering ethical, inclusive, and contextually relevant practices, the Global South can transform its educational systems and contribute to global AI governance frameworks.

11.6. Synthesis of Findings

This chapter has examined the integration of GenAI in Salvadoran higher education, highlighting its transformative potential and associated challenges across students, faculty, and administrators:

- *Students*: Socioeconomic disparities limit equitable access to GenAI tools, with a reliance on free versions of software underscoring financial constraints (Valdivieso and González, 2025). Ethical concerns about overreliance on AI and diminished critical thinking further complicate student engagement (Kazim and Koshiyama, 2021). Enhanced digital literacy and institutional policies are crucial for fostering responsible usage (UNESCO, 2024a, 2024b, 2024c).
- *Faculty*: Faculty perspectives reveal a dichotomy: While GenAI enhances personalized learning and streamlines tasks like grading, concerns about academic integrity and inadequate training persist (Rasky, 2024; Ghimire and Edwards, 2024; Walczak and Cellary, 2023). Variability in adoption across disciplines emphasizes the need for targeted support (Salas-Pilco and Yang, 2022).

- *Administrators*: Institutions face the challenge of creating governance structures that align with ethical principles while addressing socioeconomic realities. Higher education institutions need "to make information-based decisions" (Arias Ortiz *et al.*, 2024, p. 60). Policy gaps in areas such as data privacy and algorithmic transparency are particularly pressing (Dabis and Csáki, 2024; Schultz *et al.*, 2024; Wang *et al.*, 2024).

These findings underscore the necessity of context-sensitive strategies to bridge gaps in access, literacy, and governance while leveraging the transformative potential of GenAI. Higher education institutions need to keep in mind that "Good practice in human oversight could thus be achieved through a combination of preventive measures and soft, dialogue-based procedures" (Dabis and Csáki, 2024, p. 10).

11.6.1. *Future directions*

To fully realize the potential of GenAI, the following actions are essential:

1. *Invest in infrastructure and literacy*: Governments and institutions must address infrastructural inequities by enhancing connectivity and providing training programs (Jarrahi *et al.*, 2023). Latin American countries like Costa Rica offer successful examples of AI readiness through targeted investments (Arias Ortiz *et al.*, 2024; Cardozo Álvarez, 2024; Ferreira Mello *et al.*, 2024; Walczak and Cellary, 2023).
2. *Develop inclusive and ethical policies*: Policies must be transparent, adaptable, and inclusive, engaging stakeholders to address ethical dilemmas like data privacy and fairness (Kazim and Koshiyama, 2021; Krijger *et al.*, 2022; Rasky, 2024; Schultz *et al.*, 2024).
3. *Foster regional and global collaboration*: Partnerships across the Global South can amplify resource sharing and knowledge exchange, as demonstrated by regional frameworks like ILIA (2024) and the IMF's AI Preparedness Index (IMF, 2024).
4. *Support interdisciplinary approaches*: Effective GenAI adoption requires breaking disciplinary silos, fostering collaborations that recognize the diverse applications of AI in education and research (Salas-Pilco and Yang, 2022).

Future research should focus on longitudinal studies to evaluate GenAI's impact on educational equity, learning outcomes, and institutional governance over time.

11.6.2. *Concluding thoughts*

GenAI offers the potential to transform higher education globally, but its adoption must align with ethical principles and socioeconomic realities. For the Global South, particularly in regions like Latin America, this means addressing infrastructural disparities and fostering inclusive policies to ensure that technology acts as a democratizing force.

Salvadoran universities, such as the Universidad Centroamericana José Simeón Cañas (UCA), have demonstrated the capacity to lead by integrating localized, culturally sensitive approaches to GenAI adoption (Valdivieso and González, 2025). By prioritizing equity and collaboration, these institutions can provide a model for how GenAI can empower students and faculty alike, fostering innovation while addressing ethical concerns.

In a rapidly evolving global landscape, GenAI represents both an opportunity and a responsibility. Institutions must leverage this technology to democratize education, reduce inequities, and prepare for a future where AI enhances human potential, ensuring its benefits are accessible to all.

Bibliography

Aldosari, S. A. M. "The future of higher education in the light of artificial intelligence transformations." *International Journal of Higher Education* 9, no. 3 (2020): 145. DOI: 10.5430/ijhe.v9n3p145.

Almaraz-López, C., Almaraz-Menéndez, F., and López-Esteban, C. "Comparative study of the attitudes and perceptions of university students in business administration and management and in education toward artificial intelligence." *Education Sciences* 13, no. 6 (2023): 609. DOI: 10.3390/educsci13060609.

Aparicio-Gómez, O. Y., Ostos-Ortiz, O. L., and Abadía-García, C. "Convergence between emerging technologies and active methodologies in the university." *Journal of Technology and Science Education* 14, no. 1 (2024): 31–44. DOI: 10.3926/jotse.2508.

Arias Ortiz, E., Dueñas, X., Giambruno, C., and López, A. *El Estado de la Educación en América Latina y el Caribe 2024*. IDB, 2024. DOI: 10.18235/0013171.

Baker, J. "The technology–organization–environment framework." In *Information Systems Theory*, edited by Y. Dwivedi, M. Wade, and S. Schneberger, 231–245. New York, NY: Springer, 2012. DOI: 10.1007/978-1-4419-6108-2_12.

Bannister, P., Alcalde Peñalver, E., and Santamaría Urbieta, A. "A systematic review of generative AI and (English medium instruction) higher education." *Aula Abierta* 52 (2023): 401–409. DOI: 10.17811/rifie.52.4.2023.401-409.

Bansal, G., Mitchell, A., and Li, D. "A panel report on higher education in the age of AI from the perspective of academic leaders in the Midwest U.S." *Communications of the Association for Information Systems* 54 (2024): 360–375. DOI: 10.17705/1CAIS.05413.

Bissessar, C. "To use or not to use ChatGPT and assistive artificial intelligence tools in higher education institutions?" *Equity in Education & Society* (2023). DOI: 10.1177/27526461231215083.

Bond, M., Khosravi, H., De Laat, M., *et al.* "A meta-systematic review of artificial intelligence in higher education: A call for increased ethics, collaboration, and rigor." *International Journal of Educational Technology in Higher Education* 21, no. 4 (2024): 1–11. DOI: 10.1186/s41239-023-00436-z.

Cardozo Álvarez, R. "América Latina y la adopción de la IA." *DW* (2024). Available at: https://www.dw.com (Accessed: 20 August 2024).

Chávez Solís, M. E., *et al.* "Inteligencia artificial generativa para fortalecer la educación superior." *LATAM Revista Latinoamericana De Ciencias Sociales Y Humanidades* 4, no. 3 (2023). DOI: 10.56712/latam.v4i3.1113.

Chen, A., Liu, L., and Zhu, T. "Advancing the democratization of generative artificial intelligence in healthcare: A narrative review." *J Hosp Manag Health Policy* 8 (2024): 12.

Dabis, A. and Csáki, C. "AI and ethics: Investigating policy responses." *Humanities and Social Sciences Communications* 11, no. 1 (2024). DOI: 10.1057/s41599-024-03526-z.

Davis, F. D. "Perceived usefulness, perceived ease of use, and user acceptance of information technology." *MIS Quarterly* 13, no. 3 (1989): 319–340.

Domingo-Coscolla, M., Bosco, A., Carrasco Segovia, S., and Sánchez Valero, J. A. "Fomentando la competencia digital docente en la universidad: Percepción de estudiantes y docentes." *Revista de Investigación Educativa* 38, no. 1 (2020): 167–782. DOI: 10.6018/rie.340551.

Dotan, R., Parker, L. S., and Radzilowicz, J. G. "Responsible adoption of generative AI in higher education: Developing a 'Points to Consider' approach based on faculty perspectives." *Proceedings of AI in Education Conference* (2024). DOI: 10.1145/3630106.3659023.

Ferreira Mello, R., Freitas, E., Dwan Pereira, F., Cabral, L., Tedesco, P., and Ramalho, G. *Education in the Age of Generative AI: Context and Recent*

Developments. C.E.S.A.R. Whitepaper, 2024. Available at: https://arxiv.org/pdf/2309.12332.

Füller, J., Hutter, K., Wahl, J., Bilgram, V., and Tekic, Z. "How AI revolutionizes innovation management — Perceptions and implementation preferences of AI-based innovators." *Technological Forecasting and Social Change* 178 (2022): 121598. DOI: 10.1016/j.techfore.2022.121598.

García, J. "Nayib Bukele contrata un asesor en inteligencia artificial: El Gobierno aseguró que busca 'ser una potencia tecnológica en la región.'" *El Diario de Hoy* (2024). Available at: https://www.elsalvador.com.

Gellai, D. B. "Enterprising academics: Heterarchical policy networks for artificial intelligence in British higher education." *ECNU Review of Education* 6, no. 4 (2023): 568–596. DOI: 10.1177/20965311221143798.

Ghimire, A. and Edwards, J. *From Guidelines to Governance*. Springer, 2024. DOI: 10.1007/978-3-031-64312-5_36.

Gibson, J. J. "The Theory of Affordances." In *The Ecological Approach to Visual Perception*. Boston: Houghton Mifflin, 1979.

Heeks, R. "Digital inequality beyond the digital divide: Conceptualizing adverse digital incorporation in the global South." *Information Technology for Development* 28, no. 4 (2022): 688–704. DOI: 10.1080/02681102.2022.2068492.

Hernández, M. and Gonzalo Panela, C. *La Inteligencia Artificial en la Educación Superior*. OBServatory de OBS Business School, 2023. Available at: https://marketing.onlinebschool.es/Prensa/Informes/Informe%20OBS%20-%20La%20Inteligencia%20Artificial%20en%20la%20Educaci%C3%B3n%20Superior.pdf.

Hernández-León, N. and Rodríguez-Conde, M. "Inteligencia artificial aplicada a la educación y la evaluación educativa en la universidad: Introducción de sistemas de tutorización inteligentes, sistemas de reconocimiento y otras." *RED. Revista de Educación a Distancia* 24, no. 78 (2024). DOI: 10.6018/red.594651.

Holmes, W., Iniesto, F., Anastopoulou, S., *et al.* "Stakeholder perspectives on the ethics of AI in distance-based higher education." *International Review of Research in Open and Distance Learning* 24, no. 2 (2023): 96–117. DOI: 10.19173/irrodl.v24i2.6089.

Holmes, W. and Tuomi, I. "State of the art and practice in AI in education." *European Journal of Education* 57 (2022): 542–570. DOI: 10.1111/ejed.12533.

ILIA. *Índice Latinoamericano de Inteligencia Artificial*. 2024. Available at: https://ilia.cenia.cl.

IMF. *Gen-AI: Artificial Intelligence and the Future of Work*. IMF, 2024. ISBN: 9798400262548.

Jarrahi, M. H., Askay, D., Eshraghi, A., and Smith, P. "Artificial intelligence and knowledge management: A partnership between human and AI." *Business Horizons* 66, no. 1 (2023): 87–99. DOI: 10.1016/j.bushor.2022.03.002.

Kallunki, V., Kinnunen, P., Pyörälä, E., Haarala-Muhonen, A., Katajavuori, N., and Myyry, L. "Navigating the evolving landscape of teaching and learning: University faculty and staff perceptions of the artificial intelligence-altered terrain." *Education Sciences* 14, no. 7 (2024): 727. DOI: 10.3390/educsci14070727.

Kazim, E. and Koshiyama, A. "A high-level overview of AI ethics." *Patterns* 2 (2021): 100314. DOI: 10.1016/j.patter.2021.100314.

Krijger, J., Thuis, T., Ruiter, M. D., Ligthart, E., and Broekman, I. "The AI ethics maturity model: A holistic approach to advancing ethical data science in organizations." *AI and Ethics* (2022): 1–13.

León Rodríguez, G. de la C. and Viña Brito, S. M. "La inteligencia artificial en la educación superior. Oportunidades y amenazas." *INNOVA Research Journal* 2, no. 8.1 (2017): 412–422. DOI: 10.33890/innova.v2.n8.1.2017.399.

Long, P., Siemens, G., Conole, G., and Gasevic, D. *Proceedings of the 1st International Conference on Learning Analytics and Knowledge (LAK11), Banff, AB, Canada, Feb 27-Mar 01, 2011.* New York: ACM, 2011.

Mah, D. K. and Groß, N. "Artificial intelligence in higher education: Exploring faculty use, self-efficacy, distinct profiles, and professional development needs." *International Journal of Educational Technology in Higher Education* 21 (2024): 58. DOI: 10.1186/s41239-024-00490-1.pdf.

Mahat, M. "Purpose, process, place, pedagogical affordance and product (5Ps) of student learning in higher education: Beyond Beckers." *Facilities* (2022). DOI: 10.1108/F-06-2022-0086.

Mairal, R. "What should the University of the future look like?" *On the Horizon* 31, no. 1 (2023): 62–70. DOI: 10.1108/OTH-08-2022-0050.

McCarthy, A. M., Maor, D., McConney, A., and Cavanaugh, C. "Digital transformation in education: Critical components for leaders of system change." *Social Sciences & Humanities Open* 8, no. 1 (2023): 100479. DOI: 10.1016/j.ssaho.2023.100479.

McGuire, A., Qureshi, W., and Saad, M. "A constructivist model for leveraging GenAI tools for individualized, peer-simulated feedback on student writing." *International Journal of Technology in Education (IJTE)* 7, no. 2 (2024): 326–352. DOI: 10.46328/ijte.639.

Ngo, T. T. A. "The perception by university students of the use of ChatGPT in education." *International Journal of Emerging Technologies in Learning (iJET)* 18, no. 17 (2023): 4–19. DOI: 10.3991/ijet.v18i17.39019.

Nguyen, T. T., Holmes, W., and Anastopoulou, S. "Ethics and AI in education: A global perspective." *International Journal of Educational Technology* 42, no. 5 (2023): 601–616.

O'Dea, X. "Generative AI: Is it a paradigm shift for higher education?" *Studies in Higher Education (Dorchester-on-Thames)* 49, no. 5 (2024): 811–816. DOI: 10.1080/03075079.2024.2332944.

Ofosu-Ampong, K. "Beyond the hype: Exploring faculty perceptions and acceptability of AI in teaching practices." *Discover Education* 3, no. 1 (2024). DOI: 10.1007/s44217-024-00128-4.

Okuogume, A. and Toledano, N. "Co-creation in sustainable entrepreneurship education: Lessons from business–university educational partnerships." *Sustainability* 16, no. 2272 (2024). DOI: 10.3390/su16062272.

Panke, S. and Oeeshi, I. J. "Part II: AI in higher education." *AI in Education* (2023). Available at: https://edtechbooks.org/ai_in_education/part_iii_ai_in_higher_education.

Pinto, C., Nicola, S., Mendonça, J., and Velichova, D. "Best teaching practices in the first year of the pilot implementation of the project DrIVE-MATH." *Teaching Mathematics and Its Applications: An International Journal of the IMA* 38 (2019): 154–166. DOI: 10.1093/teamat/hr.

Rasky, E. *Generative AI Policy in Higher Education.* Centre for International Governance Innovation, 2024.

Ruiz-Rojas, L. I., Salvador-Ullauri, L., and Acosta-Vargas, P. "Collaborative working and critical thinking: Adoption of generative artificial intelligence tools in higher education." *Sustainability* 16, no. 13 (2024): 5367. DOI: 10.3390/su16135367.

Saarsar, P. "Exploring the constructivist approach in education: Theory, practice, and implications." 05 (2018): 717–725.

Salas-Pilco, Z. and Yang, G. "Digital equity in higher education: A Global South perspective." *Journal of Inclusive Technology* 34, no. 3 (2022): 401–423.

Sánchez Forero, V. "Estos son los países mejor preparados para la adopción de la inteligencia artificial." *La República*, 9 November 2024.

Schultz, M. D., Clegg, M., Hofstetter, R., and Seele, P. "Algorithms and dehumanization: A definition and avoidance model." *AI & Society* (2024).

Tornatzky, L. and Fleischer, M. *The Processes of Technological Innovation.* Lexington: Lexington Books, 1990.

UNESCO. "Artificial Intelligence in Education." 2024a. Available at: https://www.unesco.org (Accessed: 27 April 2024).

UNESCO. *AI Competency Framework for Teachers*. 2024b. Available at: https://unesdoc.unesco.org/ark:/48223/pf0000391104.

UNESCO. *Global Citizenship Education in a Digital Age: Teacher Guidelines.* 2024c. Available at: https://unesdoc.unesco.org/ark:/48223/pf0000388812?posInSet=9&queryId=N-1f50443f-1a37-4556-b418-38def1ebaf16.

Upadhayay, A. R. "Artificial intelligence: Opportunities and challenges for the Global South with a focus on Nepal." *NCWA Annual Journal* 55, no. 1 (2024): 44–52. DOI: 10.3126/ncwaj.v55i01.62979.

Valdivieso, T. and González, O. "Generative AI tools in salvadoran higher education: Balancing equity, ethics, and knowledge management in the global South." *Education Sciences* 15, no. 2 (2025): 214. DOI: 10.3390/educsci15020214.

Walczak, K. and Cellary, W. "Challenges for higher education in the era of widespread access to generative AI." *Economics and Business Review* 9, no. 2 (2023): 71–100. DOI: 10.18559/ebr.2023.2.743.

Wang, H., Dang, A., Wu, Z., and Mac, S. "Generative AI in higher education: Seeing ChatGPT through universities' policies, resources, and guidelines." *Computers and Education: Artificial Intelligence* 7 (2024). DOI: 10.1016/j.caeai.2024.100326.

Wu, I.-L., Hsieh, P.-J., and Wu, S.-M. "Developing effective e-learning environments through e-learning use mediating technology affordance and constructivist learning aspects for performance impacts: Moderator of learner involvement." *The Internet and Higher Education* 55 (2022): 100871. DOI: 10.1016/j.iheduc.2022.100871.

Zhang, Y., Ma, C., Li, Y., and Liu, H. "Study on the coupling of higher education and artificial intelligence from the perspective of organizational ecology." In *Proceedings of the International Conference on Artificial Intelligence and Education.* Springer, 2024. DOI: 10.1007/978-981-97-2116-0_6.

Part 4

Innovative Learning and Collaborative Intelligence: Shaping the Future of Human–AI Interaction and Analytics

https://doi.org/10.1142/9781800616578_0012

Chapter 12

Application of the Neolearning Methodology in a Networked Corporate University

Angela Maria Fleury de Oliveira[*], **Patrícia de Sá Freire**[†], **and Rivaldo Arruda**[‡]

Federal University of Santa Catarina, Florianópolis, Brazil

[*]*angelafleury48@gmail.com*
[†]*patriciadesafreire@gmail.com*
[‡]*rivaldoarruda99@gmail.com*

Abstract

The COVID-19 pandemic caused a shortage of qualified professionals, affecting companies' ability to meet their needs. To fill these gaps, many resorted to building Networked Corporate Universities (NCU), understanding that they could accelerate the qualification/requalification processes of their teams. The following research question was raised: "How can the neolearning methodology be effectively applied in a NCU to develop leadership skills and generate value for the organization?" In light of this question, the general objective of this study was to investigate the application of the neolearning methodology in a networked corporate university, focusing on the development of leadership skills and the generation of value for the organization, which were the main findings and implications of the study. Neolearning consists of learning to learn by doing, bringing together the four pillars of UNESCO, the 4 Is, the concepts of experiential learning, active methodologies, and taking care of the relational processes between individual, group, and organization. The knowledge application stage in a program of this NCU took place through Challenge-Based Learning (CBL). The research method used was action research in the Leadership Development Program (LDP) of a NCU — UCR, a pilot project for the application of the neolearning methodology.

Keywords: Four pillars of UNESCO, active methodologies, challenge-based learning, networked corporate university, 4Is, neolearning.

12.1. Introduction

The first two decades of the 21st century were marked by rapid economic, cultural, technological, environmental, and political changes. These changes have impacted organizations and the ways they are structured to generate results. New customer demands and technologies that alter processes have been transforming the business landscape. Additionally, easier access to external markets has required organizations to invest in keeping their employees up to date and preserving their competitive edge (Tapscott, 2009).

In a context of great complexity, it is essential that the identification of employees' competency development needs is aligned with educational solutions that will support this transformation. For this purpose, an integrative theory is needed, such as neolearning, which brings intentionality, connection, and reciprocity between teachers and learners to transform the corporate environment (Silva and Freire, 2017).

Educational solutions based on neolearning should propose challenges that take participants beyond their current level of knowledge and skills. Learning objectives must be defined and collaboratively agreed upon by all those involved in the change process. In the present study, the knowledge application stage is based on one of the pillars of neolearning, which is the experiential learning theory, in this case, challenge-based learning (Nichols, Cator, and Torres, 2016).

Corporate education systems have sought new ways to define what is important to learn (critical knowledge), how to engage learners, and which techniques and practices are becoming key to the quality of teaching processes (Moresi, Barbosa, and Braga Filho, 2018).

Another issue that arises is how to prepare enabling contexts, where the "learning experience" effectively leads to the results expected by the organization (Choo, 1998). Kolb's learning cycle (1984), based on the notion of "experience," is one of the most cited in educational research, and therefore must be mentioned. "Learning is the process whereby knowledge is created through the transformation of experience" (Kolb, 1984, p. 38). For Kolb, experience is not knowledge but the foundation for creating knowledge.

Experiential learning theory presents a holistic, integrative perspective on learning that combines experience, perception, cognition, and behavior (Kolb, 1984, pp. 20–21). Conversely, learners need four different types of abilities related to experiential learning — reflective observation, concrete experience, abstract conceptualization, and active experimentation — to make decisions and solve problems (Kolb, 1984, p. 30). Neolearning brings these theories to corporate learning journeys, where experience design, didactic resources, and the interaction between teacher and students significantly impact results. This new teaching-learning methodology prepares professionals for the qualification and requalification of their skills, integrating intentionality into the educational action, along with engagement and motivation for participants to learn (Sanchez, 2013).

In summary, considering the publications on neolearning (Bresolin, Freire, and Pacheco, 2021), the theoretical assumptions of this methodology will be considered during this action research, including the theoretical and practical foundation for applying andragogical principles (Knowles, Holton III, and Swanson, 2011), heutagogical principles (Blaschke, 2012), experiential learning theories (Kolb, 1984; Kolb and Kolb, 2017), and expansive learning (Engeström, 1987; Engeström and Sannino, 2010), in addition to using agile and active methods, educational technologies, and different teaching and learning strategies to meet various learning styles.

The action research presented in this chapter demonstrates the application of the neolearning methodology in a Leadership Development Program within a Networked Corporate University (NCU). The program included 37 leaders (Biologists, Geologists, Archaeologists, Administrators, Psychologists, and Educators), among approximately 700 employees. The company has 25 years of tradition in planning and executing high-quality environmental projects. Classes took place once a month, lasting 4 hours, in a hybrid format (in-person/virtual) on the Teams platform. The total of 32 hours was divided into 8-hour thematic modules: 2 hours at the start of the module, 4 hours in remote activities, and 2 hours for module closure. The entire learning design was planned based on the neolearning methodology. The program also included 32 hours for knowledge application, using the Challenge-Based Learning (CBL) method over approximately six months. At the end of this learning journey, the results were presented in a earning forum, where applied knowledge was institutionalized and became part of the organization's processes (Crossan, Lane, and White, 1999).

This study seeks to answer the following research question: How can the neolearning methodology be effectively applied in a NCU to develop leadership skills and generate value for the organization? The overall objective of this study was to investigate how applying the neolearning methodology in a NCU, focusing on developing new leadership skills, generates economic, financial, and image value for the organization. To this end, action research was used as a method, allowing an iterative and collaborative approach to implementing and evaluating the Leadership Development Program (LDP) in the NCU.

This article is organized into five main sections. The introduction presents the context and relevance of the study, highlighting the need for new educational approaches in the corporate environment. The second section presents the neolearning methodology with its methods, techniques, practices, and principles that support the actions. The third section details the action research method used to implement neolearning in the NCU. The fourth section presents the results, including qualitative and quantitative data and findings from the pilot project. The discussion of results relates these findings to existing literature, analyzing their implications and limitations. The fifth section presents the final considerations, summarizing the main conclusions of the study and suggesting directions for future research.

12.2. Neolearning Methodology

Neolearning is defined as an andragogical methodological platform of experiential and expansive teaching and learning, establishing innovative paths for the learner–teacher–institution triad, creating multiple roles for both the teacher and the learner, dynamically and institutionally, utilizing active and agile methods to reduce the distance between stakeholders in the innovation ecosystem, promoting learning environments that facilitate the development of skills, and establishing a co-creation process of knowledge to transfer it into practice (Bresolin, Freire, and Pacheco, 2021).

The andragogical principles defined by Knowles, Holton III, and Swanson (2011) form the basis for youth and adult learning as they consider and respect the individual's self-concept, self-direction, autonomy, and prior experiences during the learning process. The six principles are presented in Table 12.1.

Heutagogy is understood as an extension of andragogy, taking self-directed learning a step further by addressing the concept of self-determined learning. The focus is on developing autonomous and self-determined learners, emphasizing the development of the capacity to perceive context and apply acquired skills, preparing them for workplace complexity and motivating continuous learning (Blaschke, 2012). Thus, heutagogy can be applied in virtual learning environments, as it underpins the planning and execution of educational programs in remote and distance learning settings.

From the studies on andragogy and heutagogy emerged the categorization of the 7As of neolearning — autonomy, self-direction, self-identity, self-concept, self-motivation, self-management, and

Table 12.1. Andragogical principles for youth and adult learning.

Principles	Description
1. The learner's need to know	Adults need to know why they need to learn something before they begin to learn it.
2. The learner's self-concept	Adults are responsible for their own decisions and develop a need to be seen and treated as self-directed.
3. The learner's prior experience	This is related to each individual's self-identity, emphasizing individualized teaching and experiential learning strategies.
4. Readiness to learn	Adults are ready to learn and apply knowledge in real-life situations.
5. Orientation to learning	Adults are motivated to learn when they perceive that learning will help them perform tasks or deal with problems they face in life.
6. Motivation to learn	This is related to external and internal motivational factors, with internal factors providing greater motivation for learning.

Source: Knowles, Holton III, and Swanson (2011).

self-determination — which need to be managed during the macro processes of planning, execution, and evaluation of educational programs for the development of young adult professional learners.

Among the learning theories that are based on the 7As are experiential learning and expansive learning.

Experiential learning theory provides neolearning with the foundation for the process of learning through experience, identifying learners' different learning styles and the different roles played by teachers. According to Kolb's perspective (1984), individuals are capable of learning from their experiences, which form the basis for creating knowledge. The experiential learning cycle consists of four modules: concrete experience, reflective observation, abstract conceptualization, and active experimentation. Thus, for this theory, knowledge creation results from the combination of experience that is appropriated and transformed by the learner throughout the cycle (Kolb and Kolb, 2017).

The contribution of expansive learning theory to neolearning lies in the expansion of the learning object to include the relationships between the educational institution's context and the practical application context, as learning extends beyond the classroom environment and expands into learning networks (Engeström, 2002).

The expansive learning cycle consists of a sequence of seven actions: questioning, analyzing the situation, modeling a new solution, examining and testing the new model, implementing the new model, reflecting on and evaluating the consolidation process in the new practice so that it becomes stable and belongs to the new system. This involves forming a theoretical concept of the new activity, based on grasping and modeling an initial simple process, which gives rise to the new activity and generates its various concrete manifestations (Engeström and Sannino, 2010).

Expansive learning theory supports networked learning by proposing co-production and problem-solving projects, along with network stakeholders and ecosystems, both internally (between units, different areas, and departments) and externally (with other universities, institutions, organizations, or society). Besides the theoretical elements, neolearning proposes constitutive elements that guide multilevel planning and evaluation, the development of learning and knowledge paths, the interdisciplinary composition of the curriculum, the application of active and agile methods, the selection of teaching and learning strategies, the choice of educational technologies, the creation of collaboration environments and knowledge co-production, the different roles played by the teacher, and the respect and consideration for learners' characteristics to accommodate different learning styles (Bresolin, Freire, and Pacheco, 2021).

The neolearning methodology considers the characteristics of digital learners and the new skills required by a digitally transforming society. This is because digital learners have characteristics, learning styles, expectations, knowledge, and experiences that need to be considered during the learning process. Furthermore, they seek practical learning applicable to real life, with an innovative methodology that motivates them to pursue new knowledge (Bresolin and Freire, 2021).

The andragogical approach (Knowles *et al.*, 2011) and theories of experiential learning (Kolb, 1984; Kolb and Kolb, 2017) and expansive learning (Engeström, 1987; Engeström and Sannino, 2010) underpin the different stages of a class that we call the neolearning cycle. The cycle consists of five integrated, dynamic, and fluid modules for the development of the technical, digital, or socio-emotional skills of digital learners. The description of each module and the related competencies are presented in Table 12.2.

Table 12.2. Competencies developed in the application of the neolearning cycle.

Module	Description of the Neolearning Cycle Module	Competencies Developed by Digital Learners
Retrieve	Elicit individual experiences and knowledge about the content to be worked on, as a memory trigger for learners' tacit and implicit knowledge.	Context analysis; communication; collaboration; creativity; initiative; problem-solving; teamwork; social and emotional skills for group work; time management; people management; autonomy and responsibility for one's own learning; openness to new experiences.
Reflect	Analyze the retrieved experiences and knowledge through questioning or criticism of some aspects of practice, and what they know or do not know about the content to be worked on.	Ability to observe and critically analyze situations; observation of different alternatives and perspectives; communication; active listening; negotiation; critical and analytical thinking; systemic vision; social and emotional skills; time management; people management; emotional stability; self-control of feelings and emotions.

(*Continued*)

Table 12.2. (*Continued*)

Module	Description of the Neolearning Cycle Module	Competencies Developed by Digital Learners
Know	Research the possibilities and opportunities of what could be different by acquiring new knowledge and experiences based on evidence.	Scientific, critical, analytical, and lean thinking; logical reasoning; emotional intelligence; emotional stability; self-control of feelings and emotions; autonomy; responsibility; self-management of learning; pursuit of new knowledge.
Test	Experience theoretical models in a simulated environment to practice applying different ideas to solve real-world problems.	Innovation; creativity; entrepreneurship; problem-solving; adaptability; flexibility; communication; collaboration; negotiation; leadership; teamwork; social skills; emotional stability; emotional intelligence; time management; people management.
Apply	Implement the new knowledge generated from tests in a setting close to reality, involving learners in a contextualized learning situation of collaboration and co-creation with actors from social and work practices.	Networking; collaboration; co-production of knowledge; tolerance for differences; emotional stability; emotional intelligence; self-control; communication; openness to new experiences; adaptability; flexibility; learning to learn; autonomy and responsibility for one's own learning and professional trajectory; application of knowledge in practical performance.

Source: Bresolin and Freire (2019).

Thus, the understanding of the Principles and Guidelines of the Neolearning Cycle developed by Bresolin and Freire (2022), based on Kolb (1984), Kolb and Kolb (2017), Engeström (1987), and Engeström and Sannino (2010), was part of the foundation for the creation of the NCU and the co-creation of the LDP, the subject of this neolearning methodology application (Table 12.3).

The articles published by Bresolin and Freire (2021, 2022) and Bresolin, Freire, and Pacheco (2021) were seminal in the research proposal, providing the foundational theoretical framework for new conceptions in the search for robustness in connecting NCU and the neolearning methodology.

Table 12.3. Principles and guidelines of the neolearning cycle.

Module	Principles	Application Guidelines
Retrieve	Simulated experiential activities retrieve learners' previous knowledge and experiences, confronting what they already know about the object to be studied.	Value, respect, recognize, and utilize learners' prior experiences in the learning process; create meaning for learning based on existing knowledge and mental processes; encourage questioning about some aspects of practice and existing knowledge and possible applications; promote divergent knowledge so that the learner perceives different types of solutions for the same problem.
Reflect	An open space for reflection, observation, discussion, and analysis of the lived experience, without criticism or determination of right and wrong, provides the freedom necessary to identify gaps to be filled and motivation to discover something new.	Provide space for learners to share their experiences and express their thoughts and reflections on the object of study; promote moments of individual and group reflection on the shared experiences; ask questions, encourage questioning, generate discussions, and share opinions about the events experienced in the previous module; develop learners' ability to observe their experiences from different perspectives to foster critical reflection on contextual aspects; highlight elements of practice associated with theories to be worked on later, without judging right or wrong; motivate what is yet to be learned.
Know	The understanding of concepts, theories, and models underpins the generalization of knowledge to be applied in diverse experiences.	Request research on concepts, theories, and models on the subject to be worked on from bibliographic and documentary references; present theoretical foundations; relate theories to the experiences and analyses shared in previous modules; encourage logical and justified conclusions about the experience; facilitate the development of assimilative knowledge, using deduction to solve problems, utilizing the logic of an idea to create theoretical models, organize ideas, and transform them into coherent explanations.

(*Continued*)

Table 12.3. (*Continued*)

Module	Principles	Application Guidelines
Test	Experiential activities for practical application of knowledge allow testing new ideas and concepts in situations closer to reality.	Create group activities to apply the learned concepts, theories, and models in case studies, simulations, workshops, or lab experiences; promote spaces that facilitate the development of creativity and the generation of multiple ideas during attempts to apply knowledge in problem-solving and testing solutions; promote the creation of convergent knowledge, allowing the most appropriate solution for a specific problem to be found.
Apply	Supervised or monitored experiential practices provide opportunities to expand beyond the controlled environment, elevating learning to social and work practices.	Invite experts from the knowledge application field to participate as instructors in this module; create learning networks between learners and collaborators related to the practice environment, breaking the boundaries of the simulated learning environment; expand the learning object to include the relationships between the simulated context and practical application, projecting the application to social or professional practices; allow observation, reflection, and evaluation of the new knowledge consolidation process in practice; encourage the development of new models for the experienced practice so that new knowledge can be institutionalized; create space for discussion after the practical experience to accommodate and internalize new knowledge; question the lessons learned and best practices from the experience.

Source: Bresolin and Freire (2022).

12.3. Research Method

To apply the neolearning methodology in the NCU, an action research approach was chosen. This method was selected because it is a technique that allows the researcher to act throughout the research process. It aligns with the objective of this study by enabling an investigation at all stages of the process. The action research cycle comprises the following stages: problem identification, planning a solution, its implementation, monitoring, and evaluation of its effectiveness. These stages, as part of the cycle, can be repeated recurrently, continuously applying improvements (Tripp, 2005). The stages of the action research are described in the following, along with all the actions taken by the researchers using the neolearning methodology as the guiding thread of the expected transformation process. Even after the final evaluation of the LDP and delivery of results, it was still possible to continue evaluating the entire process, implementing new improvements, and conducting participants' self-assessment regarding their learning.

12.3.1. *Problem identification stage*

The first stage involved active listening with the company's managers to identify aspects of leadership development that could generate value for both business management and intra- and inter-team relationships. A semi-structured interview guide was used, exploring aspects of the current leaders' profile, such as alignment with business strategies, understanding and management of business project results, readiness to face challenges, cooperation between teams, self-awareness, internal entrepreneurship, and developing team competencies. This phase was crucial to understanding stakeholders' needs and expectations (Kormakova *et al.*, 2015). There was a weakness in understanding the integration of the various phases of a project and the expected results, which were not always aligned with what was anticipated.

12.3.2. *Solution planning stage*

During the planning stage, the solution was co-produced with representatives from the HR area, leaders, specialists, and managers. This collaborative process allowed participants to engage, becoming authors of the proposal and influencers of others. The educational solution was structured in four eight-hour stages, covering the following topics: life purpose, business management, people management, and project management. In the initial stage, a self-awareness analysis was conducted using an Artificial Intelligence (AI) tool, revealing personal characteristics, learning style, and behavioral patterns, among other aspects. The results were provided individually and collectively before the first stage — life purpose. Additionally, as part of the educational solution and the application of knowledge generated and shared during the program, one of the neolearning theories — experiential learning based on challenge analysis and resolution as proposed by Nichols, Cator, and Torres (2018) — was used. Participants identified their own challenges to resolve, which were part of their tasks and whose solutions fell within their department's scope. These challenges had to be described in writing using a specific form with questions such as the following: What is the challenge? What steps do you plan to take to solve it? What are the main difficulties to eliminate during the process? Who could be involved to help? What will be the monitoring and result indicators? What information systems will be used to collect, store, analyze, and evaluate the results? How will the information be reported, and to whom? Where will the lessons learned be recorded, and what follow-ups will be made to implement the proposed improvements? During the planning stage, there was also an oral presentation of the plan in the form of an "Elevator Pitch" lasting 10 minutes. In this evaluation, there was no novelty to present. Instead, socio-emotional skills were analyzed, such as concentration, flexibility, enthusiasm, ability to handle time pressure, and calmness in the face of challenges, among others. The results of the oral and written stages were returned to the participants, who could request an optional individual feedback session.

The learnings from this stage of challenge-based experiential learning (Nichols, Cator, and Torres, 2018) were presented in a "Knowledge Sharing Forum," where the results and value generated for the company in solving the challenge were identified. This "practiceship" lasted six months, with monthly monitoring of each challenge's status and coaching/mentoring by professors and internal specialists to address any issues during the learning journey. Classes took place in monthly 4-hour in-person/virtual meetings via Zoom. Between the first and last class, activities related to the focused content were interspersed in a learning design built to develop competencies in applying the neolearning cycle: retrieve, reflect, know, test, and apply. All activities were situated on a virtual learning platform, including records of experiences and memories of the results achieved.

12.3.3. *Implementation stage*

The implementation of the educational solution was supported by four integrative theories of the neolearning methodology: the four pillars of 21st-century education by UNESCO (Delors, 2012), the 4Is of organizational learning (Kolb, 1984), challenge-based experiential learning (Nichols, Cator, and Torres, 2016), and active methods of cooperation and collaboration (Filatro and Cavalcanti, 2018; Cavalcanti, 2023). The internal network of the business partners was trained in educational solution design to support the program. The 70-20-10 methodology (Rabin, 2016; Costa, 2014) and the 6Ds that transform learning into business results (Wick, Pollock, and Jefferson, 2011) were integrated into the implementation stage of the plan, supporting the pursuit of results for the challenges.

The projects developed in the knowledge application stage (Bresolin and Freire, 2022) were challenges proposed individually by the 36 participants of the LDP. Following the delivery of the initial execution plan, these plans were integrated into nine categories of questions focused on related topics. This thematic convergence integrated participants, the macro proposal, the required support, and connections between individuals from other themes/categories who had common interests and could contribute in some way to their colleagues. Figure 12.1 presents the categories and the number of leaders in each.

In a meeting with all 36 participants, all proposals from each category were presented in a "pitch" format, which helped retrieve, know, and reflect on all the projects to be executed (Bresolin and Freire, 2021). Many suggestions were made using "Jamboard" to include conceptual inputs, technological information, customer experiences, processes, and outcomes to improve.

This "unveiling" of collective improvement opportunities expanded the engagement and understanding of the individual challenge, allowing for the testing and application of knowledge and the identification of new concrete results collaboratively (Bresolin and Freire, 2021).

As the program evolved, new knowledge about the projects was incorporated into each participant's challenge. Here, the contribution of expansive learning theory to neolearning is clearly seen, particularly in expanding the learning object beyond the classroom environment into learning networks (Engeström, 2002). Contributions from module expert

Figure 12.1. Convergence of themes of leaders' challenges in the LDP.

teachers, internal and external mentors, and colleagues were important for executing the challenges. The activities proposed in the learning design were structured in learning paths according to the neolearning cycle modules, intentionally bringing in the complementary technical content necessary to cover the knowledge gaps identified during the active listening of the demand (Bresolin and Freire, 2022).

The company's management was committed to the program and met all requests for the acquisition of materials, machines, software, and equipment necessary for project completion. In this respect, it is noted that the management reflected on and evaluated the process of consolidating new practices to make them stable and incorporated into the new system, generating several manifestations of concrete results (Engeström and Sannino, 2010).

12.3.4. *Monitoring stage*

Throughout the learning journey, participants' behaviors regarding participation in discussions, collaboration, cooperation with colleagues, demonstrations of autonomy, commitment to deadlines, and the quality of remote activities prepared in each LDP module were monitored through weekly reports issued by the digital platform LMS. The lesson plans of the teachers were also co-constructed with the HR area and external network knowledge partners, as well as with invited expert teachers for specific interventions to ensure internal and external consistency of the intentionally focused content. All modules included real-life work situations to create meaning for the leaders. Teachers received data, information, and materials from the company to make group remote activities more engaging. The results of all activities were collected by the LMS system and addressed by the teacher in the final module class. Interactive individual and group activities were programmed for this final class using active cooperation and collaboration methods (Filatro and Cavalcanti, 2018; Cavalcanti, 2023).

12.3.5. *Evaluation of effectiveness stage*

The effectiveness evaluation was developed throughout the implementation stage of the LDP, using different formats: diagnostic, formative, summative, and self-assessment. The action research method allowed for various interventions by the researchers between content modules and in preparing the final project delivery reports. The evaluations considered content, methodology, digital processes, knowledge delivery and documentation, involvement of teachers and participants, presentation of the solution to the chosen challenge, and value generated for the company.

Regarding the LDP's effectiveness evaluation, at the end of the period, 36 projects were delivered. Of these, only 4 were not 100% completed due to the volume of data to be digitized (resulting from the company's shutdown due to COVID-19) and the failure of follow-up data in the post-training phase of the program. The results showed significant improvements in the objectives set at the beginning of the program, collected 60, 120, and 180 days after project delivery. The effectiveness results can be categorized as follows:

- **Process improvement:** There was improved management of project technical data, increasing accuracy in inter-team information, speeding up data collection and parameters for project construction, introducing new process and outcome indicators, and greater integration in monitoring databases, enhancing project management; 14 projects achieved 100% of their results against established goals based on new evidence.
- **Technical and behavioral development improvement:** The teams involved showed greater transparency in communications, evidence of positive change in accountability levels for tasks and outcomes, and improved technical processes with reduced costs and reporting errors; 12 projects achieved 100% of their results against established goals, based on improvements identified and reported by their internal and external clients.
- **Internal communication improvement:** The number of inter-area channels was reduced and certain messages were standardized with redefined decision-making flows and roles, enabling better monitoring through meetings to evaluate new process implementations, especially in more complex projects. Six projects achieved 100% of their results against established goals due to significant quantified improvements by internal clients and suppliers who received internal communications differently.
- **Partial improvements in operational field training results:** Due to the necessary infrastructure for this purpose, as well as projects involving the digitization of a large volume of data, four projects achieved 50% of their expected results against predicted goals.

The results obtained, after monitoring for 180 days post-project delivery, evidence consolidated learnings attributed to the neolearning methodology, which integrates a systemic set of theories for the stages before, during, and after digital learners' development.

Other LDP Results:

The co-construction of the NCU featured an implementation model based on the neolearning methodology, which supported outcomes related to network formation, engagement, productivity, and behavioral improvements.

Thirty microlearning modules, each lasting between 5 and 8 minutes, were co-created, with topics derived from interest research among employees. These can be categorized into 10 groups, with the number of views updated from May 2023 to June 2024 totaling over 6,247 records (Figure 12.2). LMS platform reports indicate that many microlearnings received multiple accesses from the same employee. This fact is attributed to the high level of customization of the scripts, which included much data, forms, tools, and photos from the real work context, as presented in

1	**Informational about the global context**	Ex: Digital Transformation (452), VUCA World and BANI World (850).
2	**Informational about the business context**	Ex: Sustainability in Business (212), Intrapreneurship (639).
3	**Self-learning**	Ex: How to deal with anxiety (764), Nonviolent Communication (768).
4	**Team development**	Ex: Five stages to create a team (197), Effective Meetings (381).
5	**Leadership skills**	Ex: Leadership and Decision Making (105), Value-Added Negotiation (250).
6	**Interpersonal skills**	Ex: Active Listening (86), Protagonism and Resilience (96).
7	**Intra and inter· Team skills**	Ex: How to conduct difficult conversations (605), Empathy in practice (328).
8	**Workplace communication**	Ex: Learning to deal with mistakes (184), Happiness at work (362).
9	**Learning for the future of work**	Ex: Lifelong Learning (58), Rapid Learning (78).
10	**New technologies and employee reskilling**	Ex: Artificial Intelligence (590), Exponential Technologies (143).

Figure 12.2. Number of views per grouping: Examples of microlearnings.

Source: Prepared by the authors based on Learning Monitoring Reports — LMS.

the neolearning methodology principles (Bresolin and Freire, 2022). As these were adults who already used digital platforms, all microlearnings were available on smartphones and computers, allowing employees to extend this access to their families and friends in communities, especially those far from the north and west of the country, where these innovations from the company's Corporate University became unprecedented events. This outcome is an integrated effort by the researchers and the company to support the co-construction of each learning resource and adapt it to the company's reality (Filatro and Cavalcanti, 2018; Cavalcanti, 2023). Networked expansive learning was driven by an intentional action of the researchers, and the results were collected through informal narratives from Employees, by the Business Partners of the people area, during "Care Moments," a company ritual held every Monday morning before the workday begins. This is a qualitative result that reinforces one of the integrative theories of the neolearning methodology: expansive networked learning (Engeström, 1987; Engeström and Sannino, 2010).

The microlearnings were designed based on the principles and guidelines of neolearning (Bresolin and Freire, 2022), drawing from Kolb (1984), Kolb and Kolb (2017), Engeström (1987), and Engeström and Sannino (2010).

Thus, after a brief introduction of the actor and the topic, questions were posed to utilize existing knowledge and mental processes (Retrieve Module).

Using questions, the essential concepts of the topic, methods, and steps were introduced (Reflect and Know Modules). There was a contextualization of the company concerning practices that are and could be used by employees in intra- and inter-team relationships. This was a moment to conclude the video topic, where the employee was invited to "Learn More" in the platform's workspace (Test and Apply Modules).

Questions were used to engage the employee in their own learning, along with other formats that went further: a short quiz to assess content understanding, a simple activity to expand on the topic, suggestions to meet mentors in the university network on this topic, and recommendations for short, curated texts, books, and YouTube videos.

Another practice used in this networked university was offering short, free courses by business management knowledge partners. The courses were studied to identify their alignment with business strategies and whether neolearning elements could be identified. Of the 181 courses offered, 17 were suitable for the educational project's needs and target audience. From May 2023 to June 2024, the number of views was updated to 958 records, demonstrating a high level of interest from the target audience.

In the virtual library, accessible to all employees, videos and short texts on operational, leadership, and administrative "Best Practices" were also available, recorded by supervisors and employees using smartphones and edited in the HR area. A recording studio with editing and design materials was set up in the NCU. This action increased the protagonism of employees working in the field as they felt valued and part of the company's transformation project. Eleven materials were co-created by employees from various areas and recorded 351 views during the period from May 2023 to June 2024, enhancing opportunities to develop socio-emotional skills with active methodologies through digital learning (Cavalcanti, 2023).

Onboarding training, which was previously in-person before the NCU was established, was restructured into a digital format for computers and smartphones, with support from human resources business partners, to be conducted in over 20 regions where environmental study and service projects are located.

From May 2023 to June 2024, more than 400 employees participated in this program, enhancing their sense of belonging to the company and reducing the integration time into work after the selection process. There are two types of onboarding: One is general and informative about the company, highlighting its identity, business, benefits, and the employee's roles in achieving expected outcomes. The other specifically introduces the job position and the NCU, where the employee will "enroll," presenting available learning opportunities and paths.

The neolearning methodology enabled employees, through techniques, activities, challenges, and projects, to experience new forms of experiential and expansive learning.

Teamwork, collaboration, cooperation, autonomy, accountability for the learning process, idea generation, critical thinking, intrapreneurship, and problem-solving skills were developed, which resulted in process transformations and economic and financial outcomes for the organization.

12.4. Presentation of Results

The theoretical elements considered to be the foundation of neolearning are embedded in the instructional design of each thematic learning path of the four contents addressed in the LDP, the pilot project of this action research.

One of the researchers' tasks, in their role supporting the program's technical coordination, was to collect business context data related to each LDP content, obtained through active listening during the problem identification and solution planning stages of the action research.

Documents such as climate surveys, "One Page Strategy," technical projects, exit and selection interviews, competitive environment information, and financial statements from the last three years were consulted.

In-depth interviews were conducted with the CEO, some directors, and managers to understand the context, expectations, and facilitators and barriers to applying neolearning principles in the LDP. The data obtained from this internal multilevel network were discussed with teachers and other actors involved in the delivery to co-create an integrated journey, connecting content, methodologies, and digital technologies. The structure of the didactic material was highly customized to the business reality with real data, real problems, and possible concrete solutions involving participation, collaboration, and cooperation.

The Google Meet platform, a basic digital tool supporting the program, facilitated discussions in open rooms and brought new experiences to participants, especially with the teacher entering each "digital room" to answer questions and stimulate discussions as a "live, in-person, and dynamic process." This technology allowed discussions between individuals, the group involved in a specific topic, and the organization (represented by the teacher), with concrete challenges researched in the problem identification and solution planning stages. Multilevel learning is also one of the principles of neolearning. The face-to-face/virtual events were highly anticipated and had strong attendance from learners. The 4Is of the neolearning methodology (Include, Interpret, Integrate, and Institutionalize) were "embedded" in the prepared activities: a four-hour in-person/virtual meeting via Google Meet; four remote activities, individual or group, or inter-group; and four in-person/virtual hours, closing the thematic module and retrieving the remote activities.

There was also the major program deliverable, the "Practicum" activity, which consisted of identifying a daily work challenge and structuring a plan to solve it over the six-month program duration.

Neolearning provided the necessary elements to enrich the didactic material: action scripts, points of attention, internal or external network people who could help, expected outcomes, monitoring and evaluation indicators, resources required for investment in some stages to be negotiated in advance, value generated for the individual, group, or organization, and the evaluation process to be used (e.g., ROI or impact assessment). Thus, the learner would be practicing the four pillars of 21st-century education: "learning to know" (emotional aspect), "learning to do" (functional aspect), "learning to live together" (relational aspect), and "learning to be" (rational aspect). This last exercise brings the rational aspect by reflecting on how learning affects the collective and effectively contributes to the common good (Delors, 2012).

The structuring of practical activities using the neolearning methodology organizes the action of the digital teacher/facilitator to put the student at the center of their learning, bringing other elements, technological tools, and more playful teaching resources, transforming the teacher's ability to create more stimulating and challenging enabling contexts (Choo, 1998).

The CBL methodology brings in the intentionality of the transformation effort to be undertaken by everyone involved in the NCU ecosystem.

The concepts and foundations of CBL are "intertwined" with the neolearning methodology and are described in Table 12.4.

CBL is conducted through guided processes, divided into three interdependent phases: Engage, Investigate, and Act (Nichols, Cator, and Torres, 2016):

- **Phase 1 — Engage** starts with the "Big Idea," condensed into a concrete and actionable challenge. Through group questioning processes, an essential question is developed, guiding the work toward a solution.
- **Phase 2 — Investigate** aims to seek information that supports a possible solution to the proposed challenge. This phase is also divided into three stages:
  - **Guiding questions:** They help identify the knowledge necessary to develop a solution to the challenge, prioritizing, categorizing, and creating an organized learning experience.
  - **Guided activities and resources:** These are used to answer the questions defined in the previous stage, considering all methods, tools, and people who can assist in this process.
  - **Analysis of lessons learned** in guided activities provides the basis for identifying solutions.
- **Phase 3 — Act** is the third phase of CBL, where solutions are developed, implemented, and presented for evaluation (Nichols, Cator, and Torres, 2016).

Table 12.4. Concepts and foundations of CBL.

Concepts	Foundations
Everyone is a learner	Teachers, students, peers, managers, administrators, families, and the community.
Beyond the four classroom walls	Learning enables students to use external resources and information.
Inspired and self-directed student	CBL allows students to connect the learning content with their lives, highlighting freedom and responsibility in self-direction.
Challenges create urgency and action	Study and work facilitate finding appropriate solutions for each challenge.
Challenges develop 21st-century skills	CBL was built using these skills as a guideline. Neolearning also includes 21st-century skills in its principles and guidelines, comprising five modules — Retrieve, Reflect, Know, Test, and Apply.
Space and freedom to fail	CBL provides a safe space to fail, find creative solutions, try new ideas, receive feedback, and interact.
Reflective capacity exercise	With calmness, the learner finds solutions to challenges, avoiding the urgency to present solutions without a proper foundation and depth.
Authentic use of technology	In composing solutions, technology plays a fundamental role in researching, communicating, creating, and presenting information, mastering, and transforming the learning process.
Focus on process and product	The search process is as valuable as the proposed solution. CBL allows evaluation of both processes and products/solutions derived from them.
Documentation	All resources (videos, texts, audios, infographics, and figures) can be used by learners to document work progress and enable evaluation.
Reflection	CBL enables students to reflect continuously on the learned content and the process that led them to learn.

Source: Nichols; Cator; Torres (2016).

CBL was created to be flexible and allow adaptations, such as categorizing challenges by duration and complexity.

CBL tracking and evaluation were conducted through reports related to each execution phase. In the conclusion phase, participants in the "Practicum," based on CBL, created final presentations to share knowledge with other groups using videos, PPTs, audios, written work, and photos, generating portfolios of achievements. The neolearning cycle presents stages similar to CBL, and the evaluation focuses on real-world challenges, as seen in the LDP.

Guided question scripts make the didactic material's intention to create transformation explicit. The opportunities for developing socio-behavioral skills were connected with the development of technical skills in the same learning activity. When, during the planning stage, the learner faced obstacles, they sought additional support from people they had to communicate, negotiate, argue, deliberate with, and, at times, be resilient, building conciliatory positions.

Neolearning allows these situations, especially when the teacher brings more than just concepts, but also knowledge-generating experiences for various stakeholders in a systematic way.

12.5. Final Considerations

The LDP represented an opportunity to prepare and requalify 37 managers in just six months, resulting in 37 transformed processes. The use of digital technologies and active methodologies allowed for extensive interaction among participants, as well as between participants and the teachers, mentors, and coaches who supported the program.

This research employed the neolearning method, which consists of learning by doing, and explored new strategies and online teaching practices centered on the individual learner. Four approaches were used to form the theoretical basis of neolearning: the four pillars of UNESCO, the 4Is of organizational learning, Kolb's experiential learning, and active learning methods.

The CBL methodology was chosen for the "Practicum" stage, where learners present solutions to challenges identified in their daily lives. This journey starts with concrete experience, moves through reflective observation, develops and organizes concepts internally, assimilating them through abstract conceptualization, and shares the learning outcomes with colleagues.

Thus, the acquired knowledge can be applied to new situations, characterizing the active experimentation stage.

Future follow-ups will assess the financial results of return on investment (ROI) and some projects that have generated impact in the communities where the company operates. Digital facilitators will be prepared for operational activities using the neolearning methodology, allowing more professionals within internal and external networks to benefit from learning and relearning throughout their lives.

Based on all the evidence and findings from this action research, it is possible to apply the neolearning methodology in leadership development programs in a digital environment, with the delivery of projects that bring process and productivity improvements to the company, as well as the development of technical and socio-behavioral competencies for participants.

Bibliography

Blaschke, L. M. "Heutagogy and lifelong learning: A review of heutagogical practice and self-determined learning." *The International Review of Research in Open and Distributed Learning* 13, no. 1 (2012): 56–71.

Bresolin, G. G. and Freire, P. de S. "Metodologia da Neoaprendizagem para o desenvolvimento dos Aprendentes Digitais." *Congresso Internacional de Conhecimento e Inovação (CIKI)* (2019).

Bresolin, G. G. and Freire, P. de S. "Ciclo da Neoaprendizagem para o Desenvolvimento da Criatividade e Inovação." *XIIEGEPE online* (2022).

Bresolin, G. G., Freire, P. de S., and Pacheco, R. C. dos S. *Neoaprendizagem, 10 passos para a prática andragógica, experiencial e expansiva.* Florianópolis: Editora Arquétipos, 2021. https://editoraarquetipos.com.br/produto/Neoaprendizagem-10-passos-para-a-praticaandragogica-experiencial-e-expansiva/.

Cavalcanti, C. C. *Aprendizagem socioemocional com metodologias ativas: um guia para educadores*. São Paulo: SaraivaUni, 2023.

Choo, C. W. *A organização do conhecimento*. New York: Oxford Press, 1998.

Costa, C. A. J. *O conceito 70:20:10 no Brasil — estado atual e perspectivas*. IPL Institute of Performance and Leadership, 2014.

Crossan, M. M., Lane, H. W., and White, R. E. "An organizational learning framework: from intuition to institution." *The Academy of Management Review* 24, no. 3 (1999): 522–537.

Delors, J. *Educação: um tesouro a descobrir*. 7. ed. Brasília: Cortez, 2012.

Engeström, Y. *Learning by Expanding: An Activity-Theoretical Approach to Developmental Research*. Helsinki: Orienta-Konsulit, 1987.

Engeström, Y. and Sannino, A. "Studies of expansive learning: Foundations, findings and future challenges." *Educational Research Review* 5 (2010): 1–24.

Filatro, A. and Cavalcanti, C. C. *Metodologias Inovativas na educação presencial: a distância e corporativa*. São Paulo: Saraiva Educação, 2018.

Freire, P. de S., *et al.* "Universidade Corporativa em Rede: considerações iniciais para um novo modelo de educação corporativa." *Revista Espacios* 37, no. 5 (2016).

Knowles, M. S., Holton III, E. F., and Swanson, R. A. *Aprendizagem de Resultados: Uma abordagem prática para aumentar a efetividade da educação corporativa.* Tradução de Sabine Alexandra Holler. The adult learner. Rio de Janeiro: Elsevier, 2011.

Kolb, A. Y. and Kolb, D. A. "Experiential learning theory as a guide for experiential educators in higher education." *ELTHE: A Journal for Engaged Educators* 1, no. 1 (2017): 7–44.

Kolb, D. A. *Experiential Learning: Experience as the Source of Learning and Development.* New Jersey: Prentice Hall, 1984.

Kormakova, I. *et al. Entrepreneurship Competence: An Overview of Existing Concepts, Policies and Initiatives — Final Report.* Luxembourg: Publications Office of the European Union, 2015.

Marques, J. R. "Como funciona o modelo de aprendizagem 70 20 10 nas empresas."2019.https://www.ibccoaching.com.br/portal/como-funciona-o-modelo-de-aprendizagem-70-20-10-nas-empresas/

Martins, R. "Metodologia 6Ds: conheça 6 disciplinas que facilitam a educação corporativa." n.d. https://www.gupy.io/blog/metodologia-6ds

Moresi, E., Barbosa, J., and Braga Filho, M. "O emprego da metodologia aprendizagem baseada em desafios na elaboração da revisão de literatura." *XII Congresso Ibero-Americano em Investigação Qualitativa* (2018).

Nichols, M., Cator, K., and Torres, M. *Challenge Based Learner User Guide.* Redwood City, CA: Digital Promise, 2016.

Pacheco, R. C. dos S., Freire, P. de S., Bresolin, G. G., Prado, G. M. B. do, and Izidorio, G. "Método da Neoaprendizagem para a inovação na Educação Superior brasileira: uma pesquisa ação na Academia Sapientia." *Congresso Internacional de Conhecimento e Inovação (CIKI)* (2019).

Rabin, R. *70.20.10.* Center for Creative Leadership, 2016.

Sanchez, J. "The impact of an entrepreneurship education program on entrepreneurial competencies and intention." *Journal of Small Business Management* 51 (2013): 447–465.

Silva, T. C. and Freire, P. de S. "Universidade corporativa em rede: diretrizes que devem ser gerenciadas para a implantação do modelo." *Espacios* 38, no. 10 (2017): 13.

Tapscott, D. *Grown Up Digital: How the Net Generation is Changing Your World.* New York: McGraw Hill, 2009.

Tripp, D. "Pesquisa-ação: uma introdução metodológica." *Educação e Pesquisa* 31, no. 3 (2005): 443–466.

Wick, C. W., Pollock, R., and Jefferson, A. *6ds: as seis disciplinas que transformam educação em resultados para o negócio.* São Paulo: Évora, 2011.

https://doi.org/10.1142/9781800616578_0013

Chapter 13

Collaborative Intelligence: Cultivating Human–AI Partnerships

Jeff M. Allen[*,‡], Tara L. Whitson[†,§], Mariya Gavrilova Aguilar[*,¶], and Pamela Scott Bracey[*,‖]

[*]*University of North Texas, USA*

[†]*Tarleton State University, USA*

[‡]*jeff.allen@unt.edu*
[§]*whitson@tarleton.edu*
[¶]*mariya.gavrilovaaguilar@unt.edu*
[‖]*pamela.bracey@unt.edu*

Abstract

This chapter provides a human-centered perspective on Artificial Intelligence (AI) as a transformative technology poised to reshape the workplace. It examines the historical trajectory of technological advancements and their impact on work environments. It explores how AI's capabilities in logical processing and predictive analytics can complement human expertise, even while lacking human qualities like ethical judgment and creativity. The chapter emphasizes collaboration over replacing human capabilities and proposes a conceptual framework to guide integration, balancing innovation with preserving uniquely human roles essential for fairness and accountability. Organizational adaptations, including workforce reskilling and task reorganization, are discussed, illustrating how AI can align with human efforts to accomplish strategic goals. Ultimately, the authors argue that AI necessitates a collaborative workforce model, where human–AI systems work together to drive workplace innovation, aligning technology with mission-driven organizational values.

Keywords: Human-centered AI, AI enhancement, learning, technology, workplace, ethics, wisdom, capabilities.

13.1. Background

In the rapidly evolving field of Artificial Intelligence (AI), it is easy to overlook the historical development that has shaped it over the past approximately seventy-five years. The Turing Test, developed in 1950, aimed to assess whether a machine's ability to think could be considered equivalent to the thinking of a human. This test marked the early beginnings of AI, leading to the formal coining of the term "Artificial Intelligence" in 1956. Since then, AI has advanced through notable milestones that tested machine capabilities. In 1996, IBM's Deep Blue made history by defeating world chess champion Garry Kasparov. This moment significantly raised awareness of machine potential and questions about its use.

Two decades later, in 2010, Apple introduced Siri, an acronym for Speech Interpretation and Recognition Interface, as a virtual assistant for iOS devices. Siri helps users perform tasks via voice command using natural language processing (NLP). AI's advancements in NLP were further demonstrated when IBM's Watson won the game show *Jeopardy*. In 2014, Amazon's Alexa brought AI-powered NLP into everyday households, further integrating the technology into daily life. In 2017, Google's AlphaGo defeated Ke Jie, the world's top-ranked Go player, showcasing the strategic thinking capabilities of AI. More recently, in late 2022, the launch of generative AI platforms, such as OpenAI's ChatGPT, marked a new era of rapid growth in Artificial Intelligence and its implications for society and the workplace.

These milestones have significantly influenced how humans interact with technology. While technological progress is not new, AI is the latest innovation to impact humanity profoundly. As with any significant leap forward, there is a need to reassess how this technology may influence our personal lives and workplaces.

13.1.1. *Trepidation*

"Any sufficiently advanced technology is indistinguishable from magic" Clarke (1962, p. 36). Introducing transformative technologies creates uncertainty about our role in a rapidly changing world. As new technologies emerge, individuals are required to unlearn previous paradigms and explore how these innovations will affect their lives, personally and professionally. While such advancements may appear sudden and dramatic, they are typically the result of decades of development. It is important to understand AI implications for the modern workplace and to reflect on and trace the shift from an industrial-based workforce to one centered on information and knowledge. This transition has been occurring over the past several decades. In the mid-1900s, the workforce was predominantly focused on physical labor and manufacturing. By the mid-2020s, it has shifted toward sectors like technology, communication, and information management. Each technological advancement compels society to reconsider the nature of work and the role of humans within the workforce. As we look ahead, this question arises: What roles will AI and humans play in the evolving labor market?

We will explore how the workplace has evolved to help us prepare for future changes. The introduction of the cotton gin in 1793 had an immediate and profound economic impact on the labor force. Similarly, the rise of AI is transforming the labor market, albeit in different industries and contexts. Both innovations significantly increased efficiency and productivity while reshaping the nature of work. Similarly, the steam engine, vaccines, photography, steel production, combustion engine, radio, penicillin, television, jet engine, nuclear energy, computers, space exploration, fiber optics, the internet, mobile phones, email, the Internet of Things (IoT), Machine Learning, and gene editing each brought about national and international conversations on the future of societal structure and how we work.

From an organizational perspective, such technological advancements provide a perfect opportunity for businesses to evaluate how they operate, and they often change how we work. Organizations must decide what value-added activities to prioritize, which tasks can be automated or even outsourced, and how many employees are needed to complete tasks. While the general notion at first may be to fear the uncertainty, it is a process that, if executed carefully, can propel the organization forward by allowing it to focus on what matters the most to its stakeholders and what aligns best with its mission, vision, and goals. Organizations have also been affected by significant changes in their specific industries, such as the need to upskill or reskill employees more specifically. Walmart has embarked on a three-year journey to provide associates with in-demand skills to fill 100,000 higher-paying jobs and critical roles within the company, including salaried management and hourly supervisory store roles, supply chain facilities, technology, health and wellness, and the private fleet of truck drivers (Stomski, 2024).

13.2. Purpose

This chapter offers a human-centered perspective on AI as a transformative technology that will fundamentally alter the nature of the workplace. This perspective is grounded in the historical patterns of technological changes, which, although often disruptive at first, eventually become integrated and normalized into everyday life in the 21st century. In line with decades of technological innovation, AI is expected to follow a similar trajectory — progressing through stages of adoption, implementation, adaptation, institutionalization, normalization, and optimization (Davis, 1989; Rogers, 2003) — ultimately becoming an integral part of both daily life and the workplace.

AI refers to technology systems capable of performing tasks that require human-like thinking, including learning, reasoning, problem-solving, predictive analytics, and understanding natural language. However, AI systems lack proper contextual understanding, emotional intelligence, ethical awareness, inherent creativity, and wisdom. These human attributes are vital for promoting fairness, transparency, and accountability in the workplace.

In the coming decades, shaped by AI's possibilities, the relationship between humans and technological systems within the workforce will inevitably evolve. This chapter examines the role of human wisdom in an AI-enhanced society and workplace, emphasizing how humans can contribute unique value while integrating AI systems' human-like intelligence capabilities.

13.3. Dispelling Concerns Regarding AI Replacing Humans

AI will not replace humans, but it will significantly transform knowledge-based work, requiring a reorganization of tasks. Change often brings inherent fear. For instance, the steam engine and industrial machinery of the late 1700s posed a serious threat to farm labor, as automation reduced the need for small-scale farming in favor of industrialized production. Similarly, the advent of photography in the 1830s challenged painters and portrait artists, while the airplane in the early 1900s threatened the dominance of the automobile industry. In the 1950s, nuclear power emerged as a potential competitor to the oil and gas sectors. In the 1990s, websites and search engines raised concerns about the future of traditional education and the role of teachers and trainers.

Today, AI presents yet another challenge to human roles and contributions in the workplace. However, history shows that although these technologies initially sparked apprehension, they eventually became integral to our daily lives after years or even decades of adoption, implementation, and normalization. As such technologies continue to advance in sophistication and computational power, so have considerable waves of anxiety and fear across the human workforce regarding AI's potential impact (Wong, 2024). In response, workers are increasingly encouraged to adapt their skills toward higher-level roles, such as content editing, oversight, and creative strategy that complement AI-generated outputs (Wong, 2024).

Despite advanced capabilities, AI systems are not human. AI systems are limited in grasping a contextual and profound understanding of emotional intelligence, ethical sensitivity, natural creativity, and wisdom. These uniquely human qualities are essential for ensuring fairness, transparency, and accountability within the workplace. At the individual level, employees still contend with how they can continue to meet the demands of the changing job requirements and the need for continuous learning that is even more prevalent in a rapidly changing workplace. Baskin (2023) reported that the skills of extraction and transfer will be essential to adapting to the age of AI when learning will occur nonlinearly and will require our ability to understand multiple factors and apply them to our lives.

In a world of relentless progress, learning innovation must stay one step ahead to keep us future-ready. Unlike the automated acquisition and classification of information that forms the basis of machine learning, human learning is a profoundly personalized process shaped by individual perspectives and needs. Human learning is complex, multifaceted, and challenging to diagram. Human learning is infinitely rich, more flexible, and more contextually grounded than machine learning. It is holistic and adaptive, drawing upon self-awareness, empathy, and our inherent social bonds as primates. Emotions, behaviors, thoughts, and experiences interact to contextualize and shape information, making human learning a dynamic, lifelong journey rooted in personal and ethical growth.

13.4. Workplace Evolution

Since the 1950s, the workplace has evolved from a manual service-based economy toward a digital age, an era of AI-driven environments. This evolution includes several critical milestones of innovative technology that have shaped and redefined how people work, create, collaborate, and interact. Figure 13.1 highlights key technology innovations within the workplace from the 1950s until the 2020s. We discuss each one in greater detail within this section.

The period following World War II in the mid-1940s marked a significant shift in the workforce, economic growth, and technological innovation. By the 1950s, employment patterns shifted from predominantly manufacturing and agricultural work toward service-oriented work such as retail, hospitality, and other service-based areas (Nallari *et al.*, 2011). This transition paralleled the rise of consumerism, as households sought goods and services influenced by widespread advertising. During this period, mass communication through television and radio commercials emerged, creating new marketing opportunities for organizations to reach their audiences.

During the same period, innovations in telecommunications expanded, introducing the ability to place long-distance phone calls, enabling workplaces to conduct "just-in-time" business at a greater distance. By the early 1960s, the introduction of the fax machine transformed office communication by allowing the transfer of documents through a telephone line rather than delivery by postal service.

Global events also indirectly shaped workplace evolution during this period. The Cold War, beginning in 1947 and continuing until 1991, accelerated technology innovation as the United States and the Soviet Union competed through heightened research and development. This competition drove advancements in communication technology, early computing, and even the internet for military needs, later finding a way to expand

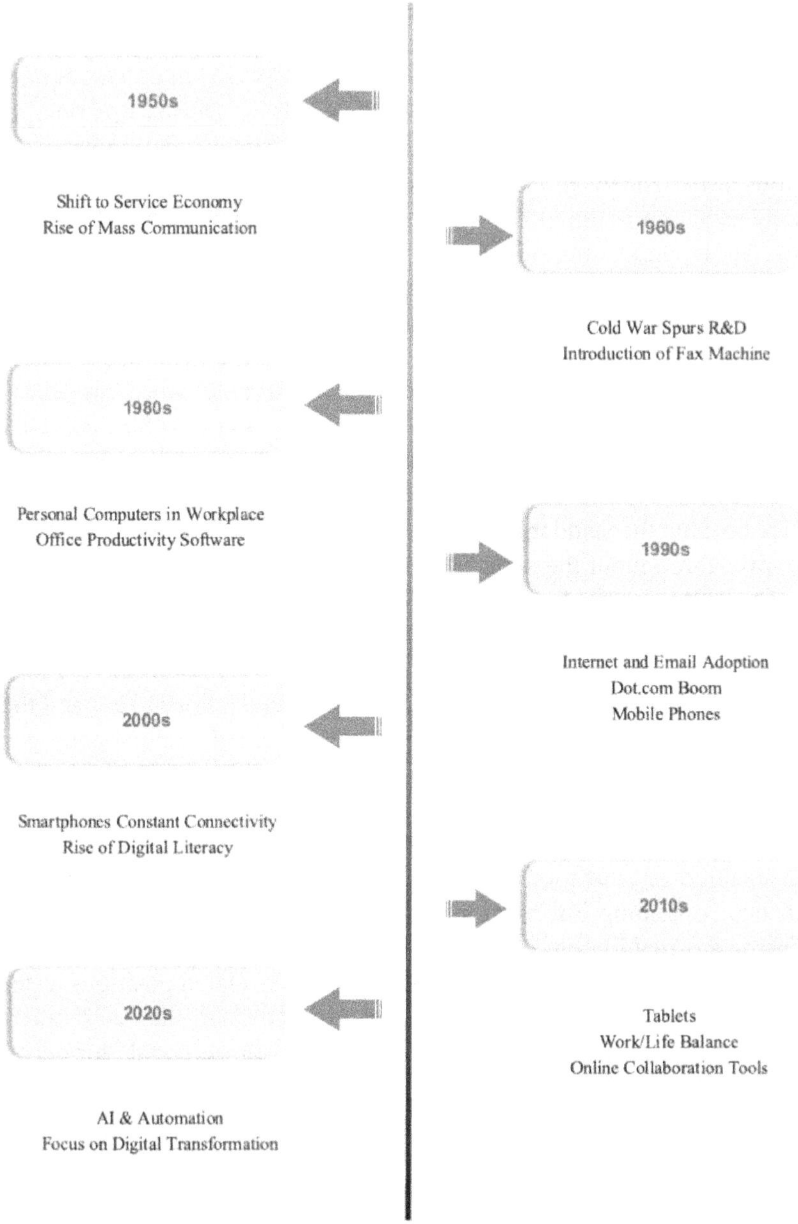

Figure 13.1. Workplace evolution timeline.

public availability for both homes and organizations (Akera, 2006; Targowski, 2005).

The introduction of the personal computer (PC) in the 1980s brought opportunities to homes, schools, and organizations. During this time, the workplace shifted from using manual processes to using computers for various tasks. The PC gradually phased out the typewriter, which had been widely used as a writing tool since its introduction in the late 19th century. IBM, Apple, and Commodore were the first companies to introduce PCs into the workplace, allowing workers to complete tasks such as word processing, data entry, and record keeping. Office productivity software was first introduced in the early 1980s with the MicroPro Internal Starburst suite, which included tools to assist with word processing, spreadsheets, and databases (Bergin, 2006). Later in the 1980s, Bill Gates announced the first Microsoft Office Suite, which initially included software for word processing, spreadsheets, and presentations. Microsoft Office became the standard for office productivity software that continues to evolve throughout the early 2020s.

The 1990s marked a defining decade for workplace evolution, with communication innovations such as the internet and mobile phones. In the mid-1990s, the internet became publicly available for home and organizational use via telephone. This access allowed organizations to expand their reach through communication channels such as email and company websites, making information sharing more efficient. Email quickly replaced slower methods of correspondence, such as fax and physical mail, because it allowed instant communication to be sent and received. The internet also enabled organizations to establish internal networks connected to websites containing information and e-commerce functionality. The late 1990s saw a rapid boom of internet-based companies known as the "dot.com boom," increasing workforce demand for IT-related positions as tech companies heavily invested in internet infrastructure and e-commerce (Doms, 2004; Hilton, 2001). Several companies emerged during this period, including eBay, a global online marketplace, and Amazon, originally an online marketplace for books.

Alongside internet availability, mobile phones and pagers became more readily available during the mid to late 1990s. This technology enabled constant connectivity and accessibility for workers after hours, laying the foundation for the always-connected workplace in later years. As such, the reliance and dependency upon technology devices within the 1990s prompted the need for digital literacy — the ability to continuously learn and use technology tools effectively. In 1997, "digital literacy" became an essential skill as the workforce began integrating computers and the internet into processes to gain and retain information (Murray and Pérez, 2014).

In the early 2000s, workplaces continued adopting internet connectivity, email, and various productivity applications. Additionally, mobile technology advanced with the release of smartphones, such as the Apple iPhone in 2007 and the Android phone in 2008. Smartphones provide users with constant connectivity to the internet, a new line of communication to transfer data, and the opportunity to access emails directly from a personal or company-issued phone device. Pocket-sized computers became another avenue for workers to connect outside the traditional workspace, allowing collaboration, communication, and productivity at a distance. There was yet to be a significant concern about work–life integration and the possible adverse effects of being constantly available for work-related communication and tasks. Along with mobile device development, the introduction of the touchscreen revolutionized mobile computing, making it possible to interact with devices more intuitively and with less action required from the user.

Additionally, innovations in web applications allowed teamwork at a distance, with the introduction of Google Docs in 2006 and Skype in 2007. Mobile technology continued to advance in the 2010s by introducing tablets to homes, schools, and the workplace. Tablets are a middle-of-the-road device between a smartphone and a personal computer, such as a laptop. Tablets are ideal for facilitating a mobile workstation and providing the ability to stay connected without being bound to a place or time. This innovation now prompts discussion on how mobile technology blurs the lines between work and personal life. Workplaces have since begun to promote work–life balance to acknowledge the importance of overall well-being to employee productivity and give way to exploring alternative work arrangements (Buick *et al.*, 2024).

The year 2020 marked a critical turning point for society due to the COVID-19 pandemic, which forced educational institutions and organizations to pivot with rapid and short assimilation to online and remote opportunities. Technologies such as Zoom, a web conferencing application, and Microsoft Teams, a group collaboration and productivity application, provided functionality for working virtually at home. While the workplace had already implemented various technologies, the quick pace and magnitude of moving practically every non-essential employee online in a matter of days was daunting. Zoom alone experienced a surge, with 10 million users in December 2019 and over 300 million users by April 2020 (Farringer, 2020). Similarly, team collaboration tools such as Slack and Asana allowed teams to collaborate on work at a distance. The call to "return to work" or "to the office" in mid-2020 will be a continuous point of conversation well into the late 2020s as the traditional workplace was reimagined to embrace flexible and adaptable work environments with tools crucial to complete work during the pandemic. While the restructured workplace offers benefits, challenges such as employee burnout and mental health issues are also present (Johnson *et al.*, 2020).

Organizations have since embraced the hybrid and remote work model and are investing in employee training programs to assist in navigating the evolving landscape (Miscovich, 2021). AI has played a transformative role as the workplace evolves, reshaping job roles and workflows and requiring employees to adapt continuously. The criticality of digital literacy is ever present and central to this evolution, requiring workers to both unlearn and relearn to enhance future success in the AI-driven, technology-advanced workplace (Zirar *et al.*, 2023). In addition, the increasing integration of AI has presented concerns about governance and ethical use. As AI becomes embedded within workflow processes in an organization, issues such as accountability, decision-making, and bias must be addressed through an AI governance framework to ensure fairness and protection of the rights of human workers and trust in the technology (Daly *et al.*, 2019; Yu *et al.*, 2018). AI brings many ethical considerations, such as data privacy, security, and discrimination (Gupta and Mishra, 2022; Lepri *et al.*, 2021). Organizations are also concerned about cybersecurity attacks, handling and storing client data, the accuracy of existing data, and the ethical implications of using data that may be imperfect to make decisions about essentially human outcomes. When ChatGPT was first introduced, employers such as PwC forbade the utilization of this technology for client work (e.g., Tadros, 2023). Many other employers, including higher educational institutions, still need an official policy governing the allowable use of Generative AI technologies. Further, AI introduces the need for ongoing ethical oversight to minimize the risk of AI replacing jobs. Addressing governance and ethical issues is crucial in a future workplace when humans and AI work together (Yu *et al.*, 2018).

Our future workplace will likely be unrecognizable compared to today. As demonstrated through workplace evolution, which we discussed in this chapter, each time since the 1950s, rapid transformation has been seen due to the advancement of technology and the impact of world events. For example, the patterns of a new technology being introduced and integrated throughout various sectors and society have shown positive effects, primarily through enhanced collaboration. The workplace of 2050 can be envisioned as a collaborative environment where humans and AI coexist to improve productivity and innovation (Zirar *et al.*, 2023). AI is expected to augment job roles rather than replace them, which leads to demand for skill development, such as ongoing reskilling and upskilling (Davenport and Mittal, 2023; Zirar *et al.*, 2023). While concerns about AI surpassing human intelligence exist (Grace *et al.*, 2018), the focus should be on developing ethics and trust with AI integration and emphasizing human well-being (Taddeo and Floridi, 2018). The future workplace will likely incorporate a flexible and accommodating structure toward differing work patterns to create a harmonious relationship between humans and AI.

13.5. The Workplace Landscape

The modern workplace is profoundly transforming, with AI technologies central to reshaping workplace dynamics and efficiencies. This shift builds upon the workplace evolution from the early 20th century to the current era of a digital-first, AI-enhanced workplace that is transitioning industries toward a future where digital literacy and AI fluency will be essential. Among the AI technologies leading this change are generative AI, conversational AI, and predictive AI (Bankins *et al.*, 2024). Generative AI systems use prompt input to create text, images, audio, and video content. This technology revolutionizes content creation by streamlining and automating creative tasks to produce content (Kanbach *et al.*, 2024). Conversational AI systems have user interaction through chatbots or virtual assistance, generally for customer service needs and to expedite the efficiency of operations. The interactions provide open-ended human-like responses to improve customer interactions and streamline customer service through real-time support (Strohmann *et al.*, 2022). This type of AI increases operational efficiency in service-related industries and the ability to support internal processes within organizations, such as human resources (Fenwick *et al.*, 2024a). Many human resource management (HRM) practices, such as updating policies and handbooks, creating job descriptions, and delivering performance appraisals, have been transformed and now rely on more advanced data analysis and faster decision-making. Thus, the functions performed by HRM professionals and the emphasis on the strategic role of HR continue to evolve. Lastly, predictive AI makes use of historical data to forecast future trends. Financial, medical, and retail industries use predictive AI to consider outcomes such as market trends and detailed analysis. For example, hospitals have recently used AI to detect the early onset of diseases, develop treatment plans, assist with patient monitoring, and even analyze X-rays and CT scans (Garcia-Madurga *et al.*, 2024).

13.5.1. *Generative AI technologies currently in use*

While each type of AI impacts the current workplace differently, the focus of this section highlights generative AI use and integration across industries. Generative AI uses machine learning and neural networks to create new content and automate a wide range of tasks, which can be tailored to specific needs. Machine learning is a branch of AI that uses algorithms to learn from data, identify patterns, and make predictions or decisions without being explicitly programmed (Brynjolfsson *et al.*, 2023). Large language models (LLMs) and technology tools powering them, such as OpenAI's ChatGPT, are an increasingly important application of machine learning. These "Generative Pre-trained Transformers" (GPTs) attempt to mimic the human brain to generate new content by predicting the likelihood of certain words being combined in sentence form.

13.5.2. *Content creation and workflow automation*

Generative AI is effective for content creation, automating the creation of text, images, audio, and video (Ooi *et al.*, 2024). This capability streamlines workflows in sectors such as communication/media, education, and marketing, where content creation is a substantial work function, allowing for faster and more responsive content production. For instance, tools such as ChatGPT or DALL-E can create draft reports, presentations, or graphics at a fraction of the time it would take a human to design manually (Ooi *et al.*, 2024). This allows organizations to increase output while reducing costs and errors (Brynjolfsson *et al.*, 2023). ChatGPT, DALL-E, Gemini, Copilot, Claude, and Jasper are current examples of leading generative AI tools. For instance, ChatGPT produces text outputs from user prompts, while DALL-E generates images from text descriptions. Beyond content creation, generative AI's adaptability extends into other high-impact areas not limited to producing text, images, or videos. Generative AI also enables deeper personalization and customized experiences tailored to individual users. This flexibility allows organizations to enhance user engagement, improve workflow efficiency, and provide relevant and targeted communication to specific users. In close relationship to marketing, GAI allows intuitive and timely interactions in customer service. With AI-driven chatbots, organizations can use large generative language models to provide messages anticipating customer needs and creating a sense of value and satisfaction (Cheng and Jiang, 2020).

13.5.3. *Personalization and customization*

Another significant application of generative AI is creating personalized content (Ooi *et al.*, 2024). This capability analyzes an individual's preferences and behavior patterns and then drafts content specifically for that user. Personalization falls into two main categories: recommendation systems and personalization algorithms (Zhang *et al.*, 2021). Well-known applications of recommendation systems are found through the shopping experience within an online store such as Amazon and streaming content such as video and audio through service providers like Netflix and Spotify, where an application is in place to analyze a user profile's patterns and offer suggestions based on the pattern of previous activity including purchases or views. This functionality uses collaborative filtering and content-based filtering, which find similarities between user profiles and the attributes of the content (Malik *et al.*, 2020). Personalized algorithms go a step further by adjusting recommended content in real-time. Typical applications are found in online advertising, e-commerce, and social media. For example, as a part of the Chrome web browser, Google Ads analyzes a user's search queries, location, and previous interactions to display personalized ads. Similarly, social media sites such as Facebook use AI for news feed display based on user profile behavior of likes, shares, and comments.

13.5.4. *Task management and workflow optimization*

Generative AI also impacts day-to-day operations through task management and workflow optimization. Applications such as Microsoft Copilot and Google Gemini can perform tasks such as prioritizing work, scheduling meetings, and organizing emails. These integrations analyze user behavior to suggest priority reminders and automatically schedule meetings using existing application capabilities, such as the calendar, task list, and email. An additional example of an application is the use of ChatGPT to analyze an email inbox, organize the emails by priority, and suggest draft responses. By streamlining routine tasks in the workplace, employees can gain more time to focus on other job duties (Rane *et al.*, 2024).

13.5.5. *Natural language processing and communication*

Generative AI advancement in natural language processing has been transformative for communication management. For example, ChatGPT's memory feature can recall previous conversations with a user, resulting in more relevant and personalized responses to communication (OpenAI, 2024). Generative AI applications can create routine communication, such as emails or messages, with customization for tone (Akdilek *et al.*, 2024). Many inefficient and time-consuming workplace practices, such as note-taking and transcribing meeting minutes, are being replaced by advanced GAI technologies such as Fathom (Fathom, 2024). Such tools easily integrate with Zoom, Google Meet, and Microsoft products, summarize the main points discussed in the meeting, and clearly outline follow-up tasks, enhancing collaboration and efficiency by holding everyone accountable and quickly moving on to the next steps.

13.5.6. *Generative AI across industries*

GAI has potential applications across multiple industries, such as agriculture, banking, communication, education, government, healthcare, human resources, manufacturing, marketing, retailing, sustainable IT management, and workplace management (Al Naqbi *et al.*, 2024; Ooi *et al.*, 2024). The following sections focus on selected industry implementations across education, healthcare, human resource management, and marketing.

13.5.7. *Education*

GAI assists educators in creating lesson plans, rubrics, assessments, and grading feedback in educational settings. These features support educators through course development and task administration, and provide additional task time to support student success (Mittal *et al.*, 2024; Yu and Guo, 2023). Students have mostly had a positive perspective toward Generative AI as it creates an opportunity for personalized learning, research, and writing assistance (Chan and Lee, 2023; Chiu, 2024). Students also favor GAI because it frees them from the toil of rote learning (Wong, 2024). Students often use ChatGPT, Gemini, Copilot, and Grammarly tools to supplement learning and complete tasks faster. Although concerns exist regarding authenticity, privacy, and ethics, successful integration is possible by establishing ethical guidelines, ensuring transparency, and providing training (Alasadi and Baiz, 2023; Yu and Guo, 2023).

13.5.8. *Healthcare*

GAI integration into the healthcare industry can potentially transform functional areas related to information management, healthcare education, and clinical workflows. An example of triage is the ability to summarize patient data from different sources to provide discharge letters (Yu *et al.*, 2023). For clinical decision support, suggestions can be formulated to improve patient outcomes and quality of services (Zhang and Boulos, 2023). Pharmacies are using GAI to review multiple sources of patient information, such as drug interactions and insurance information, with one click, allowing for extra time to see more patients (Chalasani *et al.*, 2023; Huang *et al.*, 2024). Although AI has been used in healthcare for years, particularly in imaging, GAI allows for streamlined processes in retrieving information from multiple internal databases, summarizing and generating medical reports, and providing patient education materials (Yu *et al.*, 2023). In addition, companies like Deep Scribe are using GAI, Ambient Voice Recognition, and Natural Language Processing to automatically create a doctor's note (Deep Scribe AI, 2024). Another similar tool is Unriddle, which provides AI-generated summaries of plan documents, usually consisting of numerous pages saved in PDF format (Unriddle, 2024). This saves time and allows users to quickly gain access to vital information to make decisions instead of calling insurance companies on the phone, placing users on hold, and potentially providing incorrect information.

13.5.9. *Human resource management*

The potential of GAI within human resource management has attracted high interest, with scholars and practitioners considering applications to enhance HR processes to gain efficiency (Ardichvili *et al.*, 2024). GAI in human resource management, such as ChatGPT, is being integrated into HR processes for tasks ranging from resume screening during the hiring process to employee engagement (Andrieux *et al.*, 2024; Chowdhury *et al.*, 2024). Practical usage of GAI in HR requires quality prompts and verification processes (Aguinis *et al.*, 2024). GAI has also been integrated into recruitment and employee lifecycle management by automating job postings, screening resumes, and generating personalized interview questions (Andrieux *et al.*, 2024). Such applications can also contribute to talent development by customizing training programs based on employee and organizational needs. For example, Jasper — an AI content writing tool — can create interactive content for training sessions. For performance management, GAI can analyze performance data and draft reviews for HR consideration. Specifically, Varma *et al.* (2024) conducted interviews with HR professionals and reported that AI-enabled tools make performance management more efficient. They found that AI can continuously collect performance data from multiple sources and identify trends, which can then be used to monitor and evaluate performance. Data from email, customer reviews, peer evaluations, and social media conversations can be summarized and included continuously throughout the year, making performance management more objective and evidence-based. Most importantly, such AI-enabled tools can also help determine merit raises based on performance by calibrating and calculating ratings. They are likely to be more objective and minimize errors and bias. For employee engagement, chatbots powered by GAI offer real-time feedback to employees. In addition, such tools can be used by managers who can benefit from virtual coaching opportunities and how they can approach their employees. Varma *et al.* (2024) reported that using AI-enabled tools has helped them source a larger pool of candidates and decreased recruitment speed. When making decisions related to compensation, professionals use such tools to identify market and industry trends, consider performance rating raises, and compare data across employees. Although GAI technology provides an avenue for streamlining tasks, consideration must be made to ensure compliance with the law, ethics, and discrimination, prompting the need for human review and engagement.

13.5.10. *Marketing*

Generative AI has become an essential tool in marketing, and it can create personalized content. For example, ad creation has become more streamlined using tools like ChatGPT and Jasper to create ad copies, social media posts, and other messaging. Rather than being content creators, workers should expect to be skilled as content editors (Gartner, 2024). In customer relationship management (CRM) systems used by marketing, sales, and customer service teams, GAI adds another dimension through personalized marketing. Platforms such as Salesforce Einstein and Adobe Sensei analyze data from customer behavior, such as purchase history and browsing habits, to craft highly tailored messages (Kaiser, 2019; Yu, 2019). This allows marketers to deliver curated content for individuals to strengthen brand loyalty and increase sales. Additionally, in marketing analytics, large language models are applied to assist in tasks such as strategy analysis, summary of data, and trend spotting (Robbert *et al.*, 2023). As technology advances, it is expected to further transform brand–consumer relationships and marketing practices (Jain *et al.*, 2024).

13.6. Ethical Considerations and AI

As AI becomes integral to business operations, decision-making, and employee management, it is essential to ensure that these technologies are integrated ethically in the workplace. AI has great potential to enhance efficiency, productivity, and innovation; however, without a solid ethical foundation, it can also compound issues surrounding bias, inequality, and loss of accountability — mainly due to massive amounts of the uncurated text data of real-word biases on which they are trained (Wong, 2024). Academic literature has consistently reported ethical considerations related to algorithmic bias, vulnerability, security-related issues, potential career risks, or malicious use (Garcia-Madurga *et al.*, 2024). Ethical competency in AI involves considering privacy concerns and proactively addressing broader societal implications (Moore, 2024).

13.6.1. *Ethical AI practices*

Ethical AI practices ensure that AI systems and integrations operate responsibly by aligning with societal values and supporting employee well-being. These practices include incorporating processes towards trust, fairness, transparency, accountability, and privacy within AI systems and integrations (Li *et al.*, 2023). Specifically, when it comes to decisions related to employee performance, Varma *et al.* (2024) cite ethical concerns with using AI-enabled tools in the performance management process due to issues such as potential biases being identified by proximity bias, protection of data regarding performance or other confidential employee data, as well as the general level of trust one should place in a tool if upper management cannot explain how the process works. To effectively address these concerns, organizations can adopt established frameworks that guide responsible AI development and use.

For example, frameworks such as the IEEE Ethics of Autonomous and Intelligent Systems Ethically Aligned Design (EAD) and the European Union (EU)'s Ethics Guidelines for Trustworthy AI provide foundational principles for ethical AI design and integration. The IEEE Global Initiative on Ethics of Autonomous and Intelligent Systems aims to address ethical challenges in AI development. It has created *EAD* guidelines, which propose a set of principles emphasizing human-centered values, transparency, and accountability (Chatila and Havens, 2019). This encourages developers and organizations to consider AI systems' social, economic, and cultural impacts. Similarly, the EU's Ethics Guidelines for Trustworthy AI provide a comprehensive approach to designing, developing, and deploying AI systems that are efficient, ethical, and legally compliant. This framework emphasizes that AI should acknowledge human rights, be free from unfair biases, and maintain technical reliability (Hickman and Petrin, 2021). As an example of how this applies to healthcare, Elwyn *et al.* (2024) focused on a shared decision-making model between patients and clinicians that assists in making informed preferences.

13.6.2. *Human-centric AI design for the workplace*

With ethical principles in place, human-centric AI focuses on incorporating human needs, values, and ethical considerations directly into designing and implementing AI systems. This approach ensures that AI technologies complement human skills and capabilities in the workplace rather than displacing them. By addressing employee physical and mental well-being and human-centric values, organizations can create a balanced and supportive environment for their workforce that celebrates innovation and efficiency.

Regarding physical safety, AI systems can actively monitor employees and environments in real time to detect potential hazards. For instance, personal risk assessment tools provide individualized safety recommendations that help mitigate risks across industries (Lemons *et al.*, 2024). In high-risk work environments such as construction and manufacturing, AI systems consisting of wearable sensors can be deployed to detect falls or accidents and immediately notify safety personnel for prompt response (Danilenka *et al.*, 2023). However, the successful implementation of these technologies hinges on respecting employee privacy. Wearable devices, for instance, should be minimally intrusive and compatible with existing safety protocols (Danilenka *et al.*, 2023). In such cases, AI systems can create safer work environments without overstepping boundaries by enhancing real-time safety while prioritizing workers' privacy and comfort.

Furthermore, a human-centric approach to implementing AI for workplace safety should prioritize worker well-being over productivity gains (Fenwick *et al.*, 2024a). This includes involving workers in the design and implementation process, addressing privacy and job security concerns, and ensuring that AI systems are transparent and explainable (Fenwick *et al.*, 2024a). By taking a human-centric approach to AI design in workplace safety, organizations can create environments that reduce accidents and injuries and promote job satisfaction and overall worker well-being (Fenwick *et al.*, 2024a).

Beyond physical safety, human-centric AI also addresses mental well-being in the workplace. AI's influence on workplace mental health is both a challenge and an opportunity. AI analyzes real-time data concerning employees' mental health, including mood, fatigue, and stress levels (Garcia-Madurga *et al.*, 2024). However, constant reliance on technology can create an "always-on" culture, leading to increased stress, unrealistic performance expectations, and mental fatigue (Corvite *et al.*, 2023). Workplaces that leverage AI effectively can benefit from integrations like task automation, which helps monitor mood, stress, and fatigue levels, ultimately providing recommendations to reduce mental strain. This lets employees focus on creative and meaningful work, fostering greater job satisfaction (Johnson *et al.*, 2020).

Moreover, companies can use digital mental health tools and AI-based eHealth interventions, such as mindfulness apps. Meta-analytic evidence suggests that such tools reduce symptoms of common mental health issues and improve overall well-being and productivity (Johnson *et al.*, 2020). Chatbots and AI messaging applications offer employees emotional support and counseling services. Involving employees in designing and developing these AI tools and collecting continuous feedback ensures they align with their needs and foster a healthier work culture (Fenwick *et al.*, 2024a).

In this comprehensive human-centric framework, human resources management leaders are pivotal in aligning human-centric values within AI implementations. HRM can facilitate the development of policies that protect employee privacy, address ethical concerns, and promote responsible AI usage (Fenwick *et al.*, 2024a). By embedding human-centric AI values into organizational policies and practices, HRM helps create a workplace where safety, well-being, and ethical considerations are prioritized, aligning with both employee and organizational goals.

13.7. Human–AI Collaboration

This section explores the idea that humans can undoubtedly live and thrive alone, but we will be better off if we continue to adopt and use innovation to learn, grow, and improve. Technology adoption has been explored previously. It started with fire and the wheel and has expanded to modern GAI. AI is a technology that has existed for the last 75 years, but it is only now filtering into our everyday language and daily routines with a much more robust capacity. By cultivating a workplace environment where humans and AI complement each other, collaborative intelligence paves the way for enhanced efficiency, innovation, and sustainable learning and growth in a global workplace.

The idea of human–technology collaboration is not new, but the "newness" of any technology is inherently riddled with questions and concerns. The Partnership for 21st Century (2009) introduced a framework that focused on four critical skills essential for success in the 21st century: critical thinking, communication, collaboration, and creativity. To help us better understand some of humans' capabilities and how to navigate AI in workforce situations, we explore these four areas in Table 13.1.

Humans and Artificial Intelligence systems have unique skills to guide, develop, and support the workforce in the next fifty to hundreds of years. Artificial Intelligence systems will inherently change and enhance how humans think, interact, communicate, collaborate, and create. The cooperative capability of human and AI systems will improve the responsiveness and resistance of our global workforce (Spector and Ma, 2019; Goleman, 2017; Guzman and Lewis, 2020; Jarrahi *et al.*, 2023; Berretta *et al.*, 2023; O'Toole and Horvat, 2024).

Table 13.1. Human/AI cooperative critical skills for the 21st century.

Complex Thinking	
AI role	Processes large amounts of data, identifies patterns, performs predictive analysis, and provides problem-solving assistance
Human role	Interprets complex data using ethical judgment to clean data and apply a contextual interpretation of data for decision-making
Overlap	While AI excels at large data processing and pattern recognition, human judgment and contextual analysis are needed for nuanced ethical judgment in critical decision-making
Communication	
AI role	Provides technology tools for meetings, transcription, and translation for a global and diverse workplace
Human role	Ensures that empathy, compassion, insight, and cultural and global awareness are present during personal and group meetings
Overlap	Communication facilitation is needed across geography, culture, and language. AI-provided support tools support humans' management of interpersonal relationships and personal connections
Collaboration	
AI role	Provides platforms for project management and interdisciplinary teams and individuals regardless of time or place
Human role	Understands personal connection, adaptability, and connection to perceive and interpret belief systems critical to communication across diverse departments, divisions, and organizations
Overlap	AI enhances collaboration by streamlining tasks, while human input remains essential for managing team dynamics and ensuring effective teamwork
Creativity	
AI role	Assist humans in generating new ideas through design options, pattern recognition, and processing large amounts of data
Human role	Humans drive innovative, original thoughts, expressions, and ideas that move beyond current knowledge, skills, and attitudes
Overlap	AI provides tools to enhance creativity and the creative process that supports inherent human artistic ability and creative endeavors

The overlapping and complementary relationship between humans and AI will create a transformative shift in work, problem-solving, innovation, and agility. Leveraging AI's computational strengths alongside human capacities for ethical reasoning, emotional intelligence, and cultural insight builds a future workforce characterized by adaptability, resilience, and connection. The 21st-century critical thinking, communication, collaboration, and creativity skills demonstrate how this partnership enhances individual and collective capabilities, enabling innovative advancements and enriching human experience in the global workplace. Cultivating an integrated approach to human–AI collaboration will become essential for addressing the challenges of the 21st century and beyond.

13.8. Conceptual Framework

We provided a historical overview of human and technology systems to highlight how the implementation of technology systems over the past century has contributed to a clearer understanding of workplace evolution. This analysis demonstrates how new, rapidly adopted technologies disrupt work environments but eventually become normalized and integrated into daily workplace and societal practices. Figure 13.2 presents a conceptual framework illustrating the need for humans to adapt to emerging AI systems, both in the workplace and in personal life. The following conceptual framework is partially inspired by the work of David Epstein (2019) on wicked and kind learning environments. At this model's core are three sets of capabilities, each with a broad spectrum of skills and competencies.

This conceptual framework provides a better understanding of the cooperative nature of workplace learning, productivity, and adaptability. The following sections provide a comprehensive overview of this framework.

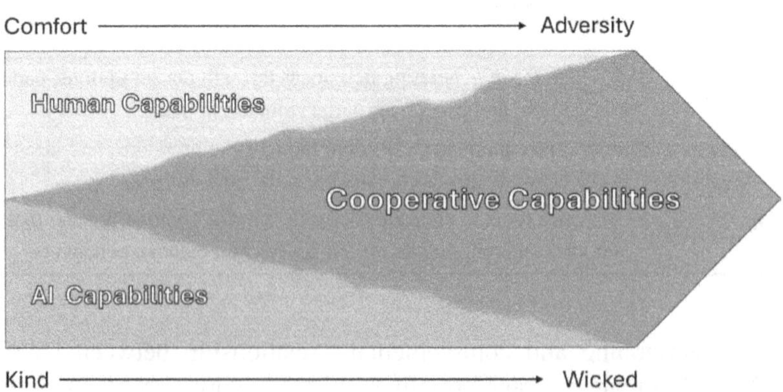

Figure 13.2. Human and AI system capabilities framework.

13.8.1. *Upper and lower spectrums*

Individuals often find themselves in a comfortable phase where they can control their physical environment, work specialization, and the resources needed to succeed. This spectrum serves as a tool for individuals and organizations to assess their current environment. At the upper boundary of the model lies a linear spectrum ranging from "comfort" to "adversity," while the lower boundary represents a spectrum from "kind" to "wicked."

When a person has a comfortable and secure job that typically aligns with their job description, they are enabling success through well-defined tasks and guidance from supervisors who set clear, achievable goals. However, as they progress along this spectrum, they may encounter increasingly adverse conditions where job stability and predictability decline. In these environments, roles can become more ambiguous, tasks evolve rapidly, and resources may become limited or uncertain. Supervisors in adverse settings may also have higher expectations, urging employees to expand their skill sets and adapt to shifting priorities. Although adverse job conditions present challenges, they can also offer significant growth opportunities, pushing individuals beyond their comfort zones and fostering resilience, problem-solving, and innovation. Understanding this spectrum allows organizations to support employees in navigating adversity better, potentially reducing burnout and promoting an adaptive learning culture.

In in-kind learning environments, the structure and predictability support steady improvement through practice and adherence to established rules (Epstein, 2019). Individuals in these settings benefit from clear, consistent feedback that directly correlates with their actions, enabling them to make reliable predictions about outcomes. Information transparency and straightforward cause-and-effect relationships empower learners to refine their skills through repetition, building confidence and expertise within a controlled, reliable framework (Allen, 2022). Therefore, environments promote mastery through structured learning as individuals can safely experiment, learn from mistakes, and gradually increase their competence without facing severe, unpredictable consequences. Wicked learning environments operate with ambiguity, where information is often hidden, unreliable, or conflicting, making it difficult for individuals to discern accurate patterns or predict outcomes. In chaotic settings, feedback may be delayed, inconsistent, or misleading, fostering counterproductive habits and impairing decision-making (Epstein, 2019). For instance, the stock market exemplifies a wicked environment where innumerable variables interact unpredictably, often obscuring cause-and-effect relationships (Allen, 2022). Even experts may need help in these settings, as their advanced knowledge and experience do not necessarily translate to superior performance. The disconnect between perceived and actual realities in wicked environments can lead to judgment errors, where the need for clarity complicates the development of expertise, making adaptive reasoning and resilience essential to navigating such adversity (Allen, 2022).

13.8.2. *Human capabilities*

Humans possess an extraordinary capacity for adaptation and resilience, allowing us to overcome even the most formidable challenges. As social primates, our curiosity, emotions, cooperation, cultural awareness, and advanced cognitive abilities equip us with self-awareness, intrinsic motivation, self-direction, and sensemaking, enabling us to navigate the complexities of life and work. Effective communication, self-understanding, intuition, empathy, storytelling, intergenerational vision, and systems thinking enhance our ability to collaborate productively and professionally, fostering opportunities for social engagement and influence.

Humans can be efficient, effective, cooperative, and productive without the aid or intervention of technological assistance. Furthermore, many core human traits may never be replicated by AI systems. As we advance with new technological systems, it is essential to continue valuing these uniquely human traits. Human intelligence is enriched by emotions, empathy, original creativity, lived experiences, individual and collective wisdom, and complex social bonds and cannot be fully replicated.

13.8.3. *Artificial Intelligence capabilities*

AI increasingly plays a critical role in the workplace (Hillen, 2024). Although AI evolves daily into a more powerful tool, it will still not replace human labor in tasks requiring emotional intelligence. Many workplace roles demand high levels of emotional intelligence, which involves appropriately recognizing, responding to, and interacting with the emotions of customers or colleagues. While AI systems can assist by providing emotional counseling and support to employees facing stressful situations (Garcia-Madurga *et al.*, 2024), they lack genuine emotional depth and adaptability through human interaction.

AI systems can effectively mimic various human tasks, such as pattern recognition, predictive analysis, language processing, data management, speech and image recognition, and certain forms of creative output. As AI advances, its ability to replicate some human-like traits such as creativity, empathy, learning, and social interaction will improve. Understanding AI's capabilities and limitations is essential, as it cannot fully replicate the nuanced emotional and social skills that are uniquely human. This perspective does not downplay AI's future potential but should highlight the complementary roles AI and human intelligence can play in the workplace.

13.8.4. *Cooperative capabilities*

In the modern workplace, cooperative capabilities highlight the potential for effective collaboration between humans and AI systems, as needed. AI can handle data-intensive tasks such as pattern recognition, predictive analysis, and language processing to enhance human productivity rather than replace it. When humans and AI systems work together, they complement each other's strengths and promote efficiency.

AI can provide computational and data processing power while humans bring unique social, emotional, and cognitive abilities, ethical judgment, and lived experiences. Humans contribute empathy, intuition, and emotional intelligence, essential for communication, relationship building, and ethical decision-making. These traits allow for a deeper understanding of social dynamics and individual needs, which AI, limited by its data-based processing, cannot fully replicate. With these cooperative capabilities, humans can guide AI usage in ways that reflect human values, building trust, adaptability, and resilience in the workplace that will help us prioritize goals and achieve relevant organizational outcomes.

While AI's ability to mimic some human traits is improving, the partnership between humans and AI remains essential. AI boosts efficiency by handling large amounts of information quickly and accurately, allowing humans to focus on complex, creative, or emotionally nuanced tasks.

13.9. Preparing for the Future

As we prepare for an even more technologically advanced future with high demand for digital literacy among current and future employees, all must strive to possess value-added skills and abilities, along with practical communication skills. Although automating work tasks may eventually create unintended issues related to unemployment and lower wages, especially among service-related professions these tasks are often done more efficiently. While it may be challenging to be sure how the global adoption of AI will heavily impact specific human jobs, jobs that require repetitive tasks are anticipated to be first on the list to be revised, including data processing, manufacturing, machine operators, journalists, accounting, and bankers (Garcia-Madurga *et al.*, 2024). Hence, data suggest that AI's revolutionary overall impact does not differentiate between traditional white-collar and blue-collar occupations (Wong, 2024).

Lifelong learning related to AI is essential for all. Organizations benefit from managers with a deeper understanding of AI technologies and analytics (Moore, 2024). Leaders skilled in effective communication can informatively address issues of concern, dispel myths and misconceptions, and cultivate positive perceptions of AI initiatives among employees and stakeholders. When drafting various documents in the workplace, AI tools often speed up the revision process and content accuracy (Hillen, 2024). HRM leaders must remain empowered to navigate the complexities of AI to make informed decisions and foster collaboration with technical teams (Moore, 2024). For example, suppose HRM professionals fail to continue to adopt AI healthily and ethically. In that case, future employees should prepare for potential recruitment bias, fear of job loss, and the promulgation of other unsound hiring practices. However, incorporating AI to maximize job efficiency could contribute to lower stress levels for employees, increased work–life balance, improved mental health, reduced turnover rates, and overall higher levels of job satisfaction. AI app developers must ensure that upcoming applications are user-friendly, multidisciplinary, responsible, explainable, and relevant (Fenwick *et al.*, 2024b). Employees must continue to strive for up-skilling and reskilling to remain relevant.

13.10. Final Thoughts

While governments across the globe continue to struggle to establish appropriate frameworks and guidelines to introduce Generative AI into public and educational sectors effectively, the relative rate of GAI's progress and workforce/academic integration far outpaces the speed of regulation (Wong, 2024). The adoption of AI also mandates a paradigm shift in employability skills and competencies due to the modern workplace evolving so rapidly (Moore, 2024). Educational programs on both secondary and postsecondary levels must overcome negative perceptions of the AI disruption in academia, incorporate ethical uses of emerging AI technologies, and tailor instruction to align with technologically advanced trends to help fulfill the need for skilled employees with continuously enhanced skills and knowledge. Furthermore, school leaders and corporate employers must be dedicated to providing additional training and development opportunities to ensure that their staff and leaders are knowledgeable in AI integration and implementation (Fenwick *et al.*, 2024b).

Future research related to the AI-driven workplace should attempt to address further concerns related to employee mental well-being, wearable devices, real-time monitoring of employees' physical health, ethical considerations, potential biases in AI algorithms, and how AI practices may vary globally or across different cultural contexts (Garcia-Madurga, 2024). Recognizing and valuing irreplaceable human traits — like creativity, individual and collective wisdom, and the capacity for meaningful connection — ensure a workplace that is both technologically advanced and human-centered and that values collaboration and integration of tools that enhance how we accomplish organizational goals.

Bibliography

Aguinis, H., Beltran, J. R., and Cope, A. "How to use generative AI as a human resource management assistant." *Organizational Dynamics* 53, no. 1 (2024): 101029. DOI: 10.1016/j.orgdyn.2024.101029.

Akdilek, S., Akdilek, I., and Punyanunt-Carter, N. M. "The influence of Generative AI on interpersonal communication dynamics." *The Role of Generative AI in the Communication Classroom* (2024): 167–190. DOI: 10.4018/979-8-3693-0831-8.ch009.

Akera, A. *Calculating a Natural World: Scientists, Engineers, and Computers During the Rise of U.S. Cold War Research*. The MIT Press, 2006. DOI: 10.7551/mitpress/1712.001.001.

Alasadi, E. A. and Baiz, C. R. "Generative AI in education and research: Opportunities, concerns, and solutions." *Journal of Chemical Education* 100, no. 8 (2023): 2965–2971. DOI: 10.1021/acs.jchemed.3c00323.

Al Naqbi, H., Bahroun, Z., and Ahmed, V. "Enhancing work productivity through generative artificial intelligence: A comprehensive literature review." *Sustainability* 16, no. 3 (2024): 1166. DOI: 10.3390/su16031166.

Allen, J. *Fostering Wisdom at Work*. Taylor & Francis, 2022. DOI: 10.4324/9781003018759.

Andrieux, P., Johnson, R. D., Sarabadani, J., and Van Slyke, C. "Ethical considerations of generative AI-enabled human resource management." *Organizational Dynamics* 53, no. 1 (2024). DOI: 10.1016/j.orgdyn.2024.101032.

Ardichvili, A., Dirani, K., Jabarkhail, S., El Mansour, W., and Aboulhosn, S. "Using generative AI in human resource development: An applied research study." *Human Resource Development International* 27, no. 3 (2024): 388–409. DOI: 10.1080/13678868.2024.2337964.

Bankins, S., Ocampo, A. C., Marrone, M., Restubog, S. L. D., and Woo, S. E. "A multilevel review of Artificial Intelligence in organizations: Implications for organizational behavior research and practice." *Journal of Organizational Behavior* 45, no. 2 (2024): 159–182. DOI: 10.1002/job.2735.

Baskin, K. "How continuous learning keeps leaders relevant in the age of AI." 2023. MIT Sloan School of Management. https://mitsloan.mit.edu/ideas-made-to-matter/how-continuous-learning-keeps-leaders-relevant-age-ai.

Bergin, T. "The origins of word processing software for personal computers: 1976–1985." *IEEE Annals of the History of Computing* 28 (2006): 32–47. DOI: 10.1109/MAHC.2006.76.

Berretta, S., Tausch, A., Ontrup, G., Gilles, B., Peifer, C., and Kluge, A. "Defining human-AI teaming the human-centered way: A scoping review and network analysis." *Frontiers of Artificial Intelligence* 6 (2023): 21–28. DOI: 10.3389/frai.2023.1250725.

Brynjolfsson, E., Li, D., and Raymond, L. "Generative AI at work." National Bureau of Economic Research, 2023. DOI: 10.3386/w31161.

Buick, F., Blackman, D. A., Glennie, M., Weeratunga, V., and O'Donnell, M. E. "Different approaches to managerial support for flexible working: Implications for public sector employee well-being." *Public Personnel Management* 53, no. 3 (2024): 377–405. DOI: 10.1177/00910260241226731.

Chalasani, S. H., Syed, J., Ramesh, M., Patil, V., and Pramod Kumar, T. M. "Artificial Intelligence in the field of pharmacy practice: A literature review." *Exploratory Research in Clinical and Social Pharmacy* 12 (2023): 100346. DOI: 10.1016/j.rcsop.2023.100346.

Chan, C. K. Y. and Lee, K. K. "The AI generation gap: Are Gen Z students more interested in adopting generative AI such as ChatGPT in teaching and learning than their Gen X and millennial generation teachers?" *Smart Learning Environments* 10, no. 1 (2023): 60. DOI: 10.1186/s40561-023-00269-3.

Chatila, R. and Havens, J. C. "The IEEE Global Initiative on Ethics of Autonomous and Intelligent Systems." *Robotics and Well-Being* 95 (2019): 11–16. DOI: 10.1007/978-3-030-12524-0_2.

Cheng, Y. and Jiang, H. "How do AI-driven chatbots impact user experience? Examining gratifications, perceived privacy risk, satisfaction, loyalty, and continued use." *Journal of Broadcasting & Electronic Media* 64, no. 4 (2020): 592–614. DOI: 10.1080/08838151.2020.1834296.

Chhatre, R. and Singh, S. "The AI Jungle Book!" *International Journal of Innovative Science and Research Technology (IJISRT)* 5 (2024): 3132–3135. DOI: 10.38124/ijisrt/IJISRT24MAY2051.

Chiu, T. K. "Future research recommendations for transforming higher education with generative AI." *Computers and Education: Artificial Intelligence* 6 (2024): 100197. DOI: 10.1016/j.caeai.2023.100197.

Chowdhury, S., Budhwar, P., and Wood, G. "Generative artificial intelligence in business: Towards a strategic human resource management framework." *British Journal of Management* 35, no. 4 (2024): 1680–1691. DOI: 10.1111/1467-8551.12824.

Clarke, A. C. *Profiles of the Future: An Inquiry into the Limits of the Possible.* Harper & Row, 1962.

Corvite, S., Roemmich, K., Rosenberg, T. I., and Andalibi, N. "Data subjects' perspectives on emotion Artificial Intelligence use in the workplace: A relational ethics lens." *Proceedings of the ACM on Human-Computer Interaction* 7, no. CSCW1 (2023): 1–38. DOI: 10.1145/3579600.

Daly, A., Hagendorff, T., Hui, L., Mann, M., Marda, V., Wagner, B., Wang, W., and Witteborn, S. "Artificial Intelligence governance and ethics: Global Perspectives." ArXiv, 2019. DOI: 10.48550/arXiv.1907.03848.

Danilenka, A., Sowiński, P., Rachwał, K., Bogacka, K., Dąbrowska, A., Kobus, M., Baszczyński, K., Okrasa, M., Olczak, W., Dymarski, P., Lacalle, I., Ganzha, M., and Paprzycki, M. "Real-time AI-driven fall detection method for occupational health and safety." *Electronics* 12, no. 20 (2023): 4257. DOI: 10.3390/electronics12204257.

Davenport, T. H. and Mittal, N. "How companies can prepare for the coming "AI-first" world." *Strategy & Leadership* 51, no. 1 (2023): 26–30. DOI: 10.1108/SL-11-2022-0107.

Davis, F. D. "Perceived usefulness, perceived ease of use, and user acceptance of information technology." *MIS Quarterly* 13, no. 3 (1989): 319–340. DOI: 10.2307/249008.

Deep Scribe AI. "About." 2024. https://www.deepscribe.ai/.

Doms, M. "The boom and bust in Information Technology Investment." *Economic Review-Federal Reserve Bank of San Francisco* (2004): 19–34. https://www.frbsf.org/wp-content/uploads/er19-34bk.pdf.

Elwyn, G., Ryan, P., Blumkin, D., and Week, W. "Meet generative AI… your new shared decision-making assistant." *BMJ Evidence-Based Medicine* 29 (2024): 292–295. DOI: 10.1136/bmjebm-2023-112651.

Epstein D. *Range: Why Generalists Triumph in a Specialized World.* Riverhead Books, 2019.

Farringer, D. R. "A telehealth explosion: Using lessons from the Pandemic to shape the future of telehealth regulation." *Texas A&M Law Review* 9, no. 1 (2020). DOI: 10.37419/LR.V9.I1.1.

Fathom. 2024. https://help.fathom.video/en.

Fenwick, A., Molnar, G., and Frangos, P. "The critical role of HRM in AI-driven digital transformation: A paradigm shift to enable firms to move from AI implementation to human-centric adoption." *Discover Artificial Intelligence* 4, no. 1 (2024a): 34. DOI: 10.1007/s44163-024-00125-4.

Fenwick, A., Molnar, G., and Frangos, P. "Revising the role of HR in the age of AI: Bringing humans closer together in the workplace." *Frontiers in Artificial Intelligence* (2024b): 1–10. DOI: 10.3389/frai.2023.1272823.

Garcia-Madurga, M., Gil-Lacruz, A., Saz-Gil, I., and Gil-Lacruz, M. "The role of Artificial Intelligence in improving workplace well-being: A systematic review." *Businesses* 4 (2024b): 389–410. DOI: 10.3390/businesses4030024.

Gartner. "Generative AI: What is It, Tools, Models, Applications and Use Cases." 2024. https://www.gartner.com/en/topics/generative-ai.

Goleman, D. *Emotional Intelligence: Why It Can Matter More Than IQ*. Bantam Books, 2017.

Grace, K., Salvatier, J., Dafoe, A., Zhang, B., and Evans, O. "Viewpoint: When will AI exceed human performance? Evidence from AI experts." *The Journal of Artificial Intelligence Research* 62 (2018): 729–754. DOI: 10.1613/jair.1.11222.

Gupta, A. and Mishra, M. "Ethical concerns while using Artificial Intelligence in recruitment of employees." *Business Ethics and Leadership* 6, no. 2 (2022): 6–11. DOI: 10.21272/bel.6(2).6-11.2022.

Guzman, A. L. and Lewis, S. C. "Artificial intelligence and communication: A human-machine communication research agenda." *New Media & Society* 22, no. 1 (2020): 70–86. DOI: 10.1177/1461444819858691.

Hickman, E. and Petrin, M. "Trustworthy AI and corporate governance: The EU's ethics guidelines for trustworthy artificial intelligence from a company law perspective." *European Business Organization Law Review* 22, no. 4 (2021): 593–625. DOI: 10.1007/s40804-021-00224-0.

Hillen, A. "Exploring artificial intelligence tool use in a nonprofit workplace." *Journal of Business and Technical Communication* 38, no. 3 (2024): 213–224. DOI: 10.1177/10506519241239661.

Hilton, M. "Information Technology workers in the new economy." *Monthly Labor Review* 124, no. 6 (2001): 41–45. https://www.bls.gov/opub/mlr/2001/06/ressum2.pdf.

Huang, X., Estau, D., Liu, X., Yu, Y., Qin, J., and Li, Z. "Evaluating the performance of ChatGPT in clinical pharmacy: A comparative study of ChatGPT and clinical pharmacists." *British Journal of Clinical Pharmacology* 90, no. 1 (2024): 232–238. DOI: 10.1111/bcp.15896.

Jain, P., Jain, P., and Jain, A. "Marketing's crystal ball: Where we are and where we could soon be with generative Artificial Intelligence in marketing." *Journal of Cultural Marketing Strategy* 8, no. 2 (2024): 134–150. DOI: 10.69554/JDOC2249.

Jarrahi, M., Askay, D. Eshragi, A., and Smith, P. "Artificial Intelligence and knowledge management: A partnership between human and AI." *Business Horizons* (2023): 87–99. DOI: 10.1016/j.bushor.2022.03.002.

Johnson, A., Dey, S., Nguyen, H., Groth, M., Joyce, S., Tan, L., Glozier, N., and Harvey, S. B. "A review and agenda for examining how technology-driven changes at work will impact workplace mental health and employee well-being." *Australian Journal of Management* 45 (2020): 402–424. DOI: 10.1177/0312896220922292.

Kaiser, Z. "Creativity as computation: Teaching design in the age of automation." *Design and Culture* 11, no. 2 (2019): 173–192. DOI: 10.1080/17547075.2019.1609279.

Kanbach, D. K., Heiduk, L., Blueher, G., Schreiter, M., and Lahmann, A. "The GenAI is out of the bottle: Generative Artificial Intelligence from a business model innovation perspective." *Review of Managerial Science* 18, no. 4 (2024): 1189–1220. DOI: 10.1007/s11846-023-00696-z.

Lemons, J., Souza, V. B. de, Falcetta, F. S., Almeida, F. K. de, Lima, T. M., and Gaspar, P. D. "Enhancing Workplace Safety through Personalized Environmental Risk Assessment: An AI-Driven Approach in Industry 5.0." *Computers* 13, no. 5 (2024): 120. DOI: 10.3390/computers13050120.

Lepri, B., Oliver, N., and Pentland, A. "Ethical machines: The human-centric use of Artificial Intelligence." *iScience* 24 (2021). DOI: 10.1016/j.isci.2021.102249.

Li, B., Qi, P., Liu, B., Di, S., Liu, J., Pei, J., Yi, J., and Zhou, B. "Trustworthy AI: From principles to practices." *ACM Computing Surveys* 55, no. 9 (2023): 1–46. DOI: 10.1145/3555803.

Malik, S., Rana, A., and Bansal, M. "A survey of recommendation Systems." *Information Resources Management Journal (IRMJ)* 33, no. 4 (2020): 53–73. DOI: 10.4018/IRMJ.2020100104.

Miscovich, P. "The intelligent, experiential and competitive workplace: Part 1." *Journal of AI, Robotics & Workplace Automation* 1, no. 1 (2021): 70–86. DOI: 10.69554/BYSC3755.

Mittal, U., Sai, S., and Chamola, V. "A comprehensive review on generative AI for education." *IEEE Access* (2024). DOI: 10.1109/ACCESS.2024.3468368.

Moore, B. "What competencies will be needed to manage Artificial Intelligence in the workplace?" *Assessment & Development Matters* 16, no. 1 (2024): 4–8. DOI: 10.53841/bpsadm.2024.16.1.4.

Murray, M. C. and Pérez, J. "Unraveling the digital literacy paradox: How higher education fails at the fourth literacy." *Issues in Informing Science and Information Technology* 11 (2014): 85. DOI: 10.28945/1982.

Nallari, R., Yusuf, S., Griffith, B., and Bhattacharya, R. *Frontiers in Development Policy: A Primer on Emerging Issues*. World Bank, 2011. DOI: 10.1596/9780821387856.

Ooi, K. B., Tan, G. W. H., Al-Emran, M., Al-Sharafi, M. A., Capatina, A., Chakraborty, A., and Wong, L. W. "The potential of generative artificial intelligence across disciplines: Perspectives and future directions." *Journal of Computer Information Systems* (2023): 1–32. DOI: 10.1080/08874417.2023.2261010.

OpenAI. "Memory and new controls for ChatGPT." 2024. https://openai.com/index/memory-and-new-controls-for-chatgpt.

O'Toole, K. and Horvat, E. "Extending human creativity with AI." *Journal of Creativity* 34, no. 2 (2024): 1–8. DOI: 10.1016/j.yjoc.2024.100080.

Partnership for 21st Century Learning (P21). "P21 framework definitions." 2009. Washington, DC: Author. https://eric.ed.gov/?id=ED519462.

Rane, J., Kaya, O., Mallick, S. K., and Rane, N. L. "Impact of ChatGPT and similar generative artificial intelligence on several business sectors: Applications, opportunities, challenges, and future prospects." *Generative Artificial Intelligence in Agriculture, Education, and Business* (2024): 27–83. DOI: 10.70593/978-81-981271-7-4_2.

Robbert, K., Penn, C., and Wall, J. "Use cases of large language models in marketing analytics." *Applied Marketing Analytics* 9, no. 3 (2023): 249–269. DOI: 10.69554/mcni7392.

Rogers, E. M. *Diffusion of Innovations* (5th ed.). Free Press, 2003.

Spector, J. M. and Ma, S. "Inquiry and critical thinking skills for the next generation: From artificial intelligence back to human intelligence." *Smart Learning Environment* 6, no. 8 (2019): 1–11. DOI: 10.1186/s40561-019-0088-z.

Stomski, L. "Walmart accelerates efforts to provide associates with skills to fill 100,000 in-demand jobs." 2024. https://corporate.walmart.com/news/2024/02/22/walmart-accelerates-efforts-to-provide-associates-with-skills-to-fill-100000-in-demand-jobs.

Strohmann, T., Siemon, D., Khosrawi-Rad, B., and Robra-Bissantz, S. "Toward a design theory for virtual companionship." *Human–Computer Interaction* 38, no. 3–4 (2022): 194–234. DOI: 10.1080/07370024.2022.2084620.

Taddeo, M. and Floridi, L. "How AI can be a force for good." *Science* 361 (2018): 751–752. DOI: 10.1126/science.aat5991.

Tadros, E. "PwC warns staff against using ChatGPT for client work." 2023. Financial Review. https://www.afr.com/companies/professional-services/pwc-warns-against-using-chatgpt-for-client-work-20230205-p5chzi.

Targowski, A. "From the Cold War to internet cathedral." *International Journal of Information and Communication Technology Education (IJICTE)* 1, no. 2 (2005): 87–99. DOI: 10.4018/jicte.2005040108.

Unriddle. 2024. https://www.unriddle.ai/.

Varma, A., Pereira, V., and Patel, P. "Artificial intelligence and performance management." *Organizational Dynamics* 53, no. 1 (2024): 101037. DOI: 10.1016/j.orgdyn.2024.101037.

Wong, W. "The sudden disruptive rise of generative artificial intelligence? An evaluation of their impact on higher education and the global workplace." *Journal of Open Innovation: Technology, Market, and Complexity* 20 (2024): 1–8. DOI: 10.1016/j.joitmc.2024.100278.

Yu, H. and Guo, Y. "Artificial Intelligence empowers educational reform: Current status, issues, and prospects." *Frontiers in Education* 8 (2023): 1183162. DOI: 10.3389/feduc.2023.1183162.

Yu, H., Shen, Z., Miao, C., Leung, C., Lesser, V. R., and Yang, Q. "Building ethics into artificial intelligence." ArXiv, 2018. DOI: 10.24963/ijcai.2018/779.

Yu, J. "Einstein analytics: Introduction." In *Getting Started with Salesforce Einstein Analytics*, 1–23. Apress, Berkeley, CA, 2019. DOI: 10.1007/978-1-4842-5200-0_1.

Yu, P., Xu, H., Hu, X., and Deng, C. "Leveraging generative AI and large language models: A comprehensive roadmap for healthcare integration." *Healthcare* 11, no. 20 (2023). DOI: 10.3390/healthcare11202776.

Zhang, P. and Boulos, M. N. "Generative AI in Medicine and Healthcare: Promises, opportunities and challenges." *Future Internet* 15 (2023): 286. DOI: 10.3390/fi15090286.

Zhang, Q., Lu, J., and Jin, Y. "Artificial intelligence in recommender systems." *Complex & Intelligent Systems* 7, no. 1 (2021): 439–457. DOI: 10.1007/s40747-020-00212-w.

Zirar, A., Ali, S. I., and Islam, N. "Worker and workplace artificial intelligence (AI) coexistence: Emerging themes and research agenda." *Technovation* 124 (2023): 102747. DOI: 10.1016/j.technovation.2023.102747.

https://doi.org/10.1142/9781800616578_0014

Chapter 14

The LAFBAH AI Framework for a Transformative National AI Strategy: Enhancing Morocco's Competitiveness and Strategic Intelligence

Abdelmjid Lafram[*,‡] **and Salah Eddine Bahji**[†,§]

[*]*School of Information Sciences, Rabat, Morocco*

[†]*Mohammadia School of Engineers,*
Mohammed V University, Rabat, Morocco

[‡]*alafram@esi.ac.ma*
[§]*salaheddinebahji@research.emi.ac.ma*

Abstract

What are the structural and transformational impacts of a national Artificial Intelligence (AI) strategy on the competitiveness and strategic intelligence of countries? This is the central question that we try to answer by focusing on the Moroccan context.

Thus, this chapter attempts to explore this question by presenting our conceptual model called the "LAFBAH AI Framework" in an integrated, structured, and innovative approach for the implementation of a holistic, visionary, ethical, and impactful national AI strategy in Morocco.

This framework is divided into leadership and vision, agile and accountable governance, future-ready skills and talent development, broad-based collaboration, advanced data and infrastructures, and human-centered approach. It aims to achieve strategic goals called the 5S: Smartness of Strategic State, Sovereignty, Security, Soft Power, and Sustainability. It sheds light on the strategic role of the state in its prospective vision, the competitive and structuring dimensions of public policies, and the design of sectoral strategies boosted by the transformative potential of AI.

Our conceptual model is the result of a reflection supported by a mixed methodological triangulation approach. It is based on an in-depth analysis of the best global practices relating to national AI policies and strategies. In addition, a focus was placed on the impact of AI on the competitiveness and strategic intelligence of countries.

By combining interviews with confirmed experts in the field of AI and a systemic approach, we diagnosed the Moroccan AI ecosystem in terms of actors and initiatives by addressing the major challenges and opportunities for an impactful, ethical, responsible, safe, and trusted AI.

This chapter also presents the key success factors of a visionary, coherent, and impactful national AI strategy while outlining the levers and the main axis of development of the Moroccan AI ecosystem. The final results of this research further advocate for a dedicated AI strategy. They also open up promising directions for thinking and research on the impact of AI on the state's strategic intelligence and its overall competitiveness.

Keywords: Artificial Intelligence, national AI strategy, LAFBAH AI framework, competitiveness, strategic intelligence, Morocco.

14.1. Introduction

Artificial Intelligence (AI), as a disruptive technology, is becoming a major driver of any country's socioeconomic development and an increasing indicator of its competitiveness. It is disrupting all sectors of activity and transforming entire sections of the global economy. Considered a key and crucial technology for the 21st century (Heumann and Zahn, 2018), presenting several incredible potentials, AI has been the subject of numerous national strategies to exploit its potential and meet major challenges (OECD, 2024).

Its transformative impact has affected every region, compelling states to envision their future, plan their strategic trajectories through AI. This enables them to improve overall performance, enhance national competitiveness, and strengthen strategic intelligence to compete effectively, position themselves globally, and create sustainable value.

Certainly, AI has undeniable positive and beneficial impacts, but, on the other hand, it also comes with risks and major challenges, both globally and nationally. In this context, many international organizations, including the United Nations Educational, Scientific and Cultural Organization (UNESCO), the Organization for Economic Cooperation and Development (OECD), and other multilateral cooperation groups, as well as alliances and regional blocks like the European Union, the G8, and the G20 (Ajaykumar, Tripathi, Basrur, Bag, and Mohan, 2024), have become involved in global AI governance and regulations.

Since Canada's first AI strategy was published in 2017, a wave of national AI strategies has emerged. These strategies have been published annually since then, culminating in new frameworks that outline each nation's ambitions, visions, key strategic goals, and priorities for the long-term development of AI. Thus, with more than seventy national AI strategies, the global AI landscape has been enriched over the years by new strategic AI frameworks and inspiring models from leading countries.

As part of its digital transformation, Morocco launched an ambitious digital strategy in September 2024 under the name of "Digital Morocco 2030," with two major objectives, namely, digitalizing public services and stimulating the digital economy. However, Artificial Intelligence is presented as just an integral part of this overall digital strategy.

It should be noted that Morocco's challenges are numerous and its ambitions in the digital field are enormous, in accordance with its strategic orientations and in alignment with Morocco's new development model.

Our research falls within this framework, aiming to highlight the transformative impact and the fundamental role of an effective and efficient national strategy of AI in strengthening Morocco's competitiveness and strategic intelligence.

In this context, we have developed a conceptual model called "LAFBAH AI Framework", which serves as a reference framework for the design and implementation of a national AI strategy adapted to the

Moroccan context. At the same time, it integrates the best international practices that can enhance Morocco's competitiveness, while establishing its regional and continental leadership and strengthening its strategic and competitive intelligence on the global scale.

To this end, we employed a systemic approach based on a theoretical triangulation of stakeholder theory (Freeman, 1984), while mobilizing the concepts of competitiveness and national strategy (Porter, 1990). In addition, we used a methodological triangulation integrating interviews with experts in the field, the documentary approach, and conceptual modeling also based on lessons learned from international good practices.

The ultimate goal is to demonstrate how a national AI strategy aligned with the strategic orientations of Morocco's new development model can be a real lever for digital transformation to boost the country's competitiveness and strengthen its strategic intelligence and resilience.

LAFBAH AI framework constitutes a strategic and holistic initiative to emphasize the urgent need for a synergistic, integrated, and well-structured approach to implementing an AI ecosystem that is both effective and efficient, tailored to the Moroccan context while aligned with leading international practices in AI practices.

Thus, to achieve this, this chapter is structured around six key sections: transformative impact of the national AI strategies on nations' competitiveness and strategic intelligence; assets, achievements, and challenges of the Moroccan AI ecosystem; the LAFBAH AI framework: a conceptual model for a transformative national AI strategy in Morocco (presentation and strategic goals); critical success factors of the national AI strategy according to the LAFBAH AI framework; the levers of a national AI strategy according to the LAFBAH AI framework; and recommendations of the key components of an integrated framework to foster the development of an AI ecosystem in Morocco.

14.2. Transformative Impact of the National AI Strategies on Nations' Competitiveness and Strategic Intelligence

As a disruptive technology, AI has become a real lever for economic and strategic transformation by fundamentally impacting all socioeconomic industries and sectors (UN, 2024). It strengthens economic competitiveness, optimizes industrial processes, accelerates time to market, improves the quality of products, services, and processes, and stimulates innovation.

Governments can harness the enormous potential offered by Artificial Intelligence to improve policy design, make better decisions, strengthen communication and engagement with the public, and accelerate and improve the quality of public services (OECD/CAF, 2022).

In addition, AI has the potential to strengthen national strategic intelligence in the sense that it enables automation, even empowerment, rapid and efficient analysis, and smart exploitation of big data to extract strategic information on economic opportunities and strategic and geopolitical risks to anticipate changes that are looming on the horizon and technological trends of various natures. It also allows for increasing resilience, vigilance, agility, productivity, growth, and inspired innovation across the private and public actors and socioeconomic sectors.

In their relentless quest for global performance and long-term competitiveness, many countries have launched their own national AI strategies by developing their own frameworks that reflect their transformative national strategic visions, technological aspirations, and specific priorities (Ajaykumar *et al.*, 2024), translating their long-term ambitions to induce the changes needed to perform, compete, and strengthen their leadership and expand their soft power.

Canada was the first country to launch its national AI strategy in March 2017. The AI Index 2024 reports that 75 national AI strategies have been unveiled (Maslej *et al.*, 2024). In the global landscape of national AI policies and strategies, several countries have adopted innovative approaches with forward-looking and ambitious visions, such as the United States of America (USA), China, Singapore, the United Kingdom, South Korea, and Germany. In addition, several scientific studies have compared these strategies in terms of vision, strategic objectives, development axes and levers, priority sectors, and their financial and economic benefits and impacts.

Regarding AI in the MENA region, it is characterized by a government-driven investment strategy aimed at fostering emerging technology sectors. AI strategies in this region focus on developing AI talent and creating a business environment conducive to AI growth. Also, governments are strongly engaged in developing AI ecosystems and integrating AI into public administration initiatives (Economist Impact, 2022).

The following examples give us a clear idea of the typical structure of national AI strategies, the crucial importance of the vision, the diversity of pillars and levers specific to each country, and the key and priority sectors targeted by each national AI strategy.

As shown in Figure 14.1, the Singapore's National AI Strategy in its 2nd updated version in 2023 titled "Singapore National AI Strategy 2.0 (NAIS 2.0): AI for the Public Good For Singapore and the World," "relies on three axes to have, activity drivers (Industry, Government, Research), Infrastructure & Environment (Compute, Data, Trusted Environment, Leader in Thought and Action) and People & Communities (Capabilities, placemaking)" (Government of the Republic of Singapore, 2023).

As shown in Figure 14.2, the UK's National AI Strategy has the vision "to make AI a science superpower fit for the next decade" Supporting the transition to an AI-enabled economy, capturing the benefits of innovation in the UK, and ensuring AI benefits all sectors and regions" (Office for Artificial Intelligence, 2021).

As illustrated in Figure 14.3, South Korea's national AI strategy, titled "Toward a Global AI Leader Beyond Information Technology: AI for All,

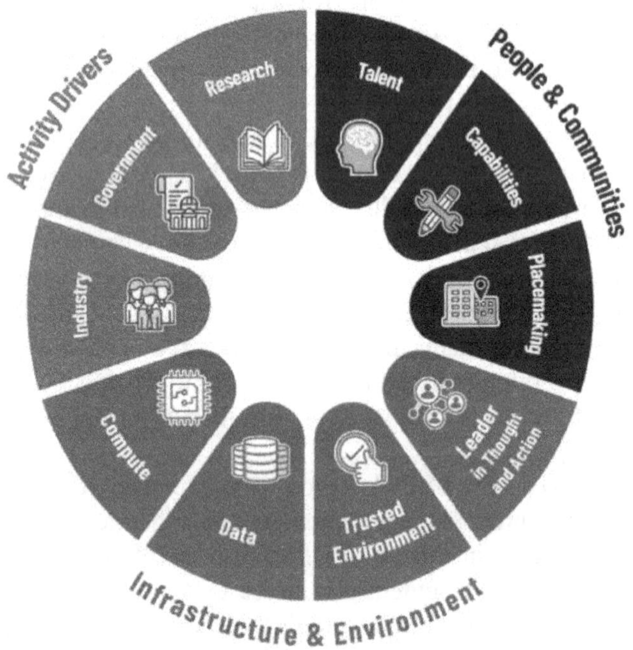

Figure 14.1. The national strategy for Artificial Intelligence of Singapore.
Source: Government of the Republic of Singapore (2023, p. 15).

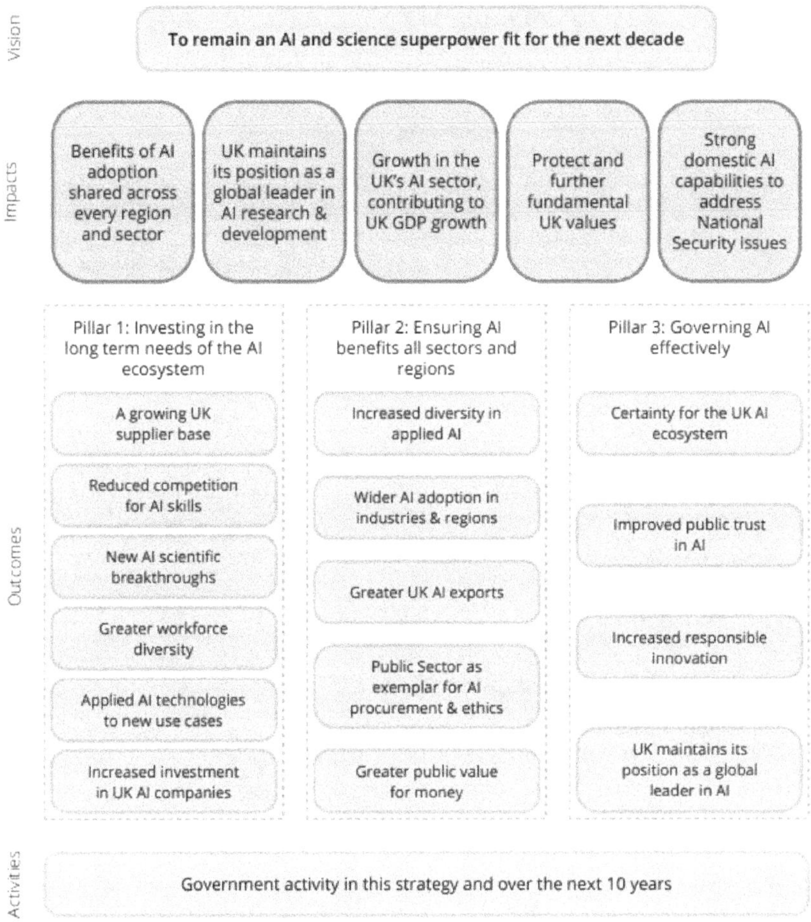

Figure 14.2. The UK's national AI strategy.

Source: Office for Artificial Intelligence (2021, p. 14).

AI for Everything," has set three major goals: building a world-leading AI ecosystem, optimizing domestic AI utilization, and establishing human-centered AI (Government of the Republic of Korea, 2019).

Furthermore, as shown in Figure 14.4, the National AI Strategy of the United Arab Emirates (UAE) involves becoming one of the leading nations in AI by building a reputation as an AI destination by 2031 (United Arab Emirates, Minister of State For Artificial Intelligence Office, 2019).

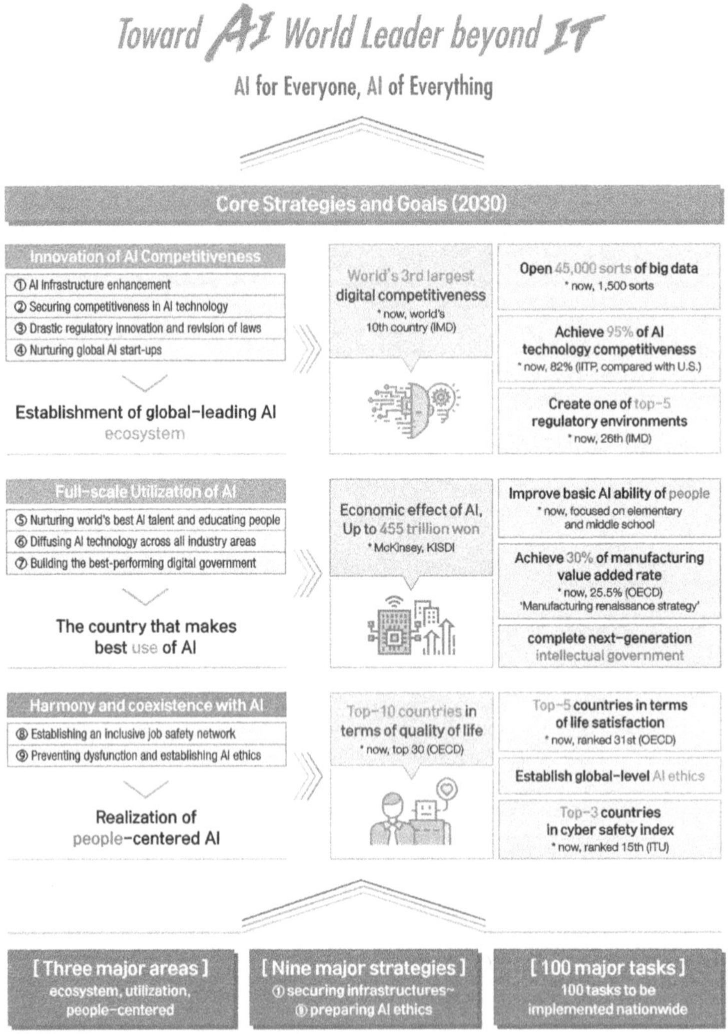

Figure 14.3. The national strategy for Artificial Intelligence of South Korea.
Source: The Government of the Republic of Korea (2019, p. 16).

Among the most studied models, we also find the American model characterized by the innovative dynamics of the private sector, the Chinese model marked by massive investment and the fundamental role of the state, and the European Union model focused on regulation and the ethical dimensions of AI.

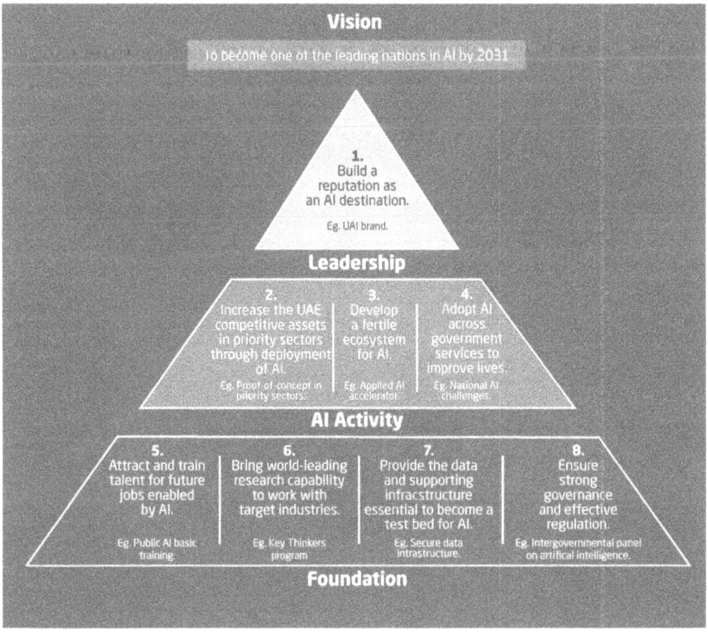

Figure 14.4. The United Arab Emirates (UAE) national AI strategy.

Source: United Arab Emirates Minister of State For Artificial Intelligence Office (2019, p. 18).

This leads us to inquire about the key topics most commonly present in national AI strategies, namely, trustworthy and ethical approaches, AI governance, AI adoption, AI procurement, civil service capacity and skills, cross-sector and cross-border collaboration and ecosystem building, experimenting and piloting, infrastructure, and data-driven public sector and open government data (OECD, 2020; OECD/CAF, 2022).

Furthermore, the analysis of these various models as well as the different national AI strategies has allowed us to clarify the key lessons and the main points, which are summarized in Figure 14.5.

The global challenges of AI are diverse and multidimensional: technological, economic, societal, political, ethical, environmental, and others. Moreover, competition among major global powers adds further complexity as they use AI to strengthen their global power and extend their digital influence.

For Morocco, these global challenges necessitate the development of a new national AI strategy that is well suited to its context and aligned with international standards, to be on the right track as recommended by

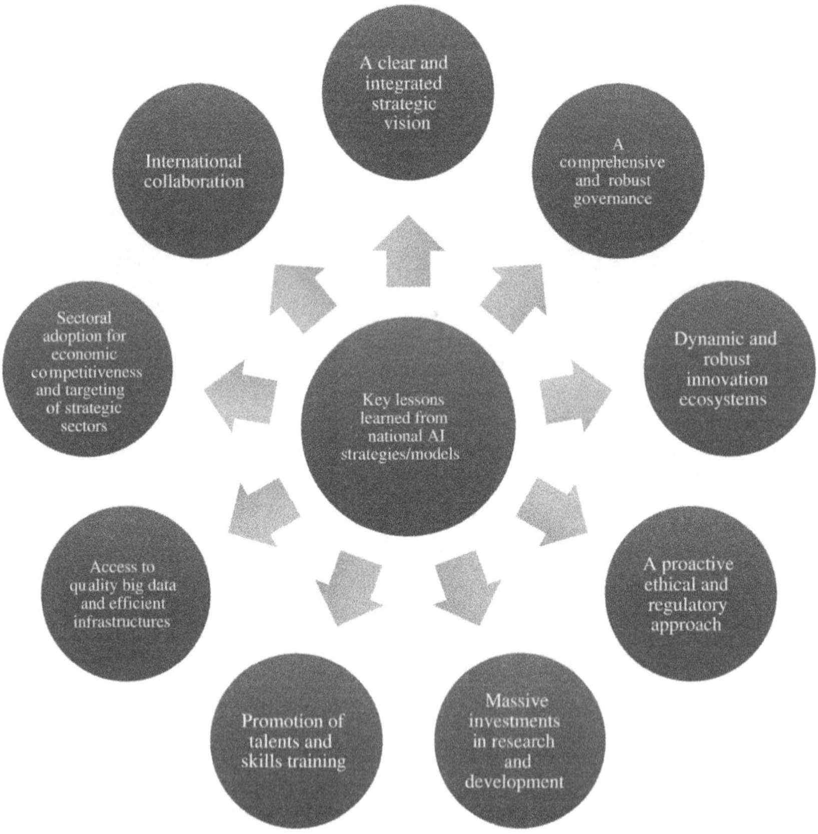

Figure 14.5. Key lessons learned from national AI strategies/models.

the World Economic Forum (2019), considering that "*A national strategy with long-term planning and a global outlook will steer the country in the right direction, not just to manage any concerns but also to make the fullest use of AI's potential.*"

14.3. Assets, Main Achievements, and Challenges of the Moroccan AI Ecosystem

14.3.1. *Assets and main achievements of the Moroccan AI ecosystem*

The Moroccan AI ecosystem is characterized by a multiplicity of public, private, associative, and academic actors working in support of the

Moroccan economy, its competitiveness and resilience, and to strengthen Morocco's strategic intelligence, its leadership, and its soft power.

The mapping of the different actors and the analysis of the major initiatives and various programs and projects launched in the field of AI show that Morocco has a favorable environment for the development and emergence of an ambitious, inclusive AI ecosystem that can ensure its African leadership and regional influence (Lafram and Bahji, 2024).

As illustrated in Figure 14.6, the main characteristic of the Moroccan AI ecosystem is the crucial advantage of having the political will at the highest level of the state to develop digitalization and enhance the digital transformation of the country. This is an undeniable asset that will certainly contribute to the launch of new ambitious programs and the implementation of a high-performance Moroccan AI ecosystem, provided the actors involved align with the strategic vision and leadership of the state.

The other asset that constitutes a major turning point in the development of AI in Morocco is its international commitment to the global governance of AI. Indeed, Morocco is the first African and Arab country to implement the UNESCO recommendation on the Ethics of Artificial Intelligence, which was adopted at the 41st session of the UNESCO General Conference in November 2021 in Paris.

In addition, one of the highlights of the AI landscape in Morocco is the creation of the "AI Movement" within Mohammed VI Polytechnic University, under the supervision of UNESCO, as the first level 2 AI center in Africa, certified as a center of excellence in the field of AI and data science on the African continent.

In addition, Morocco has launched several cooperative programs and projects at the national and international levels in AI fields and systems. These initiatives, which need to be strengthened, can provide momentum to the development of AI, both at the African and global levels.

Another major feature of the Moroccan university ecosystem is the creation of several schools, faculties, and centers focused on AI, which shows the growing interest in AI and the involvement of public authorities in the promotion and development of human skills and scientific research in the strategic field of AI.

In addition, Morocco has created several research programs to fund AI initiatives, such as the AL KHAWARIZMI program.

We can also note the initiation of a public and political debate on AI involving the public and private sectors, academia, and civil society. This

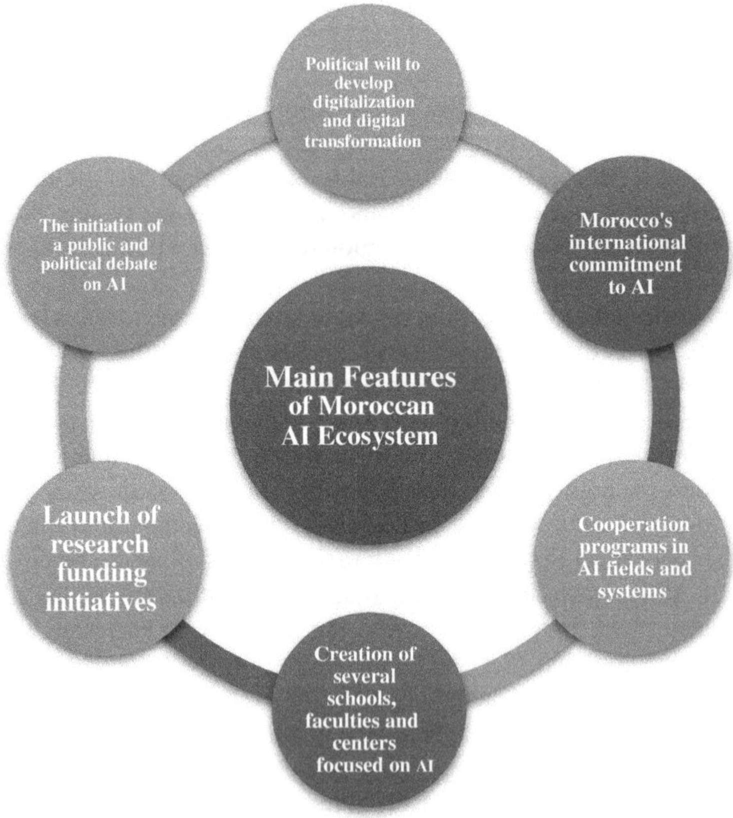

Figure 14.6. Accomplishments and advancements in AI in Morocco.

is reflected in the various events, workshops, conferences, seminars, and scientific, academic, and professional meetings organized by professional federations, ministries, think tanks, and civil society. Furthermore, several constitutional bodies and think tanks have published reports on the strategic importance of AI for the harmonious and inclusive socioeconomic development of Morocco and the strengthening of its national competitiveness and strategic intelligence.

The Economic, Social, and Environmental Council (ESEC) calls for the implementation of a national strategy for the use and development of AI aligned with the country's ambitions (CESE, 2024).

14.3.2. *Main challenges of the Moroccan AI ecosystem*

We have also identified a number of major challenges that the Moroccan AI ecosystem must overcome in order to be in line with international standards and have the expected structuring and transformative impacts. Among these major challenges, we can cite the following ones:

- **Strengthening and developing AI skills:** This challenge takes a leading position among the concerns that occupy the minds of the main AI stakeholders in Morocco. Thus, the development of highly qualified talents in AI, with the ability to design, develop, and implement ambitious projects is a major challenge. Public authorities must ensure a strong pool of qualified professionals to launch the various technological projects and implement AI-driven strategies across key sectors.
- **The challenge of technological and digital infrastructures:** This is an exceptionally critical challenge since it determines the efficiency and performance of the entire AI ecosystem in Morocco. Stimulating the development and implementation of AI cannot be done without modern, high-performance technological and digital infrastructure that is constantly evolving with the latest global technological trends.
- **The challenge of inclusion and equity:** This is a critical issue that requires also a well-adapted strategy to address the various forms of exclusion and to ensure that all socioeconomic groups are fully integrated into the country's development efforts. Giving everyone the chance and the possibility to use, develop, and implement AI with equitable access by facilitating inclusion is a challenge faced by every country wanting to move up to cruising speed in terms of the use and implementation of AI.
- **The challenge of investment and financing:** This challenge involves establishing sufficient financial resources and innovative tax incentive systems to encourage new investments. The goal is to attract both direct and indirect foreign investment that supports the country's major infrastructure projects and develops a robust, efficient, and high-performing AI ecosystem.
- **The challenge of innovation and competitiveness:** This poses several challenges for the sustainability and performance of the AI ecosystem in Morocco. It is through a creative dynamic and a synergy of continuous innovation that we can win the battle of competitiveness and be one step ahead of competing countries.

- **The challenge of data protection and confidentiality:** This is becoming increasingly essential as the use of AI becomes widespread in different sectors of activity and markets. Protecting the data of individuals and institutions and ensuring confidentiality are part of the protective role of the state and its institutions to preserve, protect, and guard against any attack or intrusion. It is a major pillar of the state's strategic intelligence.
- **Institutional and intersectoral coordination between the different AI stakeholders:** Institutional and intersectoral coordination between the different AI stakeholders: This is also a major challenge for AI in Morocco, representing a structural obstacle preventing synergy, integration, and convergence of sectoral policies and strategies, as well as the pooling of resources. Institutional and intersectoral coordination between the various public, private, non-profit, and academic stakeholders in AI is a key success factor enabling Morocco to ensure its leadership and strengthen its soft power in its various dimensions, particularly digital.
- **Ensuring the security of AI systems:** This is also among the most pressing challenges. It requires considerable effort to secure the technological infrastructure, databases, and information systems. AI requires careful preparation and rigorous planning to ensure the security and integrity of AI systems in the framework of an integrated strategy.

14.4. LAFBAH AI Framework: A Conceptual Model for a Transformative National AI Strategy in Morocco

14.4.1. *Presentation of the LAFBAH AI framework*

The LAFBAH AI framework (Figure 14.7) is a conceptual model that consists of six main elements: L, A, F, B, A, and H. Its importance lies in its ability to structure reflection, facilitate understanding, guide action, and inform the strategic decision relating to the implementation of an effective, efficient, ethical, and responsible national AI strategy in Morocco.

This framework can also be generalized and adapted to other countries to suit diverse organizational needs and contexts. It can relate to the state at the macro level but can be applied at the meso level of a sector or

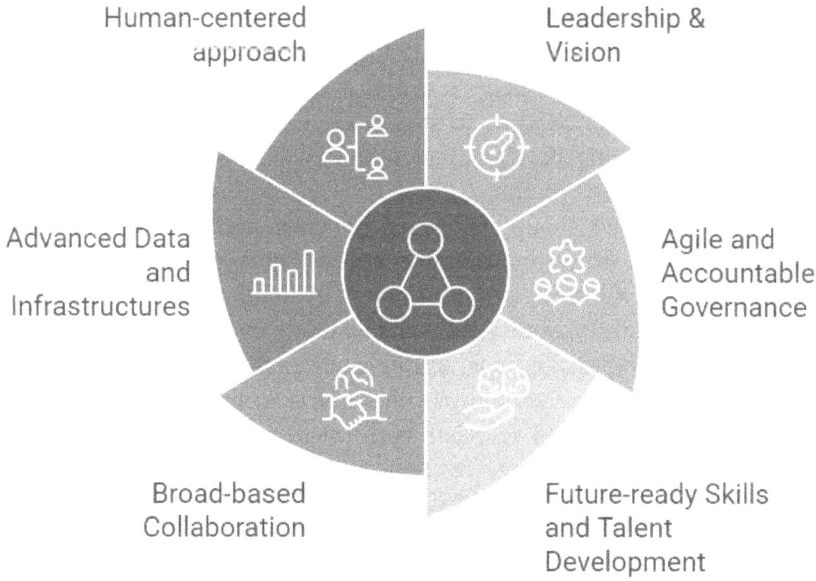

Figure 14.7. LAFBAH AI framework overview.

micro ministry level across various public agencies, offices, or enterprises engaged in the national AI ecosystem.

- **Leadership and vision**

Having a sense of leadership and vision is a fundamental condition and a necessary characteristic to give value, meaning, and direction to a country's strategic action. Visionary leadership makes it possible to mobilize, make people adhere to a collective strategic ideal, and find one's way through complexity with wisdom and intelligence. This is the main trait of a visionary leader capable of providing structured solutions and mobilizing the vital forces of a country to lay the foundations of a technological ecosystem capable of boosting AI through its strategic strength coupled with the wisdom of visionary leadership.

This is why we consider that leadership and vision constitute the basic foundation for the implementation of an innovative AI ecosystem in Morocco and can therefore play a crucial role in achieving Moroccan strategic objectives.

A clear and engaging vision, a strong commitment, and collective mobilization of all stakeholders are necessary to have the expected impact and guarantee the chances of success and competitive sustainability.

- **Agile and accountable governance**

Agile and responsible governance is vital for an effective, ethical, and responsible national AI strategy. It is also a fundamental pillar for a country like Morocco, which aims to strengthen its regional and continental leadership by pursuing strategic objectives of global competitiveness, soft power, and digital sovereignty.

This governance should be based on clear and precise principles, agile and efficient structures, and mechanisms for convergence, coordination, rigorous monitoring, and continuous evaluation, in order to boost Morocco's national competitiveness and strategic intelligence. To this end, clarity of roles and attributions, agility and reactivity, transparency and accountability, adaptable structuring, strategic steering via prospective and dynamic dashboards, and relevant performance indicators are all keywords to be favored to increase resilience, attractiveness, competitiveness, and the strategic leadership of Morocco on a regional and global scale.

AI needs specific and flexible governance, with *ad hoc* structures that deal exclusively with the development of AI in the country and ensure close coordination between all actors and stakeholders involved in the Moroccan AI ecosystem:

- **Future-ready skills and talent development**

The implementation of a national AI strategy requires future-ready skills and talent development to support its successful execution and guarantee that the nation can compete globally in the AI-driven fields and industries. Countries must invest in the education and training of their workforce with the necessary skills and expertise to drive innovation and ensure sustainable AI development. This absolutely requires an effective strategy for training tomorrow's data scientists, technologists, IT engineers, and experts.

- **Broad-based collaboration**

Collaboration must be considered in its global and holistic dimension as a central process fostering synergy and convergence of strategies and actions. This requires broad intra-departmental and inter-departmental collaboration between the public and private sectors at the national level. It is also necessary to develop programs and projects for collaboration and partnership at the international level within the framework of bilateral cooperation between Morocco and other leading countries and multilateral cooperation with other international organizations and regional blocs such as the EU and the African Union.

It should be said that the development of an efficient AI ecosystem necessarily relies on an integrated strategy of national and international cooperation to find solutions suited to Morocco's specific needs and ensure its leadership on the African continent.

- **Advanced data and infrastructures**

The optimal, effective, and efficient implementation of a national AI strategy that meets the economic, social, and environmental challenges of the future cannot be achieved without advanced data infrastructures adapted to the national needs and global ambitions of Morocco. Indeed, for increased competitiveness and good strategic intelligence, Morocco is called upon to give all the necessary importance to data and infrastructures by investing in robust and efficient systems for collecting, analyzing, processing, storing, sharing, and valorizing data.

These infrastructures must manage increasingly growing volumes of big data produced in the various sectors of activity, such as industry, health, agriculture, and education. By creating an integrated, robust, and secure data ecosystem that boosts creativity, promotes technological innovation, and ensures digital sovereignty, Morocco will position itself as a high-performance regional hub in the field of AI. This will also involve equitable access to quality data and integration of new-generation national data centers into local, regional, and national cloud infrastructures and data centers.

- **Human-centered approach**

The LAFBAH AI framework is also intended to focus on humans and their needs, rights, expectations, and their aspirations for a better life, without compromising their security, their survival, and their human tranquility. A humanized AI that makes life better, easier, and enables humans to become augmented, smarter, and freer.

Developing responsible, ethical, safe, and secure AI is closely linked to a human-centered approach. This means taking into account the needs, concerns, and expectations of individuals by opting for human-centered AI technologies that are accessible and understandable in an inclusive and humanized way.

14.5. LAFBAH AI Framework Strategic Goals: Shaping the Future through the 5Ss

- ***Smartness of Strategic State***

The Smartness of Strategic State is the first pillar of our framework. It aims to align the development of a robust and inclusive national AI ecosystem with Morocco's Strategic Intelligence and its global ambition and strategic vision to become a Smart Nation and a leading African Hub of AI. It involves crafting visionary policies and designing relevant and impactful strategies.

- ***Sovereignty***

Our model also aims to ensure the necessary conditions for preserving Morocco's sovereignty in its various dimensions: geostrategic, digital, technological, health, energy, food, etc. AI is a powerful vector of growth and innovation and a driving force for the country's development. Ensuring its security and sovereignty is synonymous with autonomy, control of its own destiny, in accordance with its values, priorities, and strategic interests.

- ***Soft power***

The soft power of a thousand-year-old country like Morocco, considered to be one of the world's oldest kingdoms, is a combination of cultural, economic, gastronomic, tourist, and sporting dimensions, combining different forms of diplomacy (economic, digital, artistic, cultural, scientific, university and academic, gastronomic, etc.). This is why we believe that our conceptual model should ultimately serve Morocco's soft power and international influence.

- ***Security***

Multifaceted and multidimensional security is one of today's major challenges. Cyber defense and cybersecurity require a strong commitment from the country's dynamic forces to make Morocco's AI ecosystem a safe and secure environment, capable of protecting the country against all the malicious cyberattacks and intrusions that are multiplying in an ultra-connected world full of risks. Securing its development model and its AI technical ecosystem is a prerequisite, bringing together everything from infrastructure to hardware and software.

- ***Sustainability***

Sustainable development is also at the top of the list of objectives, ensuring that the country's development is sustainable, harmonious, and inclusive, taking into account the needs and expectations of all fragile and vulnerable populations. Training must be extended to all social classes, and those excluded from technology must be informed, trained, and made aware, so that development benefits the entire population without exclusion. In addition, green AI must be prioritized, integrated into sustainable smart cities, and AI solutions developed for sustainable agriculture. Other solutions must be adapted for climate challenges and also aimed at saving and optimizing the use of Morocco's various natural resources in an intelligent and rational way (water, energy, raw materials, etc.).

14.6. Critical Success Factors of the National AI Strategy According to the LAFBAH AI Framework

For Morocco's national AI strategy to have the expected structuring impact, it is necessary to consider the conditions for the emergence, development, and success of an innovative, high-performance AI ecosystem by ensuring adherence to a set of key factors that we have called the critical success factors of the Moroccan AI strategy. To this end, we recommend adopting an approach we have called P3A: Prioritize, Adapt, Agile, and Evaluate (Lafram and Bahji, 2024).

Table 14.1 summarizes these key success factors and defines them in accordance with the philosophy behind our conceptual model.

Table 14.1. Critical success factors of the Moroccan national AI strategy.

Key Success Factors	Description
Holistic and global approach	The proposed strategy should be global in its vision, taking into account the interconnectivity of various sectors and global implications, aiming for a holistic, global, integrated, and coherent approach to the development and governance of AI in Morocco.
Forward-thinking	The national AI strategy should look toward the future by anticipating the various weak signals and future challenges and opportunities.
Inclusivity	Inclusiveness can be defined as the collective and intentional quest for the integration of all stakeholders in the AI ecosystem. It also involves taking into consideration all the needs, expectations, aspirations, and points of view of public, private, associative, and academic stakeholders.
Responsibility	Responsibility refers to the idea of accountability of all stakeholders in the field for the use and development of AI, in compliance with the principles, rules, standards, and practices of good governance, as well as with the regulatory and legislative requirements. These obligations relate to various dimensions, including data, infrastructures, people, institutions, flows and procedures for the use and implementation of AI technologies.

(*Continued*)

Table 14.1. (*Continued*)

Key Success Factors	Description
Innovation	The national AI strategy should be creative and focused on innovation, stimulating Moroccan competitiveness and economic development.
Collaboration and partnership	The Moroccan AI strategy should encourage co-construction with the different economic, academic and research, technological, and social ecosystems, promoting synergistic collaboration between the different actors and sectors to ensure the success of the strategy.
Adaptability and agility	The flexibility of the Moroccan AI system and its responsiveness to ultra-rapid developments and emerging challenges in the field of AI are crucial factors allowing a fluid adaptation of AI solutions to Moroccan regional and local cultural specificities.
Sustainability	Sustainability refers to a strategic vision of integrating sustainable reflexes and good practices in order to align with global recommendations in this direction and to minimize environmental impact while ensuring the promotion of green technologies for the benefit of the Moroccan economy and society.
Transparency and trust	Transparency and trust are critical and fundamental factors to consider in the design, development, implementation, and different uses of AI as a disruptive and emerging technology requiring increased trust from the general public.
Human-centric	The strategy should be centered on human well-being, meaning creation, sense of values, and human needs, prioritizing the development and deployment of AI technologies that serve the best interests of citizens.
Ethics	Respect for ethics is a key success factor in the governance of the entire AI ecosystem in Morocco. This includes maintaining and embedding strong ethical standards and principles to guide the development, deployment, and use of AI, ensuring that moral and social values are at the heart of all applications and decisions related to AI in line with the country's international commitments.

14.7. The Levers of a National AI Strategy According to the LAFBAH AI Framework

The design of our conceptual model has outlined the contours of an essentially prospective approach that has defined the essential levers of a renovated national AI strategy. As shown in Table 14.2, these levers take into account the strategic orientations of the country's new development model and are driven by Morocco's ambitious vision of becoming a regional and African hub in terms of AI.

Table 14.2. Ecosystemic dimensions and key levers of Morocco's AI national strategy according to the LAFBAH AI Framework.

AI Ecosystemic Dimension	AI Key Lever
Political and strategic ecosystem	• Development of a clear and global national vision for AI • Development of an integrated, inclusive, forward-looking, agile, holistic, responsible, and ethical national strategy • Launch of political and strategic debate on AI
Legal and regulatory ecosystem	• Establishment of a clear legislative and regulatory framework for the production, implementation, and use of AI • Development of an AI law adapted to the context and specificities of Morocco
Governance ecosystem	• Establishment of AI Good Governance Practices • Creation of a National Artificial Intelligence Agency • Promotion of the AI public–private partnership (PPP) • Creation of thematic, sectoral, and territorial commissions on AI • Creation of a labeling and certification system for products, services, platforms, and technological solutions based on AI • Creation of a Moroccan AI observatory institutionalizing the functions of monitoring, alerts, studies and analysis, and foresight on AI • Development of codes and charters on AI • Assessment and adaptation of AI policies and initiatives
The university, scientific, and innovation ecosystem	• Strengthening skills, training, and AI upskilling • Encouraging the creation of start-ups and research projects in AI fields • Investing in AI research and development

(*Continued*)

Table 14.2. (*Continued*)

AI Ecosystemic Dimension	AI Key Lever
	• Establishment of a national network for research and development in the field of AI • Establishment of a national plan for AI training and lifelong learning
International cooperation ecosystem	• Strengthening cooperation with international organizations • Encouraging international cooperation for the exchange of AI expertise, knowledge, and technologies
Technological ecosystem	• Development of an integrated AI ecosystem • Creation of new AI institutes, academies, and centers • Promoting open data governance and policies • Development of technological infrastructure • Boosting innovation and competitiveness • Promotion of technological entrepreneurship
Economic and productive ecosystem	• Putting AI at the heart of economic policies and the new development model • Making AI a powerful vector of competitiveness and Moroccan strategic intelligence • Integration of AI in key Moroccan economic sectors such as agriculture, health, industry, and financial services • Establishment of a specific AI fund • Encouraging investment in AI programs and projects • Integration of environmental and sustainability dimensions into AI systems and solutions
Cultural and social ecosystem	• Integration of cultural and social actors and the civil society collective in citizen consultation initiatives and advocacy in favor of moral, ethical, human-centered AI • Public and institutional AI information and awareness • Launch of a communication strategy to promote AI development, implementation, and use • Implementation of actions to improve the acceptability, assimilation, and integration of AI • Integration of AI into cultural and social policies and the promotion, enhancement, and preservation of Moroccan culture and cultural heritage

Based on our conceptual model, we consider that AI needs, above all, a strategic vision. AI is not only a technical and technological issue but also a managerial concern. This issue should be placed at the heart of the political and legislative agenda and public discourse. Above all, il requires sustained attention and engagement from public authorities to strengthen Morocco's leadership and strategic foresight.

The second lever is of a legislative and regulatory nature, which will lay the foundations of an integrated synergistic ecosystem of AI in Morocco according to the standards of good governance and AI governability by structuring this highly strategic field for the future of the country and its overall performance. It should be remembered that good AI governance inevitably involves adapted structures, laws, and regulations that are contextualized and relevant to the case of Morocco.

Another lever is the development of a digital ecosystem that strengthens the infrastructure and connectivity assets of AI, facilitates access to data, strengthens cybersecurity, protects personal data, and helps to create excellent clusters and high-performance research centers in the field of AI in Morocco.

The establishment of a well-thought-out strategy for cooperation and partnership at the bilateral and multilateral levels is strongly recommended in a vision of co-construction with pioneering countries in AI and other emerging technologies. It will also be a good opportunity for Morocco to reiterate its commitments and confirm its contribution to global AI governance to facilitate international collaborations between AI research structures and laboratories in different sectors of activity.

In this third millennium, collaboration cannot be done without a synergistic strategy for promoting public–private partnership (PPP) that boosts programs, projects, and initiatives of public, private, and associative and academic collaboration in the field of AI. To this end, the private sector can play a fundamental role by providing the necessary financing through PPP contracts which can have a structuring impact on major technological programs and strategic projects in Morocco.

The private sector contributes not only its significant financing capacity but also its technical expertise, its performance and flexibility in management and execution, and its monitoring and evaluation capabilities. Reskilling and upskilling are highly recommended to induce the necessary change and have sufficient talents to face the various current and future challenges of AI and conquer new African and global markets.

Innovation is another essential lever to promote open data, technological development, modernization of technological and telecommunications infrastructures, networks, cloud computing, 5G technology, and strengthening of local, regional, and national data centers.

In this context, we consider the installation of supercomputers and high-performance computing (HPC) infrastructure an essential prerequisite for research and development. Through the extension of fiber optics, Morocco can ensure rapid and stable connectivity, stimulate innovation, increase the competitiveness of businesses, and reduce regional disparities in access to digital technologies (Lafram and Bahji, 2024).

Adaptability is also necessary to ensure continuity and sustainable competitiveness, and to adapt AI policies and strategies to the Moroccan context, priorities, and ambitions.

Raising awareness and promoting the ethical and responsible use of AI are important matters for all citizens. The involvement of all stakeholders, whether public, private, associative, academic, or citizen, is highly recommended in these areas. The goal is to encourage the ethical, responsible, and inclusive use and development of AI and to raise public awareness of its benefits, but also its potential risks.

14.8. Recommendations of the Key Components of an Integrated Framework to Foster the Development of an AI Ecosystem in Morocco

What are the components of an integrated model for the development of the AI ecosystem in Morocco? It is also this fundamental question that we have tackled to bring out the essential and necessary components for harmonious, sustainable development. The objectives are mainly boosting creative energies, attracting foreign investment in AI, and creating conditions for co-construction with economic, social, academic, and other ecosystems.

These components are also necessary to ensure comprehensive governance of the AI ecosystem. They also contribute to the establishment of safeguards and guidelines for ethical and professional responsibility, and therefore an environment conducive to the integrated, ethical, and inclusive development of AI.

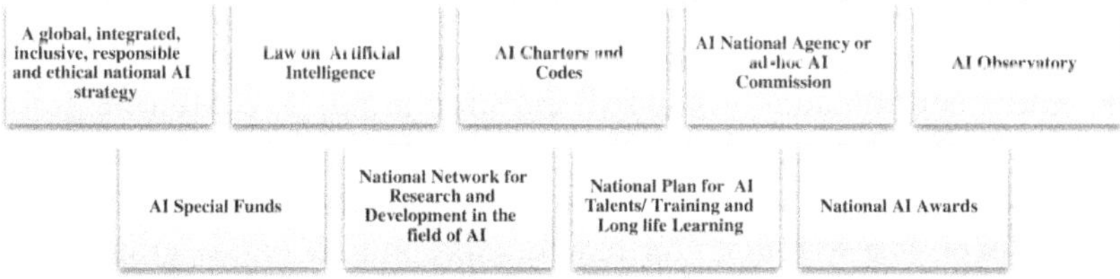

Figure 14.8. Components of an Integrated Framework for the Development of AI Ecosystem in Morocco.

In this context, we propose the components of an integrated strategic approach for the institutionalization and promotion of an inclusive and effective AI ecosystem in Morocco as shown in Figure 14.8.

Our conceptual model advocates for a national AI strategy that is comprehensive, integrated, synergistic, responsible, and ethical in essence. A clear, visionary strategy is one that ensures Morocco's regional and continental leadership in AI, fuels its socioeconomic development engine, and boosts its strategic and competitive intelligence model. This is why we have focused our model on leadership and vision, which cannot be achieved without a mobilizing, structuring, and engaging strategy.

The second foundation is a legal and regulatory arsenal adapted to the national context of Morocco, to its socioeconomic specificities, but open to technological changes. We believe that a specific law that promotes AI, stimulates creativity, and does not inhibit initiatives is a good practice to implement to frame, institutionalize, and govern the entire AI ecosystem in Morocco.

A law that defines the basic concepts, clarifies responsibilities, and resolves issues of ethics, accountability, security, protection of personal data, and other emerging and subsequent issues related to the timely use of AI in all national activities and economic sectors and interaction with other foreign ecosystems is required.

The hard law must also be associated with soft law through the promotion and development of charters and codes dedicated to AI. In fact, AI charters and codes, whether sectoral or ecosystemic, with the participation and involvement of various partners, can contribute to improving awareness of the opportunities, benefits, issues, challenges, and risks related to the use of AI in the public, private, and associative sectors, and in universities, schools, and higher education institutes and research structures (research centers, research laboratories, think tanks, etc.).

Another essential component is creating a national AI agency or an ad-hoc commission that has the attributions and the prerogative to decide, rule, guide, control, and evaluate all the structuring of AI projects, initiatives, and sectoral AI programs. We consider that good governance of AI at the national level, with territorialization of national AI policy at the regional level, is also crucial for having more impact on the ground.

AI is a strategic matter that requires close coordination between all stakeholders and an effective and proactive partnership with the various stakeholders and national and international partners. A sector as sensitive as AI cannot be left to the goodwill of the various ministerial departments working independently of each other in silos and even intra- and inter-departmental competition and between ministries and their agencies.

If there is one component that is also urgently needed it is the national AI observatory that could be attached to the national AI agency or another national structure enjoying management, steering, and governance autonomy, capable of providing it with the leadership necessary to structurally impact the AI ecosystem in Morocco. This observatory must ensure multidimensional strategic monitoring (informational, competitive, technological, legal, cultural, environmental, economic, social, societal, ethical, etc.) to provide relevant information and signals to guide or influence decisions and be one step ahead of competitors.

Having a smart, forward-looking strategy that ensures a visionary and impactful lead, in addition to a relevant and adapted legal arsenal, adapted and structuring governance, and a strategic monitoring observatory, is necessary but cannot have the expected impact without a financial effort in the form of a fund specially dedicated to AI. This fund must be consistent with Moroccan ambitions for influence, soft power, and leadership on the African continent. It must finance the major structuring projects of AI by launching ambitious initiatives and innovative and collaborative projects.

This also brings us back to the strategic importance of a national research and development network in the field of AI, with the creation of thematic research institutes in all Moroccan regions and at the national level, bringing together all researchers and multidisciplinary and transdisciplinary teams, working on themes related to AI (technical and technological issues, cybersecurity, cyber defense, development, ethical and legal issues, sociological, training, lifelong learning, e-learning, etc.)

Another key component is a national plan for initial training and lifelong training in AI. To have the expected result, it is necessary to invest in human capital, which can make a real difference. By having well-trained youth and creative, efficient, and ambitious talents, Morocco can win the battle of competitiveness. It is with this inexhaustible source of creativity and inventiveness that a country like Morocco can break into the world of AI and emerging and cutting-edge technologies.

It is also strongly recommended to launch a new ambitious national plan that integrates the public, private, and associative sectors to train a sufficient number of highly qualified engineers. This plan should also train a new generation of AI experts, developers, and senior managers capable of innovating, developing, and leading high-performance organizations and AI-driven structures. This plan should be part of a strategic and collective intelligence approach aimed at increasing national competitiveness.

This also brings us to another dimension, namely, national AI rewards to create conditions for emulation and competition. The objective is to reward excellent, creative researchers, innovative Moroccan start-ups, and the most successful companies in the field of AI. The rapid expansion of AI in Morocco should be institutionally supported by the creation of several national and regional AI awards and the promotion of incentive measures and programs. These awards will aim to reward and promote flagship initiatives, recognize innovative actions and projects, thus celebrating original solutions and major advances in AI, and strengthening a culture of excellence, innovation, and creativity within the Moroccan AI ecosystem.

14.9. Conclusion

Artificial Intelligence is now a strategic lever of influence and a vector of power, domination, and international competition. Having a national AI strategy is a necessity to position the country on the global scale, compete, and strengthen the country's strategic intelligence. For a national Artificial Intelligence strategy to have an impact and transformative effect on the competitiveness and strategic intelligence of a country such as Morocco, it is necessary to create a truly integrated and innovative ecosystem dedicated to AI, which is also adapted to the Moroccan context, capitalizes on its assets and strengths, and overcomes the gaps by addressing various challenges.

It is in this context that we have designed our LAFBAH AI framework, providing new perspectives and knowledge based on the case of

Morocco, but also focusing on strategic goals with concrete recommendations with a holistic, systemic, and structured approach.

The framework represents an important contribution in the field of national AI policies and strategies. It serves as a guide for an adaptive and agile implementation of the necessary milestones of a new AI ecosystem that boosts the strategic and competitive intelligence of the country.

The LAFBAH AI framework focuses on fundamental levers and structured mechanisms to integrate AI into all sectors and organizational processes. By adopting a structured and integrative strategic approach, AI-driven organizations can rethink and optimize their decision-making processes and practices, and quickly adapt to the multiple changes in their economic, technological, and social environments. This framework is the result of deep strategic reflection that integrates the structuring impact and the transformative and global influence of AI on the business landscape. It also aims to show public decision-makers the urgent need to have a strategy dedicated to AI with all the necessary resources to change the Moroccan AI ecosystem by transforming Moroccan organizations and companies into competitive economic players, capable of taking full advantage of the enormous potential of AI technologies to innovate, collaborate, and grow sustainably.

Bibliography

Ajaykumar, S., Tripathi, P., Basrur, A., Bag, S., and Mohan, S. *A Roadmap for AI Governance from G20 National Strategies*. Observer Research Foundation, 2024. https://www.orfonline.org/public/uploads/posts/pdf/20240430205801.pdf.

Conseil Economique, Social et Environnemental. *Quels usages et quelles perspectives de développement de l'intelligence artificielle au Maroc? Avis du Conseil Economique, Social et Environnemental* [What uses and development prospects for artificial intelligence in Morocco?]. 2024. https://www.cese.ma/media/2024/11/AVAS78VFP1.pdf.

Economist Impact. *Pushing Forward: The Future of AI in the Middle East and North Africa*. 2022.

Freeman, R. E. *Strategic Management: A Stakeholder Approach*. Pitman, 1984.

Government of the Republic of Singapore. *Singapore National AI Strategy 2.0 (NAIS 2.0): AI for the Public Good for Singapore and the World*. 2023. https://file.go.gov.sg/nais2023.pdf.

Heumann, S. and Zahn, N. *Benchmarking National AI Strategies: Why and how indicators and monitoring can support agile implementation*. Stiftung Neue Verantwortung e. V, 2018.

Lafram, A. and Bahji, S.E. "Artificial Intelligence in Morocco: Towards Holistic, Responsible and Ethical National AI Strategy for Moroccan Competitiveness and Strategic Intelligence." *Proceedings of the 20th European Conference on Management, Leadership and Governance,* Lisone, Portugal, 14-15 November 2024. ACPI, 2024.

Maslej, N., Fattorini, L., Perrault, R., Parli, V., Reuel, A., Brynjolfsson, E., Etchemendy, J., Ligett, K., Lyons, T., Manyika, J., Niebles, J. C., Shoham, Y., Wald, R., and Clark, J. "The AI Index 2024 Annual Report." AI Index Steering Committee, Institute for Human-Centered AI, Stanford University, 2024.

OECD. *A Blueprint for Building National Compute Capacity for Artificial Intelligence.* OECD Digital Economy Papers, No. 350. OECD Publishing, 2023.

OECD. *Artificial Intelligence, Data and Competition.* OECD Artificial Intelligence Papers No. 18. OECD Publishing, 2024.

OECD/CAF. *The Strategic and Responsible Use of Artificial Intelligence in the Public Sector of Latin America and the Caribbean.* OECD Public Governance Reviews, OECD Publishing, 2022. DOI: 10.1787/1f334543-en.

Office for Artificial Intelligence. *National AI Strategy.* HM Government, 2021. https://assets.publishing.service.gov.uk/media/614db4d1e90e077a2cbdf3c4/National_AI_Strategy_-_PDF_version.pdf.

Porter, M. E. *The Competitive Advantage of Nations.* Free Press, 1990.

The Government of the Republic of Korea. *Strategy for Artificial Intelligence: Toward AI World Leader, beyond IT.* National Ministry of Science and ICT, Artificial Intelligence Policy Division, 2019. https://www.msit.go.kr/eng/bbs/view.do?sCode=eng&mId=10&mPid=9&pageIndex=2&bbsSeqNo=46&nttSeqNo=9.

United Arab Emirates Minister of State For Artifial Intelligence Office. *UAE National Strategy for Artificial Intelligence 2031.* 2019. https://ai.gov.ae/wp-content/uploads/2021/07/UAE-National-Strategy-for-Artificial-Intelligence-2031.pdf.

United Nations System, High-Level Committee on Programs (HLCP) Inter-Agency Working Group on Artificial Intelligence (IAWG-AI). *United Nations System White Paper on AI Governance: An Analysis of the UN System's Institutional Models, Functions, and Existing International Normative Frameworks Applicable to AI Governance.* 2024.

World Economic Forum. *White Paper: A Framework for Developing a National Artificial Intelligence Strategy.* Centre for Fourth Industrial Revolution, 2019.

https://doi.org/10.1142/9781800616578_0015

Chapter 15

Managing Social Noise and Reducing the Impact of Misinformation on Business Practices

Manar Alsaid

Department of Information Science and Information Systems, East Texas A&M University, USA

manar.alsaid@tamuc.edu

Abstract

Today, we live in a truly integrated global village where social media acts as a glue that combines many of the social and economic aspects of life. Social media today is being transformed from communication channels to AI-driven smart marketplaces. Misinformation can significantly impact business operations, consumer trust, and corporate reputation. This chapter discusses Artificial Intelligence (AI) as a double-edged sword, where, on the one hand, it increases productivity and efficiency and, on the other hand, it increases the risk of misinformation such as deepfakes. It introduces the concept of social noise as a factor in amplifying misinformation and discusses measures that could be used to minimize the spread of misinformation. The chapter highlights the need for organizations to adopt risk management strategies, AI-based monitoring systems, and proactive communication frameworks to mitigate the effects of misinformation. By understanding the dynamics of social noise and leveraging AI responsibly, businesses can safeguard their operations against digital threats while harnessing technology for market advantage.

Keywords: Misinformation, social noise, digital marketplace, Artificial Intelligence, business practices, risk management, social media, disinformation, cybersecurity.

15.1. Introduction

The Internet brought about fundamental changes to both people and businesses alike. The sense of place, location, community, and even neighborhood was changed. The advent of the Internet and the rise of the digital world have transformed the world into a global village. It created a virtual world where people from the far corners of the world can get together, share information, exchange ideas, trade goods and services, and exercise significant influence. Social media as a type of virtual social place has become the first destination when it comes to information gathering, communication, networking, and the free market. It has become necessary for businesses to consider social media when creating their business and include social media in their marketing plan.

The digital revolution opened the door for new and exciting opportunities. Yet, it created a noisy and risky world for businesses through the increase in misinformation or disinformation in the form of propaganda, fabricated content, satire and parody, fake news, and conspiracy theories. Most of the time, "misinformation", "disinformation" is created using fabricated content with the aim of deceiving the population and the audience. Sometimes, such fabricated content is based on partially accurate information that, at some point, was manipulated and changed to suit a certain hidden agenda. Kapantai *et al.* (2021) pointed out that misinformation phenomena are based on hidden motives such as profit, ideological, and psychological factors.

After COVID-19, companies were alerted to the importance of social media and the need to evaluate new emerging risks, given the huge amount of information generated daily on social media platforms as well as the speed by which misinformation spreads online. Misinformation influences people's behaviors and it can be used and manipulated for good or bad. Understanding the new challenges and the risks associated with it is critical for business practices. A good example of the negative impact of misinformation on social media business companies is Corona beer

(Gibson, 2020). Rumors went viral on social media saying that if you drink Corona Beer, you will get Coronavirus. The company lost a lot of customers in the United States and Mexico. The company was struggling like all other companies during the lockdown. However, this rumor significantly increased risks during the COVID-19 pandemic and quickly exposed previously unknown weaknesses in the company's business disaster recovery plans.

Misinformation about products made in China being associated with COVID-19 was problematic. Misinformation regarding the type of masks that might prove to be more effective in the protection against COVID-19 negatively impacted businesses and prompted the Centers for Disease Control (CDC) to clarify information regarding the use of masks.

15.2. Digital Revolution and the Transformation of the Marketplace

The rapid digital transformation of the Internet, driven by advances in communication and information technology, has redefined the way people conduct business. Technologies such as Artificial Intelligence (AI), big data, cloud computing, and the Internet of Things (IoT) have dramatically reshaped global marketplaces. The digital marketplace has become an appealing destination for people from all walks of life. The fast adoption of technology, even in developing countries, has created an environment where people have become dependent on digital goods and services. Companies adapting to the rise of e-commerce, such as Amazon, Alibaba, and Shopify, utilize online platforms that have made it easier for businesses to reach global customers. Nowadays, consumers tend to shop online more than before. Further, they expect seamless shopping experiences, personalized recommendations, and quick delivery. Companies that were slow to adopt an online strategy failed to survive and stay in operation. For example, in the early 2000s, Toys "R" Us closed down. One reason for its failure was that TOYS "R" Us was slow to adapt to the rise of online shopping and lagged behind competitors in technology and online sales (Chakraborty, 2024).

The adoption of cashless and digital payments has made it easier for people to shop online. The use of AI and data analytics has made it possible for companies to track consumers' shopping habits. The use of automated cookies, AI-driven recommendation systems, software that compares product prices, efficiency reviews, and other services has made online shopping much easier and more convenient. The availability of 24/7 chat online and other tools designed to respond to customer questions and customer needs has transformed the definition of the marketplace. The availability of a marketplace on different social media platforms such as Facebook, TikTok, and Instagram has allowed small businesses to compete globally. Global supply chains are digitally managed, efficient, and transparent. Virtual online platforms such as Zoom, Google Meet, and Microsoft Teams have also transformed the way people communicate, consult with suppliers, and execute transactions remotely. Virtual meeting technology enables businesses to operate efficiently regardless of location. Remote work is an easy option for hiring talent worldwide without the need to relocate physically. Reducing the need for office spaces, travel, and in-person meetings has resulted in significant cost savings.

Rapid technological advancements have transformed education into a commercialized industry by expanding access to digital tools, platforms, and resources. Technology has made education accessible to a broader audience, regardless of geographical, financial, or social barriers. Online learning platforms like Coursera, Udemy, and Khan Academy (Karaş, 2024) provide affordable and sometimes free courses. These platforms may also have features like text to speech and screen readers to enhance access for students with disabilities. In addition, translation tools and AI-powered subtitles make content accessible in multiple languages, helping students overcome language barriers.

15.3. Social Media as a Marketplace

Social media started as a networking platform and over time has been transformed from a marketing tool to a digital marketplace. The digital market is shaped by financial motives rather than being a neutral ground for information. Programmatic advertising is an automated system that places ads in real time without considering whether the sponsored content is accurate or harmful. Influencers have mastered the art of feeding their audience polarizing and emotional content because that drives engagement and income. Diaz Ruiz (2023) discussed a theoretical framework to understand this market-driven ecosystem and proposed a way forward. He argued that the fight against disinformation requires one to look at the deeper market forces and create regulations that remove the financial incentives to spread falsehoods.

The architecture of digital media platforms is inherently designed to prioritize content that drives the maximum number of users and engagement, even if that content is misleading or harmful. The drive for profit is at the core: Algorithms are programmed to amplify emotional and polarizing content because it captures more attention, leading to increased ad revenue. Advertising models, like programmatic advertising, place ads automatically without considering the nature of the surrounding content, which often means that ads unknowingly fund sites that spread disinformation. Additionally, content moderation practices are presented as inconsistent and commercially motivated. Platforms face a conflict of interest as they are expected to remove harmful content but benefit financially from viral, high-engagement posts.

The overall argument is that disinformation is not just an unfortunate side effect of social media platforms but rather a feature built into the system that monetizes user engagement, even if it means prioritizing profit over disseminating truthful information (Diaz Ruiz, 2023; Vaidhyanathan, 2022; Zuboff, 2023). Digital platforms bring together various actors who learn to leverage (and exploit) market infrastructure to boost traffic to their website. The actors' behavior is influenced by social noise constraints identified in previous studies on social noise.

15.4. Misinformation and Security Challenges

As online transactions continue to grow, driven by technological advancements and changing consumer behaviors, the digital marketplace has become an appealing target for cybercriminals aiming to exploit weaknesses and access sensitive data. This makes it crucial for everyone involved in digital commerce to understand and address e-commerce security risks effectively (Smith and Carter, 2024). Fraud, threats, and cybersecurity attacks have become a concern for consumers and businesses. E-commerce has become a vital part of the global economy, offering consumers unmatched convenience and extraordinary business opportunities.

Social media offers great opportunities for engagement and brand building; on the other hand, it presents serious risks, such as the increasing rise of cybersecurity attacks, misinformation, and social noise, which can spiral out of control and cause significant damage such as fueling anger and panic among customers, investors, or employees. The fallout could cause damaged reputation, lost revenue, or even a dip in stock prices. Moreover, actors with bad intentions use generative AI to create alternate realities and viral topics, from political propaganda to health-related fake news, that undermine civil society. Kara (2024) stated that "a database contained 115 pro-Trump fake news stories that were shared on Facebook a total of 30 million times, while 41 pro-Clinton fake news stories were shared a total of 7.6 million times, Notably, social media fake news stories during the 2016 election were shared around 38 million times, resulting in approximately 760 million clicks"(P 6).

According to Morantz (2024), a Twitter account (now known as X) impersonating Eli Lilly falsely claimed that insulin would be given away for free, causing the company's stock price to drop by over 4%. Similarly, Kay Jewelers experienced a decline of 11% in its share value after fake news alleged that its rings contained low-quality gemstones instead of real diamonds. Pepsi faced significant setbacks twice: In 2016, its shares fell by 4% during the U.S. presidential election due to false claims that its CEO supported Donald Trump, and in 2018, its stock was negatively impacted by rumors that its products were contaminated with HIV-infected blood. Sometimes, a company's messages appear in conjunction with harmful content such as misinformation, conspiracy theories, or fake news. People tend to believe and share misinformation or fake news six times faster than accurate information (Beauvisage *et al.*, 2024).

The lack of control has led to many household brands aligning with false or damaging content. According to Jacob Brower, a professor of marketing, marketers are very willing to sacrifice brand safety in order to drive metrics and conversions, sacrificing long-term brand reputation in the process. Research has proven the adverse effect of such ad placements, where brands appearing near fake news are perceived as less trustworthy and consumer attitudes toward them turn more negative. The damage is amplified when ads are contextually linked to fake news, such as a mobile provider's ad near misinformation about 5G. Additionally, these ad placements can enhance the credibility of the fake news itself. During the COVID-19 pandemic, some health and vaccine companies had their ads appear alongside posts promoting vaccine misinformation due to algorithmic advertisement placements.

All of these elements — monitoring, rapid response, proactive reputation management, training, legal strategies, and industry collaboration — together form a comprehensive approach to managing the risks associated with misinformation and social noise. In a world where false information spreads faster than ever, companies need to be vigilant, strategic, and ready to defend their reputation at a moment's notice.

15.5. The Concept of Social Noise

The International Organization for Standardization's (ISO) risk framework highlighted two types of threats to an organization. Internal threats or risks, such as values, vision, mission, data, information flows, organizational structure, objectives, strategy, culture, and capabilities, and external threats or risks, such as political, economic, social, technological, environmental, trends, stakeholder relationships, contractual relationships, and networks (ISO, 2018). It highlighted that a company must understand the context in order to be able to manage risk in an integrated approach. Misinformation in the form of internal or external noise can interfere with the company's ability to understand the context. Noise interference adds uncertainty to the communication process, which can lead to potential changes or distortions in parts of the intended message. As a result, when uncertainty rises, the receivers' capacity to gather additional information to clarify or reinforce their understanding of the message may be constrained.

Social noise is a term used to refer to the degree to which the Internet and social media users participate in the magnification and the spread of misinformation. Several studies have shown that there is a strong relationship between social noise and misinformation (Alsaid *et al.*, 2024; Alsaid and Madali, 2022; Madali *et al.*, 2022; Madali *et al.*, 2023). Social noise can negatively impact business practices by magnifying misinformation, and in some cases, it could lead to the distortion of information related to business products and services. The increase in the number of false ads, rumors, and misrepresentations of business practices is alarming and risky. In this section, we will discuss the role of social noise in social media and its impact on business practices, along with methods and practices, including the use of AI techniques to counter the effect of social noise.

Businesses depend on AI-driven software for social media analysis to understand customer behaviors, track trends, track reviews, and identify misinformation. The social noise constructs identified in social noise studies could be used to guide the development of AI models for detecting and filtering misinformation. As an example, businesses using AI for brand monitoring might be able to fine-tune their models to recognize patterns of social noise that might distort their public image or affect their customer trust in the brand.

Successful companies need to recognize emerging risks, social noise, and disruptive trends, evaluate their impact, connect them to their business model, and implement necessary adjustments. Enterprise Risk Management (ERM) frameworks align with this approach, as risk management is evolving through both conventional and innovative methods. Organizations today are navigating a complex, risk-filled landscape marked by ongoing digital disruption, unexpected global events like the pandemic, and interconnected threats. While economic uncertainty from COVID-19 remains a challenge, finance executives are especially concerned about risks tied to shifts in business models. To thrive in this environment, companies need to enhance their ability to identify and manage risks, dedicating more time and resources to this effort.

This involves using a range of innovative tools, such as AI, big data, predictive analytics, and trend analysis, as well as engaging employees through crowdsourcing to gather insights. Techniques like black swan workshops, decision tree analysis, and strategic disruption planning help organizations better understand and respond to emerging risks. Additionally, companies are developing processes to monitor key trends and employing AI to scan data sources for early warning signals of potential threats (Paul, 2021).

15.6. AI as Double-Edged Sword

AI is a technology that allows computers or machines to analyze information and generate results that mimic the human thinking process. Many people fear that AI will eventually replace them in the workforce. In reality, AI has already revolutionized numerous aspects of our daily lives, and integrating it into our work and routines is no longer optional but necessary. Rather than taking your job outright, AI is more likely to replace those who fail to harness its potential with individuals who can leverage AI efficiently and effectively. Embracing AI as a tool for productivity and innovation is essential to staying relevant in today's rapidly evolving landscape.

AI technologies such as machine learning algorithms, neural networks, and deep learning have been integrated into rule-based systems, financial markets, and market trend analysis. AI software has the capability to process vast datasets to identify patterns, predict market movements, and execute trades at high speeds. This has led to increased market efficiency and the emergence of sophisticated trading model.

Digital markets implementing AI reveal six emerging areas or categories:

- AI is used in marketing research, known as psychosocial dynamics, which includes personalization, predictive analytics, chatbots, customer service, and content optimization.
- AI-enhanced market dynamic strategies are available, such as ad targeting, optimization, and marketing automation. AI-powered tools and platforms enable marketers to automate routine tasks such as email campaigns, social media management, content creation, and ad optimization (Deng *et al.*, 2019). Automating these processes allows businesses to enhance their marketing efficiency, streamline operations, and redirect human resources toward more strategic and creative activities (Rodgers and Nguyen, 2022). Furthermore, AI-driven automation facilitates real-time marketing campaign optimization, with algorithms continuously analyzing performance data to refine targeting, messaging, and delivery for maximum effectiveness (Rodgers and Nguyen, 2022).
- AI for consumer services helps to understand customer behavior and needs.
- AI is used for value transformation, ethical and responsible AI, integration with other technologies, and collaboration with AI software.
- AI is used for ethical marketing. AI providers and start-ups are all best practices for incorporating ethical and responsible AI into digital marketing initiatives.
- The sixth cluster is AI for decision-making, and it sounds like the most beneficial use in AI. AI assesses the marketing decision-making across the five stages of the marketing process, which include analysis, strategy, tactics, customer interactions, and value proposition creation. With enhanced customization, integration with other technologies, and a stronger emphasis on ethical and responsible AI, the future of AI in marketing analytics is bright (Apriani *et al.*, 2024; Labib, 2024).

Social media companies claim to uphold values like global community and democratic participation, but their reliance on digital marketing contradicts these principles. Digital marketing prioritizes wealthier users, and disinformation campaigns exploit social media's ad systems, harming democratic engagement. Despite efforts to address foreign disinformation actors, this focus overlooks how digital marketing fuels the spread of false information, highlighting the need for more comprehensive regulation.

Imagine pinpointing your unique soundscape with just a click. Social media's cutting-edge AI system makes this possible through automated noise monitoring terminals that continuously gather noise levels and audio recordings. This advanced AI does not just collect data; it enhances, cross-references, and autonomously identifies and categorizes sounds from diverse noise sources like cars, trucks, sirens, trains, and jackhammers. With over 22 years of expertise in automated environmental monitoring, social media has amassed audio data from over 2,500 noise-monitoring projects. This extensive dataset powers a highly efficient, reliable, and sophisticated automated noise recognition and classification system.

While integrating AI into various aspects of daily life offers numerous benefits, it also raises critical concerns about dehumanization and privacy risks (Lobschat *et al.*, 2021). Businesses must prioritize addressing organizational privacy issues such as data breaches, profiling, micro-targeting, surveillance, and hacking. Emphasizing ethical and responsible AI practices, particularly in safeguarding customer privacy and data security, is essential. Additionally, companies should critically evaluate AI's role in decision-making processes to ensure transparency and accountability (Lobschat *et al.*, 2021; Anayat and Rasool, 2024).

Large language models (LLMs) like ChatGPT and Copilot enhance the capability to produce convincing, inaccurate content and disseminate misinformation and disinformation. The large amount of AI-generated disinformation can destabilize political environments, impacting economic policies and investor confidence, potentially leading to devastating impacts on individuals' beliefs and behaviors, the integrity of public information, and the foundations of democracy. (Karaş, 2024; Simon *et al.*, 2023). Also, datasets and AI tools needed to produce misleading content are publicly available online. Because of their accessibility, AI can be used for various reasons by benign, normal users as well as malicious actors. Concerns over AI's possible misuse in both deliberate and inadvertent scenarios have been raised by the combination of its strong capabilities and low entry barrier (Safdar *et al.*, 2020).

AI has significantly influenced financial markets positively and negatively. While AI-driven tools enhance trading efficiency and market analysis, they also present challenges concerning misinformation. Misinformation and disinformation generated by Artificial Intelligence have undermined the global economic forum's ability to recognize and address this issue as a serious threat to international stability. Misinformation may cause businesses to make uninformed decisions, resulting in financial losses. The rapid spread of AI-generated misinformation can undermine trust in financial markets and institutions. Also, it influences stock returns negatively. The World Economic Forum has recognized this as the most critical threat to global stability in the near future. This reflects a growing understanding of the extent to which false information powered by AI can upend social and economic structures. Furthermore, widespread misinformation disrupts supply chains, leading to economic losses, reduced profitability, and weakened competitiveness (Karaş, 2024; Torkington, 2024).

15.7. Ethical and Legal Implications of Artificial Intelligence

The use of AI in content creation, information filtering, and misinformation detection brings with it a set of ethical and legal issues that must be addressed. The European Union (EU) is now shifting toward a descending co-regulation model. Notably, the Digital Services Act proposal introduces requirements for transparency and external audits of content moderation and recommender systems used by major online platforms. While the proposal primarily targets the regulation of problematic content, the EU Parliament and Council emphasize the need to promote access to reliable and trustworthy information (Bontridder and Poullet, 2021).

Deepfakes are one example of how AI can be used to create fake content. It is a method where highly realistic but fake videos are created using advanced AI algorithms such as machine learning, neural networks, and the Generative Adversarial Network (GAN). The GAN algorithm can be used to generate new types of data from existing datasets. The algorithm can be applied to different types of data, such as text, images, moving, and audio (Walorska, 2020). Misinformation, along with AI technologies, can be used to manipulate existing content effectively, alter individual opinions, and influence the public. The AI algorithm is trained to optimize engagement, regardless of the content's quality. Some of these AI algorithms are leveraged by malicious actors to effectively manipulate opinions and reach specific goals (Bontridder and Poullet, 2021; Dicke, 2001).

Besides using AI to customize content for the purpose of micro-targeting, recommendation systems, and others, AI algorithms are also being investigated to filter and detect false and misleading content. Such automated ways of detecting and regulating content using AI with minimal human intervention could be problematic and raise questions regarding issues related to freedom of speech, free expression, and information freedom in general. According to Bontridder and Poullet (2021), AI's presence on the Web boosts the creation and dissemination of disinformation. They stated that "Owing to the economic model of the web-based on advertising, tracking methods using AI technologies were developed by information and communication platforms to enable the targeting of advertisements to specific consumers for the sake of efficiency" (P4).

One of the major ethical issues of using AI for marketing is the consumers' right to correct information and their ability to make an informed decision. A corporation's major aim is to make money and maximize profit, which is why the use of advanced technology as a competitive tool is justified. Real-world applications of AI have the potential to influence decision-making in ways that raise significant ethical concerns. Autonomous vehicles, which may involve unavoidable accidents, can face the decision to either save passengers or pedestrians. The Massachusetts Institute of Technology's (MIT) Moral Machine is a platform that allows companies and users to explore AI decision-making preferences that vary across cultures and social groups by gathering public input on ethical preferences for AI decisions, showing how cultural and social factors influence responses (Karliuk, 2018). For example, the Federal Ministry of Transport and Digital Infrastructure in Germany stated that programming self-driving cars to make life prioritization decisions should be based on the law (Brown, 2016). However, China's social credit system forms the basis for the programming of self-driving cars (Karliuk, 2018).

15.8. Conclusion

In this chapter, we discussed the digital revolution and the transformation of the marketplace. We explored the current issues and the emergence of new digital technologies, such as social media as a marketing tool and as a marketplace. The chapter focused on the impact of misinformation on business practices and the use of social media and AI as marketing tools to attract customers and increase profitability. While social media offers great opportunities for engagement and brand building, it presents serious risks, such as the rise of cybersecurity attacks, misinformation, and social noise. The chapter also discussed the concept of social noise as a measure for combating misinformation. Social noise can negatively impact business practices by magnifying misinformation and could lead to the distortion of information related to business products and services. AI technology is discussed in this chapter as a double-edged sword where it is used by companies to create content, enhance recommendation systems, and reduce costs. AI can revolutionize the marketplace; however, the use of AI brings with it ethical and legal issues that must be addressed.

Bibliography

Alsaid, M. and Madali, N. P. "Social noise and the impact of misinformation on COVID-19 preventive measures: comparative data analysis using Twitter masking hashtags." *Journal of Information & Knowledge Management* 21, no. Supp01 (2022): 2240007.

Alsaid, M., Panguluri, S. P., and Hawamdeh, S. "Combating misinformation on social media using social noise and social entropy as a measure of uncertainty." *Proceedings of the Association for Information Science and Technology* 61, no. 1 (2024): 25–35.

Anayat, S. and Rasool, G. "Artificial intelligence marketing (AIM): Connecting-the-dots using bibliometrics." *Journal of Marketing Theory and Practice* 32, no. 1 (2024): 114–135.

Apriani, A., Sani, I., Kurniawati, L., Prayoga, R., and Panggabean, H. L. "The role of artificial intelligence (AI) and its benefits in digital marketing strategy." *East Asian Journal of Multidisciplinary Research* 3, no. 1 (2024): 319–332.

Beauvisage, T., Beuscart, J. S., Coavoux, S., and Mellet, K. "How online advertising targets consumers: The uses of categories and algorithmic tools by audience planners." *New Media & Society* 26, no. 10 (2024): 6098–6119.

Bontridder, N. and Poullet, Y. "The role of artificial intelligence in disinformation." *Data & Policy* 3 (2021): e32.

Borz, G., De Francesco, F., Montgomerie, T. L., and Bellis, M. P. "The EU soft regulation of digital campaigning: Regulatory effectiveness through platform compliance to the code of practice on disinformation." *Policy Studies* (2024): 1–21.

Brown, M. "Mercedes-Benz's self-driving car A.I. will kill pedestrians over drivers." 2016. Inverse. https://www.inverse.com/article/22204-mercedes-benz-self-driving-cars-ai-ethics.

Chakraborty, P. "Why toys R us failed: An Entrepreneur's analysis." 2024. Tactyqal. https://www.tactyqal.com/blog/why-toys-r-us-failed-an-entrepreneurs-analysis/.

Deng, S., Tan, C. W., Wang, W., and Pan, Y. "Smart generation system of personalized advertising copy and its application to advertising practice and research." *Journal of Advertising* 48, no. 4 (2019): 356–365. DOI: 10.1080/00913367.2019.1652121.

Di Domenico, G. and Ding, Y. "Between brand attacks and broader narratives: How direct and indirect misinformation erode consumer trust." *Current Opinion in Psychology* (2023): 101716.

Diaz Ruiz, C. "Disinformation on digital media platforms: A market-shaping approach." *New Media & Society* (2023): 14614448231207644.

Dicke, K. "The founding function of human dignity in the Universal Declaration of Human Rights." In *The Concept of Human Dignity in Human Rights Discourse*, 111–120. Brill Nijhoff, 2001.

European Commission. "Guidance on strengthening the code of practice on disinformation (COM (2021) 262 final)." 2021. https://digital-strategy.ec.europa.eu/en/library/guidance-strengthening-code-practice-disinformation.

Gibson, K. "Corona beer maker shrugs off misinformation on coronavirus." 2020. *CBS News*. https://www.cbsnews.com/news/corona-beer-virus-misinformation-on-coronavirus/.

ISO. "Risk management — Guidelines." 2024. https://www.iso.org/standard/65694.html.

Juhász, K. "European Union defensive democracy's responses to disinformation." *Journal of Contemporary European Studies* (2024): 1–20.

Kapantai, E., Christopoulou, A., Berberidis, C., and Peristeras, V. "A systematic literature review on disinformation: Toward a unified taxonomical framework." *New Media & Society* 23, no. 5 (2021): 1301–1326.

Karaş, Z. "Effects of AI-Generated Misinformation and Disinformation on the Economy." *Düzce Üniversitesi Bilim ve Teknoloji Dergisi* 12, no. 4 (2024): 2349–2360.

Karliuk, M. "Ethical and legal issues in artificial intelligence." *International and Social Impacts of Artificial Intelligence Technologies, Working Paper* 44 (2018).

Labib, E. "Artificial intelligence in marketing: Exploring current and future trends." *Cogent Business & Management* 11, no. 1 (2024). DOI: 10.1080/23311975.2024.2348728.

Lobschat, L., Mueller, B., Eggers, F., Brandimarte, L., Diefenbach, S., Kroschke, M., and Wirtz, J. "Corporate digital responsibility." *Journal of Business Research* 122 (2021): 875–888.

Madali, N. P., Alsaid, M., and Hawamdeh, S. "The impact of social noise on social media and the original intended message: BLM as a case study." *Journal of Information Science* 1 (2022): 1–15.

Madali, N. P., Alsaid, M., and Hawamdeh, S. "Social noise on social media and users perception of global warming." *Journal of Information & Knowledge Management* 22, no. 06 (2023): 2350050.

Morantz, A. "Fake news gives brands a real headache: Smith Business Insight." 2024. Smith Business Insight. https://smith.queensu.ca/insight/content/Fake-News-Gives-Brands-article.php.

Rodgers, W. and Nguyen, T. "Advertising benefits from ethical artificial intelligence algorithmic purchase decision pathways." *Journal of Business Ethics* 178, no. 4 (2022): 1043–1061. DOI: 10.1007/s10551-022-05048-7.

Safdar, N. M., Banja, J. D., and Meltzer, C. C. "Ethical considerations in artificial intelligence." *European Journal of Radiology* 122 (2020): 108768.

Simon, F. M., Altay, S., and Mercier, H. "Misinformation reloaded? Fears about the impact of generative AI on misinformation are overblown." *Harvard Kennedy School Misinformation Review* 4, no. 5 (2023).

Smith, J. and Carter, E. "*Security Challenges in E-commerce Transactions: Safeguarding the Digital Marketplace.*" No. 11673. EasyChair, 2024. https://easychair.org/publications/preprint/CgJl.

Torkington, S. "These are the 3 biggest emerging risks the world is facing." 2024. World Economic Forum. https://www.weforum.org/stories/2024/01/ai-disinformation-global-risks/.

Vaidhyanathan, S. *Antisocial Media: How Facebook Disconnects Us and Undermines Democracy*. 2nd ed. Oxford University Press, 2022.

Walker, P.L. and Irving, J.H. "Managing noise, change, and emerging risks." *Journal of Accountancy*. (2021). https://www.journalofaccountancy.com/issues/2021/nov/managing-noise-change-emerging-risks.ht.

Walorska, A. M. "Deepfakes and disinformation." Friedrich Naumann Foundation for Freedom, 2020.

Zuboff, S. "The age of surveillance capitalism." In Social Theory Re-Wired. edited by W. Longhofer and D. Winchester, 3rd ed., 203–213. Chicago: Routledge, 2023.

https://doi.org/10.1142/9781800616578_0016

Chapter 16

How Does the Use of Language Matter in Organizational Change Processes? Setting Up an AI-Based Analytics Approach

Sabine Van Almsick and Christian Stary*

Johannes Kepler University,
Business Informatics-Communications Engineering,
Business School, Linz, Austria

**christian.stary@jku.at*

Abstract

Change management requires communication. For instance, company succession is a crucial phase for medium-sized companies. Like any change process, it is characterized by a multitude of challenges, including the role of internal communication and linguistic expressions. A central concern in this context is the identification of resistance that can arise in managing change. The use of language plays a crucial role in verbal resistance. It manifests itself in employee discussions as well as in internal chats and emails. Corresponding data serve as an indicator of potential difficulties in the change process. In order to recognize and address verbal resistance, we introduce a design science approach focusing on a systematic analysis of internal change communication. It includes social business platforms for formal and informal communication, as these promote the understanding and implementation of corporate goals. In this chapter, we capture the initial design science cycle as it targets the identification of performance indicators for the way language is used in organizational communication as a part of an organization's culture. It is also investigated how these indicators relate to traditional KPIs, such as sales figures. The subsequent design cycles apply AI-based data analytics, such as semantic clustering, to develop a communication-based resonance and feedback system that includes early warnings of resistance to change in management processes. Intervention mechanisms can then be based on organizational communication evidence. It is expected that a targeted communication strategy and the early recognition of resistance are essential factors for a successful transition in company succession or when a company is sold.

Keywords: Organizational communication, socio-semiotics, big data, analytics, machine learning.

16.1. Introduction

How communication matters in organizations has been investigated with respect to recession, increased global competition, and restructurings (cf. Young *et al.*, 1993) as well as managing change and collective learning (cf. Daft *et al.*, 1986) for several decades, including the Luhmann perspective on organizations as communication (cf. Fleischmann *et al.*, 2013a, Schoeneborn, 2011). Thereby, communication is considered a means to tackle employees' concerns effectively with respect to (re)organization and related resistance to change (Sabino *et al.*, 2021). It is related to an organization's culture, which "includes a jointly shared goal of organization that is common to everybody and the social network" (Takala *et al.*, 2011).

In change processes, the context, in particular the value of interactions (Stary, 2014) and work processes (Fleischmann *et al.*, 2012, Fleischmann *et al.*, 2013b), including the negotiation of these processes (cf. Lazega, 1992, Oppl *et al.*, 2014), seems to be of utmost importance. For instance, when we consider business succession for medium-sized companies, it is likely to come with organizational culture change. In cultural change, the role of organizational communication and the specific use of language by the organization's members play a crucial role (Matos Marques Simoes *et al.*, 2014). According to KfW's Research on Succession Monitoring in 2023, around 125,000 medium-sized companies are due to be handed over every year, with the proportion of owners seeking succession planning increasing from 35% to 41%, closely linked to the aging of the entrepreneurial community and resistance during the succession process and, thus, affecting cultural rituals (cf. Deal *et al.*, 2000).

Verbal resistance, which manifests itself in employee discussions as well as in internal chats and emails, is an indicator of potential difficulties in the change process. The ability to recognize and address this resistance is crucial for the success of the succession (Coch *et al.*, 1948). Hence, a systematic and analytical approach to internal communication may help organize and improve change management processes. Such an endeavor needs to take into account social business aspects, including platforms for formal and informal communication. They promote the understanding and implementation of corporate goals. Analyzing communication helps one find out whether a targeted (communication) strategy and the early recognition of resistance are essential factors for successful transitions in company succession or change in company ownership (cf. Sabino *et al.*, 2021).

The presented study aims to investigate the language dimension of technology-based communication used along with change (management) processes. In order to gain insight, we will focus on AI-based analytics, as it has been applied in a variety of contexts effectively, such as human resource management (Albassam, 2023), urban planning and design (Kamrowska-Załuska, 2021), energy management (Kumari *et al.*, 2021), and healthcare (Lokesh *et al.*, 2022). Its use concerns voluminous and numerous flows of data capture, aggregation, analysis and visualization, and the application of techniques to gain insight with accuracy and trustworthiness (LaValle *et al.*, 2011).

The introduced research design aims to provide insight into how organizations use verbal communication. We target salient communication issues that occur along change processes. Of particular interest is the respective use of language that diffuses across organizational units and finally becomes routine in organizational communication. Thereby, we address the following research question: "How can organizations use AI-based analytics with respect to organizational communication for effective change management?" It is investigated how far AI-based analytics utilization can reveal patterns of language use and finally influence organizational communication in the course of change (management) processes.

In Section 16.2, we contextualize verbal organizational communication by framing it with organizational culture. In Section 16.3, we detail the iterative research design to measure verbal communication in social media and emails, and subsequently apply language-based AI analytics.

Section 16.4 concludes the chapter with implications of the presented research approach.

16.2. Organizational Culture and the Use of Language

According to Pacanowsky *et al.* (1983), who have an anthropological perspective, communication corresponds to language use rather than information transfer, which leads to understanding organizations as social systems. Hence, an "organization emerges in communication, which thus furnishes not only the site of its appearance to its members, but also the surface on which members read the meaning of the organization to them. As its site, communication may be studied as conversation; as surface the appropriate object of study for the communication researcher is the set of texts produced by organizational members" (Taylor, 1999, p. 21). The use of language in organizations finally impacts the language in business communication (Du-Babcock, 2007).

Internal organizational communication is a significant success factor for an organization (Zinke-Wehlmann *et al.*, 2021). Communicative processes within an organization not only generate knowledge but also promote the understanding and effective implementation of corporate goals. In addition, these processes form the basis for negotiating explicated goals and for developing and maintaining corporate culture. The latter manifests itself in the specific behaviors, norms, and practices that characterize the work and interaction environment within the company (*ibid.*).

Ways of speaking, communication, and thus also the way of giving feedback or expressing resistance are part of the corporate culture. Organizational culture is considered the collective set of assumptions, expectations, and practices that guide people when interacting in an organization (Brown *et al.*, 1994) and when establishing rituals (Deal *et al.*, 2000). It reflects the shared vision, mission, and goals of the organization, as well as the norms and rules that govern its operations (Schall, 1983). Organizational culture shapes an organization's identity and history and is perceived through the motivation of its members, the satisfaction of interacting, and finally the performance of each member (Nordby, 2021).

Considering language as part of an organization's culture brings into play the fact that culture presents itself in different ways (Schein, 1995). Schein's modeled 3 levels represent "the visibility of a cultural phenomenon for the observer" (*ibid.*, p. 29). The top and most visible level of his model includes all visible, audible, and tangible phenomena. These comprise the appearance and furnishings of the office building, rituals, legends, ways of speaking, and clothing as examples. "The most important finding about this level of culture is that it is easy to observe but difficult to decipher" (*ibid.*, p. 30). This finding makes communication and thus also (written) language challenging research targets.

Nevertheless, for the successful course of a change project, it is crucial to identify any form of resistance (including verbal one) at an early stage and to respond to it. Failure to do so can result in significant delays, serious blockages, and costly failures in operation. Therefore, dealing with resistance constructively is a key success factor in change management (Doppler *et al.*, 2019, p. 354).

Resistance manifests itself in different ways, as summarized in Table 16.1. We list verbal forms of resistance in the first column. Talking and verbalizing in the form of contradiction or evasion are manifestations of resistance and can therefore be an indicator of the impending failure of a change process, such as a succession plan or a change of managing director.

Table 16.1. Manifestations of resistance.

	Verbal (Talking)	Non-Verbal (Behavior)
Active (Attack)	Contradiction	Excitement
	Counter argumentation	Unrest
	Accusations	Argument
	Threats	Intrigues
	Polemic	Rumors
	Stubborn formalism	Clique formation
Passive (Escape)	Evasion	Lack of interest
	Silence	Inattention
	Trivializing	Fatigue
	Fooling around	Staying away
	Ridiculing	Internal emigration
	Debating unimportant things	Illness

Source: Authors (Based on Doppler *et al.*, 2019, p. 357).

Verbal resistance is not only reflected in face-to-face conversations among employees but can also be found in chats or internal emails. These exchanges are usually not accessible to management or the change team, so that resistance mainly occurs between colleagues. Respective indicators are valuable in order to question measures or initiate interventions if necessary.

16.3. Setting Up Speech Metrics and (AI-Based) Analytic Methods

We first introduce the design science approach to research, before discussing methodological approaches toward AI-based analytics of language culture.

16.3.1. *Design science*

Design science has attracted increasing attention in the last decade (cf. Hevner, 2007, Baskerville *et al.*, 2018). Its dual but iterative nature with respect to design artifacts and design theory equally supports practical development and the conceptual understanding of a problematic situation and resolving it.

The Relevance Cycle (Figure 16.1) applied to the objective of this research connects the environment of a change (management) project with its verbal communication activities. The Rigor Cycle relates these activities to the knowledge base informing the project and serving as development memory. The Design Cycle iterates between the core development activities building and evaluating artifacts. This intermediate position ensures that (i) artifact development remains in the context of the process started, (ii) each development cycle is informed by scientific theories and domain-specific practice, and (iii) the results can be documented in a structured form. Hence, each design cycle result can be traced back to its starting point and related to previous design cycles. In this way, each step in developing an analytical and a communication transformation space becomes transparent.

The design science framework (Figure 16.1) has been operationalized by Peffers *et al.* (2006). It captures the development stages as shown in Figure 16.2: (i) identification of the problem, (ii) definition of objectives for a solution, (iii) design and development of artifact, (iv) demonstration

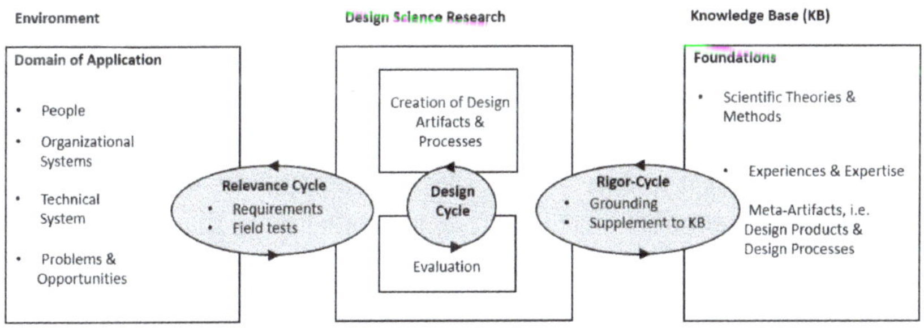

Figure 16.1. Design cycles embodied in pragmatic and methodological context.
Source: Authors according to Hevner, 2007.

of artifact use to solve the problem, (v) evaluation of the solution, (vi) communication of achievements:

- **Identification of the problem and motivation:** The research problem needs to be identified and the value of a solution needs to be justified. Initially, the concepts of organizational communication and change management can be specified and promoted by strategic foresight rather than elaborated requirements. For structuring development, cultural value drivers and properties need to be elaborated and related to language-based communication in change (management) processes. They serve as a baseline for organizational transformation, in particular through attribute-based analytics, learning models, and dynamic adaptation.
- **Definition of objectives for a solution:** The solution needs to facilitate the transformation of organizations through informed AI-based analytics of communication supporting business operations. Developers can use language attributes representing communication acts and design analytical (earning) models in the course of change processes, and utilize them for adaptation and prediction. Particularities of domains and industrial sectors, such as service industries and related communication systems, need to be recognized and taken into account.
- **Design and development of artifact:** An artifact can be a model, a concept, a method, an object, an application, or a combination of those. For AI-based analytics, a digital representation of a verbal communication system is required that allows stakeholders in the course of change (management) processes to redesign their organizational communication in an interactive and adaptive way.

- **Demonstration:** Each design science cycle uses the current version of the artifact to exemplify whether and how the addressed problem is solved in practice. In our first case, a concession case serves as demonstrator. It is selected due to its technological and organizational challenges. Existing findings with respect to the applied solution concept are taken into account. They stem from related work that is analyzed in the Definition of Objectives of a Solution and is utilized for Design & Development (see Figure 16.2).
- **Evaluation:** In each of the design science cycles, the current solution is evaluated based on the objectives and the requirements developed so far. It is checked whether the results from the use of the artifact in the demonstration case meet the requirements. As the directed backward links from Evaluation indicate, either the artifact requires further refinement and/or adjustment or the objectives need to be reconsidered in terms of revisiting the conceptual foundation of the approach and requirements before starting a new design cycle.
- **Communication:** All collected information and achievements are communicated, including the problem, the artifact, its utility, and effectiveness, to other researchers and practitioners. It feeds to the Knowledge Base (see Figure 16.1) and enables a complete picture of findings through the Rigor Cycle. Both conceptual and experiential findings are captured, allowing for reflecting on the process of finding a solution (i.e., meta-findings are represented and preserved, too).

The result of the design science cycles is always a purposeful artifact. In our case, it is an operational framework, i.e., a procedure involving the representation of verbal communication in organizations and methodological tool support of effective change (management) processes on the basis for AI-analyzed language use. Like other design science projects, the endeavor finally focuses on social systems and their members. The outcome of this work will be used by organization developers applying AI-based analytics to organizational communication.

The focus of this work is the verbal interaction between people in the course of change processes and the representation of the underlying communication system or schemes featuring mutual understanding for effective transformation. One needs to consider communication activities integrated with handling technology artifacts when developing an AI-based analytics solution. The context of iterative development of a solution is formed by previous experiences, evolving needs/requirements, conventions, and standards. They are the basis of reflection and design.

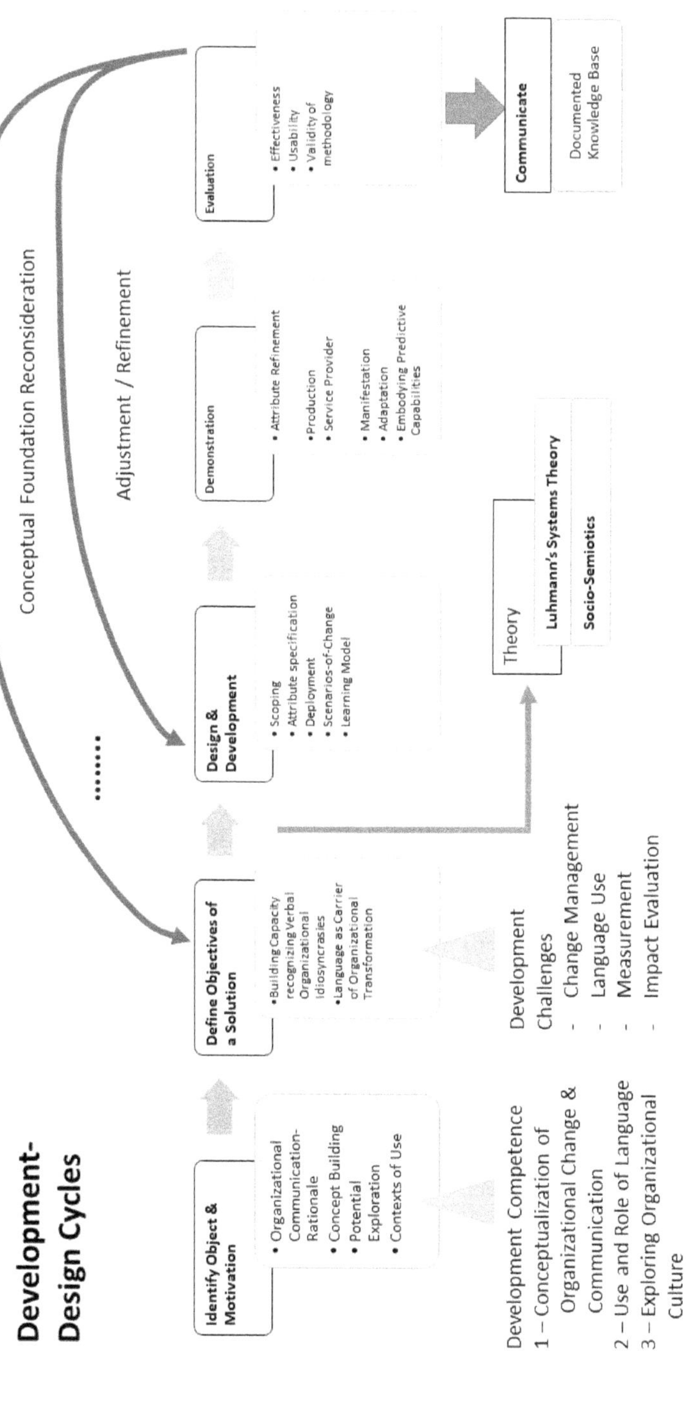

Figure 16.2. Design science-based research on organizational communication space.

16.3.2. *Method candidates for data analytics*

Studying organizational culture and communication involves traditional data collection approaches, comprising surveys, interviews, focus groups, observations, and audits (cf. Zamanou *et al.*, 1994; Hargie *et al.*, 2004; Driskill, 2018). They provide qualities for assessing both organizational culture and communication and help to identify operational strengths and weaknesses, as well as gaps or opportunities for the improvement of change processes (Lewis *et al.*, 2012).

However, the context of analysis is formed by the alignment of organizational culture and communication issues with the vision, mission, and goals of an organization. Organizational culture and communication need to be consistent across different levels and locations, which affects the adaptability of the organizational culture and communication to changing environments, together with the engagement of all stakeholders in establishing a certain organizational culture and effective communication. Finally, it has an impact on performance, operational quality, and innovation, which have also been part of analytic approaches (Al Bogami *et al.*, 2024).

The following list captures method candidates relevant for AI analytics and big data. There are different models from linguistics available for text analysis to measure the use of language. Due to the large amount of expected text in each application of our research, we initially aim to analyze text on a meta-level. This form of text capture is called "distant reading" (Biemann *et al.*, 2022) referring to Moretti (2013): "For automatic content-based research in large text corpora, a distinction must be made between the macro view and the micro view (cf. Jockers, 2013) based on Moretti's concept of distant reading (Moretti, 2013). The macro view makes it possible to structure very extensive text corpora, e.g., by clustering similar texts or identifying topics and their distribution in the text corpus. The macro view thus supports the search for relevant information and contexts in a very large search space" (Biemann *et al.*, 2022, p. 6).

Each of the following methods is designed to gain a better understanding of the corporate language culture in the form of communication indicators or visualizations:

Topic modeling provides probabilistic data. Topic models are based on the assumption that every word is assigned to a topic area and that the underlying topic areas, the topics, can be derived from the distribution of thematically related words in a text (Biemann *et al.*, 2022). The basic principle of topic models is that documents are viewed as a set of topics. Topics are represented as a distribution of words (Petz, 2019). Applications like R, Python, and the web-based TopicExplorer use topic model methods (Papilloud *et al.*, 2018).

A widely used topic model is the LDA (Latent Dirichlet Allocation) as introduced by Blei *et al.* (2002), and succeeded by BERTopic, Top2Vec, and NMF (Non-negative Matrix Factorization) (Papilloud *et al.*, 2018). The LDA model aims to "automatically discover topics from a collection of documents" (Petz, 2019, p. 224), which makes it a candidate to tackle organizational communication on a meta level.

BERTopic and LDA have been contrasted recently by Azuero (2024), revealing advantages and disadvantages. Egger and Yu (2022) have also compared topic models, namely, LDA, BERTopic, Top2Vec, and NMF. They concluded that "applying BERTopic to generate insights from short and unstructured text offers the most potential when it comes to embedding-based topic models" (*ibid*., p. 13). For further evaluation and measurement of language, they recommend that research continually look at new algorithms. "However, it is still critical to note that the nature of social media differs in terms of user demographics, text presentation, or rhetoric, amongst others. Thus, future research should continue to explore the effectiveness of topic modeling algorithms across other platforms" (*ibid*.).

The benefits of topic modeling to handle the objectives of the presented research are that it can be used to identify topics that occur in communication frequently. It should also be used to recognize how topics change over time and whether the change in topics is reflected in business indicators.

Stylometry is another method for analyzing texts, as defined by Schöch (2014): "Stylometry is one of several methods that can be assigned to the field of quantitative text analysis. The term stylometry refers to computer-aided methods for collecting stylistic features and their frequencies in texts, as well as using these features and frequencies to classify texts" (*ibid*., p. 133). He could identify the following fields of application:

- *author attribution* for texts whose author is unknown or disputed;
- *chronological classification of individual texts* by authors in their overall work;
- *digital forensics* to detect plagiarism and to authenticate texts.

According to Schöch (2014), stylometry enables one to look at certain text features in order to determine the relative similarity or the difference between different texts. Texts are then classified or grouped on this basis. A variety of measures can be taken into account, including the average length of words and sentences, the proportion of certain word classes in the overall text, and N-grams of letters, words, or word classes. Stylometry networks (Eder, 2017) are used to represent stylometry features and their mutual relationship.

In addition to providing a comprehensive feature list, Chanis *et al.* (2025) compare five different machine learning training algorithms that are used to prepare the basic language model: Logistic Regression, Decision Trees, Random Forest, Gradient Boosting, and Naïve Bayes. Training the language model serves as preparation for applying vectorization techniques, in order to run stylometry algorithms, such as the successfully applied Burrows Delta algorithm (Büttner *et al.*, 2017).

Network analysis deals, among other elements, with relationships between content items, such as actors communicating in an organization. Digital tools can be used to visualize these relationships. Thereby, "quantitative aspects of the relational system, primarily the number of nodes, connecting lines and links, emerge clearly, which can serve as the basis for a qualitative analysis. Network analyses are made easier by digital programs, but can also be carried out manually" (Schumacher, 2018, §1).

Sentiment analysis aims to analyze the moods expressed through or addressed in a text. Sentiment analysis can follow different methodological approaches. Rule-based approaches require "a lexicon and weightings for the wordlist to calculate the overall polarity of the text" (Li, 2024, p. 4). Machine learning-based approaches require "training with manually tagged labels in order to learn new dataset by supervised learning" (*ibid.*) and have been applied in several variants for sentiment analysis (Ligthart *et al.*, 2021). Finally, there exist hybrid approaches.

A common but essential feature of sentiment analysis is sentiment polarity. According to Li (2024), sentiment polarity of textual data is defined as "the result of analysis expressed in terms of a numerical value obtained by the algebraic sum of opinion contained in each entity of the sentence, document, or message. The sentiment polarity can be determined as positive, negative, or neutral" (Li, 2024, p. 61).

16.3.3. *Methodological setup and informed method selection*

The above-mentioned approaches provide measurable items for texts. The texts, e.g., of emails, to be analyzed are each provided with time stamps so that the measured values can be arranged and displayed on a timeline. In this way, a timeline for a particular mood in texts (sentiment polarity) or the occurrence of certain topics (topic modeling) can be set up per day or per week, applying the respective measurement method.

This way of recording enables the documentation, visualization, analysis, and interpretation of changes. For instance, a change of language use or tone in internal e-mail communication over time is an indicator for the management team or the stakeholders of a change project to look closely at collaboration. A negative polarity of what is written could be an indicator of resistance.

Resistance, such as in the form of language, has been highlighted by Doppler *et al.* (2019) (see also Table 16.1). A suitable method for measuring polarities is sentiment analysis. It supports the identification and analysis of expressions (sentiment expressions) that refer to or represent a subjective state of mind or an evaluation of objects, events, or opinions (sentiment targets). Typical measurement dimensions are polarities such as positive–negative for polarity analysis or subjective–objective for subjectivity analysis (Biemann *et al.*, 2022).

For the successful course of a change project, it is crucial to identify any form of resistance at an early stage (cf. Sabino *et al.*, 2020), and to respond to it constructively (Doppler *et al.*, 2019) and effectively (cf. Ford *et al.*, 2009). Ignoring it can result in significant delays, serious blockages, and costly failures (cf. Pardo de Val *et al.*, 2003). The importance of recognizing resistance in mood-related statements is why sentiment analysis will be chosen as the first step in the subsequently described research setting, analyzing email communication with respect to the polarity of texts.

16.4. Implementing the Design-Science-Based Research Approach

In this section, we detail the initial phases of the Design-Science-based Research (DBR) approach and take a closer look at the first design cycle by instantiating the generic scheme of Figure 16.2. We structure this section according to the activity bundles described in Section 16.3.1.

16.4.1. *Identification of object and motivation*

We target change management support through AI-based analytics for SMEs that have already implemented or will implement a succession plan. The case that motivated the research concerns an owner-managed company around 170 years in business and willing to host the demonstrator in the first design cycle. Its production unit is located in Germany. The current workforce comprises around 500 employees, of whom around 250 work in the administrative area. According to the management, employee turnover is low.

In order to develop change management support for the management team, the marketing and the human resources department as primary stakeholder groups, the focus is on analyzing the development of email communication over the last 10 years. In that period, there was a generational change in company management from father to son, which was accompanied by challenges in the communication culture and employee management. Analyzing collected email data should be aligned with a selection of business key indicators for the same period. Significant change processes include modifying the management structure. The timeline of the change processes provides the relevant context for the analysis.

Based on the initial interview with the primary stakeholder groups, they see potential in recognizing changes in the company's verbal communication culture in order to be able to intervene in a timely manner when changes occur in the company. The stakeholder groups want to be able to monitor whether there are departments in which changes occur in the tone of text-based communication. The period of time in which the change occurs is also important. Finally, the stakeholder groups want to know which direction these changes in the tone of communication are taking (sentiment polarity).

The identification of measurable verbal communication indicators, e.g., sentiment polarity from the sentiment analysis, should help analyze the changes and derive further indicators for the company. When existing business indicators can be set in relation to the anaysis, the organization's culture along change processes can be better understood.

16.4.2. *Definition of objectives for a solution*

From the interviews and the provided company data, the initial requirement for designing an artefact has been derived, namely, to detect changes in the tone of text-based organizational communication.

Hence, the first design cycle requires a setup that demonstrates how data for tone changes can be collected and documented along a timeline in order to carry out a trend analysis. Running a demonstrator requires the structured evaluation of support tools for collecting and documenting measured values.

16.4.3. *Initial design cycle*

- **Design and development of an artifact:** The first design activity scopes the artifact in terms of a method and corresponding (type of) tool support, in order to meet the requirement. As already argued, the design of the artifact includes AI tools that exist for sentiment analysis of the provided data. In a workshop, the results of the literature research for tools will be presented to the stakeholders, and one or more tools will be selected to run the demonstrator.
- **Demonstration:** For a selected dataset, sentiment analysis for a specific period of time will be performed. The selected AI tool will be utilized for collecting, presenting, and interpreting the data.
- **Evaluation:** The evaluation phase targets the testing of the tools and analysis functionalities by each stakeholder group, i.e., management, marketing management, and human resources department. It will be checked whether the measurement options of the sentiment analysis tools are compatible with the stakeholder requirements to identify changes in mood. For further work, it will be discussed whether and which analysis tool should be tested in the next step, also considering the social process of data analytics (cf. Sodero *et al.*, 2019). One result of the first design cycle may also be that further research is necessary to find a more suitable way of analysis and a corresponding analysis tool.
- **Communication:** The results of the evaluation phase will be summarized in a presentation for the stakeholder groups. All experiences with sentiment analysis and the corresponding tool will be documented, together with the collected data and their interpretation. Aside from the functions the analyzed tools provide for sentiment analysis, a structured review of their support will be prepared for the stakeholder groups. It lists the type of data that can be measured, the methods that can be used for the measurement, and what restrictions or limitations the measurements have with respect to the development of language-based communication indicators.

16.5. Conclusion

Setting up an AI-based analytics approach to interpret the use of language in organizational communication in change processes is a multifaceted task. We have exemplified it for the context of company succession, which is a crucial phase for medium-sized companies. The central concern, namely, the identification of verbal resistance, can be tackled by sentiment analysis. The introduced design science approach focuses on the systematic preparation and collaborative design of a method-driven artifact. The outcome can be used as guidance by organization developers who design AI-based analytics for organizational communication. Further design cycles and use cases, either to meet the initial requirements or to incorporate novel ones, will be performed.

Bibliography

Al Bogami, M., Sharawi, O., and Muhammad Khan, R. "Organizational Culture Adaptability by Leaders and its Influence on Firm Performance." In *Proceedings 14th International Conference on Industrial Engineering and Operations Management*, 2024. DOI: 10.46254/AN14.20240610.

Albassam, W. A. "The power of artificial intelligence in recruitment: An analytical review of current AI-based recruitment strategies." *International Journal of Professional Business Review* 8, no. 6 (2023): e02089.

Azuero, M. "Topic Modeling and Sentiment Analysis for Predicting the Direction of Movement of the S&P 500 Index Based on Financial News." Master Thesis, Johannes Kepler University Linz, 2024. https://epub.jku.at/obvulihs/content/titleinfo/10132574.

Baskerville, R., Baiyere, A., Gregor, S., Hevner, A., and Rossi, M. "Design Science Research Contributions: Finding a Balance between Artifact and Theory." *Journal of the Association for Information Systems* 19, no. 5 (2018): 358–376.

Biemann, C., Heyer, G., and Quasthoff, U. *Wissensrohstoff Text. Eine Einführung in das Text Mining*. 2nd ed. Springer Vieweg, Wiesbaden, 2022.

Brown, A. D. and Starkey, K. "The effect of organizational culture on communication and information." *Journal of Management Studies* 31, no. 6 (1994): 807–828.

Büttner, A., Dimpel, F. M., Evert, S., Jannidis, F., Pielström, S., Proisl, T., and Vitt, T. "Delta in der stilometrischen Autorschaftsattribution." *Zeitschrift für digitale Geisteswissenschaften* 3 (2017).

Chanis, I. and Arampatzis, A. "Enhancing phishing email detection with stylometric features and classifier stacking." *International Journal of Information Security* 24, no. 1 (2025): 1–16.

Coch, L. and French Jr, J. R. "Overcoming resistance to change." *Human Relations* 1, no. 4 (1948): 512–532.

Daft, R. L. and Huber, G. P. "How organizations learn: A communication framework." Defense Technical Information Center, TR-ONR-DG-18, Dep. of Management, College of Business Administration, Texas A&M University, 1986.

Deal, T. E. and Kennedy, A. A. *Corporate Cultures. The Rites and Rituals of Corporate Cultures*. Life Perseus Books Publishing, Cambridge, Massachusetts, 2000.

Doppler, K. and Lauterburg, C. *Change Management: Den Unternehmenswandel gestalten*. 14th ed. Campus Verlag, Frankfurt/Main, 2019.

Driskill, G. *Organizational Culture in Action: A Cultural Analysis Workbook*. Routledge, New York, 2018.

Du-Babcock, B. "Language-based communication zones and professional genre competence in business and organizational communication: A cross-cultural case approach." *Journal of Asian Pacific Communication* 17, no. 1 (2007): 149–171.

Eder, M. "Visualization in stylometry: Cluster analysis using networks." *Digital Scholarship in the Humanities* 32, no. 1 (2017): 50–64.

Fleischmann, A., Kannengiesser, U., Schmidt, W., and Stary, C. "Subject-oriented modeling and execution of multi-agent business processes." In *2013 IEEE/WIC/ACM International Joint Conferences on Web Intelligence (WI) and Intelligent Agent Technologies (IAT)*, Vol. 2, 138–145. IEEE, New York, 2013a.

Fleischmann, A., Schmidt, W., and Stary, C. "Subject-oriented BPM = socially executable BPM." In *2013 IEEE 15th Conference on Business Informatics*, 399–407. IEEE, New York, 2013b.

Fleischmann, A. and Stary, C. "Whom to talk to? A stakeholder perspective on business process development." *Universal Access in the Information Society* 11 (2012): 125–150.

Ford, J. D. and Ford, L. W. "Decoding resistance to change." *Harvard Business Review* 87, no. 4 (2009): 99–103.

Hargie, O. and Tourish, D. "How Are We Doing? Measuring and Monitoring Organizational Communication." In *Key Issues in Organizational Communication*, edited by O. Hargie and D. Tourish, 234–251. Routledge, London, 2004.

Hevner, A. R. "A three cycle view of design science research." *Scandinavian Journal of Information Systems* 19, no. 2 (2007): 87–92.

Jockers, M. L. *Macroanalysis. Digital Methods and Literary History. Topics in the Digital Humanities*. University of Illinois Press, Urbana, 2013.

Kamrowska-Załuska, D. "Impact of AI-based tools and urban big data analytics on the design and planning of cities." *Land* 10, no. 11 (2021): 1209.

Kumari, A. and Tanwar, S. "preveal: An ai-based big data analytics scheme for energy price prediction and load reduction." In *2021 11th International Conference on Cloud Computing, Data Science & Engineering (Confluence)*, 321–326. IEEE, 2021.

LaValle, S., Lesser, E., Shockley, R., Hopkins, M. S., and Kruschwitz, N. "Big data, analytics and the path from insights to value." *MIT Sloan Management Review* 52, no. 1 (2011): 21–32.

Lazega, E. *The Micropolitics of Knowledge – Communication and Indirect Control in Workgroups*. Aldine de Gruyter, New York, 1992.

Lewis, L. K. and Seibold, D. R. "Reconceptualizing organizational change implementation as a communication problem: A review of literature and research agenda." In *Communication Yearbook 21*, edited by M. E. Roloff, 93–151. Routledge, New York, 2012.

Li, J., ed. *Advances in Sentiment Analysis. Techniques, Applications, and Challenges*. IntechOpen, South Africa, 2024. https://directory.doabooks.org/handle/20.500.12854/135417.

Ligthart, A., Catal, C., and Tekinerdogan, B. "Systematic reviews in sentiment analysis: a tertiary study." *Artificial Intelligence Review* 54, no. 7 (2021): 4997–5053.

Lokesh, S., Chakraborty, S., Pulugu, R., Mittal, S., Pulugu, D., and Muruganantham, R. "AI-based big data analytics model for medical applications." *Measurement: Sensors* 24 (2022): 100534.

Simoes, P.M.M. and Esposito, M. "Improving change management: How communication nature influences resistance to change." *Journal of Management Development* 33, no. 4 (2014): 324–341.

Moretti, F. *Distant Reading*. Verso, London, 2013.

Nordby, H. "Communication and organizational culture." In *A Closer Look at Organizational Culture in Action*, edited by S. D. Göker, ch. 7, 95–110. InTechOpen, London, 2021.

Oppl, S. and Stary, C. "Facilitating shared understanding of work situations using a tangible tabletop interface." *Behaviour & Information Technology* 33, no. 6 (2014): 619–635.

Pacanowsky, M. E. and O'Donnell-Trujillo, N. "Organizational communication as cultural performance." *Communications Monographs* 50, no. 2 (1983): 126–147.

Papilloud, C. and Hinneburg, A. *Qualitative Textanalyse mit Topic-Modellen. Eine Einführung für Sozialwissenschaftler*. Springer Fachmedien, Wiesbaden, 2018.

Pardo del Val, M. and Martínez Fuentes, C. "Resistance to change: A literature review and empirical study." *Management Decision* 41, no. 2 (2003): 148–155.

Peffers, K., Tuunanen, T., Gengler, C. E., Rossi, M., Hui, W., Virtanen, V., and Bragge, J. "The design science research process: A model for producing and presenting information systems research." In *Design Science Research in Information Systems and Technology (DESRIST 2006)*, 83–106, 2006.

Petz, G. *Opinion Mining im Web 2.0. Ansätze, Methoden, Vorgehensmodell.* Gabler, Wiesbaden, 2019.

Sabino, L. R., Reis Neto, M. T., Morais, G. M., and Santos, V. F. D. "Leadership, communication, and resistance influence organizational performance." *Latin American Business Review* 22, no. 3 (2021): 265–286.

Schall, M. S. "A communication-rules approach to organizational culture." *Administrative Science Quarterly* (1983): 557–581.

Schein, E. H. *Unternehmenskultur: Ein Handbuch für Führungskräfte.* Campus, Frankfurt/Main, 1995.

Schoeneborn, D. "Organization as communication: A Luhmannian perspective." *Management Communication Quarterly* 25, no. 4 (2011): 663–689.

Schöch, C. "Corneille, Molière et les autres. Stilometrische Analysen zu Autorschaft und Gattungszugehörigkeit im französischen Theater der Klassik." In *Literaturwissenschaft im digitalen Medienwandel*, edited by C. Schöch and L. Schneider, 130–155. PhiN-Beiheft 7/2014, 2014. https://web.fu-berlin.de/phin/beiheft7/b7t08.pdf.

Schumacher, M. "Netzwerkanalyse." In *forTEXT. Literatur digital erforschen*, 2018. https://fortext.net/routinen/methoden/netzwerkanalyse.

Sodero, A., Jin, Y. H., and Barratt, M. "The social process of Big Data and predictive analytics use for logistics and supply chain management." *International Journal of Physical Distribution & Logistics Management* 49, no. 7 (2019): 706–726.

Stary, C. "Non-disruptive knowledge and business processing in knowledge life cycles–aligning value network analysis to process management." *Journal of Knowledge Management* 18, no. 4 (2014): 651–686.

Takala, J., Sivusuo, H., Leskinen, J., and Hirvelä, J. "How to communicate and implement strategies in a strong organization culture?" *Tehnički Vjesnik* 13, no. 1, 2 (2006): 49–55.

Taylor, J. R. "What is "organizational communication"? Communication as a dialogic of text and conversation." *The Communication Review* 3, no. 1-2 (1999): 21–63.

Young, M. and Post, J. E. "Managing to communicate, communicating to manage: How leading companies communicate with employees." *Organizational Dynamics* 22, no. 1 (1993): 31–43.

Zamanou, S. and Glaser, S. R. "Moving toward participation and involvement: Managing and measuring organizational culture." *Group & Organization Management* 19, no. 4 (1994): 475–502.

Zinke-Wehlmann, C. and Friedrich, J. *Social Business Transformation: Werkzeuge für erfolgreiche digitale Zusammenarbeit in Unternehmen*. Springer Vieweg, Wiesbaden, 2021.

https://doi.org/10.1142/9781800616578_bmatter

Index